HTML5 Advertising

John Percival

apress·

HTML5 Advertising

ISBN-13 (pbk): 978-1-4302-4602-2

ISBN-13 (electronic): 978-1-4302-4603-9

President and Publisher: Paul Manning
Lead Editor: Louise Corrigan
Technical Reviewer: Richard Carter
Editorial Board: Steve Anglin, Ewan Buckingham, Gary Cornell, Louise Corrigan, Morgan Ertel, Jonathan Gennick, Jonathan Hassell, Robert Hutchinson, Michelle Lowman, James Markham, Matthew Moodie, Jeff Olson, Jeffrey Pepper, Douglas Pundick, Ben Renow-Clarke, Dominic Shakeshaft, Gwenan Spearing, Matt Wade, Tom Welsh
Coordinating Editor: Kevin Shea
Copy Editors: Thomas McCarthy, Kim Wimpsett
Compositor: SPi Global
Indexer: SPi Global
Artist: SPi Global
Cover Designer: Anna Ishchenko

"Do what you love and you'll never work a day in your life." **Thanks, Mom. Love you.**

Contents at a Glance

Contents

Foreword

We are currently experiencing the initial stages of an unavoidable shift within the digital advertising industry. Specifically, there is a push toward widely adopting open web standards such as HTML5 and moving away from closed, third-party options such as Adobe Flash. With Flash long being the main delivery mechanism of all nonstatic digital advertising, this is a monumental change of direction that at least in these early, beginning stages poses far more questions and challenges rather than easy answers and quick solutions. An entire industry is currently faced with having to completely change direction and redefine its core creative technology. For those of us who are involved with the creation and deployment of digital advertising, it has become quickly apparent that there is a strong and urgent need for guidance in this area as well as for the formalized establishment of industry standards, specifications, and best practices that will facilitate the industry to effectively transition toward this next-generation advertising format and designate HTML5 as the new *de facto* standard.

Installing HTML5 as a replacement for Flash within digital advertising may eventually become everything that we believe it will be; however, right now the subject seems to pose far more questions than answers. There are several industry-specific issues and obstacles that need to be adequately addressed before HTML5 can truly be considered a scalable and standardized solution. These issues include concerns relating to overall file size, bandwidth consumption, inconsistent and fragmented feature support within browsers, and acceptable optimization and performance across browsers, as well as the lack of suitable content creation tools for designers. From the content creation perspective, designers are now forced to contemplate starting over completely and developing an entirely new skill set. This can be a very daunting and intimidating task, and without any relevant direction or suitable industry resources, the average designer who creates digital advertising is most likely left feeling very confused and overwhelmed. This book comes to the rescue and effectively fills the void by providing relevant guidance, insight, and advice. John does a magnificent job of identifying the key challenges and then presenting suitable solutions that are easy to understand and digest even for novices.

I truly understand just how useful and valuable of a resource this book will be for designers who are transitioning to HTML5 and away from Flash, because that is the exact path I have already traveled. I have been working within the digital advertising industry for the past seven years now, and during that time, I have been fortunate enough to have accumulated a great deal of relevant industry knowledge and technical experience. When I began my career at AOL, I was hired as a Flash developer, tasked with creating highly immersive, interactive, and rich advertising experiences. Over the years I was able to successfully push the boundaries of what was possible within digital advertising by leveraging my strong design skills as well as my vast knowledge of Flash and ActionScript. By all accounts I was very good at what I did, and I thought I had it all figured out. Boy, was I wrong! When Apple decided that Flash would not be supported on the iOS operating system, it changed everything, not just within the digital advertising industry but within the web development world as a whole. Suddenly, I was no longer the confident and experienced interactive development expert I thought I was. I wasn't even sure whether I was going to have a job in another couple of years. Suddenly, everyone was talking about moving toward HTML5, and I had never even heard of it. I was definitely feeling confused, lost, and even a little scared. That said, rather than give up and begin looking into a new career, I decided to investigate this new HTML5 technology and see what all of the fuss was about. What came next was months and months of extensive research, trial and error, and testing, followed by more testing. There was plenty of frustration, sleepless nights, and more cursing than I'd like to admit. I learned a great deal through this process and was able to eventually become as proficient with HTML5, JavaScript, and CSS3 as I had previously been with Flash; however, it was definitely not easy. In the end, my career was saved, my friends and family still loved me, and all was right with the universe once again. That being the case, the journey was long and hard, and I could have definitely benefited from some help and guidance along the way. Do you know what I could have really used the most? This book!

Plenty of HTML5 resources are available these days, but none is completely devoted to the perspective of a designer who creates digital advertising for a living. This may seem like a small niche to some; however, this is a very significant group of folks because they are the ones who are supporting the multibillion-dollar digital advertising industry. It is extremely important that these designers are able to effectively and efficiently transition to HTML5 so that they can continue to deliver standards-compliant advertising units that adhere to established specs and best practices and that do not negatively affect the user or the publisher. It's truly in the best interest of the industry as a whole to ensure that this happens, and that's why this book is so valuable and necessary during this crucial time. This book will undoubtedly prove to be an invaluable resource for Flash designers interested in learning about the usage of HTML5, CSS3, and JavaScript for digital advertising purposes. John clearly and articulately covers a great deal of ground within these pages. The reader will receive a thorough education on the campaign process, ad requirements, all of the relevant HTML5 APIs and related functionality, working with JavaScript and CSS3, handling media assets, web standards, optimization techniques, several advanced topics such as communication between domains, mobile and in-app advertising, and a lot more! John does an excellent job of providing a holistic view of HTML5 advertising, and this book is really the only resource that the reader will need in order to get started. As someone who now leads a large team of interactive designers and developers who are entirely focused on all forms of digital advertising for both desktop and mobile, I can ensure you that John's book will be required reading for all of my employees.

Most recently I have found myself working very closely with the IAB and was recently named cochair of the HTML5 Digital Advertising Working Group. This group of industry experts is currently working to establish the first-ever HTML5 digital advertising specification and best practices for the digital advertising industry. During my time spent working with this group of experts, I have found John to be one of the most knowledgeable, friendly, and collaborative individuals I have ever had the pleasure of working with. His great knowledge and enthusiasm for HTML5 advertising really comes through in these pages, and the amount of information that he has packed into this book will make your head spin! This book is extensive in its breadth and effectively covers all aspects of HTML5 advertising, from defining industry terminology all the way to specific technical tips and tricks that designers can utilize in order to take full advantage of HTML5 and all of its vast capabilities. Even better, John does not simply provide a generic overview of the new HTML5 APIs and other related technologies; he ties everything directly into advertising and explains why it is relevant and how it should be used within the context of our industry. John has done an amazing job of documenting and capturing everything that a transitioning designer would need in order to effectively begin working with the emerging technology of HTML5 within the context of digital advertising. He effectively breaks down the barriers and provides the reader with the required information and skills they need in order to build up their knowledge so that they can comfortably and confidently approach this exciting new phase of their career. John has done all of the legwork for all who are just now approaching the subject, and his hard work will make their lives drastically easier. No longer will designers find themselves in a position where they are forced to learn everything on their own without any guidance, direction, or validation. No longer will designers find themselves contemplating career changes or crying into their keyboards late at night out of frustration. With this book sitting on their desks, designers will finally have the resource they've been missing and that will allow them to make the leap into HTML5 advertising. Trust me, I know what I'm talking about. I've been there and done that.

Cory Hudson
Creative Director, AOL

About the Author

John Percival is an established creative director and web technologist who resides in the Philadelphia area. He specializes in digital media production, multiscreen development, interactive design, and video creation/delivery. He currently keeps busy in the digital advertising space, working for many Fortune 500 clients and leading agencies solving complex problems with emerging technology. John has been in the digital space for nearly a decade, has led teams big and small, and has a strong background in audio and video production as well as motion graphics. John is an industry speaker, technical author, and member of the IAB's various working groups and committees. When he's not online or wiring up his house, he can be found playing the drums or starting projects that consume most of his free time.

About the Technical Reviewer

Richard Carter is a web designer and front-end developer and creative director at Peacock Carter Ltd., a web design agency based in Newcastle upon Tyne, England.

Richard is the author of four books to date on theme integration with open source content management and e-commerce systems, and he previously reviewed Apress' *The Definitive Guide to Drupal 7*. He blogs at www.earlgreyandbattenburg.co.uk and is on Twitter as the imaginatively named @RichardCarter.

Acknowledgments

I'd like to thank a variety of people who have either directly or indirectly helped in writing this book: Alison Mazurek, Louise Corrigan, Kevin Shea, Richard Carter, Todd Pasternack, Craig Furlong, Rob Avery, Chris Deely, Daniel (Tree) Sandler, Nick Fox, Joe Brust, Rodrigo Brinski, Ben Fiore, Wade Neumeister, Ray Matos, Ian McLean, Brendan Reiley, Nathan Carver, Joe Lazlo, Chris Menaj, Jessica Anderson, Sabrina Alimi, Yolanda Brown, the IAB's HTML5 working group, and a very special thanks to Cory Hudson for writing the foreword.

Introduction

Why write a book geared toward advertising with a focus on HTML5? Well, for most of 2011, my job was to create, debug, and make informed decisions on HTML, CSS, and JavaScript in the emerging browser market, and boy was it frustrating! During December of that year, I had some free time to myself, and took the time to draft an outline to a book that I would want to read, based on all the troubles I faced throughout the year. Needless to say, I had lots to say, so that outline grew to be 20+ pages, covering all topics around advertising in the digital world and more importantly how it's being drastically altered by HTML5.

In the beginning of 2012, I ended up pitching the outline to a few folks in an effort to gauge interest from other people in the industry, and from what I found quickly, I wasn't the only one thinking about this stuff! In Q1 of 2012, I felt confident that I had developed a strong enough outline on the content, and I was really excited to write this thing! So, after signing with the kind folks at Apress, I began to write, develop, and test for most of 2012. I guess you can say I was pretty fed up with hearing things like "Will Flash deliver on tablets?" or "Why do I need to have five versions of my ad for this responsive site?" Note: if these questions seem new to you, don't be alarmed; I'll cover all these topics throughout the book. Needless to say, the need in the industry was strong!

With that said, let me be the first to welcome you to the crazy world of digital advertising (if this is new to you). This industry is fast-paced, cutting-edge, and growing constantly. If there is one thing that's consistent with it, it's that it changes rapidly. I've been in this industry for nearly a decade and can attest that it requires someone with high-energy, quick timing and often someone who can deal with stressful surroundings. If you're looking for a career change by reading this book, I feel you should know the important stuff up front. With that out of the way, let's take a look at the next logical question:

What is HTML5?

The W3C states the following:

> HTML5 is being developed as the next major revision of HTML (HyperText Markup Language), the core markup language of the World Wide Web. HTML5 is the proposed next standard for HTML 4.01, XHTML 1.0 and DOM Level 2 HTML. It aims to reduce the need for proprietary plug-in-based rich Internet application (RIA) technologies such as Adobe Flash and Microsoft Silverlight.

This is a great universal outline, but I'd like to elaborate on it for you as it relates to the context of this book.

HTML5 is a specification for the new and emerging open Web. It's often a widely used term to loosely describe the ability to target platforms where Flash is not accepted. However, in reality, HTML5 is much more than that (http://platform.html5.org). It's an evolving standard built on many web features that we've grown accustomed to in rich platforms, like Adobe's Flash environment. Since HTML5 relies on the native qualities and APIs of the browser, it provides a faster and higher-performing approach to web and ad development because it offers the same robust experiences we've become used to seeing with plug-ins like Flash. Conversely, since HTML5 is an evolving specification, managed by two consortiums (W3C and WHATWG), with two different agendas for the specification, it means it's a moving target to deploy toward because there is plenty of room for fragmentation and interpretation among the marketplace regarding which browsers and devices can utilize which feature sets of the new specification and, much more importantly, when.

HTML5 is the future of the Web but more importantly the present of web advertising, especially if you want to target users in the endlessly growing mobile and tablet landscape, which is becoming a frequent request as more clients make the shift from proprietary platforms such as Flash to the open web standard for more reach and penetration. It will be many years until the advertising space has fully adopted HTML5 as its main platform for delivering and rendering ads, but this book is geared to surveying the current landscape, making some educated assumptions, and adding some developer assistance as the shift happens.

Before we dig in, I'll review what this book is and what it is not in order to set expectations accordingly. First, you must understand that the HTML5 specification is not set for completion and finalization for years to come. On top of that understanding, the browser manufacturers will have to release final updates and bug fixes before full adoption within the market occurs and emerging features can be used safely across browsers.

Second, this book assumes you have some basic knowledge of the Web and development, which means you understand HTML, CSS, JavaScript Flash, and the use of APIs because there are code samples throughout.

Next, you shouldn't be using a dated browser and attempting to work with HTML5 and the code samples in the chapters. IE6, I'm looking at you! If this seems strange to you, trust me you'll understand more as you read the book. So, be sure to download one of these browsers before continuing:

- *Chrome*: http://google.com/chrome

- *Mozilla*: http://mozilla.org/en-US/firefox

- *Opera*: http://opera.com

- *Safari*: http://apple.com/safari

- *Internet Explorer*: http://ie.microsoft.com

Next, this book is not a beginner's guide to coding or ad development but a guide to assisting web developers who understand code practices and how it relates to advertising on the Web, while also providing insight as to why certain things occur in the complex world of advertising.

Finally, with this book, you'll learn about HTML5 and its effects on web advertising but at the end of the day, I want you to understand how to take advantage of this cool technology within the browsers that support it. Also, I'd love to include every facet of advertising technology with regard to HTML5 in this book, but truth is there is just too much out there that's evolving and changing, and that's a good thing! This industry is moving so fast that any attempt to document some features would do a disservice to you and myself for wasting effort. Before we start, if you're interested in where the HTML5 specification develops from, please visit the following sites because the information there is always changing:

- http://whatwg.org

- http://w3c.org

With that primer out of the way, let's move on to Chapter 1 and start learning about the future of digital advertising.

■ ■ ■

The Campaign Process

Welcome to HTML5 advertising. The goal of this initial chapter is to get a complete, end-to-end view of the entire campaign process before we dig into the big stuff. Understanding the campaign process will provide insight into how everyone works together to get campaigns out the door on time. Furthermore, this book also aims to clarify where creative and development fit into the scheme. After breaking down the process into its vital parts and deconstructing them one by one, we'll tie everything back together again to present you the big picture.

This chapter's sections will outline many things, from typical media buying and creative development to launching a campaign and reporting on campaign performance. Technology, terminology, process, and general industry acronyms (which are likely confuse new readers and users)—all these will be reviewed. Also reviewed will be different ways to approach the development of a campaign—through discussion of brand time versus direct response creatives and the importance of clear calls to action and by keeping the user experience in mind at all times. We'll discuss fundamentals of brand storytelling and how advertisers use it to engage potential customers. We'll also provide both an understanding of creative specs and limitations as they relate to publishers and directions on where to go next when launching a digital advertising campaign. Lastly, we'll quickly summarize what we've covered and familiarize you with the terminology. Ready to get started? Then let's begin . . .

Digital Strategy

Since you're reading this book, you may have wondered, "How are those ads that I see online made?" or "Who actually comes up with them?" In online advertising, digital strategy is concerned with an approach to developing a creative marketing message for a brand or advertiser that aligns with the their goals, vision, and business objectives. This strategy could take the form of a message you're familiar with; something like "Back to School Sale" or "Memorial Day Sale." Digital strategy, usually the first step in the process, allows creative agencies to create mock-ups and designs and pitch new ideas to their clients (advertisers). Depending on the agency's size and structure, this process will typically involve a creative or art director and one or more copywriters, project managers, and technical gurus, all working to sell the idea so effectively that the advertiser buys into the marketing message. Though Figure 1-1 should give you a better idea of how this works, keep in mind that every agency is run differently. So consider this just a sample.

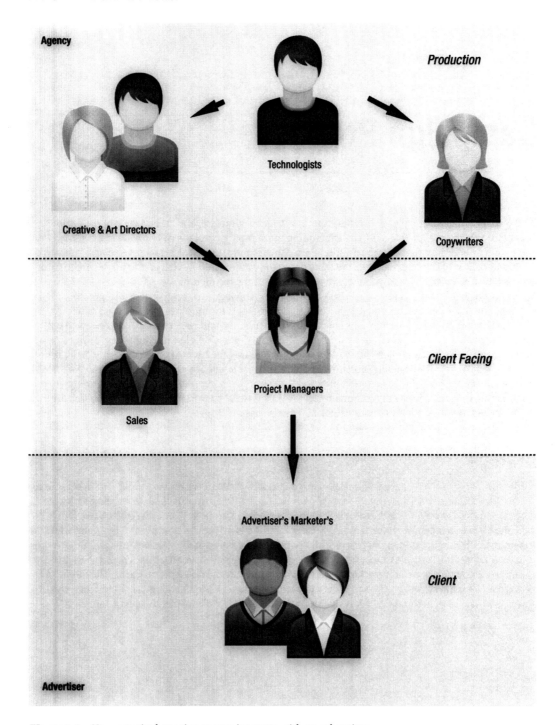

Figure 1-1. *How a typical creative agency interacts with an advertiser*

The effort may require weeks, if not months, of development and planning to ensure that the pitch is conveyed correctly to the client. In some cases, an agency may invest all this time only to see its ideas shot down by the client for any of several reasons: because they didn't align with the client's objectives, because execution costs were too high, or worse still, because petty differences between agency teams ruined the pitch. This last situation is the most unfortunate, in that when it happens, great ideas could go to the grave much too soon. In the end, this process exists to develop the campaign—that is, the overall marketing message the advertiser wants to communicate to audiences and potential customers. The campaign may exist solely online or may be broadened to other distribution channels, including broadcast television, print, and billboards.

Another important part of the digital strategy process involves inclusion of previous campaign intelligence. Let's say you are an advertiser called Joe's Hardware, situated in the American Northeast. In July you had an online ad campaign to sell snow shovels. In analyzing the campaign's performance, you'd most likely realize that the shovels didn't sell very well. Once you realize that it was probably a mistake to sell snow shovels in mid-July, what you've learned can be used to turn your next campaign into a better-performing one. (Obviously this example is oversimplified, but its lessons can be applied to more sophisticated campaigns.)

Note Since dynamic campaigns allow analysis of information in real time, the creative messaging can be adjusted while the campaign is in progress. There's no need to wait until the campaign's end to use what's being learned to make changes. There will be more on this in Chapter 11.

Digital strategy aims at identifying the marketer's challenges, developing a unified solution to them, and delivering a message effectively to the target audience. Taking these points and properly executing each will lay the groundwork for a successful online advertising campaign.

Media Buying

Now that you've had a look at what goes into generating a successful campaign and know something of the parties involved, let's look at what usually is the next step: purchasing media for a particular campaign.

Note Media purchasing can happen at any stage of a campaign's life, but for this chapter's purposes, we'll assume the purchase was made after the strategy was developed.

First, let's define what we mean by media, in relation to the digital advertising industry. In short, the term refers to the planning, implementation, and purchasing of ad inventory through various publishers or networks or the like. Places where media purchases for digital campaigns take place include but are not limited to

- publisher web sites: USA Today, ESPN, BBC, The Guardian (UK), etc.
- web portals: Yahoo, MSN, AOL, etc.
- ad networks: The Deck, Google AdSense, Chitika, etc.
- video players: YouTube, Vevo, Tremor Video, etc.

Publisher Web Sites

Publisher web sites are the most traditional online media buys; leaderboard ads at the top of a page and square ads along a site's right or left hand side are typical examples. These are traditional because they've been around the longest. Anyone with a popular blog or site can sell this form of ad inventory. In fact, `buysellads.com` and similar sites help content producers and advertisers to do so. Anyone who is getting a bunch of unique visitors to a web page and wants a form of passive income should consider including advertising. The New York Post web site (`www.nypost.com/`) is a typical example of an ad experience on a publisher's web site.

Web Portals

Web portals are virtually analogous to publisher web sites in terms of their ad inventory. They differ in being gateways to other sites or to subsections of site information. Web portals include AOL Travel, Yahoo Music, and many others. AOL's subsections include AOL News, AOL Music, AOL Travel, and AOL Money. Each subsection, being tailored to a specific user interest, and could include section-specific advertising inventory.

Ad Networks

An ad network, is a collection of publisher sites for which advertising can be bought and sold on a group basis, can be big or small. Its key function is accumulating ad inventory from a contributing list of publishers and matching it with the advertiser's requirements. Going through an ad network allows the advertiser to reach more web properties than can be reached by just going through publisher sites one at a time. A very good example of a successful ad network is The Deck (`http://decknetwork.net/`).

Video Players

Video player media buys are quite new on the scene. They are what you'd see if you viewed a popular video on YouTube or another content provider that shows ads to viewers in order to provide them free content. This would be the typical 15- or 30-second in-stream video spot that plays before the content. Typically, the video autoplays; it disables users' ability to skip to the content until the ad has played. Video player advertising can also be a lower-third type of ad unit, traditionally called a "post-roll," which appears over the player content

The Media Buyer

Securing any or all of the above-mentioned outlets is a job of its own. This is where a media buyer comes into the mix. The media buyer plays a vital part in the overall campaign process: the media buyer, usually as part of a media agency, specializes in securing appropriate media outlets. One of the media buyer's jobs is ensuring that the inventory purchase aligns with the advertiser's overall vision. For example, if I'm the advertiser Titleist Golf Balls, I'd want my media buyer to place my brand all over the golf sites and related networks. It wouldn't make much sense to show golf ads at, say, a dog show.

Publisher Inventory

As you might guess, the above-described purchasing outlets are all based on available publisher inventory. This can badly limit a media buyer and be subject to many variables, including but not limited to

- day of the week or time of day
- popularity of content
- percentage of views needed

Let's quickly look at this situation as it relates to a traditional form of media buying for broadcast television. It's fair to assume you will pay much more for a 30-second ad spot in the second quarter of the Super Bowl than you would for the same spot on some random channel on late-night television. Put otherwise, as the popularity of a site's content increases, more advertisers will want to run ads on it. So keep posting good content on that blog of yours!

Can you see why it's often tough for media buyers to secure inventory on popular sites? Since the media buyer's job is to hunt down and gather all the media appropriate to communicating the advertiser's message within the allotted budget of the plan, it's really nothing but old-school supply and demand in a new guise.

CPM and Roadblocks

You may be wondering by now, if media is sold based on the popularity, how does this relate to actual dollars? Well, in the digital advertising industry, this amount is assessed by the number of views an ad gets. A view is called an impression. A media buyer, looking at the media sheet, will tally all the different places the ad campaign will run to generate an estimated impression volume. The cost, based on every thousand impressions, could be anywhere from a fraction of a cent (for less-popular content) to several dollars or more, depending on the many variables already mentioned.

Since cost per impression—also called cost per mille (from the Latin "mille," meaning "one thousand")—is higher on sites that see a lot of traffic, getting prime inventory on CNN, the New York Times, the BBC, and similar sites can be difficult. It's especially difficult if you want to be the only advertiser in view that day. For example, an advertiser such as Apple will typically buy what is called a "roadblock," or "takeover," on days it runs campaigns. No conflicting advertiser's messages will be shown in conjunction with the brand's messages.

A roadblock is really the pinnacle buy, and it's unsurprising that it usually comes at a very high cost. What makes this buy special is that it normally allows you the freedom to do whatever you want with the publisher's page content. This may include full-screen video, manipulating page elements that interact with the ad unit, sometimes even a longer duration of ad animation time. A roadblock, when tastefully done, can provide a brand experience like no other.

Real-Time Bidding

At the beginning of this section, I mentioned that media buying is typically done after the campaign's digital strategy is developed and the advertiser's message is finalized. While this is true in most cases, another form of media buying is becoming ever more popular among advertisers. This new technique of media buying, real-time bidding, is done via a demand-side platform, or DSP. A DSP is also known as a trading desk for media buying. This means that when an ad creative is already developed and eagerly awaiting a place to run, the media can be bought or sold via this trading desk so that it can secure ad inventory on the site and run the ad at the exact time of purchase. Obviously, this is true only if the advertiser was the highest bidder. RocketFuel (`http://rocketfuel.com`) and similar companies are hired by media agencies and advertisers to manage purchase of media inventory on publisher's sites in real time to eliminate wasted ad spend. I like to think of it as the eBay for ad buying, only it happens much quicker and often becomes more cost effective for the advertiser.

Publisher Specs

Depending on the media buy, ads need to be developed in different sizes to satisfy all the placements within the publisher's available inventory. This is why it's very important up front to understand where the ad will be delivered before any development is done. It's even more important if the ad has specific functionality and rich features such as expanding real estate or forced video playback. Since certain sites won't allow these features, it's in the best interest of the advertiser to understand the requirements beforehand. Misunderstanding the publisher's requirements may lead to a reduced ad experience or a late campaign launch.

Now, I know what you're saying. "Why would I want to reduce my creative? I want to make the biggest splash I can and wow my target audience!" Well, that's all well and good if you can, but at the end of the day, if the publisher won't run your ad because of a certain feature set, you won't be making any splash at all. Publishers are a hard group to budge; it's their content and their user base, after all. Would you invite someone into your living room and give him free rein to rearrange the place, add things, even remove them? Probably not—unless you got some sort of benefit in return. I like the saying, "No matter how much you love Pizza, you'll never give the delivery guy the keys to your house". So for your own sake, please examine your media plan carefully; note what is and isn't accepted and where it's accepted before any development begins. You might consider having a one-on-one call with your publisher to iron out any unresolved details prior to campaign launch.

Ad Sizes

As just mentioned, different publishers require differently sized ad units to satisfy their inventory. A typical ad size for desktop display is 160 pixels in width by 600 pixels in height; this is what is called a 160 × 600 ad unit or skyscraper. Other typical sizes are 300 × 250 and 728 × 90. For mobile it's pretty standard to see 300 × 50 and 320 × 50. But note that each publisher's requirements are different; they can vary drastically from one site to the next. The spec sheet associated with the media plan should provide technical details for creative development. Be sure to request this sheet from publishers and ad networks before building out the creative; doing so will save you time in the long run. I've seen more often than you might think, where a creative is built and an attempt is made to traffic it to the pub's site, only to find that they won't accept its sizes and feature set.

Responsive Design

Understanding the media plan is really important, but so is understanding why publishers can't or won't take certain formats or features within an ad unit. Their reasons could be related to technical limitations within their site's architecture; for instance, it might not accept specific HTML elements, CSS styling, or JavaScript commands. When this occurs, the best thing to do is set up a kickoff call with the publisher to iron out any and all details before you begin.

One developing design pattern is responsive web design (RWD); it's also known as adaptive web design. A thing to consider about RWD is that the ad layout may need to cater to the site's layout. Thus, a 728 × 90 ad unit may need to be developed for a 300 × 250 size as well as a 160 × 600 size—and all within the same ad tag. The publisher's requirements are paramount here; they should be discussed before development and design begins. RWD is becoming a huge area of interest in the web world due to the ability of so many phones, tablets, and televisions to access websites. Publishers don't want to increase their operational workload or worry about developing a different version of their site for each and every device that can access it. So they rely heavily on cascading style sheets (CSS) and JavaScript to manage site layout variations dynamically, regardless of the screen requesting the content.

Using CSS media queries (more on this topic in Chapter 3), a publisher can tailor content in such a way that it's formatted correctly for the device or screen accessing it. For example, if I were viewing www.bostonglobe.com full-screen on my 27-inch Apple iMac desktop computer, my full-screen width would be 2,560 pixels, whereas if I were viewing it on my iPad in portrait orientation, the screen width would be 768 pixels. This value, when used to check against the CSS media query for screen width, allows a publisher to adapt its site layout dynamically and re-align content. It's still the same site and URL, but the layout changes, which can result in the images shown in Figure 1-2.

Figure 1-2. *How* www.bostonglobe.com *displays at 2,560 pixels on Apple iMac and at 1,024 pixels on Apple iPad in landscape orientation*

Dynamic adaptation for web sites is a breath of fresh air for any publisher's web site developers and designers. It's a bit of a nightmare, however, for digital advertising folks, the reason being that at any time the display changes, whether I'm scaling the window on my desktop or switching orientations between landscape and portrait on my tablet, the ad inventory on that particular page can change or request another ad, possibly firing off duplicate impressions if the ad is request happens more than once. This could result in removal of the 300 × 250 ad shown in Figure 1-2 ("4 story high tides"). This also begs the question whether impressions need to adapt to the new layout as well, doesn't it? If the Boston Globe is in my media plan, how can I be sure that the smaller displays will reach my target audience? This is an interesting question, one that the industry is having a tough time trying to standardize, as it affects both visual ad layouts and reporting concerns.

My hope is that as mobile ad serving grows increasingly popular and becomes a prime focus in advertisers media plans, ad-serving companies and publishers will develop a consistent way to adapt and tailor their ad views for multiple screens and devices, regardless of the distribution channel. More than likely, this will take some time to develop and even more time to be fully adopted, but a standard will eventually be born. Luckily, digital advertising has an organization to help with these standards.

Note   For more information on this topic, look at the section titled "Responsive-ize it" at www.ravelrumba.com/blog/responsive-ads-real-world-ad-server-implementation/.

IAB

In the digital advertising space there is an established bureau to help the industry cure its headache and fragmentation-related problems, whether they be mobile, display or even connected televisions. The Interactive Advertising Bureau (IAB) provides standardization in ad sizes, specs, and metrics agreed on by many publishers, ad servers, creative agencies, and active members of the IAB's working groups. It provides scale across media buys and ad networks by leveling the playing field. Because it sets practices known throughout the industry so adoption is more prevalent.

IAB Guidelines for Specs and Sizes

The IAB focuses on creating a comprehensive and evolving chart for developing ads and ad formats for all distribution channels. Table 1-1 offers a sample of the IAB's spec and size requirements for many desktop ads.

Table 1-1. *Some of the IAB's Size Guidelines for Desktop Displays*

Size	300 × 250	180 × 150	160 × 600	728 × 90
Initial size load	40 KB	40 KB	40 KB	40 KB
Max. frames/sec.	24 fps	24 fps	24 fps	24 fps
Animation time	15 sec	15 sec	15 sec	15 sec

■ **Note** For current information on IAB's display guidelines, visit
`www.iab.net/guidelines/508676/508767/displayguidelines`

As you can see from the table, these guidelines outline initial size of the ad, the frame rate of the ads animation and even duration time of the animation. The IAB continues to change, just as the industry it supports does. It regularly holds discussions and meetings in order to advance the industry's interests.

Another useful tool for assessing your ad's suitability in relation to IAB guidelines is Adobe's Adthenticate. This online tool provides a comprehensive suite of analytics for your ad creative, whether it is a Flash SWF file or an actual ad tag. An ad run through the process will generate a detailed report indicating whether the ad passes or fails with regard to the IAB specifications. More information on using this tool can be found at `https://adthenticate.adobe.com`. The tool is designed to eliminate guesswork between creative development and publisher specs so there is no confusion and no repeat work is needed.

Creative

OK, back to the campaign process. You've seen where advertisers want to spend their media dollars; now an ad needs to be designed and developed. At this point, in order to develop the ad effectively and convey the advertiser's (client's) message clearly, you should have a clear understanding of all the publisher's requirements and specs.

The creative is the actual element that gets rendered to the publisher page on day of launch. It's the SWF file or HTML that conveys the advertiser's message—rather, it's the file that visually conveys the advertiser's message. What is the advertiser's main focus? Is it to provide a direct response creative or just to keep the user within the ad experience with a brand-time initiative for the longest time possible? The goal is to create the advertiser's vision in an inventive and scalable ad unit, one that will run across every publisher site in the media plan. In industry terms, this is the LCD (lowest common denominator) spec for creative development. Developing and designing to this spec will allow for ultimate scale and fewer issues along the way.

Creative Development and Design

In this phase, the advertiser's creative agency will go back to the mock-ups and designs pitched during the digital strategy section. The agency will bring in creative and technical team members (that's you!) to design and build the final ad experience for the advertiser. This involves leveraging design skills with technology and code. Designers use Adobe Photoshop and similar tools, and technologists leverage code languages like JavaScript to pull off the execution.

Because ad experiences vary and marketers always want the newest thing, the technology changes at such a rapid pace that it's sometimes hard to keep up with it all. I stay ahead of the curve by reading up on new techniques and experimenting with different code languages. Find what works for you and keep at it. Depending on an ad's complexity and an advertiser's requirements, design and development can take several weeks to finish, so this activity can be done in conjunction with other campaign requirements, such as finalizing the media buy. To some, creative development is the most important process in the campaign; it's what tells the advertiser's message. Others say that it's the media buying and optimizing the target audience. I myself feel nothing goes far without an amazing creative message. With a compelling creative, you can make people want something they didn't want before. If you can achieve this with a mass audience, then it doesn't really matter where the ad runs. But keep this in mind: when was the last time you went online to look at the ads? At any rate, when a campaign is both effective and timely, it always performs very well.

Brand Time vs. Direct Response

An advertiser has many options when it comes to communicating with an audience. It can provide an ad experience that includes a game or video, which typically rolls into a brand-time initiative. Or it can allow the viewer or user to click something or fill out a form and submit information in the hope of getting potentially useful personal information (this form of advertising is called direct response). Certain options work better on certain screens and with certain advertisers. Stats from an ad-serving company, PointRoll, show that brand time works better on tablets and large screens and direct response works really well on mobile phones. PointRoll suggests that the big screen and tablets are more of a lean-back approach to advertising, whereas mobile is more of a utility-based experience. It gets users' attention quickly and while they are on the move.

Another focus for the advertiser in creative development is having a clear call to action. If you want your audience to do something, tell them! If you want them to watch a video or click a button, you'll gain higher response rates by instructing the audience to do it. In addition to keeping the CTA (call to action) clear, certain publishers won't allow you to develop a creative that doesn't follow the message it's attempting to communicate. For example, say I develop an ad where the CTA states "Click here for a free coupon!" Yet when the viewer clicks, a video pops open with no link to a coupon. A publisher will usually protect its audience by not running such a misleading ad campaign as this.

As this is all part of the user-experience aspect of the creative, you'll want to do your absolute best to develop an ad campaign that makes sense to your audience visually as well as functionally. The key is to remember the user; keep his or her overall experience in mind at all times.

Storytelling

Another prime focus of advertisers is the ability to tell a story with one or multiple ad campaigns. Many advertisers use cross-screen initiatives to communicate the message. This transmedia approach lets advertisers deliver a single cohesive message to a user via multiple screens and devices. Perhaps it's instructing a user to visit a web page in a broadcast spot for more information, or it's uploading a photo from your phone for a chance to see yourself on television and win a prize. The possibilities are virtually endless with this form of engagement, and the ROI (return on investment) for advertisers is enormous. With information about their user base they normally wouldn't get, they can more easily target individuals listening at given times and on given devices or screens.

Creative LCD

As already mentioned briefly, the goal in this development process is to create an LCD spec so the ad can run flawlessly across every publisher and ad network on the buy. This is where a creative agency has many hard choices to make. In order to raise the bar creatively, it—you—may need to ignore or break some publisher spec, but in order to run the campaign everywhere, you'll need to follow the lowest spec. It's a tough call to make, especially if you are trying to be innovative in the space.

Note   Innovative advertisers will work with ad servers to ask for special publisher allowance to run their creative.

This requires a one-off conversation with the publisher to hash out any concerns they may have about the ad's execution prior to running. Many different things could be settled, such as how much file size (or k-weight) the ad can have and what features the publisher will allow. In most cases, demonstrating the creative will help the publisher sign on or off on the execution. Worst thing that can happen is that they ask you to revise a few things.

These one-off conversations always occur, yet members in the space feel differently about them, depending on which side of the fence they're on. On the one hand, the conversations can allow an advertiser or creative agency to be super innovative, to break rules that once applied to everyone. On the other, they set a poor precedent for other advertisers looking to do similar things, and because it's not a public standard, other agencies will have to ask for the same special permission.

At the end of the day, the process is political and money driven. "Hey, welcome to advertising!" If you have a close relationship with a publisher or pour lots of dollars into a campaign, chances are you'll be given the OK to do whatever the hell you please. Being a job on its own, the process typically involves getting an ad-serving vendor such as PointRoll (http://pointroll.com), Media Mind (www.mediamind.com), or Crisp Media (www.crispmedia.com) to get that grant of permission and run a large, innovative digital ad campaign. These companies focus on developing strong publisher relationships so that advertisers and creative agencies can focus on being creative and continue to invent.

Ad Serving

Once the creative is designed, developed, and advertiser-approved, it's usually passed to an ad-server. The ad server's job is to do just what it's name states: serve the ads the creative team designs and develops. Once the ad-serving company gets the creative, it goes through an asset-intake process, where the creative assets are analyzed and processed to ensure all files are present and within spec and follow general best practices that adhere to publisher guidelines. If it is determined that the creative files are completely out of spec, they will usually be returned to the agency that developed them for further optimization. If the assets require only minimal work—adjusting a size or shaving some k-weight—the ad-serving company will typically do the work for the creative agency, whether to satisfy the client or ensure continued work or float the costs based on other revenue streams.

Tracking

Once the assets are given the sign-off, they're sent to the ad developers and engineers to install tracking and metrics for reporting purposes. Tracking is the additional code implementation into the creative assets in order to fire off an impression per view, a click for buttons and interaction beacons to track user interaction. For the ad server, the tracking is typically installed by way of an API (Application Programming Interface). APIs come in many forms but in this case it's the communication layer between the ad creative and the ad-serving platform.

Here are some tracking metrics an ad server might capture:

- impressions

- clicks

- interactions or activities

- interaction time

- video metrics

    - play/pause/stop/restart/replay

    - starts and completion rates

Depending on the necessities of the creative, other tracking requirements could be data collects, such as e-mail addresses, names, and phone numbers. This information is a user-controlled process: the viewer needs to enter information into a form field within the ad.

Third-Party Tracking

Another tracking concept in digital advertising involves third-party redirects and third-party tracking validation. A third-party tracking situation is one where another analytics company, in order to verify metrics, places tracking pixels within the creative, along with the ad servers. Platforms used in third-party tracking include Dart, Atlas, and ComScore 1x1's, to name a few. Typically, DoubleClick's Dart, Microsoft's Atlas and ComScore provide tracking pixels within a creative that they're not hosting and serving. 1x1's are invisible GIFs (image files) that fire when a user views an ad or performs some type of interaction. This could be one or several pixels depending on the advertiser's needs for the campaign.

The other form of third-party tracking uses redirects. Redirects are engaged when a user performs a click through action within the ad unit and the user is channeled through a redirect server location before it lands on the final destination. Advertisers can include as many redirects as they wish to validate the click-tracking within an ad unit.

Note Traditionally, the more redirects you add to a URL string, the more discrepancies in reporting you are likely to see. Also, URLs could be cut off due to browser limitations; the user would end up on a bad landing page.

Figures 1-3 and 1-4 show how one-click action by a user can actually ping a few different locations before it presents a landing page. Figure 1-3 illustrates what is called an in-band click redirect. In-band is the older of the two methods requiring a "daisy chain" effect to ping servers.

Figure 1-3. *How an in-band click redirects work*

The second method, out-of-band click redirects, pings all the servers at once (see Figure 1-4).

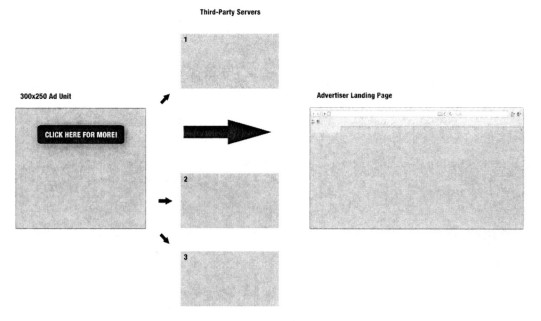

Figure 1-4. *How out-of-band click tracking works*

■ **Note**   For more information on how to set up appropriate click tracking, see the IAB's click measurement PDF: http://www.iab.net/media/file/click-measurement-guidelines2009.pdf.

Optimization

Upon completion of the tracking, one additional level of creative optimization is needed to ensure all creative meets k-weight specs and doesn't hog CPU power of a users machine. An optimization check ensures that the ad will run flawlessly on multiple machines, platforms, publishers, and devices. The optimization process can include rewriting code, compressing bitmap images, converting images to vector artwork, simplifying vector artwork, and staggering the loading sequences based on user interactions. It can take quite a bit of time, depending on the number of ads and which devices and screens are targeted (as ultimately dictated by the media plan). These tests are frequently rigorous, since each ad has to run on multiple computers and operating systems in real time and is reliant on the length of the ad animation or video duration. Thus, the number of optimization steps can grow pretty quickly.

Tags

After the creative runs a thorough round of prerelease quality assurance checks, the ad-serving company will create ad tags out of the creative assets in order to ensure the creative performs accurately in its new ad-serving environment. The creation of ad tags typically involves upload into a content management system (CMS) that the ad-serving company operates. Whether it be static images, HTML, or Flash files, the creative assets get compiled and stored in the system. Depending on the publisher's specifications, the ad server will generate any of several different tag types and formats, including the following:

- iframe tags
- JavaScript tags
- Flash SWF tags
- image and click tags

■ **Note** Iframes are used to embed one HTML document inside another one.

For richer executions some publishers may require a file that lives on their servers; it allows the ad server to communicate with the domain that the publisher's site is on. This is a requirement when "iframe busting" (an industry term) is needed. Iframe busting allows an ad tag to render outside the publisher's desired iframe for the ad; this in turn allows the ad server to interact directly with the publisher's content. This type of execution should be set up in advance with the publisher to ensure that all parties are on the same page and that this file is in place at the time of ad serving. Permission for this type of execution is usually granted only to trusted ad servers, as breaking the iframe creates the ability to do damage if one wanted to. Figure 1-5 shows how an ad tag will treat iframes both "busted" and "non-busted".

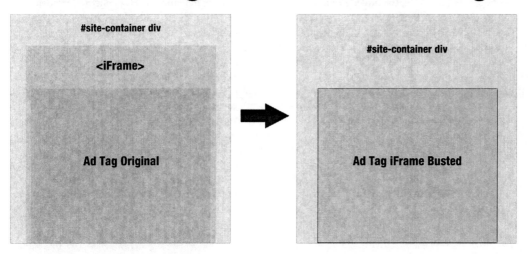

Figure 1-5. An ad tag can break free of an iframe when a publisher's hosted file is in place

Quality Assurance

Once the ad tags are generated and analyzed by the ad server, a final round of tracking quality assurance (QA) is run to ensure that all the impressions are firing off and metrics are being accounted for. Assuming the tracking calls are good to go, the unique tags are sent off to each and every publisher on the media plan. Upon receiving the tags, a publisher will perform its own QA to ensure they operate smoothly with other site content in a live environment. It may take a publisher a few days to complete this process, depending on its ad operation's size and the number of tags to be scheduled.

At this phase, the publisher will usually offer a test page to the ad server so more QA can be done at the ad server's end. The test page typically mirrors what the page will look and function like on the day the ad goes live. The page used is often the home page with the usual dummy copy—content of the "lorem ipsum" type—instead of actual editorial content. This test is performed solely because anything can happen in the live environment. You could have other ads competing for computer processing power or a hidden navigational menu that is knocking your ad 20 pixels down. Whatever the case may be, this test is performed to eliminate any remaining mystery that could derail a campaign launch. This could result in a lot of back-and-forth involving the ad server, the publisher, and the creative agency, depending on whose domain the issue is in. The back-and-forth can be time-consuming for sure, but its important to hash out issues that may come up during the campaign before the launch. Think of it as test-driving a car before it's taken out on the track.

Campaign Launch

When the publisher and ad server give a final thumbs up to the supplied tags, they're scheduled by the publisher for a specific launch date and set live. Finally, one last round of checking goes into the tags while they are live in the real-world environment by the ad server, publisher, creative agency, and most importantly, advertiser. All the checks have been put in place to assure that the performance remains smooth throughout the course of launch.

Analytics and Reporting

At the campaign's beginning and end, the advertiser and media agency will request the ad server and any third-party measurement companies to run their analytic reports. This is done at the beginning to ensure that all analytics are being tracked successfully and at the end to aggregate all the results and metrics. The ad server's reports will tally the totals to date; the tally includes but is not limited to impressions, clicks, activities, video metrics, click-through rate (CTR), view-through rate, interaction time, and conversions. These results are offered to all requesting parties as the final report, from which they can get a clear picture of the campaign's overall performance.

The information in this report is invaluable for the advertiser; it outlines the key performance indicators (KPIs) of the campaign, whether they relate to driving brand awareness or interaction rate. A report could be issued as a Microsoft Excel document, a CSV, XML or JSON file or even centrally located on the ad server's CMS application via a user-controlled analytics dashboard.

Once the report is sent out and reviewed by all parties, the ad server bills either the publisher or the media agency, based on a CPM model, on the basis of the total impressions served and possibly labor in development. This is the stage in which media and creative can learn what worked and didn't work for their advertiser and apply the recently acquired knowledge toward making a better campaign in the future. This sort of number crunching and statistical analysis can be fed back to the folks heading up digital strategy and, even more importantly, the advertiser.

Payment

Based on the overall budget dictated by the advertiser's total digital spend, the media agency will have a specific amount to devote to securing the appropriate media inventory. Another budget is assigned to creative and technological design. The media budget will go to paying the publisher for the ad inventory and possibly the ad server for the production and serving of ad tags. For the creative and technology development, those payments are sent to the creative agency, possibly the ad server as well, for any tasks needed to optimize assets.

Note   Depending on the campaign, certain one-off vendors—technology partners, enablers, data providers—may be needed. Their presence would result in additional fees.

Based on the agreed CPM, the advertiser, media agency, or publisher will float the cost. Sometimes deals are made between the ad server and media agency on the basis of a certain number of impressions being met. Because the ad server bills off a CPM model as well, if a given number of impressions, x, are guaranteed, the ad server may cover all production-related costs. Having the client shoot for a tentative impression count—for example, 10,000,000 at $1.00 CPM or 50,000,000 at $.50 CPM—is a great way to go if you want to increase your overall volume. If the agreed impressions are not met, the media agency pays additional fees to make up what was not accounted for to the ad server.

Sometimes, things just don't go as planned, and people have to eat the costs of missed impressions due to technical or administrative limitations. These mishaps come at the cost of a make-good. Make-goods are often payable when the ad-serving company does something to hinder the release of tags on time to the publishers. This is also the case if a publisher double- or triple-books ad inventory at a specific time that the plan initially asked for. This make-good typically comes by way of free ad serving or an agreed-upon amount of additional impressions covered by the ad server. The publisher's terms may be slightly different; it may offer another day of ad inventory or an ad slot on another section within its site or network at a reduced rate or even free, depending on its relationship with the client.

As you can see, a lot of hands are reaching into the advertisers spending pot. Since every single campaign is different, depending on the tools and people needed, awareness of budget constraints is a must in determining what is needed to get a campaign out of the gate. It essential to ensure success, to reduce make-goods, and to schedule accurate launch dates.

Targeting Audiences—a Smarter Future

As technology becomes more sophisticated and media buying ever more intelligent, advertisers are able to purchase audience segments very easily and target their audience accordingly. Audience segments are typically sold as a group of generalized individuals that will most likely view an ad and react positively to its branded messages. Companies employ many different systems to gain information about users. Such information includes but is not limited to

- location

- online behavior and browsing history

- demographic information

- publisher passed data

This information is either served directly by the ad server's ad tag or derived from browser cookies, which were once dropped on users by sites they visited. The benefit and power in this is that viewers can get tailored messaging with information personalized to their liking. Advertisers adore this tool: they gain vital information about their customer base and its buying habits and location. They acquire the power to influence their viewers, especially when they include social channels like Facebook and Twitter in the mix.

There is a famous saying: "With great power, comes great responsibility." It's certainly true in online advertising. As user privacy is a huge concern when dealing with such data, the next sections will be geared toward showcasing how information is accessed, collected, distributed, and used.

Privacy

Online privacy is currently a huge topic, not just in the industry but even at government level in the United States and Europe. Like it or not, Google, Yahoo, MSN, Microsoft, and many other companies have information about you. Believe it or not, you yourself handed it over to them, more or less. A quick question: do you have a Gmail, Yahoo, or MSN mail account? Do you use social networks—Facebook, Google+, and so on? I assume the answer to at least one of those questions is a resounding, yes. The truth is, when you sign up and provide information to these social networks and publishers, you are essentially trading the information for use of their tools and services. You effectively make yourself Google's and Facebook's product to advertisers. These services sell audience information to advertisers because they know what your likes and dislikes are, how old you are, and even where you live. This may be a bit scary, even Big Brotherish, but really, you never get anything for free. So choose wisely before you hand over your information.

For more information on how the U.S. government is helping web users understand their rights, visit `http://onguardonline.gov`.

Cookies

So you may be asking yourself, if I don't sign up for those services, how can they get my information? You don't need to surrender all your information to be tracked online. All by itself, online behavior is an extremely valuable metric for advertisers. Have you ever shopped on Amazon or another shopping site and then later viewed a couple of web pages and realized that the product you originally looked at on Amazon was now being advertised to you wherever you went online? If you have, you're not alone. This happens because you had a cookie dropped in your browser storage.

Every browser has some memory dedicated to storing files in its local cache. They can be stored to optimize viewing web sites that you frequent. Depending on what domain the cookie was dropped from (in this case Amazon), different sorts of information bits are stored about you as viewer. In Amazon's case, this information could be what product you saw, what color it was, what time of day you viewed it, or a plethora of other information.

Once the cookie information is in your cache, you take it everywhere you go on the Web. Sort of like a digital shopping passport! This information can be shared with data providers (Blue Kai and similar companies) who use it to pinpoint even more information about you as you browse. The more you browse, the more information is accumulated about you and your browsing behavior: what your potential likes and dislikes are, what time you normally search the Web—the list goes on. This information can even be paired with a unique ID number and loaded in databases for lookup and retargeting. AdTruth (`http://adtruth.com`) and companies like it are worth checking out. This information is not, strictly speaking, personal; it's just information about you and your online behavior. But again, data providers can sell the information to advertisers to help them target an audience by groups or segments—potentially down to individuals.

If you are a Firefox browser user, there is a really nice browser add-on called Collusion. It helps visualize what is going on when you are browsing the Internet (see Figure 1-6).

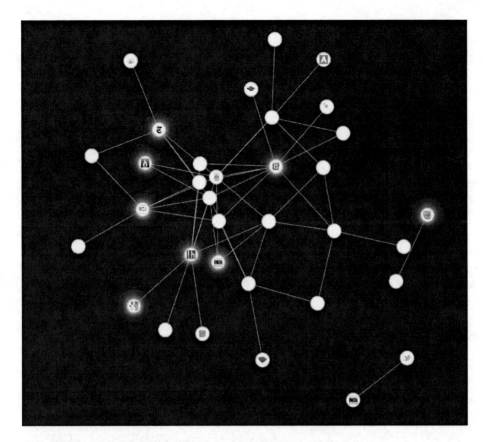

Figure 1-6. *What the Firefox browser add-on Collusion looks like*

As you can see, Collusion shows what sites are sharing information about you as you browse the Web and, what is more important, how they access each others information. The image in the figure was taken by going to five different web addresses. It's remarkable to see how much can be collected without a user doing much other than typing in URL's. An advertiser can see that some publishers are setting cookies on users to track certain information. Then that information can be sold to make better media buys and/or tailor the creative messaging within the ad itself.

___

■ **Note**   Learn more about Collusion at its web site: `www.mozilla.org/en-US/collusion/`.

___

Publisher-Passed Data

As you now know, when you use Gmail or Yahoo Mail or something similar, you essentially allow the use of your information for advertising purposes. Publisher-passed data allows publishers to put an encrypted string of information into the ad server's ad tag and allows the ad server to determine what viewer it has and craft an appropriate advertising message. This information could include age, geographic region, zip code, gender, and even interests among many other inputs.

Say that, from my e-mail and browsing history, Yahoo knows I am 18 years old and interested in electronics. If an advertiser is promoting new products to me, Yahoo can pass information to the ad server that my known interest is electronics and that I am 18. The ad server has inputs to determine an accurate output message, perhaps a video game system and an iPod—who knows? You've gotten the idea by this point and are probably asking yourself, "Wait, advertisers have all this information about me?" The answer to that varies, but at least they don't have any personal identifiable information (PII).

PII

Personal identifiable information (PII) is intelligence about a user or a user's activity that would give away his or her exact identity. This includes but isn't limited to name, address, credit card number, and social security number. Media agencies and publishers want to get as much information as they can about their audience in order to make smarter business decisions and make advertiser's dollars work harder by targeting people that will listen. When dealing with an audience's personal information, they must be in accord with federal law on online privacy and not use this detailed information in malicious ways. The only way information of this sort can be transferred via an ad unit is through use of an opt-in process. It could be a check box selection before submitting a form in an advertisement or even signing up for a free service.

Luckily for viewers and users, the law also requires an opt-out process. Fundamentally, the opt-out process is set up to allow users to disallow the sharing of their information on such sites and networks as Google and Facebook after they've signed up for the free service, willingly or otherwise. The opt-out process is a tricky one in that it begs the question whether what applies to one publisher applies to the next. Also, what happens to all the information that they already have about you?

What's Next for Privacy?

My instinct tells me that new rules, policies, and guidelines for Internet and online advertising privacy will appear sooner or later; probably very soon. Congress has actively sought representatives from all the leading online properties and advertising outlets with whom to discuss this topic and related matters and ultimately attempt to figure out whether companies can police themselves or will need the U.S. government to step in. Another issue is that the whole world is online, and privacy laws are not standard from one country to another.

Anyone with questions regarding privacy online should contact the ad server, the IAB, the IAB UK, or a local political representative. There should be a clear benefit in how information about an audience is used to deliver tailored and relevant advertising, and you should voice concern if you feel your rights are being jeopardized. As advertising and technology continue to get smarter, it's sensible for you to do the same.

Terminology Review

You've been exposed to a ton of industry buzzwords and lingo in this chapter. The purpose was, not to confuse, but to educate, in the event you have to communicate with team members or prospective clients. Use Table 1-2 to review the key words and acronyms covered thus far in this chapter.

Table 1-2. *Campaign Process Terminology Review*

Word	Definition or Meaning
creative pitch	Where a creative agency develops a marketing message and pitches it to the client, the advertiser.
media buying	Where a media agency secures ad inventory on various publisher sites and ad networks to satisfy the launch of an ad campaign.
impressions	The number of times an ad has been rendered to a screen through the life of a campaign.

(continued)

Table 1-2. (*continued*)

Word	Definition or Meaning
CPM	Cost per mille (thousand); referring to calculation of impressions served.
roadblock (or takeover)	Typically, when an advertiser buys an exclusive spot on a publisher's page, is the only advertiser on a given day, and has complete control creatively.
DSP	Demand-side platform (or trading desk); it allows the purchase of media in real time via an auction.
placement	A particular ad on a specific section within a publisher's page or ad network.
CSS	Cascading Style Sheets; they dictate the look and feel of a page or ad.
JavaScript	A tool that handles the functionality and logic of the page or ad.
IAB	Interactive Advertising Bureau; an organization dedicated to the growth of online advertising and to development of standards for it.
LCD	Lowest common denominator; referring to development of an ad that will run well across an entire media buy.
CTA	Call to action; having a clear call to action in your creative will ensure that your users know how to interact.
k-weight	The binary weight of the ad unit—40 KB, for example—that will be rendered on the publisher page.
CPU processes	The central processing unit, which often spikes when a taxing creative, often involving heavy graphics, animation, and code, is rendered to the page. These factors can slow a user's machine down and hinder the overall user experience.
third-party	1x1 tracking pixels from third-party ad vendors to perform validation on metrics within online advertisements.
CMS	Content management systems, typically used by an ad-serving company to house creative and create ad tags. Also used for inventory and aggregation of analytics.
iframe busting	The term used when publishers allow ad creative to work outside the designated ad iframe on the page.
CTR	Click-through rate; it determines the rate at which clicks were measured for a particular ad campaign divided by the number of impressions served.
interaction time	Time spent interacting within the ad experience. This could be when a user has expanded ad real estate, watched a video or plays a game.
conversions	User that perform a desired action. For example, clicking for more or clicking a button to a landing page.
cookies	The file that is dropped in browser storage with information about a user's online behavior. This information can then be accessed by other vendors.
PII	Personal identifiable information; any information that specifies the identity of a user viewing or interacting with an ad. Examples are name, address, SSID.
opt-out	A process in place that allow users to disallow information sharing to advertisers.

Summary

This chapter has reviewed in exhaustive detail what goes into a typical advertising campaign process. You've seen how agencies develop strategies to achieve an advertiser's goals, vision, and business objectives. Also discussed was how media is found and purchased, whether by means of traditional buying or through a trading desk using the real-time bidding approach. You saw, too, how creative design and development are handled and how digital storytelling is a key element in a successful campaign. You took a look at how an ad server receives assets and adds tracking to leverage information about a viewer and tailor messaging. You saw how analytics and reporting from the ad server equate to payments as well as knowledge and insight into future campaigns. Many industry terms were introduced; many key points about the industry, including privacy and publisher specs, were discussed. For you to go over this information is extremely important; the rest of the book will touch on concepts and terminology outlined here.

It's time now to take what you know about the campaign process into Chapter 2, where we take a deep dive into understanding what brought us here today and look at the technology that started it all. It's a bit of a history lesson, but it sets the stage for how HTML5 became so prevalent in 2012 and how advertising needed to adjust and follow suit.

If you're ready, let's continue . . .

CHAPTER 2

■ ■ ■

Evolution of Advertising Technology

Now that you have a strong understanding of the campaign process, it's time to understand what the technologies and businesses are that drive us to where we are today. The industry, as discussed in the previous chapter, is constantly going through rapid changes, and as an HTML5 designer and developer, it's important for you to understand all of this. Advances in technology, improvements in processes, and gains in overall efficiency appear with predictable regularity. With new browsers being developed, technical specifications being written, and new plug-ins being deployed at a dashing pace, there's never a shortage of important aspects to consider.

For starters, let's discuss the foundation of the preceding and current Web, how content is rendered to the screen by means of varying technologies, and improvements seen nowadays that would have been unthinkable years back. Let's also take a look at the beginnings and transitions from HTML to the Flash platform and at the business behind the technologies used on the Web, as well as dive into where the new hotness that is HTML5—and look at it all from an advertiser's perspective.

This chapter will discuss how HTML5 was brought onto the scene, what it aimed to accomplish, and how one influential pioneer rushed it onto the mainstream market. At this chapter's close, there'll be a terminology review to go through some terms that may be unfamiliar. Finally, there'll be a summary of what has been learned thus far as we head into the core of this book and learn still more about how advertising is developed and designed with the emerging web standards: HTML, CSS, and JavaScript.

Early Web and HTML

First, as clichéd as it sounds, let's take a trip down memory lane and discuss the foundation of the World Wide Web. It was the 1990s—the era of Pearl Jam, jean jackets, and, what's more important, the early Web. It all began with an MIT grad and computer scientist by the name of Tim Berners-Lee, who created the World Wide Web specification and proposed hypertext markup language (HTML) as the structural language that all browsers would eventually comprehend to render elements to the screen. The World Wide Web Consortium, or W3C, states that

> *HTML is the language for describing the structure of Web pages.*

In addition to the HTML building blocks, style and function are also needed. Cascading Style Sheets (CSS) maintains the style, and JavaScript is the language that controls the logic and functionality (also known as the "behavior" within the page) of the web content the user sees. There is also the Document Object Model (DOM), which is an object hierarchy for reading and editing objects in the browser stack. For those who are serious about web development, DOM, a huge topic on its own, is well worth understanding.

Hindsight reveals that the early Web was patchy. Browsers were primitive by design, and trying to figure out the market share of the installed user base was a big challenge. This made web development on browsers a total mess; each had its own limitations and code base under the hood. Think of it in the context of television sets, with the TV as your browser; depending on the set's manufacturer—Sony, LG, Samsung, whatever—the program being watched would need to take into consideration all of the different TVs and adapt accordingly. This sounds totally unrealistic now, but that's just what the early Web was like. This is why the HTML spec was pretty simple to start with. It needed adoption first; then it could iterate and become more progressive.

Advertising with HTML

Everyone now recognizes that web pages are developed and designed with HTML, CSS, and JavaScript. As the Internet became more mainstream, it was only a matter of time before advertisers got into the market. It reminds me of the question, "Where can't you see advertising?" with the answer being, "In your sleep." As almost everyone had an opportunity to be online at some point throughout the 1990s and into the 2000s, advertisers needed to get onto publisher pages so that casual web surfers—a vast potential viewership—would see their ads.

Naturally, in the beginning ads were very basic; just static images at first. Think of the early AOL startup page on a 56k dial-up modem; you know, the one that you had to unplug your phone to use (if you were tech savvy, you had a phone line splitter). Depending how far back you think, the ad inventory was scarce if present at all.

Note The Internet Wayback Machine allows you to enter a URL into its database—for example, AOL.com—and review previous versions of the site throughout the years. The ad slots do not render, as these campaigns are long over, but you can get an idea as to where and how ads were used then. Visit it here (note that all sites aren't supported): http://archive.org/web/web.php.

Pop-up Ads and Subsequent Evolution

We all know how deeply pop-up advertising messages were hated and how much they plagued the Internet early on, so I'll spare you more words of hate and offer something of an educational lesson instead. In short, an annoying pop-up ad is only a snippet of JavaScript code executing. In JavaScript, the following code opens a new browser window and takes the following parameters, or arguments or URL, name, specs and replace.

```
window.open(URL,name,specs,replace);
```

With the preceding code, a new window is spawned when a user views a page where this code is present. Since it was notoriously annoying to have many new windows open as a user casually browsed the Web, browser developers implemented what are known as pop-up blockers to keep any window.open(. . .); code from executing without the user actually clicking on something first. This was a great improvement in the overall user experience online; it forced advertising to be maintained within the specific real estate of the page it was intended for. Given that effect, advertisers were very limited as far as different forms of advertising online. They knew that, due to the popularity of the "new" screen, they wanted to be in the digital space, but they didn't quite know how to measure their return on investment. Typically, they ran simple ad campaigns; nothing extraordinary, because of the creative limitations and the fact that they could never measure campaign performance. For media buying, this was a much different approach and a new type of media inventory to secure for advertisers. For the longest time, they had only needed to worry about TV as their main screen, and they had Nielsen (nielsen.com) and other companies to analyze the success of their television campaigns.

Pioneers in the space, seeing the advertisers' frustration as a huge opportunity to capitalize on, began to add metrics and creative enhancements to their relatively simple campaigns. In the beginning, the creative of the ads and metrics was extremely meek and primitive, being either static or having only slight, if any, movement, utilizing animated GIFs, and measuring only on impressions and clicks. Also, since browsers were fragmented in the adoption of the users, ad designers had to leverage browser-specific code to maintain how an ad would look in various environments. This additional effort, just to get a simple campaign out the door, proved to be a time-consuming process.

Rich Media

As advertisers increasingly asked for more creativity and measurement from their online ad campaigns, a new form of online advertising was required—Rich Media Advertising. Since online ads were pretty much static in the early Web, the arrival of interactivity, rollovers, and expanding ad experiences met with real popularity and rapid adoption in the advertiser market, which saw them as bringing a new, much-needed window for creative reach and a way to effectively measure online success.

On the other hand, the media vendors saw this as a shift in the way advertising was created, bought, and sold in the space. As you may guess, early rich media ads were developed using traditional HTML, CSS, and JavaScript techniques. Figure 2-1 shows the very first Rich Media ad—for the movie Erin Brockovich, created and served by the company PointRoll (`pointroll.com`).

Figure 2-1. *The first Rich Media ad*

Things have changed a bit since then, of course, but in the online space at the time, this was truly groundbreaking. For the first time a user could roll over the ad unit and have it expand to a much more robust experience. The traditional Call to Action (CTA) for "click here" was revamped to display "mouse this ad", inviting users to interact by simply rolling over the ad unit to get more content. It's also helpful to note that even in the demonstration environment, there are messages to handle the browser differences and inconsistencies. In most cases, if you could not see the rich ad experience, the ad server company served you a static or a default ad instead (see Figure 2-2).

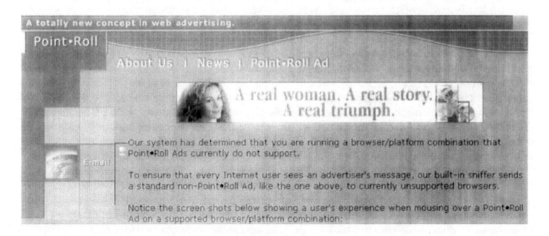

Figure 2-2. *The first Rich Media ad's backup static or default ad*

The ad-serving platform would be smart enough to determine whether or not the user could render the ad in its rich form by using what was called the "user has" rule. This technique analyzed the user's system and browser and detected to what level the user's machine was capable of rendering the unit. This sort of dynamic adjustment was really unheard of prior to Rich Media. Additionally, in the event that the user saw a static ad instead of the rich one, the ad platform would report impressions differently; in most cases the static impressions would be offered at a reduced CPM to the advertiser.

Tracking and Measurement

Throughout early Rich Media ads, tracking and measurement were pretty minimal yet effective enough to tell a story for the marketer. Advertisers, however, wanted to know more about their customers if they were going to sink more media dollars into this space. As more money eventually flowed into the industry, rich media became the common approach to online advertising.

Since advertisers were now able to measure how many people interacted, expanded, and closed an ad, they could include photo galleries, e-mail forms, and other creative elements to engage the audience, all the while reporting on everything and having it conveyed back to the advertiser for valuable brand insight. As time passed, this approach to advertising became solid enough to sustain advertisers' interest, but HTML, CSS and JavaScript had limitations when it came to creativity and to what could be done within the native browser environment.

Luckily for advertisers, there was a nifty little browser plug-in gaining traction in the market. The famous "skip intro" plug-in created by Macromedia allowed developers to easily create rich animation and add video and interactivity. Simply put, this plug-in single-handedly changed the face of online advertising forever.

Flash

Throughout the 2000s, digital advertising was pushed as far as it could go with animated GIFs, HTML, CSS, and JavaScript. Frequently, some simple interactivity and animated GIFs would be the creative extent of a campaign. Marketers and advertisers pushed the envelope creatively, but the limitations of the browser were much too significant. Advertisers just couldn't do things directly inside the browser that they wanted to accomplish. The response to this limitation was Macromedia's Flash Player.

Flash allowed for gorgeous, highly interactive content within the browser by use of an installed plug-in. The Flash Player swiftly moved to the forefront; its popularity and ubiquity made it the prime platform for moving online advertising forward. It finally gave developers and designers a cross-browser way to easily develop online experiences and deploy everywhere, consistently. Before it came along, such things were really unheard of.

Flash was the answer to many problems, creatively and from a business standpoint, due to its rapid development environment. By use of the plug-in, web developers were confident that the same experience would be had regardless of browser manufacturer, operating system, or version. A market once dominated by static ads and basic HTML-driven experiences quickly transitioned to Flash, thanks to its ease of use and large installed user base.

Flash's market penetration would grow to a percentile in the high nineties in major markets around the globe. No other browser plug-in had so much reach. In addition to enhancing graphics and interactivity, in time it would come to support bidirectional streaming of video and audio content, something that a browser alone couldn't dream of doing (at least back then).

While many developers and designers loved Flash for its ease of use, others disliked it for its easier programming language, which allowed immature developers to build inefficient and poorly designed programs or experiences. Flash's JavaScript-like language, ActionScript, permitted code to execute on animation frames, and because of the poor coding techniques tied to early Flash users, it slowed browser experiences and often even crashed browsers due to the hogging of computer resources. Since ads could be developed in a fashion that would slow down users' machines and overuse system resources, Flash typically got a bad rap from the hard-core software developer community.

Adobe

As Macromedia's Flash continued to grow in both web development and online advertising, Adobe, seeing the enormous opportunity with Flash, ended up acquiring Macromedia and all of its products on December 3, 2005, for a whopping US$3.4 billion. With Adobe's acquisition of Flash and its first company release of version 9, Flash had many years of developer interest, installed user base, and platform development already. So Adobe continued to invest heavily in Flash as the pinnacle way to develop and deploy rich Internet applications and advertising on the Web.

Flash Player Ubiquity

By version 9, the market that had the Flash Player installed was astounding. By June 2008, 98.4 percent had a Flash Player version of 7 or higher installed. With these numbers, advertisers looked solely to the Flash platform for executing their rich experiences on the Web. Not only did they leverage it within online advertising campaigns, but they also realized the power in the platform for creating their branded web sites, landing pages, and other web properties.

Other plug-ins in the space—including Java applets and the newer Unity player—have never seen such high penetration rates, which is why advertisers don't currently look to them as ideal platforms for far-reaching online advertising.

■ **Note**   You can see the current Flash Player Penetration Rates here:
`http://www.adobe.com/products/player_census/flashplayer/PC.html`.

Flash Player Video

From this moment on, a lot changed on the Web; advertising, the days of thumbnail-sized videos, and video player differences were now a thing of the past, thanks to Flash and faster machines. As of Flash Player version 6, released in March 2002, video could be included from within the compiled Flash file (SWF) itself; as of version 8 it could support streaming video content from servers. At a high level, this changed the way marketers and advertisers developed online ads forever! Entertainment advertisers could now produce their movie trailers for the Web, and it could now be watched even within an ad unit.

Video on the Web was and still is a huge topic. With more and more advertisers and people wanting web video and with the technology finally up to speed, YouTube and other billion-dollar businesses were created. With dial-up Internet access a distant memory and more and more people becoming users of broadband Internet and getting download speeds of 10 to 30 megabytes per second and with enhancements to the Flash player as of version 10.2, video could now be full-screen HD and offloaded to the GPU of the user's machine, which allowed for smoother playback; meanwhile, the CPU was freed up to do things like resource allocation and code execution.

From a publisher's perspective, since video was being streamed into the ad unit, it came at no additional cost to the overall k-weight size in the creative advertisements. Now advertisers could do more within the ad and not worry about a poor user experience or even breaking specs. As HD video on the Web became the norm, companies like Akamai created true streaming HD networks and delivery solutions for delivering and analyzing video performance.

Advertising with Flash

With the Flash Player reaching nearly 100 percent of all desktop machines in major markets, advertisers saw the opportunity to create compelling and interactive rich media with full-motion graphics and dynamic data on a single unified platform. Marketers were totally hooked; Flash was the answer to all the problems that had existed in previous versions of HTML. With the evolution of the creative, tracking followed suit; growing much more sophisticated, it proved a better return on investment (ROI) for advertisers and media buyers.

Ad-serving companies could track anything: a view, a rollover, even video milestones and completion rates. Basically, if you could think of it, they'd track it. With Rich Media leveraging the Flash Player, metrics and creativity soared to new levels. Flash allowed for deeper tracking and analytics integration with use of APIs. Flash's ActionScript APIs were developed to provide communication with ad-serving platforms, which allowed for more integrated tracking across campaigns.

As was discussed in the previous chapter regarding browser cookies, Flash also has its own way of storing data on its internal cache. Local shared objects—known as Flash cookies—allowed developers to store up to 100 kilobytes of data by default to provide richer experiences within ads. However, the legal issues around privacy still arise in advertising, whether it's browser- or Flash-based cookies. One thing is for certain, though: with Flash, rich media advertising was really born; rich motion graphics, video, dynamic data, and much more could finally be done within the browser by using a true ubiquitous plug-in.

HTML5

So now we know that Flash has made the biggest impact in online advertising thus far, and we're not far off from seeing how HTML5 will do it again. Sure, HTML has been through a couple of versions and even a few variations to date (XHTML), but we're now in the midst of the fifth release. As of 2012, the HTML5 draft isn't set for public finalization for many years yet, but advertisers are looking to leverage the new power of HTML5 to create their next innovative advertising campaigns, taking what Flash did within the plug-in but doing it all within the browser, natively. The HTML5 spec has had a lot to learn from Flash, so it's pretty important to see its significance within the overall picture.

Such HTML5 features as the canvas element, drag-and-drop, and the video element all evolved from experience with the Flash Player and what the browser couldn't handle on its own. Think about it: there was no cell phone before the pay phone! You must understand that the Flash Player did what the browser couldn't do for roughly ten years, so it's pretty exciting to see where we will end up, what with coming back to web standards and HTML5 after all this time with Flash.

HTML5 may seem like the new kid on the block, but in reality the W3C and working-group members drafted the first spec in January 2008. Since then it's been through many revisions and public "last calls," where members inside and outside the W3C voted on the completeness of the current spec.

Why HTML5?

One may well ask, "What rushed HTML5 onto the scene so quickly?" or "How come Flash was fine for so long and all of a sudden, HTML5 was the main focus for everyone online?" There is a simple answer. On June 29, 2007, Steve Jobs of Apple changed the world with the release of the iPhone, complete with a browser that would not support the Flash Player. Now, I say change the world for a variety of reasons—first, it would be the first smartphone to have the full web browsing experience with a glass touch screen. Second, it would change the Web forever, since before its release nearly all web sites were powered with at least a small bit of Flash content for graphics, video, or dynamic content. Finally, along with the Web, digital advertising would follow suit because nearly all digital campaigns to date had been created in Flash.

Many folks have mixed feelings about Apple's decision not to support Flash on the iOS operating system. Some say it was business related; others focus more on the overall performance and battery life on smartphones and tablets. I myself don't care too much if Flash, HTML5 or something else is the new standard. The same thing went on years back when everyone transitioned over to Flash. At the end of the day, working with web standards and removing any dependencies from external plug-ins will always bring you out on top in the long run. As with all respectable technology of its time, it eventually comes to an end and eases the fragmentation for everyone. For more insight into Steve Jobs's perspective on the Flash platform, check out the now-infamous post "Thoughts on Flash" (apple.com/hotnews/thoughts-on-flash).

HTML5 Adoption

Now you may be saying, "OK, so Apple pushed through HTML5 by removing Flash Player on the iPhone, but what about the other browsers?" This is a great question but one that isn't easily answered. First, as mentioned in the previous section, HTML5 is in a working spec state, meaning it's not complete. Even as I write, it's still evolving.

So adoption is fragmented, and support is often limited but growing. Apple's first release of the iPhone implemented only some features of the new web standard; in reality, HTML5's adoption is still, to this day, very fragmented. In the desktop space, browsers are all at varied levels of HTML5 compliance, and compliance is always changing because the spec is not finalized. You see how confusing this can get? If you visit beta.html5test.com, you'll be able to see how your browser ranks against the current HTML5 spec. Chances are it is subpar in the overall scope of HTML5, with some features completely unsupported. You may ask, "Why still choose to use it?" Well, it's OK! In fact at the time of this writing, only the bleeding-edge beta browsers, like the Chrome Canary, Firefox, and Webkit Nightly builds, support most of the latest and greatest features (but not all). Current HTML5 adoption is nominal; you can see how much of a headache it is for developers and designers to create a unified experience in this fragmented area. It's very reminiscent of the early Web; still, we need to start taking advantage of HTML5's features if we want penetration on mobile and tablet devices. For advertisers, this is a must!

HTML5 Video

One small feature of HTML5's overall feature set—it was dubbed in some blogs and news forums the "Flash Killer"—is HTML5 video (it will be covered in more detail in Chapter 7). I'd like to take a minute to set the record straight, as many educated developers have done before. First, because Flash is a platform, it requires a plug-in to play video within your browser. Flash can support progressively downloaded video as well as streaming. It can also support video from various protocols and adaptively change during playback. Second, as HTML5's video element is a tag within the HTML markup, dealing with this tag at the present time has limitations. For example, pretty much each browser takes its own file wrapper and codec to render the video correctly. This proves to be a huge task for video transcode jobs, and anyone attempting to have video within their creative. Also, as there is no standard for streaming video through HTML5, more development is needed in that realm as well.

A very comprehensive article written by online video great Robert Reinhardt outlines the fragmentation around HTML5's video element, not to mention the overall support for HTML5 (see "The World of Pain That Is HTML5 Video": `transitioning.to/2012/01/the-world-of-pain-that-is-html5-video/`). Things like streaming and adaptive bitrate are all things outlined within the article.

HTML5 vs. Flash on Mobile

For advertisers in the modern world, mobile is a key platform to target, and it's important to know what evolving tech can achieve here. It's pretty safe to say that mobile was indeed primitive in the beginning, when the only smartphones were Nokias, Palms, and Blackberrys and their web browsers were . . . well, for lack of a better word, awful. Around the late 2000s, since the arrival of the Apple iPhone, mobile has become a huge market. Many people saw this coming. Thanks to the iPhone's web browser, it offered something of an actual web experience with full functionality, unlike earlier devices that offered the Web but in a different view. Web developers and designers, heavily invested in Flash, needed to ensure that the decision makers on the business end understood that their online initiatives would need to support the growing market share of HTML5 on mobile devices—and OH BOY, was it growing!

There is a lot of confusion within the industry as it relates to the HTML5/Flash debate. Many startups in the field saw this; they raced into this market, using fear as fuel, to provide services that eased this transition, which in turn moved HTML5 along even faster. Companies like Adobe and Google started making tools that would take Flash timeline animation and repurpose it into HTML, CSS3, and JavaScript animations for emerging browsers to render without use of the Flash Player plug-in.

With Apple's iOS taking up a massive share of the mobile operating system market, Google's Android and Blackberry's Playbook were being released with support for Flash. Adobe's credo would be that users of these devices would get the "complete web experience" and that Flash Player would be supported and installed on mobile devices in their product road map. In fact, Adobe released this statistic outlining the future support of Flash Player on mobile into 2015 (see Figure 2-3).

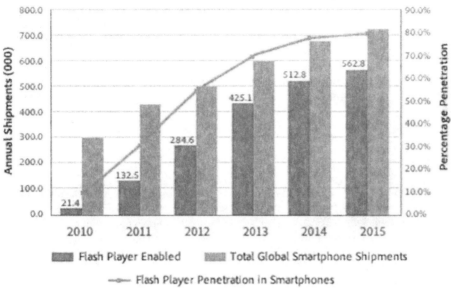

Flash Player Smartphone Penetration 2010-2015

Figure 2-3. *Showcasing the projected Flash Player penetration rate in smartphones (Credit: Adobe)*

Adobe, which had huge ambition for Flash support on mobile devices, felt that with the huge backing in the Android and Blackberry market, Apple would eventually give in to supporting Flash on iOS; for some time, that wasn't something to giggle over. Apple, it was said, actually gave Adobe a chance to prove that the mobile Flash Player could be performant on their phones and not overly tax the user's device in such a way that it would eat up battery life and ultimately crash the application. Whether this happened or not is unknown to me, but Adobe's take is much different on this matter.

This is where the politics behind the age-old HTML5 vs. Flash business comes into play. Hopefully, with the information outlined thus far, you can draw your own educated conclusion. That said, in late 2011 Adobe released a public statement that they company would finally sunset the Flash Player on mobile and focus efforts on web standards leveraging HTML5. This caused many repercussions. For starters, Adobe's faithful developer community felt betrayed and backstabbed; they thought their future on mobile was murdered. Also, many in the industry saw this as Adobe's white flag of surrender to Apple. If you look at the business decisions around it, however, Adobe took an altogether different approach for the company. Adobe also stated that it would continue to support native mobile applications built on Adobe's Integrated Runtime (AIR).

▪ **Note** At a high level, Adobe AIR is essentially a framework that leverages a code base and structure very similar to what is used in the Flash Player. With AIR, developers can build native applications on desktop and mobile devices using the same practices they did building rich Internet applications with Flash Player. In fact, at the time of writing, Adobe AIR is on its 3.2 release and continues to be supported in many distribution channels, including desktop, mobile, and TV.

With AIR's approach to building native applications, when a developer's application gets compiled, it is actually rewriting the code from native ActionScript into native Objective-C or Java for the iOS and Android operating systems. This means that the AIR compiler and packager will actually write everything to the assembly of the device, which is extremely low-level code, lower than the APIs available to iOS or Android developers building for native applications. It's damn close to machine code! 1's and 0's, my friend; that's all.

Evolving Advertising on Mobile

With the news outlined by Adobe, development on mobile had to move into the approach of using web standards and completely separating from the Flash Player. This caused a huge shift in an already new market, and mobile advertising needed to follow suit. The industry once dominated by Flash thought that it had a saving grace in the Android operating system and Blackberry, and it really thought that iOS would come around eventually and accept it as well.

Needless to say, that didn't happen, so the mobile advertising ecosystem started relatively small. As advertisers knew that they wanted to be in the space, they looked to their creative agencies and third-party ad servers for help in navigating the even more fragmented space and enabling an expressive ability to solidify an actual mobile ROI. However, the division between software, hardware, OS versions, and software development kits (SDKs) was fearful to invest actual media dollars into. It just didn't make any sense, operationally, for a developer to create a Flash and HTML5 version of the same ad, not to mention all the different sizes to support, all the different screen real estates on mobile, and the different SDKs to interface with. It's exhausting just thinking about it!

This posed a huge problem in the advertising industry. Remember from the last chapter that we briefly discussed responsive design and tracking requirements; currently this portion of the online advertising industry is still very much fragmented. To place it into perspective, what happens on publisher A's page may not be the same for publisher B. So what happens when you try to buy media across an ad network? How are you supposed to add scale to your workload when you have all of these different variables to worry about?

Transition to HTML5

As the market scrambled to figure out in which unified direction to head, many popular browsers and mobile devices transitioned (or are in the process of transitioning) to an all-HTML5-centric platform, leaving advertisers and marketers needing to follow suit in order to get their brand message across to their end users, regardless of screen or device accessing the content. In addition, it's becoming very clear that Flash was in fact a really well designed rapid development environment—nothing like HTML5, CSS3, and JavaScript to date, but I feel that will change as the tools become developed and fragmentation eases—so the current state advertisers are frustrated with the operational timing and costs in order to achieve the same experiences the Flash Player did so well for so long.

IAB Enhancements and SDK Providers

Throughout all of the confusion, fragmentation, and operational woes, the IAB has aimed to assist and support in the transformations involving HTML5 and mobile by developing a few enhancements. With the varied support in mobile applications, media buyers could not secure inventory at scale because there was no assurance it would work across everyone's application. Throughout the mobile ecosystem there are many different ways of serving ads inside those apps everyone knows and loves on iPhones and Android devices—Angry Birds, Words with Friends, and Draw Something, for example. The ads seen in these places get into the free applications by way of an SDK. These SDKs provide the communication channel between the ad creative (HTML5, CSS3, and JavaScript) and the application's code base, either Objective-C or Java. Think of it as the translator between two different languages.

Developed out of industry need, the open rich media mobile advertising (ORMMA) draft was created as an initiative to standardize the way mobile rich media ads are displayed across various platforms. There are other SDK providers in the space that have their own solutions. To name just a few, there are Apple's iAds, Google's AdMob, Medialets, Millennial Media, Opera's AdMarvel and RadiumOne. It's easy to imagine how much more fragmentation this adds. Without a standard there's no way to provide scale in a media buy or development! Mobile rich media ad interface definition (MRAID), the JavaScript API endorsed by the IAB, is based strongly off the learnings and developments in the ORMMA initiative. MRAID is a pure JavaScript-based API that communicates with publishers' applications in an approach similar to ORMMA's, but it is much simpler in that it exists only to provide a few levels of functionality in all mobile rich media ads. Last of all, the Mobile Rising Stars are formats developed by industry

29

members and adopted by the IAB as universal mobile rich media advertising formats. These formats are intended to be scaled across publishers; that is, publishers should adopt their spec if they are certified with the IAB.

Note We'll cover SDKs and in-application advertising in more detail in Chapter 9.

Development Tools

We've talked a bit about the troubles within company operations and how the IAB is attempting to provide ease through standardization, but we haven't yet discussed, from a creative standpoint, the tools that have emerged on the scene to ease developers' and designers' workloads when creating rich media ads. Development tools from Adobe, such as Wallaby, Edge, Shadow, and even Flash, have definitely showcased how Adobe, as a company, is really focused on the emerging web standards and is out to give developers the best tools possible for creative design across the HTML5 browser market (see more about these in the "Adobe" section).

A newcomer to the scene, Sencha, has also developed many advancements in this area, what with Sencha Animator and even more with the HTML5 enterprise application market, with ExtJS, and with Sencha Touch. Sencha Animator is a desktop application that eases development for HTML5, CSS3, and JavaScript creatives. The tools can be used for anything from simple to complex animations to easily including interactivity, custom-executing JavaScript, and cross-platform video, all within one clean user interface very familiar to users of Adobe's Flash Professional. Both companies (and others not mentioned here) have created these tools to help alleviate the operational costs of building ads and even rich web applications on the new browsers. (To learn more, visit Sencha.com and Adobe.com to view current product downloads.)

Note We'll dig much deeper into the mobile toolsets and programs in Chapters 8 and 9.

HTML5 Business

Unsurprisingly, HTML5 is a business as much as it's a progression in web technology. The following sections will provide insight into different companies' positions on HTML5 and how they fit into the environment and, ultimately, support the growing specification. In addition, these sections will give an idea on where they fit within the advertising sector. After reading this section, you should have a much clearer understanding of who the big players are in the space, as well as who the newcomers are, and be a better-prepared HTML5 advertiser. Also, throughout this book, we'll take a look at all the companies looking to assist in HTML5 advertising creations.

Apple

Apple has long been associated with innovation, technology, and online enhancements. With the iPhone and iPad partly responsible in shifting the Web towards HTML5, it seems only fitting to start with this company and outline their objectives as they pertain to HTML5 and emerging web standards. As you remember from what's gone before, many thank Steve Jobs for pushing the impending web standard that is now called HTML5. Every book about Steve Jobs tells how focused he was on perfection. Perhaps it was this perfectionism that skyrocketed Apple's market share and capital gains in the past couple of years. When, following a protracted battle with cancer, Jobs passed away in 2011, Tim Cook became CEO of the biggest and most profitable company in the world.

Tim Cook's core vision is very much aligned with Steve's. New versions of the iPad, the iPhone, and the Mac have been released on schedule, and Apple's market share continues to rise. The hardware Apple releases continues to get faster, more powerful, and more mobile. Having these sophisticated devices enables developers and designers to really raise the bar as it relates to HTML5. As for HTML5, Apple members are active in the W3C and continually building their browser, Safari, into an HTML5, CSS3, and JavaScript powerhouse.

Safari is a fast browser built using Webkit, which is an open source project based in Apple's hometown, Cupertino, CA. Each new stable Safari release usually does not include all the latest and greatest offered through HTML5, but users can always download Webkit Nightly, which is a bleeding-edge version of Apple's Safari browser to experiment with features that may (or may not) make it into the final HTML5 spec.

iAD

iAD is Apple's ad network for developing and delivering rich media across applications throughout their app store; it has some pros and cons. On the positive side, it's one standard, developed by Apple to be created once and deployed across their huge ad network. Second, iAD offers a suite of software to use to create really rich ads with extreme ease. However, it is Apple, and Apple is known somewhat as a "walled garden"—you need to follow all of Apple's rules to access inside, and once inside there is only a specific set of features to play with. Also, being locked into a suite of software tools developed by Apple, I've noticed that the k-weight of iADs are absolutely huge, especially for a mobile device; this is something that seems like a huge oversight in my opinion. Aside from that, iAD once started with a minimum campaign entry budget of a million dollars. However, due to the lack of participants, Apple recently dropped its ticket price, yet again, to $100,000. We'll look at how Apple plans to enhance its tools and the iAD platform in and for the future, but we'll focus more on iADs in Chapter 9.

Google

Much like Apple, Google has had a long history on the Web. Starting out as a search engine, it has moved into many different web markets: social, mapping, analytics, browsers, and mobile. Much like Apple's Safari browser, Google's browser, Chrome, is built on the Webkit engine, and Google's emerging web browser, Chrome Canary, supports many bleeding-edge HTML5 features that may or may not make it into the final HTML5 specification.

AdMob

Among Google's mobile efforts is its ad network, AdMob. Acquired in November 2009 for $750 million dollars, AdMob has its own list of mobile publishers that leverage the AdMob SDK and allows advertisers to run across the AdMob network and maintain the same functionality across applications. Along with its ad network, Google also runs the Android operating system for mobile devices. Android has a huge market share within the mobile ecosystem, but its focus on openness creates its own microfragmentation in the market. Android devices can vary in screen size. the browser, video players, and other feature sets, as well as the version of the operating system, can vary, too, since the system is open. Apple, unlike Android, has a controlled development environment, which lets developers know what they're getting into by explicitly keeping the operating system closed.

The final thing to mention about Google is its Dart Programming Language. Dart is Google's method of executing and replacing JavaScript within its Chrome browser more rapidly, as well as solving some of JavaScript's problems. Dart is an object-oriented programming (OOP) language with a C-style syntax. Dart is either to be compiled into native JavaScript or to work directly within the Dart Virtual Machine on the latest browsers that support it. As of March 2012, Apple, Mozilla, Microsoft, and Opera have no plans of implementing Dart into their browsers. However, keep this language in mind if or when you deploy to browsers that support DART. It could prove to be beneficial in future development.

Adobe

There's been a lot on Adobe and the Flash Platform in the preceding sections. Adobe has long had its roots in the Web with the Flash Platform, and the Flash plug-in went through some changes (to say the least). However, Adobe, an active member in the W3C and working groups, is still committed to the emerging web standards and is offering up various additions to the HTML5 draft, such as CSS Regions and CSS Shaders, which aim to provide layout and rich cinematic features via CSS styling.

Apps for Developers

In addition, Adobe has released some helpful applications to the developer community, apps focused on design and development for HTML5, CSS3, and JavaScript, including Edge, Wallaby, Shadow, and even Flash Professional. Edge, a tool very similar to Flash, creates timeline-based animations. The main difference between them is that Edge exports for direct use inside the latest browsers without use of a plug-in. Wallaby is a tool that will allow Flash designers and animators to take their .fla file and export it to native HTML5, CSS3, and JavaScript animations. Shadow is a multidevice developing suite; it allows developers full control over how content will look on various displays. Finally, Flash Professional has support for exporting to the HTML5 canvas object and creating Sprite Sheets.

In addition to the desktop applications, Adobe has also released Touch Apps for tablet and mobile devices. Touch Apps include Photoshop, Proto, Ideas, and Debut; they allow designers and developers to create on the go and seamlessly marry what's been created back to their desktop using their Creative Cloud tool. Creative Cloud is essentially a global sync for all of a developer's creative assets. Adobe has also made huge acquisition deals in PhoneGap and Typekit. PhoneGap allows web developers the flexibility to package their HTML5, CSS3, and JavaScript files for native use on mobile devices as applications. Typekit, on the other hand, is a huge web font library geared toward allowing designers using CSS Web Fonts to do so with the utmost of ease. Finally, Adobe's Flex Platform was donated to Apache as open source software completely driven by the developer community now.

■ **Note** To view Adobe's take on the emerging Web, visit beta.theexpressiveweb.com.

Mozilla

Mozilla is a company focused on open source development and involvement from the greater web community. Mozilla is behind the very popular browser Firefox and the not-so-popular e-mail client Thunderbird. Mozilla, a nonprofit company, is focused on building the Web through openness, security, and a mantra of being built by people who care more about the Web and less about the business side of things.

Mozilla, much like other companies, has produced features for the HTML5 working draft and developed a bleeding-edge browser, called Firefox Nightly, for testing the latest features. Like Chrome Canary and Webkit Nightly, this browser may include features that never actually make it into the final HTML5 spec, but it also includes a package of wonderful web inspector tools, called Firebug, for the browser. Using Firebug, developers can easily debug HTML, CSS, and JavaScript on live pages. Lastly, Camino is Mozilla's Mac OSX-focused browser; it aims to deliver an open browser to Mac users.

Microsoft

Microsoft is pretty much a household name. It has created the Windows operating system, the Xbox 360, and the web browser Internet Explorer (IE). For many years IE was the de facto standard browser, since it shipped natively with Windows PCs. However, as browser companies emerged and as Microsoft dropped a bomb of a browser with IE version 6, many users shifted gears to Firefox or Chrome or even became Apple users and adopted Safari as their main web browser. As Microsoft heads into adopting the next generation of web standards, they still have a lingering customer base on Windows XP, which supports only up to browser IE8. Thus, XP users will never have an emerging browser unless they update to Windows 7 or the latest 8 or install Google's Chrome Frame into their browser.

■ **Note** For more on Chrome Frame, visit `google.com/chromeframe`.

Users running Windows 7 and above can use IE9, but it supports only some HTML5 features. In fact, many suggest that IE9 is anything but an emerging browser supporting the latest web standards. See `people.mozilla.com/ ~prouget/ie9`. Also, IE9 is soon to be outdated, what with the release of Windows 8 and IE10. IE10 will be Microsoft's first major contender in the emerging web browser market, as it will support many of HTML5's feature sets. It is also slated to support the latest HTML5 spec and offer what is called a plug-in free browser, to be called "Metro" or what was formally known as Metro. Metro is essentially the new and quite famout "start" menu from Windows. The Metro-style apps will support HTML5, CSS3, and JavaScript from a front end, as well as various Microsoft technologies from a back end. There has also been talk that certain PCs will begin shipping with Kinect cameras inside the computer, offering yet another way to interact with the content on screen. Really, what does a browser without plug-ins mean? Simply, that no Flash, no Unity, and no other plug-ins will be supported. Time to learn web standards, don't ya think?

Sencha

Sencha is the new kid in town as far as technology goes. Based in California, Sencha makes JavaScript-based frameworks for desktop and mobile called Sencha Touch and ExtJS for HTML5 web-application building. Their web-development apps can easily be combined with Adobe's PhoneGap (or another packager's device) that ports HTML5, CSS, and JavaScript files over to native files, which the device can run externally of the browser environment. Developers often use Sencha's tools to rapidly build applications for the Web and deploy to app stores like Apple's App Store and the Android Marketplace.

In addition to this enterprise application focus, Sencha also runs a product called Sencha Animator, which is its solution for timeline-based animations using web standards and CSS3 based graphic animations. Like Adobe Edge and Flash, Sencha provides an interface for dealing with rich graphics, animation, and even video, all within the browser environment. Animator is targeted heavily toward the mobile industry; in addition, it offers native support for ORMMA and the MRAID API. On the business end of things, since the recent layoff of many of Adobe's Flash employees, several people, shifting gears from Adobe, have moved down the street to work on Sencha's emerging products. My bet is Sencha will become a bigger player in the space as time progresses.

RIM

Research In Motion (RIM), known for the Blackberry operating systems, has been in the security business and enterprise world a long time, but Blackberry browsers, also for the longest time, have been primitive in mobile, to say the least. Until recently RIM didn't offer the true web experience, but lately it has started making consumer-friendly Playbook, Torch, and Curve tablets and phones, with enhanced browsers, touch screen support, and even Flash support. However, in 2011 RIM decided to pull out of the consumer market and head back into the enterprise market due to its rapid decline in market share.

Blackberry, soon to release version 10 of its operating system, supports another marketplace application called Blackberry App World, but it remains defeated in the mobile and tablet market among consumers. Its main competitor, Apple, leaves it with minimal market share.

Opera

We can't forget about the Opera browser. Even though it's not huge in the U.S. market, it has enormous support in European and African markets (especially with Opera Mini), since mobile Internet is more prevalent there due to the lack of wired connections. Opera started out in 1994, first developing web products, then the Opera browser, and most recently Opera for mobile devices. Opera provides robust tools for developers, including Dragonfly (Opera's Firebug equivalent), Mobile Emulators, TV Emulators, OperaDriver, and OperaWatir.

> **Note** To view more of Opera's developer tools, visit `opera.com/developer/tools`.

In addition to mobile browsers, Opera also owns AdMarvel, a mobile ad serving company and SDK provider. AdMarvel offers mobile publishers the ability to traffic ads through the AdMarvel platform.

Others

There are many other browsers, device manufacturers, and software manufacturers out there in the HTML5 and mobile ecosystem. These sections were geared at just painting a bigger picture and attempting to understand all the moving parts. There are devices from Kindle, Nook, HTC, Motorola, Samsung, and Asus in the market, mostly using the open Android operating system and supporting at least some HTML5 features within their browsers. With the open Android operating systems, as well as the varying screen sizes, mobile developers and designers have a really hard time trying to standardize the deployment of their products. Luckily for you, you'll have a book that outlines everything for you! ☺

> **Note** To view the W3C's monthly stats on browser, operating system, and screen resolution market share, visit `w3counter.com/globalstats.php`.

What's Next?

Obviously there is a lot here to digest, and you may need to review this chapter again as well as do some research on your own to really understand how everything has evolved and how each company fits into the puzzle. This chapter's point wasn't to make your head spin, but I can completely understand your frustration in trying to remember everything. Between the technology, politics, and fragmentation across devices, this history lesson has, I hope, given you a deeper awareness of the big picture. In reality, the landscape changes so frequently that, even since the time of writing, many things will have undoubtedly changed or been updated. Companies change their strategy, get acquired, develop new devices, or add more divisions into the mix. The HTML5 draft will soon get standardized; only then will it require full adoption by all the browser manufactures. It's just the nature of the beast that it will take some time to accomplish. I'll try to provide useful links throughout to material where you can find the latest, most up-to-date information regarding important topics so you can reference things as they change in the future. You can see that the mobile market really accelerated HTML5 in technology and advertising. As we talk more about HTML5 and its impact on advertising, we'll discuss the important facets of the faster JavaScript-executing browsers, how ad servers are handling the responsive Web, the inevitable increase in k-weight and file size, file loading issues, overall adoption, user experience, industry fragmentation, and how to navigate professionally in this ever-changing market. Remember that this chapter was intended only to give you the background to where we have gotten today.

Terminology Review

Much as in the last chapter, we've seen a lot of new acronyms, concepts, and words. Let's quickly review some of the covered terminology as it relates to chapter two.

Table 2-1. *HTML, Flash and HTML5 Terminology Review*

Word	Definition or Meaning
API	Application programming interface
CSS3	CSS level 3 additions to Cascading Style Sheets specification
CSS Pre-Processor	A language that uses variables, constants, and mixins but complies with true CSS so the browser will understand
DOM	The Document Object Model
GPU	Graphics processing unit
HTML	Hypertext markup language; the language of the Web and browsers
HTML5	Hypertext markup language, version 5
Java	The native programming language of Google's Android
JavaScript	The code base in all browsers to handle functionality and logic
Objective-C	The native programming language of Apple's iOS
Static (Default)	The failover image that will serve when a user cannot view a rich ad

Summary

In this chapter, we've reviewed in abundant detail what has brought us into HTML5's presence. Now that we've worked at developing an understanding of the technology and business rules that navigated HTML5 in this direction, it's time to dig into the working specs to understand how the advertising industry is handling these changes. We'll be taking a much different approach in the following chapters, digging more into the actual practice of using HTML, CSS, and JavaScript as they relate to the emerging Web and advertisements.

Heading into the next chapter, I hope you now have a basic knowledge of code coming from a Flash or Actionscript background and understand that HTML5 is not a formal standard just yet. It's still being developed, and the W3C and WHATWG is figuring out what is to remain and what should be removed or added later into their respective specifications. There is much more to cover as we learn more about HTML5 as it relates to advertising, so prepare to take notes, bookmark some pages, and follow along with some examples. Finally having gotten an understanding of the campaign process, industry, and technology, you're ready to really dig in now. I'm fired up, so let's begin!

CHAPTER 3

Advertising with Web Standards

This chapter will discuss the new and useful features of HTML5 and open web standards that you can leverage in your next advertising campaign. The thing to remember going forward is that HTML5 is not about advancements in HTML markup alone; it also pioneers new JavaScript APIs and CSS features, among other technologies. Some HTML5, CSS3, and JavaScript techniques will be examined, and you'll see how they can be used together to enhance creative development in the modern browser market.

As you know, advertising on the Web has gone through many stages: static imagery, animated GIFs, basic HTML ads, rich features with Flash. Now HTML5 and the modern web stack are building a new stage in the progression. As this book proceeds, I'll cover some of the common pitfalls that designers and developers run into as the emerging web standard comes to fruition, and you'll see how you can use this new spec right now while providing graceful failbacks for users with older browsers.

I've discussed how rich media advertising came about in the HTML5 advertising world; so let's assume from this point forward that all advertising on the Web will be considered "rich" and highly interactive. This chapter is pointed at getting you completely up to speed with certain nuances when dealing with advertising using emerging web technologies. I'll cover some of the new features in HTML5, leveraging APIs, and optimizing your code to run efficiently across publishers.

First things first, however. Make sure you're working with the latest version of Safari, Internet Explorer, Chrome, Opera, or Firefox. Since I'll be taking a first look at some code in this chapter, it's important that you have a modern browser to follow along. Consider this chapter a primer, as it will give a full view into the landscape that is HTML5 and its affect on web advertising as a whole. Every chapter going forward will focus on diving deeper into the technology that is discussed here, but this is where you get your feet wet. So let's dig in!

HTML5 Advertising

HTML5 has brought—at the time of writing, is *still* bringing—many enhancements to the creation of web content. This book's focus is on how HTML5 and its various technologies are impacting the online advertising market, but I strongly suggest you learn more about HTML5 markup and how it's impacting the Web as a whole. Tags like `<article>`, `<aside>`, `<details>`, `<header>`, `<footer>`, and `<section>`—as well as `<canvas>`, `<video>`, `<audio>`, and some others we'll cover in detail later—are new to the HTML5 specification. With these new tags, developers and designers can create semantic and logical markup natively in the browser. Be sure to check out the latest take on HTML5 from W3C(w3.org/TR/2011/WD-html5-20110525) and WHATWG (whatwg.org/specs/web-apps/current-work/multipage) with regard to how it impacts the Web as a whole. That said, emerging and competitive browser vendors are now incorporating HTML5 features, allowing developers to define the structure of a document with these soon-to-be standard HTML semantics.

Using <div>

Since knowing what element to wrap your ad content in is really what's focused on here, some HTML5 features—those that relate to the advertising space—are more important to recognize than others. With the previous versions of the HTML specification, the structure of the document was typically marked up with <div> tags, along with specific IDs and classes, so publishers could inject ad code within a specific section in their page markup. Using <div> tags, publishers and content developers can section their page out for headers, navigation, ads, and other specific content. For example, having a <div> container called header, footer, or ad can provide a pretty standard structure when developing web site properties. Take the example in Figure 3-1, from the publisher Yahoo.

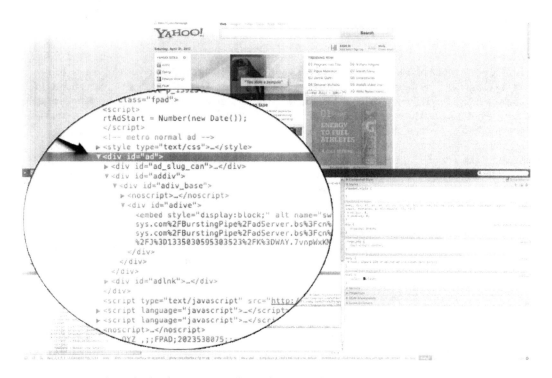

Figure 3-1. *Markup of Yahoo's page using Chrome's inspect element function*

Figure 3-1 showcases that Yahoo in fact uses an ad container div with the ID called "ad". This tells other developers that this section of the page is designated for an ad (an ad slot). If you were to inspect any page, you'd find that other divs in the markup specify other elements like "y-header" and "y-footer", which are the specific naming conventions given to Yahoo's markup.

New Ad Container Options: <section> and <aside>

With the new HTML5 markup elements, developers can leverage two new ad container elements: <section> and <aside>. The section element aids in portioning out the page for specific content. For example, you could section your page for ad content, blog posts, or even pictures. For a publisher, it can be an especially good idea to have ad content live inside wrapper divs with specific IDs. This is helpful since there are no other associated semantics with the ad on the page in conjunction with the rest of the content.

The `<aside>` tag, which represents a section of a page content loosely connected to the content around the `<aside>` element, means that if the ad server contextually served the advertising message, the `<aside>` tag would be an accurate container for the ad to live inside of. This would most likely only work if the publisher had specific ad inventory slotted out for contextual experiences. Take a look at the example in Figure 3-2 on a sample HTML5 page 3.

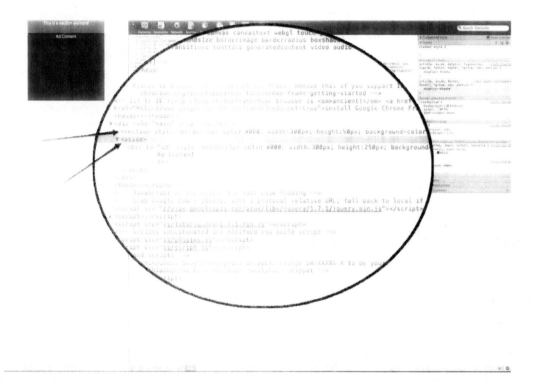

Figure 3-2. *Markup of section and aside elements in the browser*

Data Attribute

Another interesting feature in HTML5 is the new data attribute. This attribute addition may seem a bit crazy at first, but it offers some really good use cases, especially in the advertising space. Using the data attribute in your ad's markup, you can customize specific values on a certain element. For example, in ad serving, what is called a macro is often used to replace a variable with other values at ad serve time; how it is used depends on the publisher the ad is being served toward and on other information we can learn before rendering the ad to the page. This macro value, which is very similar to a variable in traditional coding languages, will typically look like $MACRO$, ??MACRO??, or something pretty similar depending on the ad-serving company and its ability to parse on a specific character in order to insert a value. The macro value can be added to the ad's markup via the data attribute; when the ad is served, that attribute will get replaced by the value that should be there, per the information the ad server gathers. Listing 3-1 showcases how this would work by replacing a click URL for an ad to enable the same ad creative to serve many publishers. The fact that the click URL can dynamically change based on the ad servers helps if you want to traffic the same creative across multiple publishers but still want to have unique click URLs.

Listing 3-1. An Example of an Ad-Serving Macro

```html
<!DOCTYPE HTML>
<html>
<head>
<meta http-equiv="Content-Type" content="text/html; charset=UTF-8">
<style type="text/css" media="screen">
#clickBtn {background-color:#000; width:100px; height:20px; color:#FFF; cursor:pointer;}
</style>
</head>
<body>
<div align="center" id="clickBtn" data-link=$MACRO$ onClick=window.open(macroValue)>Open Macro</div>
</body>
<script type="text/javascript">
var macroValue = document.getElementById('clickBtn').getAttribute('data-link') //returns value to be
replaced by ad server
</script>
</html>
```

At ad serve time, the $MACRO$ value gets replaced by what the ad server defines. This case could have something that states $MACRO$ = http://www.google.com or http://www.bing.com. In short, the rules for the data attribute state that any attribute that starts with "data-" will be treated as a storing area that the end user won't see. Again, this is pretty valuable when you're trying to specify explicit information about an element without changing its look or feel.

HTML5 Considerations

It should be noted that HTML5's new markup additions are a huge step forward in assistive technologies in that they allow machines to better interpret the structure of the document for parsing and interpretation. However, as ads tend to live only for the life of their campaign, usually a couple months at most, it's frequently better to deliver ads within a good ol' common div tag with specific IDs and classes applied. I've found that that's the commonest approach of publishers and ad networks anyway.

It should also be noted that each publisher will have its own implementations for constructing ad inventory throughout its web content. That being said, the best advice I can give is to reach out to the publisher directly to learn whether they're using HTML5 elements, a div with overflow set to none, or even an iFrame as the ad's wrapper element. While this may not be a huge concern for every campaign, the more complex and interactive campaigns may require manipulation of the site's elements or busting out of an iFrame so this information can be vital. For more information on what HTML5 building blocks to use, or if you are just a bit confused by all of this, take a peak at the image in Figure 3-3 from html5doctor.com.

HTML5 Element Flowchart
Sectioning content elements and friends

By @riddle & @boblet
www.html5doctor.com

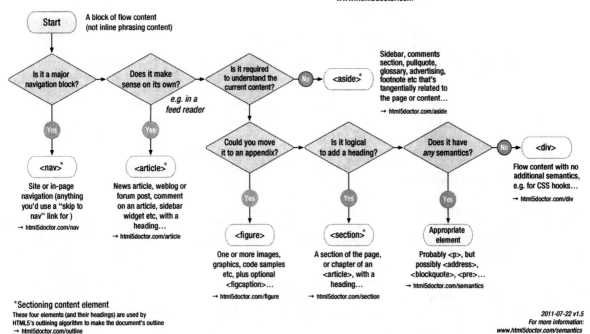

Figure 3-3. *The HTML5 Doctor's HTML5 Element Chooser Flowchart*

HTML5 already has a plethora of new elements, and by the launch of the final spec, to be decided at a future time, there could even be more. More of the new and updated elements will be covered throughout the book.

■ **Note**   For the latest, most up-to-date information on the HTML5 element index, visit
`html5doctor.com/element-index`.

For web creators, the new semantic markup in HTML5 is really invaluable when creating web content that is well formed and structured and search engine friendly. It improves overall search engine optimization (SEO), as a search giant like Google can parse the page's content much more efficiently, separating the page's content from its structure. It also helps developers keep to a standard naming practice when developing across properties, as tag names will now be the same moving forward. For instance there'll now be header and footer tags, just like head and body tags.

■ **Note**   HTML5-compliant browsers do not need quotes around attributes. For example, `<div id="ad"></div>` can
now be written `<div id=ad></div>`.

41

Safe iFrames

As mentioned briefly above, busting out of an iFrame is something that may need to happen to ensure an ad provides a rich experience across a network's or publisher's page. However, rendering the ad onto the publisher's document could produce namespace conflicts and reference variables. For example, if the ad has an element called photo-gallery and so does the web page, any manipulations done to that element could pass to the ad experience or even break the page contents. This wasn't an issue back in the Flash (SWF) days of ad creatives as the SWF element was inherently sandboxed from the publisher's page. There has to be a better way to serve rich experiences with HTML that can be sandboxed from the publisher's content, right?

If you think that wrapping the ad content in an iFrame will solve all this mess, you'd be absolutely correct. However, an iFrame limits the richness of the experience, as it confines the ad to a specific area on the page; also, it's a bit of a memory hog for pages, as it creates a new instance of the document, one that may not be wanted or needed. (Think of what happens if multiple iFrames are on the page or even nested within each other.)

Traditionally, using a publisher side script, the ad can check to see whether this script is in place and bust out of the publisher's designated iFrame. This is absolutely necessary, as most rich ad experiences require expanding and closing functionality. However, once the ad is busted out and written to the main document of the publisher's page, the same rules apply to CSS inheritance and JavaScript variable scoping. Thus confliction and styling issues could arise—indeed, they most certainly will.

Building on the knowledge that iFrames can sandbox you from publisher content, how can a common API, one that allows this iFrame to expand and contract as well as gather valuable metrics into the ad experience, be provided? Well the IAB and various working group members are working on an initiative called Safe iFrames, which is intended to be a protocol between the publisher and ad and be a common API that allows "rich" ads to be sandboxed inside of iFrames and still access specific expanding and contracting commands, among others. The publisher will effectively add some code to the iFrame to allow the ad to call pub-side functions for expand and collapse. While the approach needs standardization and adoption to be a scalable method, it holds some promise for dealing with page content and ad confliction. (I've mocked up a simple example to show that you can expand or collapse the actual iFrame at jsbin.com/omodus/5.) Keep in mind that this would involve special code on the publisher's end; it would control the functionality and animation of the iFrame on the page, not the third-party ad server tag.

Note There is even the possibility of publishers' using the MRAID API to serve ad tags through. Look for more information on the MRAID spec in Chapter 9.

Many more features of HTML5 as it relates to advertising are discussed later in the book. HTML5 is about updating and pushing the Web as a whole forward; advertising is a key part of that process. Anything that is updated in the browser will have an impact on advertising.

Advertising with CSS3

As you've just learned with HTML5, many enhancements to the overall structure of the page have been added, deleted, or modified. Along with the markup structure, of course, goes style. CSS has long been the backbone for styling within the browser, and as modern browsers adopt CSS3 features, a lot of manufacturers, including Google, Apple, and Mozilla, are leveraging the latest CSS3 additions to handle web animations and presentations as never before. Because CSS3 is such a powerful design toolset, designers can now leverage it for creating rich, print-worthy graphics directly within the browser. They no longer need to rely on Flash or use images to create the design they're after.

A few things will always be necessary with CSS, since each manufacturer has its own interpretation and adoption rate for the latest CSS3 spec. First, vendors often have variability within their environments. This inconsistency comes at a cost for designers in the form of CSS resets, which are required to reset rendering elements across browsers. A very useful tool for emerging browsers is Nicolas Gallagher's `Normalize.css` (necolas.github.com/normalize.css), which makes all browsers, both old and up to date, render elements consistently without applying unwanted styling.

A good tip is to reset from your ad's top level element down. What this means is that if you have your entire ad wrapped in a div element acting as the ad's container, you can apply a class to that div called "adContainer". Now in the CSS document, you can add specific resets or styling simply by writing:

```
#adContainer .adBanner {

}
```

This way only the elements within the ad markup are targeted and this keeps a clear separation between publisher page content and ad content.

In addition to resets, if browsers you're deploying toward happen not to be HTML5-compatible, you'll need graceful failovers to style the page correctly. A really great example of this is on the site `CSS-Tricks.com`. The site actually degrades very nicely in an older browser like IE6 but takes advantage of emerging CSS3 features when a user's browser supports and is capable of the enhanced experience. This technique, known as progressive enhancement, can be applied in your advertising creatives as well. If you're running a campaign that needs to target any and all users and isn't specified to a browser version, HTML5-compliant or not, always build the ad experience with the older user in mind. Maintain the core functionality and messaging and build richer features that newer browsers can handle on top of them.

At-Rules

The CSS spec also has what is known as an at-rule index. At-rules are used for handing CSS documents in various ways and instructing the CSS parser. Here are a few popular at-rules.

- `@charset`: This specifies the character set of an external style sheet.

- `@import`: This imports an external style sheet file to the current style sheet.

- `@media`: This specifies the media to which the style should be applied.

- `@page`: This specifies margin values for the page box in style sheets for paged media.

- `@font-face`: This defines custom font properties.

All the rules above allow designers to create specific visual experiences based on the machine or device requesting the stylized content.

As you've seen in brief, CSS media profiles are used for the different displays that will request web content to be rendered. Screen, Print, Handheld, and TV (to name a few modes) allow visually based content to dynamically update on the device requesting the content. This characteristic can be tremendously useful if you're deploying a cross-device campaign as it allows a designer to take into consideration many different displays during the design phase. Also, CSS can be used as an external link via the `@import` rule set (see above) or added to the HTML document as a linked file. But it can also be used as inline styles on the HTML elements. There are debatable pros and cons for uses in both techniques, too many to list here. You should weigh your options accordingly when starting development.

My personal way of development is to externalize style from form and function. Doing so allows for easy layout updates without touching markup or JavaScript. On the other hand, some ad platforms require that your CSS remain inline and bundled with the inline HTML markup. This situation, obviously much harder to scale, is sometimes a requirement; so be sure to keep your styling formatted nicely, since you may need to go back to the code and perform updates and revisions. However, if you are allowed to externalize your CSS files (and I really hope you can), one of my favorite CSS developing tools is `bearcss.com`, which allows uploading of your raw HTML markup and builds a boilerplate CSS template for you to style on. It's a huge time-saver, as you don't need to rewrite a bunch of element declarations after building the markup.

Vendor Prefixes

As the CSS level 3 spec gets adopted in union with HTML5, each browser manufacturer is using its own prefixes to distinguish what is emerging from what is standard inside the browser's rendering engine. Thus, using emerging CSS features, you'll need to include prefixes for Webkit, Mozilla, Microsoft, and Opera—assuming, that is, that you'll be targeting all browsers in your next HTML5 campaign (that's usually the case). A few examples of vendor prefixes are, respectively, `-webkit`, `-moz`, `-ms`, and `-o`; using these prefixes as you build with the emerging CSS spec will ensure you've got the latest bleeding-edge CSS3 feature set within your respective browser environments.

⬛ **Note** As the spec is adopted across browsers, the need for these prefixes will diminish, the result being that developers will have to go back into the code base to remove them so that nothing breaks down the line once support drops for the prefixed version of the code.

As we all know, ads usually have a much shorter life cycle than traditional web content, but it's very important to keep vendor prefixes in mind as you deploy content. Failing to do so will be a real pain if you want to build something now that's sustainable for the future. Think of anything with a vendor prefix as a sneak peak at what's to come although the feature you're using could be removed in later versions of the browser. A really good tool to use as you develop with this budding standard is `prefixer.com`. Prefixer allows you to develop with CSS. With one click of a button, it translates all the necessary vendor prefixes for you automatically—another huge time-saver! For the latest CSS3 spec, visit the W3C current drafts at `w3.org/Style/CSS`.

Media Queries

A very important function of CSS, one that's been around since version 2 but gets lumped into CSS3, is the ability to leverage media queries. A media query allows you to do just as what the term states: query the device or screen for the media it supports. Useful media examples include device width, device height, pixel density, and orientation. These features are tremendously important in mobile development and are the foundation of responsive web design. By making use of them, developers can create a CSS document that dynamically adjusts web content to the device accessing it. A few really great responsive web design frameworks are Foundation (`foundation.zurb.com`), 320 and Up (`stuffandnonsense.co.uk/projects/320andup`), and the Golden Grid System (`goldengridsystem.com`). These tools provide a blueprint for developing a single unified experience across screen.

This approach is great in the web development world, but note that when building ads with this format in mind, it's almost certain that k-weight will increase, as you're taking into consideration more than one screen—and that means more CSS declarations. Before development, I'd recommend reaching out to your publishers to determine whether they want a responsive ad layout or new tags generated for all screen variations. In reality it comes down to what the publisher wants. Often it'll be more ad inventory to sell, so they'll fire more than one impression if the user reorients their device or scales their browser on a responsive layout. The ad inventory will change rather than adapt, which will result in what seems like more ad inventory for the publisher and will require an ad server to generate separate tags for each size; the publisher or first-party ad server will need to adjust accordingly. A good practice is to strip out the CSS content into its necessary parts and load external style sheets specific to the device by using media queries. This way you don't bring in unwanted CSS code for a user viewing on a mobile device that doesn't meet the media query rules applied—or even worse, a device with very limited bandwidth. Using our earlier example, Listing 3-2 leverages media queries for a tablet device and a television and takes its orientation into consideration.

Listing 3-2. A Media Query Example

```html
<!DOCTYPE HTML>
<html>
<head>
<meta http-equiv="Content-Type" content="text/html; charset=UTF-8">
<link rel="stylesheet" media="all" href="base.css" />
<link rel="stylesheet " media="all and (orientation:portrait) " href="tablet_portrait.css">
<link rel="stylesheet " media="all and (orientation:landscape) " href="tablet_landscape.css">
<link rel="stylesheet" media="tv" href="tv.css" />
</head>
<body>
<div align=center id=clickBtn data-link=$MACRO$ onClick=window.open(macroValue)>Open Macro</div>
</body>
<script type="text/javascript">
var macroValue = document.getElementById('clickBtn').getAttribute('data-link') //returns $MACRO$
</script>
</html>
```

Since doing this obviously takes additional development and design time, make sure your team is aware; use this method only when you know your ad will be running across publishers that require a responsive layout. (For more information on the CSS3 media queries visit w3.org/TR/css3-mediaqueries.)

■ **Note**   In HTML5 doc parsers, it is no longer required to include type="text/javascript"; this is now assumed by default. Thus, writing <script></script> will now work.

Responsive ads have time to grow before they become a reality. It comes down to how publishers and ad servers gather metrics on an ad—and that can change. This is a bit of a paradigm shift in thinking; traditionally, ad servers and publishers bill clients based on impressions and break down the ads that account for those impressions into size categories to get a more granular look into the campaign's performance. However, if you have one ad tag on the page and allow the creative to resize and do a relayout accordingly, no other tags need to be accounted for. This is a dream for ad ops guys or gals—they don't have to worry about which tag goes to which property on which distribution channel. No matter if it's a smartphone, tablet, desktop, or television—its all the same tag, and so operational scale on ad trafficking is a huge win! However, clients will surely want to learn what size ad was getting the most views, as this will help determine the user base of screens accessing the ad. The following model (see Listing 3-3) helps break this down a bit more; it allows the tag to track one major campaign impression and fire off supplementary impressions based on the creative size rendering to the user's screen.

Listing 3-3. A Responsive Ad Example

```javascript
var publisherSize;//Get this value from the publisher's page.

window.addEventListener('load', function () {
//fire off uber impression
var img = new Image()
img.src = 'http://imptracker.adserver.com';
//Pass publisher's layout to the checkSize function
checkSize(publisherSize);
}, false);
```

```
function checkSize (creativeSize) {
                //Check the size to fire off supplementary impression
        switch (creativeSize) {
            case "300x50" :
                http://sizetracker.adserver.com/300x50
                break;
            case "300x250" :
                http://sizetracker.adserver.com/300x250
                break;
            case "728x90" :
                http://sizetracker.adserver.com/728x90
                break;
        }
}
```

Since every creative is different, this example does not take into consideration the CSS styling rules to be applied or all the ad sizes as they are dependent on the publisher's page, but it does showcase how to gather the same rich metrics for an ad that adapts to its viewer's screen. If the ad were to get a string value from the publisherSize variable, the ad server would be able to fire off the correct size impressions to report on.

Selectors

Another interesting part of the CSS specification is selectors. Selectors allow you to target specific elements in your markup in various ways. You can target them by ID, class, tag name, type, even attributes, along with specific values. Here are some common examples of CSS selectors.

- *: targets every single element in the document.
- #ad: targets elements by ID.
- .center: targets elements by class.
- header: targets elements by tag type.
- div + p: targets elements only preceding div.
- footer > a: targets direct children of footer.
- a[title]: targets elements by the attribute title.

    *Note that the elements above are examples only, be sure to update with your own elements.

The above examples are some common cases of how CSS selectors work in the real world. I'll be using them in examples later in the book—but note that there are many more than those covered in this chapter. So I'd strongly suggest taking a look at the W3C's current document on CSS selectors.

Note   For more information on the CSS3 selectors, see w3.org/TR/selectors.

Pseudo Classes

Another interesting feature of CSS is pseudo classes. Pseudo classes are much like selectors, but they have an additional layer to react to layout or interaction. Here are some of the CSS pseudo classes.

- :active: an active element

- :focus: an element that has focus

- :visited: a visited link

- :hover: an element that is hovered over (keep in mind this does not work on touch devices)

- :selection: an element that is currently selected by the user

- :checked: a form element that is checked

- :nth-child(n): an element that is the nth sibling (you can also use odd/even keywords in place of *n* here)

- :nth-last-child(n): an element that is the nth sibling, counting from the last sibling

These pseudo classes are very helpful in manipulating your ad layout. Use them for anything from hovering over a CTA element and changing its scale to styling an unordered list with even and odd numbering. In the following chapters, pseudo classes and selectors will be used to target our elements.

Note For more information on the CSS3 pseudo classes, visit coding.smashingmagazine.com/2009/07/13/css-3-cheat-sheet-pdf.

Pseudo Elements

Last, there are also pseudo elements in CSS; they allow designers to target elements relative to their own markup and design. Here are a few of them.

- ::first-letter: targets the first letter of text

- ::first-line: targets the first line of text

- ::before: targets before an element

- ::after: targets after an element

Using pseudo elements, you can quickly get magazine and newspaper-like type layouts with extreme ease. If you want to make the first letter in a paragraph bold or simply increase its font size, pseudo elements are where to look. As with everything emerging, be sure to check browser compatibility before using these features in your campaign or if older browsers are being targeted.

CSS Preprocessors

Lately, web advancements in code development have really taken off! It seems everyday another boutique meta language is being created. One of these languages would be a code preprocessor and developer-created custom tools to generate CSS and HTML markup code in new ways. Some of these advances are SASS, LESS, and HAML, which are CSS and HTML preprocessors.

SASS

SASS, or syntactically awesome style sheets, is a metalanguage: it sits on top of normal CSS development. SASS, initially designed by Hampton Catlin, aims to describe the CSS document with more structure and style than traditional CSS development. Using SASS requires a compiler to translate SCSS files into normal CSS files so the browser can understand them and do its job. A popular SASS compiler is Compass, found at `compass-style.org`. SASS allows developers and designers to rapidly produce dynamic code and to update and change it easily; since it accepts the inclusion of variables, mix-ins, and arguments, it's a truly logical and dynamic approach to developing CSS. For example, you can set a background color as a variable called `$bg-color: #ffffff;` and as your paying client constantly wants to change the background from white to black, it would be very easy for the developer to go back into the SASS code base and update that one line to #000000 and have it proliferate throughout all the content that is referencing that variable. This is where the true power of SASS comes into play!

LESS

LESS, by Alexis Sellier, is another dynamic style sheet language; it allows designers to leverage features similar to those of SASS—variables, mix-ins, nested rules, math, and functions with arguments. The main difference with LESS is that it works in both client-side and server-side environments ("client-side" means in the user's browser, whereas "server-side" means the hosting server performs the actions). In fact, the W3C is even contemplating including variables natively in the CSS spec in the coming future (see `dev.w3.org/csswg/css-variables`). That may or may not pan out, but if you can't wait, these hipster languages will get you started. There are other CSS preprocessors—Stylus is one—but I hope you get the picture of what they aim to solve by now. If you're building much larger and more complex ads, ads that mirror rich application development, using a preprocessor may make your life easier in the long run.

▪ **Note**   For more information on using LESS, visit `lesscss.org`.

HAML

Last of all, since we're on the topic of preprocessors, I'll mention the HTML Abstraction Markup Language (HAML). HAML is a preprocessor specifically designed for HTML markup; it can help speed up your markup development. I won't go into more detail, but to see if HAML is right for you, visit `haml-lang.com/try.html` and give it a whirl! The whole premise of these new coding languages is to do more by writing less. I mean, really, a CSS variable? That's really awesome!

Advertising with JavaScript

As I've already said, you'll be seeing a lot on JavaScript in the rest of this book. You may remember that JavaScript not only handles the behavior of the page; it can also control function and interactivity as well. It's important to note that with HTML5, we now have more JavaScript APIs than ever before to take advantage of. Also it's important to note that JavaScript is an interpreted language—not a compiled one like Flash's Actionscript or Objective-C.

In this case, the browser is instructed to run commands as it understands them, written left to right and top to bottom. This may be a whole different way of thinking if you're coming from a Flash development world, as you will almost always run into issues where JavaScript commands are being interpreted on elements that haven't even been created in the markup yet. Because of the common "null object reference", this will generally result in errors and break the code in your ad. Again, this is much different than ActionScript, since the compiler packages up to ensure that all elements exist so properties can be manipulated on them.

Some very popular JavaScript syntax elements are `getElementById();` and `getElementsByTagName();`—these JavaScript commands allow for selecting elements in the DOM tree. In addition, there is now also `getElementsByClassName();` and the new `querySelectorAll();` and `querySelector();` which allow developers to query the DOM for any element they wish to pass in as an argument as a CSS selector. This is super helpful for targeting elements directly and can be used instead of a popular JavaScript library like jQuery. Whether you're new to

JavaScript or not, before digging into it, I'd recommend reading the quick post by Rebecca Murphey called "A Baseline for Front-End Developers" (rmurphey.com/blog/2012/04/12/a-baseline-for-front-end-developers). She outlines the importance of building, testing, and process automation; these are things that every developer can relate to.

> **Note** The DOM tree is the markup of elements in the document. For more information on the DOM tree, visit w3schools.com/htmldom/dom_nodetree.asp.

Minify

When you're dealing with JavaScript, HTML and CSS, it's always nice to have a minified version and an archive version. The minified version should be used in campaign production environments; it reduces the code to a single code block with less k-weight than the archived version by removing line breaks and white space and by replacing verbose names with single letter references. The archived version should always be your wordy, cleanly legible code base—that is, something you can go back to in a couple years and quickly understand it to make updates.

Minifying code is especially useful when it's being deployed to mobile devices and tablets that could be on 3G speeds or less. Some developers even automate the process of compiling all their JavaScript files and minifying them. Tools like Apache's ANT, Maven, and Grunt can help you streamline this process when you're getting JavaScript ready for deployment. Conversely, if you ever want to unminify JavaScript code, an extremely useful tool is jsbeautifier.org; it allows you to view code in a much more formatted and digestible way. An example would be jQuery's library minified (code.jquery.com/jquery-1.8.2.min.js) and unminified (code.jquery.com/jquery-1.8.2.js) versions.

Async

In HTML5 compliant and modern browsers, JavaScript has now offered an async attribute to loading script files; async is used when script files are to be loaded in parallel and asynchronous to the other scripts loading on the page. These are scripts that have no dependency on the rest of the page content. This is especially useful in helping load a page more quickly or when an external script is not responding. Having the script load with async allows the page to render yet not be held up trying to execute a script that has failed. The main takeaway with async is avoiding parser block—the situation where the document stops rendering until script files are done. This usually results in no elements being rendered to the screen because most script files are added to the head of the document and the parser can't get past it. For JavaScript ad tags, using async can ensure that your ad script doesn't delay the rendering of the publisher's page until after all your ad content comes down. To get a better understanding on this feel free to check out some of the examples from The Deck and BuySellAds.com (css-tricks.com/thinking-async). Listing 3-4 outlines the use of async in an ad call.

Listing 3-4. Using Async JavaScript in an Ad Call

```
<!DOCTYPE HTML>
<html>
<head>
<meta http-equiv="Content-Type" content="text/html; charset=UTF-8">
<script async src='http://code.someAdTag.js'></script>
</head>
<body>
</body>
</html>
```

Defer

In addition to `async`, you're very likely to see more scripts that are dependent on other scripts. You could be referencing an external library or another dependency, like page content, that's present before the ad executes. You can use a new JavaScript attribute called `defer`, which instructs the DOM parser to load scripts in the order they're interpreted. For example, you may want to load a larger deferred script before loading another script that references the previous one. Using the `defer` attribute more often, you'll notice fewer errors when dealing with the sequencing of script files. Listing 3-5 outlines how to use the `defer` attribute.

Listing 3-5. Using JavaScript's defer Attribute

```
<!DOCTYPE HTML>
<html>
<head>
<meta http-equiv="Content-Type" content="text/html; charset=UTF-8">
<script defer src='http://code.one.js'></script>
<script defer src='http://code.two.js'></script>
<script defer src='http://code.three.js'></script>
<script defer src='http://code.four.js'></script>
</head>
<body>
</body>
</html>
```

Keep in mind neither `async` nor `defer` blocks the DOM parser, resulting in a better experience for users viewing the page content. It also goes to mention that defer occurs before the DOMContentLoaded event from the browser.

requestAnimationFrame

HTML5 welcomes users with a `requestAnimationFrame` for dealing with JavaScript animation, versus the old way of using `setTimeout` or `setInterval`. Use of `requestAnimationFrame` explicitly tells the browser what your intentions are for animation. Traditionally, developers used the code shown in Listing 3-6 for moving something on the page.

Listing 3-6. JavaScript setInterval

```
<script>
window.setInterval(function() {
   //move and repeat.
   console.log('animate');
}, 1000 / 60); // 60fps.
</script>
```

Now, we can use `requestAnimationFrame`, as shown in Listing 3-7.

Listing 3-7. Using requestAnimationFrame

```
<!DOCTYPE HTML>
<html>
<head>
<meta http-equiv="Content-Type" content="text/html; charset=UTF-8">
</head>
<body>
```

```
    <div id='box' style='position:absolute; background-color:black; width:50px; height:50px;'></div>
</body>
<script>
var globalRequestAnimationFrame = window.requestAnimationFrame || window.mozRequestAnimationFrame ||↵
window.webkitRequestAnimationFrame || window.msRequestAnimationFrame;
window.requestAnimationFrame = globalRequestAnimationFrame;

var theElement = document.getElementById('box');
var movement = 0;

function animate(timestamp) {
    //move something the new way
    movement += 5;
    globalRequestAnimationFrame(animate);
    theElement.style.left = movement + 'px';
    console.log(movement);
}

//kick animation off
globalRequestAnimationFrame(animate);
</script>
</html>
```

Using requestAnimationFrame allows the browser to intelligently offset the animation to the GPU (where doing so is supported); this makes for smoother animation and also detects when a user is not viewing animated content on, say, a hidden browser tab. The browser's throttling down the animation's frame rate saves resources; it automatically picks back up should the user return to that tab. This is a world of difference from using setTimeout; as the browser can really understand a designer's intentions, it allocates resources appropriately. (Since requestAnimationFrame is still an emerging feature and not a finalized spec, be sure to include vendor-prefixed versions.)

XML

XML (extensible markup language) has long been a language of the Web and many other software programming languages. XML's true beauty is in not being specific to any language. Completely agnostic, it describes rules that are readable both by a human and by various coding languages. Using an XMLHttpRequest, XML is the response when working with an HTTP web service call. XMLHttpRequest is subject to the same origin policy, which for security reasons allows requests to be made only from within the domain of the page content. That is, you can't access information from twitter.com or google.com using XMLHttpRequest. That said, an XML response is typically not the favorite when dealing with JavaScript developers. Typically, developers ask to have their web services respond in JSON format.

JSON

JSON (JavaScript object notation) is a name/value pair object that is handled natively inside of via JavaScript. What makes it so highly useful is that it's extremely lightweight and legible. JSON is very helpful for responses when using APIs for web services in mobile devices. Also, JavaScript with padding or JSON-P treats JSON as native JavaScript, which means you won't run into cross-domain policy issues when requesting services from external domains. JSON is becoming a standard response for Twitter and other popular API services because of its fast response and clean readability. Listing 3-8 demonstrates a basic and easily understood JSON structure.

Listing 3-8. A Basic JSON Structure

```
"people": [
        {"name": "John",
        "age":"28",
        "title":"Developer"
        },
        {"name": "Alison",
        "age":"26",
        "title":"Teacher"
        }]
```

In web advertising, developers are always working with external APIs to bring more relevance to ad units. A typical request is to pull an advertiser's recent news via an RSS feed into the ad unit. A good tool to use for this purpose in JSON format is one from the founder of jQuery, John Resig: RSS2JSON (ejohn.org/projects/rss2json).

■ **Note** We'll cover JSON in more depth using API's in chapter 11.

JavaScript Libraries

Because writing native JavaScript can be cumbersome at times, many talented developers have created libraries and abstractions for working with and writing native JavaScript. Most of the time using a JavaScript library in the ad environment means you're adding additional code bloat to your ad. Keep in mind that you can do everything these libraries do in native JavaScript, so always weigh the pros and cons of relying on a library to get the job done. That said, probably the most popular library is jQuery.

jQuery

jQuery is huge among the developer community base, and it has a very clean and simple coding language. In fact, I've seen firsthand many Actionscript developers head toward working with jQuery when moving from Flash to JavaScript development. That approach has some pros and cons, though. On the one hand, jQuery has a very simple syntax, one that AS3 developers find themselves at home in. On the other hand, jQuery has its downsides in the advertising world because it will increase overall k-weight and may be unnecessary for simple ad creations. If you notice that you're using jQuery to simply animate a few items on-screen and to easily reference DOM nodes, you really should stop using it. If you absolutely *must* lean on jQuery for cross-browser compatibility or something similar, the best thing ad servers can do is provide an option to use it or not, depending upon whether the publisher's page has incorporated it. Since jQuery is so popular—I mean really, really popular—there is a good chance that you, as a developer, won't have to include it in a redundant fashion for your ad content. Simply leverage jQuery if the publisher already has it loaded. Do a quick conditional check, something like the one in Listing 3-9.

Listing 3-9. A jQuery Conditional Check

```
<script>
(function(window){
    var latestVersion = "1.8.2";//update to jQuery's latest version
    var libraries = {
        pubjQuery: window.jQuery || window.$,
```

```
        iFramePubjQuery: window.parent.jQuery,
        googjQuery: "https://ajax.googleapis.com/ajax/libs/jquery/" + latestVersion + "/jquery.min.js",
    }
    for (var libs in libraries) {
        var lib = libraries[libs];
        console.log("Possible Libs: " + lib);
    }
    if (libraries.pubjQuery || libraries.iFramePubjQuery) {
        console.log("Publisher Has jQuery - We're Good!");
    } else {
        loadScript(libraries.googjQuery);
    }
    function loadScript(_script) {
        var script = document.createElement("script")
        script.type = "text/javascript";
        script.defer = true;
        script.src = _script;
        document.getElementsByTagName("head")[0].appendChild(script);
        console.log("We choose " + _script);
    }
})(window);
</script>
```

This conditional can be used in the ad to detect whether the page has jQuery included. If it doesn't, the ad server can bring it in before the ad loads because it could be dependent on it. Another good recommendation in using jQuery is pulling it from Google's CDN. This will more than likely already be cached on the user's machine (everybody uses Google); so no additional downloading will be required. This is a huge optimization technique—and why do more than you have to, right?

Since there is a good chance some if not all of your publishers will be leveraging jQuery, be sure to ask if they have modified versions of the library loaded before using them within the ad experience. There is a really good chance that a publisher could be loading jQuery version 1.8.2 but in fact it's a variation of that library. This fact alone could steer many ad developers away from using the library from the publisher.

In web development and content creation, jQuery is great. It's relatively lightweight when compressed and minified for its feature set. It has a huge developer following that constantly supports the code base, and it's even backed by major companies like Adobe and Google. That said, in advertising it can produce unnecessary code bloat and heavy load times if it's not fully needed. Rapidly developed JavaScript libraries can be a huge advantage, especially if you're just trying to prototype something to test functionality. However, bear in mind that keeping code minimal and lean makes for faster code execution and better performance, especially on mobile devices.

Some very popular JavaScript libraries, listed in Table 3-1, provide useful features for handling variances across browsers and dealing with such specific features as touch events, video, canvas, and offline storage. There'll be more on some of these libraries in later chapters.

Table 3-1. Some Useful JavaScript Libraries for Various Use Cases

JavaScript Library	Description
CraftJS	`http://craftjs.org/`
HandlebarJS	`handlebarsjs.com`
HammerJS	`eightmedia.github.com/hammer.js`
PhantomJS	`phantomjs.org`
Lawnchair	`westcoastlogic.com/lawnchair`
EaselJS	`createjs.com`
ProcessingJS	`processingjs.org`
LocacheJS	`locachejs.org`
RequireJS	`requirejs.org`
HeadJS	`headjs.com`
VideoJS	`videojs.com`
RevealJS	`lab.hakim.se/reveal-js`
UnderscoreJS	`http://underscorejs.org/`

Note   There are many more JavaScript libraries — in advertising some are more useful than others—but there are way too many to name here. Check out `javascriptlibraries.com` for a good list or see *Smashing Magazine*'s breakdown of the 40 most useful JavaScript libraries: `coding.smashingmagazine.com/2009/03/02/40-stand-alone-javascript-libraries-for-specific-purposes`.

JavaScript Compilers

Remember reading about SASS and HAML for CSS and HTML development? Well don't forget about JavaScript and its little JavaScript compiler language, CoffeeScript. CoffeeScript is aimed at exposing the good parts of JavaScript in a much simpler way. CoffeeScript compiles down to JavaScript as speedily as a developer could code by hand—or more so. It's also guaranteed to pass JavaScript Lint or any other JavaScript tester; that's really helpful when you're passing script files among team members. You wouldn't believe how many tools and compilers are out there that will compile to native JavaScript. Many say that in order to build complex web applications, such as Google's Gmail and Maps, you need another layer of construct on top of native JavaScript. In fact, for most advertising campaigns, doing so may be a bit of overkill but if you're dealing with a very deep and complex campaign with many moving parts, it may be worth giving CoffeeScript a look. Also, take a look at Google's Dart and Closure Compiler to get an idea on the level of abstraction I'm talking about.

Note   For a comprehensive list of JavaScript compilers, see `github.com/jashkenas/coffee-script/wiki/List-of-languages-that-compile-to-JS`.

Polyfills

A polyfill, or polyfill, is a piece of code (or plugin) that provides the technology that you, the developer, expect the browser to provide natively. Flattening the API landscape if you will.

—Remy Sharp

Polyfills handle browser differences where support for a bit of technology isn't present. When you run an advertising campaign, your user base will be on several different browsers and devices. A polyfill is code to handle these discrepancies. Some typical polyfills deal with emerging features supported in the latest HTML5-compliant browsers, such as the <canvas> element and video and offline storage. Polyfills are extremely important to use if your campaign needs to run across browsers and devices. (This information should be outlined in your initial media plan.) If you are just running an ad targeting a single device or browser, you will generally not need to add a polyfill, as you can set client expectations to what is currently available on that browser.

Note that there is a very useful online tool called caniuse.com (I'll be mentioning it frequently in the book). It breaks down current feature support across all major modern browsers and even gives insight as to what features will come in future releases. My advice? Bookmark it!

One thing to note is that adding a polyfill will almost always add additional k-weight. Publishers may not find this an ideal situation, so be sure to flag it as you become aware of it. However, in time, as the HTML5 spec finalizes and browsers adopt the updates and changes, the need for polyfills will diminish, much like the need for vendor prefixes, and so the need to add polyfill k-weight bloat will be eliminated. For now, polyfills are integral to the creative development process and should be used as campaign objectives dictate.

Some really helpful polyfill tools are yepnopejs.com and afarkas.github.com/webshim/demos. However, keep in mind that most of these are built on top of jQuery or Modernizer, which add additional k-weight. The best solution is to show your clients what can be done currently. If a campaign needs to run across devices and browsers, you will almost always need to leverage a polyfill or else significantly scale back the creative design and functionality. Again, I suggest using caniuse.com, which keeps tabs on what features are available and when.

Browser Extensions

Browser extensions for web development can help you tremendously when you're building a campaign. They allow you to get inside the browser and figure out how and why certain things happen to your ad creative. This section reviews use and installation of some very useful extensions for the Webkit, Mozilla, Opera and IE browsers.

When developing for emerging browsers, every developer needs the bare essentials of browser extensions. They can help debug and breakdown your creative development much more effectively, as they render in the browser what you'll eventually deploy.

Some extensions are so useful that I'd go so far as to describe them as mandatory. One such is Firebug (getfirebug.com). Firebug provides a suite of tools similar to what Google's Chrome browser provides when you right-click and inspect elements on a page (also known as the browser's web inspector tool). Another useful plug-in for Mozilla browsers is HttpFox (addons.mozilla.org/en-US/firefox/addon/httpfox), which analyzes the HTTP traffic in your browser. This is very useful when debugging certain API calls to and from a server. These tools are all vital in the debugging of code, whether it be HTML markup, CSS style and animation, or JavaScript. Other popular browser extensions are Adblock Plus (adblockplus.org) and similar ad blockers, which kill the rendering of advertisements in the browser. I don't encourage you to install this extension, as it blocks any and all ads and even some crucial web content not related to advertising. However, its good to understand that these exist, and it will be interesting to see how future ad blockers will behave (they've traditionally been used to kill domains of Flash content). If a blocked domain is providing useful content to a user, that content will also be blocked, creating a failed experience for the end user. My guess is that these extensions need to get much smarter if they want only to effectively block advertising for their install base. Otherwise, publisher content and other vital web content will be hidden from the user.

Debugging

As any developer will tell you, debugging code takes up easily half, often most, of the time spent working. Debugging is the process of validating code and checking for errors and bugs. Depending on the complexity of the ad unit, it could be a pretty lengthy process. Unit testing every function requires extreme patience as well as refactoring, which can be a very time-consuming process. Luckily, developers today have many enhancements and tools that to prior developers were just a dream. Using these tools you can debug anything in your markup, style, and script. You can manipulate elements directly on the DOM and get your feedback in real time. Tools like Charles (for the Mac; charlesproxy.com) and Fiddler (for Windows; fiddler2.com/fiddler2), monitor web traffic much as HttpFox does. These proxy tools are vital for debugging desktop and mobile devices as well as testing web service calls. They can provide valuable insight into what your browser's network traffic is performing from requests to responses—very helpful if you're making external HTTP calls and need to validate the responses. It can help you understand if your errors are client-side or server-side. Yet for me, probably the most important tool in modern browsers is the web inspector. As I mentioned in the previous section, Web Inspectors provide a lot of testing and debugging tools for developers and they come with all modern browsers by default.

Among the common problems I've seen when developers are debugging code especially when coming from the Flash/Actionscript world of using trace statements—are popping alerts for JavaScript testing. Popping an alert box is performed by writing a command—alert('hello world');—in your script; this will cause the code to stop executing. As you saw when reviewing async and defer attributes, the DOM parser will be blocked, which will keep your code from executing until the user clears the alert window. So it's best not to throw alerts and pause the parser. Rather, use the JavaScript console in modern browsers if you're looking for a similar experience to Actionscript's trace statement. From there, you'll be able to print output logs to the console and view what's happening under the hood of the browser, how its executing your ad code. Instead of alerts, use a throw() statement or even a log statement by calling console.log(); for normal trace output statements, console.warn(); if you are looking to handle warning signs, use console.error() when testing code for potential errors. With all of these debugging commands, you'll be able to easily navigate your JavaScript code and determine where errors are occurring or optimization can happen.

When you use console.log, console.warn, and console.error, each command writes different colored code in the browser's console viewer to differentiate them. This is very helpful because you could have many commands, depending on your ad code's complexity. There are also many other developer tools out there, and every developer has a special "go-to" tool. Some I've found helpful are Dom Monster (mir.aculo.us/dom-monster) and JsPerf (jsperf.com). Dom Monster is great because it's a nice little bookmark for your browser, and JsPerf is great for writing test cases against code snippets. My advice is to get your feet wet building with these tools till you find one that works for you.

Note For information on accessing developer tools in Chrome, visit developers.google.com/chrome-developer-tools/docs/profiles.

Advertising Best Practices

Since "best practices" is a pretty clichéd term in every industry, forgive my using it if you have a gripe with it. Moreover, at the moment no one can handle applying "best practices" to something that's not final. However, there are some useful tips that will, I hope, keep you from getting into a bind. The IAB even states on its creative guidelines page:

> *Prior to the wide adoption of devices like the iPhone™ and iPad™, Flash™ formatted creative was widely accepted and easily displayed across the industry. In today's market, adjustments have to be made to accommodate ads across multiple display devices. HTML5 has provided one solution, but is not yet widely adopted and requires different creative specifications than Flash formatted creative. Requests were made to call out a separate category of creative specs to accommodate HTML5 ads, but for this release of creative guidelines, it was decided to keep the specs "technology neutral." An addendum for HTML5 for display advertising best practices is currently being pursued.*

As you can see, it's really hard to speak of "best practices" about something that's still emerging. Myself and various other working group members are working hard to develop a formal overview on HTML5 and advertising. When the spec becomes final, the IAB will surely update this guideline. (Visit `iab.net/guidelines/508676/508767/displayguidelines` for more information on this topic.)

Borders

The first ad best practice to cover is that a publisher will normally request that all creatives include a 1-pixel black border if the ad color is not noticeably different from the page background color. If a 1-pixel boarder around the unit is needed, all you'd have to do is add CSS on the ads `div` container so its clearly separated from the publisher's page content.

Tracking

HTML5 ads have the ability to track users, just like publishers have been able to do using Flash. Now agencies can utilize Google analytics and URL shortening links, such as `Bit.ly`, which allow for tracking clicks. Ad designers can embed these free analytics platforms into their creative code and get valuable insight into a user's location, behavior, and technology. With HTML5 ads, there is much discussion about ad-serving companies using the HTML5 ping attribute for tracking URLs. That this attribute can store a value and "ping" it to a redirect server is useful for tracking purposes. (There is more about this at `lists.whatwg.org/htdig.cgi/whatwg-whatwg.org/2005-October/004926.html`.)

Click Tags

One specific form of tracking in ads involves what are known as click tags. They allow the ad server to inject specific values at serve time into the URL destination of a click. (This is very similar to the macro approach outlined in Listing 3-1.) A click tag can be assigned in multiple ways depending on the ad server, but it's almost always added in campaign creatives. They can be written in any variation required by the ad server—`clickTAG`, `ClickTag`, `clickTag`, or something else. Check with your ad-serving provider during creative development so the correct variable is used. Let's take a look at working with click tags (see Listing 3-10).

Listing 3-10. A Click Tag Example

```
<!DOCTYPE HTML>
<html>
<head>
<meta http-equiv="Content-Type" content="text/html; charset=UTF-8">
</head>
<body>
<div id='clickBtn1' onClick=window.open(clickTag1)>CLICK HERE!</div>
<div id='clickBtn2' onClick=window.open(clickTag2)>CLICK HERE!</div>
</body>
</html>
```

As you can see, working with click tags is pretty simple. Depending on the ad server, the URL's location during development will be `clickTag` and the number you want to use. In this case, there are two, so I simply call them `clickTag1` and `clickTag2`. At ad serve time, the click tag value will be replaced by whatever value is defined at the ad server. This will keep specific tracking and redirects intact when the creative is sent to various publishers and ad networks on the media buy.

File Size

File size considerations are possibly the biggest shift when working with HTML based ad creative as opposed to Flash SWF's. Flash was very good at packaging the creative assets all within a small SWF file container using a proprietary compression format. This compression really squeezed the file size down significantly for ads with animation, fonts, images—you name it. Because of this, the IAB and various publishers have adopted smaller k-weight footprints for rich media ads, usually anywhere from 40kb up to 100kb if you're lucky. Because we're no longer contained in the SWF wrapper, two things need to occur. One, we as developers and designers need to optimize much more out of the programs we're using for our creative. This could be optimizing image compression out of Adobe's Photoshop or even minifying the code base before uploading to our hosting. Second, the IAB and it's various publishers will need to update the guidelines for file size. We as an industry can't progress our creative innovation when there is an unrealistic expectation of what can be done within a certain file size limit. In the interim as this gets updated, designers and developers can use appropriate optimization techniques such as the usage of sprite sheets, code minification and compression, measuring file size via GZIP (wire weight), and leveraging CDN hosted JS libraries (All of which you'll learn in more detail throughout the rest of this book).

Asset Delivery

Ad development, much like web development, requires many different components to produce the final piece you see in a browser. Be sure that when you are requesting creative files from an agency or client, you always ask for these:

- images—PNG, JPG, GIF (animated and static)
- layered source files (Photoshop documents)
- HTML, CSS, and JavaScript files
- audio and video files (if required)
- fonts and/or (CSS web fonts)
- storyboards (PDFs)

Whether you're on the publisher, agency, or ad-serving end, this will help you keep your sanity in trying to wrangle all the different formats and files and attempting to make updates and revisions later in the process. Ensuring that all of these files are accounted for during an initial asset intake process ensures that turnaround times and client expectations won't get compromised due to missing files and/or unnecessary back-and-forth communication.

Element Names

Keeping naming conventions specific and fully worded helps reduce the risk that ad code will conflict with a publisher's page code. Using elements without specific names could result in code execution conflict or possibly even incorporating scripts and styles from the publisher's page in your ad content. For example, if the publisher's page has a div called `container` and so does the ad code and you have JavaScript code executing on that DOM element, there is a good chance that the ad code could conflict with the publisher's. The same thing could happen when styling is applied. It's best to keep div tags and others very descriptive of the ad platform. Personally, I like to apply my own prefix to the elements. For example, if I have an ad container, I'll look to see what ad server is serving the creative and add the name to the respective elements. If DFP is serving the ad, it would be something like this: `<div id=dfp_adContainer></div>`; or if it's PointRoll, it would be `<div id=pointroll_adContainer></div>`. This way, there is a good possibility that no other elements are on the page with that prefix. If you need to get even more granular, include the size of the ad as well as the ad server's prefix name.

Same In–Same Out Rule

Advertising usually also follows a "same in–same out" rule. This is the functionality of the ad unit and how it expands and contracts based on user interaction. For example, if a user clicks or taps to expand the ad creative, the user should click or tap to close out. The same rule applies to using mouse-over interactions in desktop. Note that all publishers that support rich media advertising campaigns typically follow this rule.

Mobile

If your ad agency is ready to start constructing HTML5 ads, it's a good chance that you and your clients also focus on penetration and reach in the mobile market, since Flash isn't supported on iDevices. Mobile is still a small market in the grand scheme of things, but it's growing very quickly. In 2011, mobile advertising was up 149 percent over 2010's numbers; overall, advertising will very soon shift away Flash entirely and leverage HTML5, CSS3, and JavaScript for creating experiences. For an A/B comparison, take a look at this ad sample from the folks at Sencha: `dev.sencha.com/deploy/css3-ads`. Can you tell the difference between Flash and CSS3? Chances are you can, but as more HTML5 browsers become the norm, expect to see more Flash-like experiences being developed with web standards. Also, use `html5readiness.com` to keep up to date on overall browser acceptance.

Images vs. Icons

For mobile devices, especially with varying pixel densities, it makes more sense to leverage the browser to create graphics and use fewer bitmap images where possible. Why? Because one way or another, images are absolutely horrific when they're scaled. Scaling up results in loss of image fidelity and overall quality; scaling down results in unwanted aliasing, which will reduce the overall sharpness of the image. With this in mind, Drew Wilson created a font icon library, Pictos (`pictos.cc`), for various screen layouts and overall design. Many web publishers use these icons today. If you're being pressed to use images because there is absolutely no way your client will rest for font icons, I'd encourage you to use a service, such as Sencha's Image Service, a proxy service that allows designers to optimize images requested by multiple devices and screens. (Go to `sencha.com/learn/how-to-use-src-sencha-io` for more on this technology.) Conversely, you can use a service like Resize.ly (`resize.ly`), which is a cloud-based image-resizing tool. In short, if you can get the browser to do the hard work while you take full advantage of CSS3, you'll be better off than by making multiple HTTP requests to get images from the server. Be sure to use images intelligently and target users on desktop only. If you are running a campaign on mobile, ask yourself whether images are needed, and if they are, how many? In most cases users on mobile or low-bandwidth devices will benefit more from one-image or no-image loads. Again, be sure to use CSS, SVG, `canvas`, or other alternative means on mobile. You'll learn more about each of them in later chapters.

Site Events

In advertising, site events allow tracking from an ad unit to a publisher's page; this process is otherwise known as a conversion. For an advertiser adding site events represents real ROI (return on investment); it shows where users click from and how they arrive at the advertiser's site. However, since cookies are used to track site events, there are limits on how conversions on iOS devices are handled, since the iOS default setting doesn't allow third-party cookies to be dropped unless a user has visited the domain. This is a huge challenge in the industry; many ad-serving companies want to tell this story to the advertiser but have to find other means. Many think HTML5 local storage can provide this mechanism for tracking conversions (you'll get a closer look at working with it later in this book). Others argue how this will change things in the future. Will publishers act as ad-serving first-party cookie drops on behalf of the ad server? Will third-party ad servers go away? One thing is for certain: limitations and future issues with privacy are in the forefront of everyone's mind as HTML5 becomes bigger in the advertising market.

Define Your Reach

HTML5 ads will take time to become the standard, but I'm positive you'll see more and more in coming years—especially as we head into 2013. We are slowly seeing the shift from Flash content to HTML5 on the mobile and desktop Web as more marketers realize that it's not cost effective to build two versions of the same ad experience to reach every screen. Until the full switch is made, you can do many things to get moving in the right direction in HTML5 advertising. First, you've done the best thing so far by reading this book but also start developing for the emerging web; learn what features you can use now by going to caniuse.com frequently. Then encourage the use of Google's Chrome Frame, which allows IE6 and other older browsers to work with new HTML5 features (it works by injecting an invisible rendering frame into a user's IE browser). Next, educate others to begin leveraging the open web. We all can't push the industry forward if there are agencies and ad servers still supporting the dated plugin model. Last, always include graceful failovers especially while in this transitional period. Hitting 100 percent of your user base will be damn near impossible given a campaign's turnaround time, so be sure to do everything you can to address discrepancies before they become issues. Remember, after you define your target reach, build with the oldest browser's user base in mind; iterate on top of that initial foundation with more elaborate features as newer browsers support them. This way all users, old and new, get an experience they're capable of handling. Not every browser is created the same, so neither should every ad experience. Once the browser landscape flattens and HTML5's features become widely adopted—we'll be able to ignore the development woes for older browser versions our users may be on.

Summary

This chapter has reviewed web standards with HTML5, CSS, and JavaScript and their effect on advertising as a whole. You should now be fully briefed in core ad development practices as we prepare to dive into the nuts and bolts of HTML5 advertisements. In the following chapters, the canvas element, use of web fonts, SVG, animations, presentations, forms, drag-n-drop, web workers, media, offline storage, and much more will be covered in detail. You now know both the base language of the industry and some really helpful best practices for getting started. Finally, if you are curious as to how to help with the specs discussed in this chapter or if you have questions on transitioning into HTML5, visit whatwg.org/mailing-list#specs and lend a hand in development. There's still time to shape what the new Web will become! Let's get started.

CHAPTER 4

Using Canvas, SVG, and Web Fonts

We've already covered basic web standards, emerging browsers, and how advertising fits into the big conversation called HTML5. Now it's time to dig a bit deeper into the technologies that drive HTML5, including the new canvas element, SVG and Web Font support. We'll kick things off by talking about one of the biggest advancements in HTML5 specification first, canvas.

The canvas element is the new display API for dealing with graphics directly within the browser. If you're coming from a Flash background working with the display list API, canvas will be a welcomed adjustment in making the transition. This element can provide full animation, image manipulations, and obviously a drawing tool and do it all from within the native browser environment, without the need of a plug-in like Flash. We'll dig a bit deeper into providing use cases and examples for dealing with the canvas element as it relates to advertising as well as taking a dive into the tools and API's, which can help Flash developers make the transition into using this for their creative development. For the CSS side of things, we'll discuss how web fonts can provide rich font rendering directly within the browser via normal CSS syntax. We'll also discuss Font Squirrel and how this and other tools can help convert many font formats to browser-friendly formats. Finally, we'll review how scalable vector graphics (SVG) can be interpreted by HTML5 markup within the browser and how for icons and symbols SVG provides many benefits over traditional imagery. As a follow-up to the last chapter's discussion of images vs. icons, you'll get great insight into optimizing graphics for any screen. In short, this chapter is chock full of useful tidbits, so be sure to pay attention and follow along.

Canvas

The canvas element, used to render graphics in modern browsers, is arguably one of the biggest additions to HTML5's specification. It's a particularly large inclusion to the spec with regard to advertising, since with it one can finally paint graphics as rich as Flash did—but natively, directly inside the browser! Originally developed by Apple in 2004, the tag "canvas" was used in the Mac OSX operating system's dashboard widgets and in its browser, Safari. Soon after, the Web Hypertext Application Technology Working Group (WHATWG) added it to the HTML5 standard, and it was later adopted by Firefox, Opera, Google and eventually Microsoft.

The canvas element brings many great things to a browser by rendering graphics, animation, and even interactivity. There are many different ways of working with the canvas element; the following sections will dive a bit deeper into working with it. Setting up the canvas element in your markup is really quite simple. It's a tag, just like any other you'd use: <div>, <img>, <body>. Listing 4-1 outlines how to create the element.

Listing 4-1. How to Create the Canvas Element

```
<!DOCTYPE HTML>
<html>
<head>
<meta http-equiv="Content-Type" content="text/html; charset=UTF-8">
</head>
```

```
<body>
<canvas id="adCanvas" width="100" height="100"></canvas>
</body>
</html>
```

As you can see, it's fairly simple to create the tag in HTML5. If you open your favorite text editor, input the Listing 4-1 code, save it as `canvas.html`, and open it in your favorite modern browser, you'll notice that nothing is rendered to the screen. Don't be alarmed; think of it as an artist placing his canvas on the easel—and this time you're the artist, though you haven't actually started to draw anything yet. To draw on `canvas`, you'll need to leverage the real power of this new HTML5 element; that's in its API, which is all JavaScript. JavaScript controls the painting of graphics, animation, and interactivity. (It's best to think of the element as a container or shell for graphics that you will create by leveraging JavaScript.)

Before heading into JavaScript implementation of `canvas`, note that the element has a few DOM attributes, including width and height, within the HTML markup.

Note   DOM refers to a page's document markup, which is made up of elements, attributes and tags. The `canvas` element is part of the DOM structure, which can have various attributes, including `ID`, `Class`, `Height`, and `Width`.

More importantly, `canvas` has several methods for drawing paths, shapes, gradients, and characters, as well as adding images and compositing. And that's only for starters! The element can be instructed to do many things besides detecting user input and rendering complex animations—interactive games, for instance. It can even be used multiple times either in the browser, by creating a stack of `canvas` elements, one on top of another, to represent a complex image composite, or even on different areas of the page. It's really up to you, as developer and designer, to leverage this powerful new addition to the Web.

Let's build on the code in Listing 4-1 to render a green square to the screen by adding some simple JavaScript code. Try to follow along in your text editor in Listing 4-2.

Listing 4-2. Using Canvas to Render a Green Square to the Screen

```
<!DOCTYPE HTML>
<html>
<head>
<meta http-equiv="Content-Type" content="text/html; charset=UTF-8">
</head>
<body>
<canvas id="adCanvas" width="300" height="250"></canvas>
</body>
<script type="text/javascript">
//get a reference to the canvas
var canvas = document.getElementById('adCanvas');
var context = canvas.getContext('2d');
//draw a green square
context.fillStyle = 'green';
context.fillRect(0, 0, 250, 250);
</script>
</html>
```

Once you refresh your page, you should get an image of a small green square, as shown in Figure 4-1.

Figure 4-1. *A 250 × 250 square made with the canvas element*

If you see the square, you're ready to review what's going on. If you don't, be sure you're using a modern browser, one that supports canvas, and double-check your code.

Note   Check for canvas support at caniuse.com/#feat=canvas.

First, let's create a variable that gets a reference to the canvas element in the DOM. In this case, give it the ID "adCanvas" by writing <canvas id="adCanvas" width="300" height="250"></canvas> in the markup. Once that reference is there, add a 2D context to the canvas so canvas knows how to paint graphics. In short, the 2D context represents a flat Cartesian coordinate system where the origin (0,0) is at the top left corner of the canvas, with x values increasing when going right and y values increasing when going down—similar to what you may have learned in algebra.

Having gotten this element and context, let's start "painting" on the canvas. To do so, tell the fillStyle property to render in green (it can also take a hex and RGB value), and then call the method fillRect to render a rectangle by passing in specific parameters or arguments by writing context.fillRect(0, 0, 250, 250);. In Figure 4-1, a square was created by passing in 0 for its x-coordinate, 0 for its y-coordinate, and 250 for both its width and height. This value takes a floating-point number; that is, not having it paint on a whole integer, like 10, will result in subpixel aliasing. This could be problematic if you're trying to maintain sharpness with your art. (If you want to dive into the other properties and methods for working with canvas, check out the comprehensive cheat sheet at roblaplaca.com/examples/canvasHelloWorld.

Note   The only context support available when this book was printed was 2D. There's more about 3D and WebGL in Chapter 12.

This may look pretty simple, but it's powerful. Keep in mind, too, that you've seen just the beginning of what this element can do. There are many use cases to cover; going forward, I'll showcase examples of leveraging canvas in practical approaches, especially as it relates to building online advertisements, including graphical animation, and handling user inputs.

Illustrator to Canvas

You may already be asking yourself, "Wait, why do I need to draw on the canvas programmatically using JavaScript? I'm a designer; can't I use my normal design tools?" You're not alone in asking this question; there is a very nice tool, one developed specifically for designers' use, called Ai ➤ Canvas (`visitmix.com/labs/ai2canvas`); it allows designers to design in the vector-based programs they know and love, especially Adobe Illustrator.

> *The Ai ➤ Canvas plug-in enables Adobe Illustrator to export vector and bitmap artwork directly to an HTML5 canvas element that can be rendered in a canvas-enabled browser. The plug-in provides drawing, animation and coding options such as events so that you can build interactive, well-designed canvas-based web apps.*

> visitmix.com/labs/ai2canvas

In a creative department, this tool is exceptionally helpful when you're working on a team where designers need to provide concepts and mocks to developers. You can have your designers work in Illustrator and your developers work in JavaScript. The tool offers a clear separation between design and function and helps when, down the road, clients need to make changes (they always do). In addition to drawing in this fashion, using Illustrator, this plug-in allows for animation, event handling, and even debugging. (Pretty sweet, if you ask me, plus it's all offered for free.) These features make this plug-in a valuable addition to any designer's tool belt. Since it's appropriate for certain applications, I'd suggest you check it out if you are serious about using canvas to work with highly visual and complex art. Keep in mind, though, that as the graphics get more complex, the k-weight is sure to increase, as will the unoptimized JavaScript that the plug-in will generate. So plan your execution correctly, and keep your client and publisher are aware of what you're doing, particularly if k-weight constraints are tight.

Flash to Canvas

If you work in Flash or know people who do or did, they will tell you that it was a groundbreaking platform as far as making innovative rich graphics for the Web is concerned. As you now know, the canvas element is a warmly welcomed addition, since it lets designers and developers make advantageous use of graphics in HTML5 ads. Now, in the latest Adobe Flash Professional CS6, designers can work with the canvas element more easily, thanks to a library and toolkit called CreateJS.

CreateJS

CreateJS has a bunch of great things in its suite of offerings.

- EaselJS (covered in detail shortly)
- TweenJS (for animations)
- SoundJS (for HTML5 audio)
- PreloadJS (for preloading assets)
- Zoe (a sprite-sheet generator)

■ **Note**   TweenJS, SoundJS, PreloadJS, and Zoe won't be covered in this chapter. You can learn more about these libraries at `http://createjs.com`.

For designers and developers, the CreateJS framework, developed by Grant Skinner, provides a complete set of JavaScript libraries for graphics, animation, sound, and preloading to assist in constructing HTML5 content.

EaselJS

EaselJS is a JavaScript library, part of CreateJS, that allows Flash designers and developers to create graphics in the Flash authoring environment. Using EaselJS, you gain access to a bunch of similar syntax from Actionscript 3.0 while leveraging JavaScript for creating native browser graphics and animation. According to Grant Skinner, EaselJS exercises the developments of ten-plus years of Flash's display list API; he wanted to port it over to a comprehensive JavaScript library to be used for working with the canvas element in HTML5. In its syntax, EaselJS is very similar to working with the display list API in ActionScript 3 (AS3), as Listing 4-3 demonstrates.

Listing 4-3. An Example of EaselJS

```
<!DOCTYPE HTML>
<html>
<head>
<meta charset="UTF-8">
<title>EaselJS</title>
<script src="easeljs-0.4.2.min.js"></script>
<script src="BoxBlurFilter.js"></script>
<style>
* {background-color: #000;}
</style>
</head>
<body onLoad="init()">
<canvas id="canvas" width="1024" height="768"></canvas>
</body>
<script>
var stage,
      canvas = document.getElementById("canvas"),
      context = canvas.getContext("2D"),
      logoImage = new Image(),
      logo,
      fps = 30,
      speed = 0.2;

function init() {
      stage = new Stage(canvas);
      //Keep a local image or you'll get the following error:
      //Unable to get image data from canvas because the canvas has been tainted by
cross-origin data.
      logoImage.src = 'logo.jpg';
      logoImage.onload = function () {
            logo = new Bitmap(logoImage);
            logo.cache(0, 0, logoImage.width, logoImage.height);
            logo.regX = logo.image.width * 0.5;
            logo.regY = logo.image.height * 0.5;
            stage.addChild(logo);
```

65

```
            Ticker.setFPS(fps);
            Ticker.addListener(window);
        }
    }
}
function tick() {
        var splitX = (stage.mouseX - logo.x) * speed;
        var splitY = (stage.mouseY - logo.y) * speed;
        logo.x += splitX;
        logo.y += splitY;
        logo.updateCache();
        logo.filters = [new BoxBlurFilter(5000, 5000, 2)];
        stage.update();
}
</script>
</html>
```

OK, that's quite a bit of code to work through, but anyone coming from a Flash or ActionScript background will attest that, as far as syntax is concerned, it's pretty much as close as it gets in JavaScript. In the `init` function, the similarities to Flash are very great. So if you're working with graphics in HTML5, I'd strongly suggest taking a look at EaselJS—not just for its ease of use but also for its light footprint. It comes in only around 45 kilobytes—usually enough to bring in a bit of overhead to pull off some really amazing graphics, assuming that the publisher doesn't have this library included in its site by default.

Let's break down the code sample in Listing 4-3. First, set up the `canvas` element and create some variables by writing `var stage, canvas = document.getElementById("canvas")`, `context = canvas.getContext("2D")`, `logoImage = new Image()`, `logo`, `fps = 30`, `speed = 0.2;`. For the occasional JavaScript user, nothing so far is new. Second, create the `init` method by writing `init();`, which will kick things off. Then pass the `canvas` element to the stage object, as specified in EaselJS—again, very similar to ActionScript. Third, create the image and assign it to a Bitmap object by writing `logo = new Bitmap(logoImage);` and add to the stage by calling the `addChild` method (another ActionScript code snippet). The last portion is what drives the animation. The Ticker object is essentially the application's heartbeat; it gets called at a certain number of frames per second. In this case, 30, as defined in the variable above by writing `Ticker.setFPS(fps);`. The `tick` method gets called in every frame of animation. Apply the logo movement based on users' mouse coordinates, and apply a nice motion blur filter by calling the `BoxBlurFilter` in the EaselJS framework, which is found in the `tick` method and Wahlaa!. You've just created your first canvas based animation using EaselJS. Obviously there is much more to this library and I encourage you to try out more on your own time by digging into the docs [http://www.createjs.com/Docs/EaselJS]. Perhaps, start by taking a previous Flash based ad unit and convert it over. If you're serious about working with the `canvas` element, I strongly recommend you get very familiar with EaselJS. It will make development when working with the `canvas` element a lot cleaner, especially if you're from a Flash/ActionScript background.

Other JavaScript Libraries

You may or may not be aware that many other JavaScript libraries can work with the `canvas` element, not just EaselJS. It's important to understand the others in the marketplace, because there's a good chance you'll come across them working in future campaigns or when assets get handed off between agency and ad servers. Let's look at two popular ones: KinectJS and ProcessingJS.

KinectJS

KinectJS (`kineticjs.com`) is a `canvas` JavaScript library that extends the two-dimensional context of `canvas` by enabling path and pixel detection for desktop and mobile. You can add things on `canvas` and then add event listeners to them—move them, scale them, and rotate them, independently of other elements, to support animations, interactivity, and transitions. KinectJS can handle many types of interactivity events, including mouse clicks, touches, taps, and drags. With its rich feature set and small file size (66 kilobytes), you're sure to see this library in many advertising campaigns that utilize the canvas element.

ProcessingJS

I'd like to touch on another library, but it's certainly not the last in the long and growing list of canvas JavaScript libraries on the market. ProcessingJS (processingjs.org) is formulated from the Processing language, which is a Java-based visualization language that has been used in many feature films to create node-based, "networky," and abstract elements. ProcessingJS's library is powerful; it can create some pretty compelling creative experiences (processingjs.org/exhibition). I'm including this library because it's both amazing and heavy—so very heavy that I'd advise against using ProcessingJS in advertising environments as the code base. It's a staggering 400-plus kilobytes in size just to include the library, not to mention your own codebase to work with the canvas element. Keep this in mind as you and your client build experiences using canvas. Just because it looks great to you doesn't mean all your users will get the same experience, especially when file size is this large.

These libraries are out there, most of them free to use. I mention them just to showcase that there are many options, but not every single one is suitable for the advertising space. So keep in mind the overall user experience, load time, and publisher k-weight restrictions. Working backwards from the defined pub spec will allow you to choose the correct library, should you need to go down that path.

Canvas Examples

So far I've covered working on the canvas element a bit, as well as external JavaScript libraries that can speed up development time when working with this new element. You've seen what it can do and how it can help your creative process and even some limitations when working with it in advertising. In the next few sections, we'll cover working with the canvas element without the need for third-party plugins. This will allow you to get your hands dirty quickly without needing to rely on external libraries. That said, if you do use a library, the syntax will undoubtedly change when you use them, so be sure to check out the API documentation before digging in.

Lines

Lines are used all the time in advertising campaigns. They're great for presenting a path—map directions, vector drawings, even charting a graph. The use cases for lines within the ad's creative are extensive. Listing 4-4 shows how to render a simple line using HTML5's canvas element.

Listing 4-4. Rendering a Line with Canvas

```
<!DOCTYPE HTML>
<html>
<head>
<meta http-equiv="Content-Type" content="text/html; charset=UTF-8">
</head>
<body>
<canvas id="adCanvas"></canvas>
</body>
<script>
//get a reference to the canvas
var canvas = document.getElementById('adCanvas');
var context = canvas.getContext('2d');
```

67

```
var adWidth = 300;
var adHeight = 250;

canvas.width = adWidth;
canvas.height = adHeight;
context.moveTo(0,0);
context.lineTo(adWidth,0);
context.moveTo(adWidth,0);
context.lineTo(adWidth,adHeight);
context.moveTo(adWidth,adHeight);
context.lineTo(0,adHeight);
context.moveTo(0,adHeight);
context.lineTo(0,0);
context.stroke();
</script>
</html>
```

This code outlines a dynamic way to add a border to advertisements. Start off by getting a reference to the canvas element and call it canvas. Next, set a 2D drawing context and declare two variables, adWidth and adHeight. These values will dynamically update the canvas element to the desired dimensions. This example makes use of the common ad size 300 × 250. Finally, use the drawing API of canvas to move and add a line around the whole element by using the sequence of methods lineTo and moveTo, which render the image in Figure 4-2.

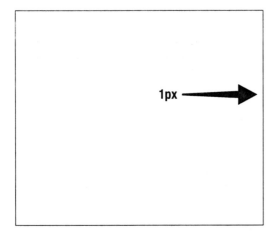

Figure 4-2. *Creating a 300 × 250 border using the canvas element*

As you see, drawing a dynamic ad border using the canvas element is fairly simple. (This can be really helpful, as publisher and IAB specs require you to add a 1-pixel border around advertisements.) It doesn't end there, though. Play around a bit with lines to see what else you can come up with. Keep in mind that anything you can do with your design tools, you can pretty much do using canvas, even adding Bézier curves and arcs. If you need a jumping-off point, start at the W3C schools "try it" editor (w3schools.com/html5/tryit.asp?filename=tryhtml5_canvas_line).

Shapes

If you can create lines, you can create shapes (no shocker here!). Let's take a look at creating complex shapes using canvas. Having successfully rendered a green square to the screen, let's make a star shape (see Listing 4-5). To save on space from here on, I will omit the full HTML markup and focus on the JavaScript portions.

Listing 4-5. Using Canvas to Make a Star Shape

```
<script>
//get a reference to the canvas
var canvas = document.getElementById('adCanvas');
var context = canvas.getContext('2d');
//draw a star
context.save();
context.beginPath();
context.moveTo(92.0, 1.1);
context.lineTo(120.1, 58.1);
context.lineTo(183.0, 67.2);
context.lineTo(137.5, 111.5);
context.lineTo(148.2, 174.1);
context.lineTo(92.0, 144.6);
context.lineTo(35.8, 174.1);
context.lineTo(46.5, 111.5);
context.lineTo(1.1, 67.2);
context.lineTo(63.9, 58.1);
context.lineTo(92.0, 1.1);
context.closePath();
context.fillStyle = 'rgb(255, 255, 0)';
context.fill();
context.stroke();
context.restore();
</script>
```

You may have noticed that the dimensions of the canvas element needed to be increased to 200 × 200 to view the full star. Keep this in mind if you try to paint something larger than the canvas dimension supports, as your painting will render off the element and produce clipping.

Looking at Listing 4-5, you can see that the same methods are being used to draw lines, but this time there's a bit more complexity in where the starting and ending points are placed. You can also see that a fillStyle method has been added and given a value of yellow in the RGB (red-green-blue) space. If you're following along, you should get the image in Figure 4-3 in your browser.

Figure 4-3. A star produced using the canvas element

This may all seem pretty simple, but its actually quite powerful. You can now let the browser do all the hard work, instead of bringing in large bitmap graphics that will incur longer load times for your end user. Keep in mind that if it's a vector shape, you can more or less re-create it using the canvas element

Gradients

Another feature of the canvas element is its ability to use gradients. Gradients are useful for filling in shapes from one color to another or building on multiple color values in a stack. Gradients are widely used in many things online. For the longest time developers and designers created and repeated a 1-pixel-wide strip of the gradient using CSS. Now, with native gradient support on the canvas element, the browser can again handle the heavy lifting. This is exceptionally important to note when a client hands you Photoshop documents and you need to re-create an exact representation in the browser while minimizing the k-weight. Instead of bringing in bitmaps from the PSD, tell the canvas to handle it. It can be somewhat time-consuming, but the end result is worth the wait. Gradients can be *Linear* or *Radial* or have multiple color stops between 0 and 1.

The main difference between a linear and a radial gradient is where the gradient begins. Figure 4-4 displays the visual difference between them.

Figure 4-4. *The difference between a linear and a radial gradient*

Listing 4-6 makes a linear gradient fill for the star shape in Figure 4-3.

Listing 4-6. A Linear Gradient Fill Using Canvas

```
<script>
//greenish gradient
var gradient=context.createLinearGradient(0,0,200,50);
gradient.addColorStop(0,"#FFFF00");
gradient.addColorStop(1,"#00FFFF");
context.save();
context.beginPath();
context.moveTo(92.0, 1.1);
context.lineTo(120.1, 58.1);
context.lineTo(183.0, 67.2);
context.lineTo(137.5, 111.5);
context.lineTo(148.2, 174.1);
context.lineTo(92.0, 144.6);
```

```
context.lineTo(35.8, 174.1);
context.lineTo(46.5, 111.5);
context.lineTo(1.1, 67.2);
context.lineTo(63.9, 58.1);
context.lineTo(92.0, 1.1);
context.closePath();
context.fillStyle = gradient;
context.fill();
context.stroke();
context.restore();
</script>
```

Even a quick look at the bolded code shows that making a gradient is as simple as calling the createLinearGradient method on the 2D context object and passing in the correct parameters. Once the gradient is created, add color stops by calling the method addColorStop and specifying a float offset (0-1) and a color value in hex format. Thus, you can specify a stop at 0.2, 0.4, 0.8, and so on, to get complete granularity and flexibility. Finally, adding that new gradient value to the fillStyle of the stars shape produces the output shown in Figure 4-5.

Figure 4-5. *Creating a linear gradient*

Images

While it's better to let the canvas element handle graphic compositing in your advertisement, you sometimes can't get away from using bitmap images, as when you're working with a retail client that wants to show off new products or with an automotive company that wants to feature the latest model vehicles. With this in mind, let's move into the realm of working with images on the canvas in HTML5. Working thus, developers can easily paint an image bitmap onto the canvas (see Listing 4-7).

Listing 4-7. Canvas Bitmap Images

```
<script type="text/javascript">
//get a reference to the canvas
var canvas = document.getElementById('adCanvas');
var context = canvas.getContext('2d');
```

71

```
//draw image
var img=new Image();
img.src="test.jpg";
img.onload = function(){
    context.drawImage (img,0,0);
};
</script>
```

As you can see from the listing script, I created a new image object, img, and assigned its source to test.jpg (note that this will change with whatever image path you use). Once the image is loaded, it will fire the event onload, which will execute the function to call drawImage and paint the image onto the canvas element.

Events

As you've become aware, the canvas element is a great feature in HTML5 for rendering both vector and bitmap graphics to the screen. But it's not finished there. The canvas can also react; it can handle events from the browser or from user inputs, including mouse, touch, and DOM events. Listing 4-8 showcases how the canvas can react to many events by logging output into the JavaScript console in your browser.

Listing 4-8. Using Canvas to Log Output into the JavaScript Console

```
<script type="text/javascript">
//get a reference to the canvas
var canvas = document.getElementById('adCanvas');
var context = canvas.getContext('2d');
//Mouse Events
canvas.addEventListener('click', function(evt){
    console.log('Click: ' + evt);
});
canvas.addEventListener("mouseover", function(evt) {
    console.log('MouseOver: ' + evt);
});
canvas.addEventListener("mouseout", function(evt) {
    console.log('MouseOut: ' + evt);
});
canvas.addEventListener("mousemove", function(evt) {
    console.log('MouseMove: ' + evt);
});
//Touch Events
canvas.addEventListener("touchstart", function(evt) {
    console.log('TouchStart: ' + evt.touches.length);
});
canvas.addEventListener("touchmove", function(evt) {
    evt.preventDefault();
    var touch = evt.touches[0];
    console.log("Touch x:" + touch.pageX + ", y:" + touch.pageY);
});
canvas.addEventListener("touchend", function(evt) {
    console.log('TouchEnd: ' + evt);
});
```

```
canvas.addEventListener("touchcancel", function(evt) {
    console.log('TouchCancel: ' + evt);
});
</script>
```

User input is being handled on mouse clicks and touch events, and the output is logged to the JavaScript console. Keep in mind that you can extend this to a user painting with their mouse or even finger, should the device support it. Having user inputs with the canvas element provides interactivity, a great feature to incorporate into your creative. It could involve starting or stopping animation in the canvas or even interacting with a game inside your ad unit. Keep this in mind when building ads that require interactivity and user input.

Saving

Now that you know how to provide interactivity by controlling user input, let's attempt to save the image on our canvas to our local drive. To save the canvas as an image, set the image source to the image todataURL. From there, a user can save it to a local machine. Pretty cool! Especially when you want the user to customize something within the experience and take the art away or share it via email or on a social networking site.

■ **Note** The toDataURL() method will throw a SECURITY_ERR exception if the canvas has paint from other domains.

Listing 4-9 showcases how to use canvas to save an image format via the toDataURL method.

Listing 4-9. Using Canvas to Save Images

```
<script type="text/javascript">
//get a reference to the canvas
var canvas = document.getElementById('adCanvas');
var context = canvas.getContext('2d');
var img=new Image();
img.src="test.jpg";
img.onload = function(){
    context.drawImage (img,0,0);
};
//Mouse Events
canvas.addEventListener('click', function(evt){
    console.log('Click: ' + evt);
    // no argument defaults to image/png; image/jpeg, etc. also work on some. image/png is the only
one that must be supported per spec.
    try {
        window.location = canvas.toDataURL("image/png");
    } catch (error) {
        console.log(error);
    }
});
</script>
```

You can now save images in your canvas container! This is really helpful if you are creating an interactive ad unit that you want the user to draw or to create something with, if you want the user to have the ability to save it to their machine or share it with another web service. As in Listing 4-9, paint the image to the canvas, and on mouse click

73

call the method toDataURL, which saves the canvas as an image with a default mime type of png. You can also save in other formats, such as jpeg and gif, as well by setting the correct mime type.

Animations

Having the canvas element handle animations is another huge plus for designers—particularly animators. Animations can be handled in several different ways in the browser. Listing 4-10 shows the most logical approach in HTML5-compliant browsers, the requestAnimationFrame method.

Listing 4-10. Using Canvas for Animations

```
<script>
var canvas = document.getElementById('adCanvas');
var context = canvas.getContext('2d');
var gradient = context.createLinearGradient(0, 0, 200, 200);
gradient.addColorStop(0, '#000000');
gradient.addColorStop(1, '#999999');
context.fillStyle = gradient;
var x = 0, y = 0;
var shapeWidth = 50, shapeHeight = 50;
var speed = 12;
function animate() {
reqAnimFrame = window.mozRequestAnimationFrame || window.webkitRequestAnimationFrame ||
window.msRequestAnimationFrame || window.oRequestAnimationFrame;
    reqAnimFrame(animate);
    x += Math.round(speed);
    if (x <= 0 || x >= canvas.width - shapeWidth) {
        speed = Math.round(-speed);
    }
    draw();
}
function draw() {
    context.clearRect(0, 0, 500, 170);
    context.fillRect(x, y, shapeWidth, shapeHeight);
}
animate();
</script>
```

As can be seen in the listing, the canvas element handles animations by utilizing requestAnimationFrame pretty easily; it tells the browser you are intentionally trying to animate something. First, grab the canvas element and add its 2D context (nothing new there). Then add some setup vars (variables) to control x, y, width, height, and speed of the animation. Next, set up a function called animate, which calls itself every time the frame is requested and calls the draw method.

Note   Functions are called methods when they are attached to an object.

Finally, inside the draw method are two methods, clearRect and fillRect, that are responsible for clearing and drawing the square to the screen. Just remember to include the entire list of vendor prefixes for the requestAnimationFrame (for the time being) if you're targeting requirements include all the modern HTML5 browsers.

Advanced Canvas

From the brief examples above, you should now have a pretty good understanding of what the canvas element can do and the many enhancements it brings to the HTML5 spec. The following are some of the more advanced canvas examples to check out on your own time.

- impactjs.com
- craftymind.com/factory/html5video/CanvasVideo.html
- gyu.que.jp/jscloth
- fir.sh/projects/jsnes
- spielzeugz.de/html5/liquid-particles.html
- nihilogic.dk/labs/canvas3dtexture_0.2
- williammalone.com/articles/create-html5-canvas-javascript-drawing-app

When exploring new libraries and tutorials, keep in mind the file weight and overall performance, especially when viewing demos and attempting to reference them for your ad creatives. Keep in mind, too, that no one is going online to view your ad, so try to avoid overkill. It's often best to just give viewers a taste, one that will drive them to a fuller experience on a landing page. An ad that's too elaborate can tax a user's machine or even crash it, depending upon the device, the machine's limitations, even the publisher the ad is running on. Last, take a look at html5rocks.com/en/tutorials/canvas/performance for tips on maximizing your canvas performance on the Web, including layering canvas elements for complex graphics and avoiding unnecessary stage changes.

Canvas Browser Support

Since the canvas element is an emerging feature of the HTML5 spec, many older browsers do not support it. Thus, you'll need to use polyfills and shivs for browsers that can't support the new element, should you need to design for them. For example, Flash can be a graceful failover for targeting desktops and display. To detect modern browser support in desktop and mobile, use a library called Modernizr (modernizr.com). Modernizr is more or less geared towards web content development where k-weight isn't a major issue. In online advertising, having your ad creative include Modernizr can increase k-weight significantly. Find out if your publisher includes Modernizr and if it can provide the proper "hooks" for the ad to tie into. If you can leverage it, Modernizr is sort of a Chinese restaurant menu for feature detection; you only include what you absolutely need to check for—and that can save on the overall k-weight. In an ideal world, publishers and ad networks would include this library by default so ads can hook into useful features that site content is already checking for. Be sure to reach out to your publisher to find out whether its page is using Modernizr and whether the ad creative can detect supported features. Listing 4-11 shows an example of using Modernizr for canvas, without including the library.

Listing 4-11. Using Modernizr for Canvas Detection

```
if (Modernizr.canvas) {
    // canvas is supported-do canvas stuff
}else{
    //canvas is not supported use Flash or something similar as a failback
}
```

As you see, an ad designer could use this very easily by simply including a conditional (if/else) statement, if a publisher already includes it into their site.

You may be asking, what about older browsers, like Microsoft's IE6 through IE8? Well, they can benefit from leveraging ExplorerCanvas (`excanvas.sourceforge.net`), which is a polyfill for working with browsers that do not support the new element. The canvas element can also be used in a bunch of different ways. Stacking multiple elements on top of each other to form a final composite is one way, and it avoids canvas state changes. Painting on the canvas is an expensive operation, since some browser's handle all of its processing power on the machine's CPU. However, as versions of modern browsers, like Chrome version 18+, provide hardware-accelerated GPU support for the canvas element, performance and rendering will speed up enormously. As more browsers adopt these features, they will be exceptionally helpful in deploying to mobile devices, where taxing the CPU can eat up a battery's life and ultimately crash browsers. (A very good write-up on canvas performance is found at `html5rocks.com/en/tutorials/canvas/performance`.)

Animated Gifs

Have you ever heard the saying, "Just because you can do something one way doesn't necessarily mean it's the best way to do it"? One often-overlooked component in browser animation is the good old animated gif format. Yes, I know, it's a slightly mature and primitive method for creating animation on the Web, but it still holds some appeal today. As you may remember, animated gifs were pretty big back in the days before Flash advertising. Remember from Chapter 1 the static HTML or HTML ads that animated by means of a simple gif image? Animated gifs can be useful in a pinch for animating a sequence of images quickly or if you just don't know much about working on the canvas (though, that shouldn't be an issue any longer!). It's also a great workaround for translating frames of a video into an image sequence so developers can simulate autoplay on iPhones and iPads and similar devices (Apple prohibits the autoplaying of video as it eats up a customer's data plans). Also, animated gifs are accepted everywhere, on pretty much every browser. Software like Adobe's Photoshop and Adobe Fireworks can create animated gifs very easily with only a little work. Some online web services are even easier:

- Gifninja: `gifninja.com`

- Mothereffing animated gif: `mothereffinganimatedgif.com`

You'll find that not everything needs the canvas element for every type of animation, especially since it's an emerging feature. Animated gifs are still a useful and viable feature to leverage; so take advantage of them for their ease of use in creating and their overall file size when rendered. However, if you're looking to wow your client with richer animations, you'd best explore with the canvas element. I suggest getting an understanding of the campaign's goals and requirements from the publisher or ad network before you commit to one feature or another. Who knows, you may be able to easily leverage both by developing with canvas in mind first and gracefully degrading to an animated gif experience on users' browsers that can't support the HTML5 experience. Work with your first- and third-party ad server to provide user agent detection and serve the creative and tags appropriately. To take advantage of an animated gif failover for the canvas element, wrap the animated gif image in the canvas tag; for example, `<canvas><img src='animated.gif'/></canvas>`. For browsers that support canvas, the inside element (in this case the img tag) will be omitted; otherwise, for browsers that do not support canvas, the tag is recognized, and the image will render to the screen.

Canvas in Advertising

So great, you've learned all the amazing features and enhancements available to designers and developers who operate with the new canvas element, but how does everything play out in the advertising space? Well, the canvas element brings many new enhancements for advertising. For starters, for the first time one can create Flash-like graphics directly inside the browser without use of a third-party plug-in. As modern browsers become ubiquitous, there'll be one set of standards for creating graphics on the web. In addition, canvas is great on mobile and tablet devices; support is very strong across manufacturers, operating systems, and browsers. Browsers on mobile devices will soon all take advantage of hardware support via the Graphics Processing Unit (GPU) to speed up rendering and tax the CPU much less. Canvas is a huge game changer for online advertising and for the Web as a whole. Examples of campaigns using the canvas element can be found at the following URLs:

- `http://bit.ly/QIpVJa`
- `http://bit.ly/OAf8BX`

I expect to see more ad designers and developers leveraging canvas in the near future for their HTML5 campaigns. In short, canvas will be here for the long haul. It will be a customary element for working with graphics on the Web—but yet again, bear in mind that it is still emerging. Thus, leveraging it for any and all animations and graphics within a campaign may not be the smartest thing to do unless you have a failover in place.

SVG

As you've seen, the canvas element is great for creating rich graphics and animations in HTML5, but there's another graphical language that's been around for quite some time (since 2003): SVG. SVG (scalable vector graphics) and its now supported inline via HTML5. ("Inline" means SVG content can be included simply by adding <svg> tags within the HTML markup.)

Let's first break down what SVG does. Scalable vector graphics are essentially XML markup defining a set of strokes, fills, and graphic instructions in a way that the browser can understand. At any size or zoom level, SVG will render the art to the screen sharply. Within an advertising campaign, it is exceptionally important to maintain legibility for brand names, logos, typefaces, and overall copy. In the mobile device ecosystem with varying pixel densities, SVG will still also render crisp to the screen, so use SVG when and where you can.

SVG is powerful yet simple in that its vector-based—which means that strokes and fills are rendered mathematically onscreen by coordinates. Contrast this with bitmaps, which are rendered in pixels, whose presence can lead to subpixel aliasing and the creation of feathered or blurred images if they don't reside on a whole pixel. Native SVG support is an important enhancement to the HTML5 spec; it allows designers to create in Adobe's Illustrator (or whatever their vector tool of choice is) and export for the screen by saving their work as an SVG file. This file format is a W3C specification and is widely supported across browsers. SVG is really good at saving on art's k-weight as well as its legibility and overall fidelity. See Figure 4-6, which shows the Pepsi logo (from brandsoftheworld.com).

Figure 4-6. *The SVG and IMG versions of the Pepsi logo*

Figure 4-6 places a vector (SVG) version above a bitmap (IMG) version. You can see that the SVG version is as crisp as the bitmap image, and it will remain crisp regardless of scale on the image or zoom level on screen, whereas the bitmap will degrade in quality with scaling up. In addition, the SVG version is 8 kilobytes, as opposed to 12 kilobytes for the IMG image. This may not seem like a big deal, but as you add more images with more color values and graphics get more complex, you'll quickly notice that this approach can save an abundance of file size in your ads. (You'll find more examples of SVG uses at bogotobogo.com/svg.html. Remember to always check for browser support, using caniuse.com/svg-html5, before launching a campaign in HTML5 that leverages SVG.)

RaphaëlJS

I'd like to draw your attention to a powerful JavaScript library called RaphaëlJS (raphaeljs.com), which can streamline your workflow with vector graphics on the Web. RaphaëlJS uses the SVG W3C Recommendation, where objects you create in its library are also DOM objects; thus, you can attach the usual JavaScript event handlers to them for user input or other events. RaphaëlJS is also pretty much cross-browser-friendly as Firefox 3.0, Safari 3.0, Chrome 5.0, Opera 9.5, IE6.0, and all newer versions of these browsers support it. However, within the advertising realm, RaphaëlJS is a bit large unless you have room to play with k-weight. Since it sits at approximately 89 kilobytes minified and over 200 kilobytes unminified, it could break the bank with some publishers. So be mindful before going down this path, as it may be tough to retool the creative or get the publisher to budge on the specs.

SMIL

SMIL (Synchronized Multimedia Integration Language) allows for animation in the SVG element. According to the Mozilla Developer Network (developer.mozilla.org/en/SVG/SVG_animation_with_SMIL) SMIL provides the ability to animate an element's numeric attributes, transform attributes, and color attributes and motion path. Listing 4-12 demonstrates how to leverage SMIL within SVG.

Listing 4-12. Leverage SMIL Within SVG

```
<svg width="300px" height="100px">
    <rect x="0" y="0" width="300" height="100" fill="white" stroke="white" stroke-width="1" />
    <circle cx="0" cy="50" r="50" fill="green" stroke="white" stroke-width="1">
        <animate attributeName="cx" from="0" to="300" dur="1s" repeatCount="indefinite" />
    </circle>
</svg>
```

In this listing, a green circle is being moved across 300 pixels within 1 second, and the process is repeated forever. This is pretty simple to accomplish if you take a look at the bolded line of code. Test the listing in your browser; you'll notice that SVG animation is surprisingly fast. There are many more features to take advantage of—this simple code shows animating on the x value only—so be sure to check out the URL [http://srufaculty.sru.edu/david.dailey/svg] and learn more as well as start experimenting. Try adjusting color, animating along a set path, and even manipulating the shapes while animating. Last of all, always use caniuse.com/svg-smil to check for overall support before leveraging the SMIL manifest.

Canvas and SVG

You may be thinking, "I have the canvas element and SVG support, but which one do I use?" Well, from an end user's visual standpoint, they are similar in what they can handle, but they differ greatly in technology. Both support layout, gradients, animation, user input, and masks, but one is driven by a JavaScript API, and the other is formed from XML markup. A benefit of SVG is that it can be styled via CSS because there are actual DOM elements within the document's markup, whereas with canvas being just one object (container) in the DOM, CSS styling is prohibited, unless you're targeting just the canvas element itself. In short, you should really leverage both, depending on the requirements of the creative and the campaign's reach. For an extremely detailed and thorough write-up, go to the Opera browser's developer site (dev.opera.com/articles/view/svg-or-canvas-choosing-between-the-two).

SVG in Advertising

Having SVG in web standards advertising is a pretty big deal. I've used vector art in Flash for many years to save on file size, and the same applies for development in the browser now. Not only does SVG render simple and complicated vector drawings by describing a bunch of mathematical coordinates directly within the browser markup; it's also very important in brand identity, maintaining image fidelity, and font rendering (as the following section explains). In addition, SVG can be saved via programs designers are already using. This makes the learning curve much easier to cope with. SVG renders quickly and, as you've seen, combines well with its SMIL animation counterpart. So I strongly suggest you explore SVG for your advertising campaigns, especially when graphics are mandatory, target screens are varied and file size limitations come into play during development and testing on publisher pages.

Web Fonts

Heading into creative development with HTML5 with CSS3, let's shift gears a bit and learn more about rendering fonts to the screen using CSS3 web fonts. For a long time fonts on the Web were horrible; there were only a select few "Web safe" fonts available: Arial, Courier, Times, Verdana, etc... While this was good in that it provided a consistent experience for the end user, it severely limited designers' creativity. Designers wanted to duplicate their level of print creativity on the Web, but they couldn't unless they saved typography designs as images or leveraged Flash when it became the advertising standard. Saving as images was a pain—updates weren't easy to make since they were often made into images, and with more image files coming down to the end user, longer load times resulted. Moreover, you could certainly throwaway the possibility of dynamic text content with designed typography. When Flash became the standard, brands and marketers fell in love with its rich font rendering and ability to offer dynamic text with a brand's exact font.

Strictly speaking, web fonts aren't really new; they've been in CSS level 2, but limited browser adoption and fragmented vendor support sabotaged their ability to shine with designers. In the latest CSS level 3 spec (CSS3), the inclusion of web fonts brings the ability to render any of the designer's fonts via CSS by including an at-rule set for font face. Listing 4-13 shows a rock-solid way to include web fonts—specifically, Oxygen, a font in Google's free web font library—in your CSS styling.

Listing 4-13. Using CSS3 Web Fonts (HTML)

```
<!DOCTYPE HTML>
<html>
<head>
<meta http-equiv="Content-Type" content="text/html; charset=UTF-8">
<link href='http://fonts.googleapis.com/css?family=Oxygen' rel='stylesheet' type='text/css'>
<style rel='stylesheet' type='text/css'>
html, body {
    font-family: 'Oxygen', sans-serif;
}
</style>
</head>
<body>
</body>
</html>
```

■ **Note** Google's list of open source and free web fonts can be found at google.com/webfonts.

Notice that I've linked to the external CSS file hosted on Google's domain. Once loaded, the new font family Oxygen can be added to the style sheet or as an inline style within our HTML markup. Simple enough? Listing 4-14 looks at what's going on in the Google-provided style sheet we're linking to.

Listing 4-14. Using CSS3 Web Fonts (CSS)

```
@font-face {
    font-family: 'Oxygen';
    font-style: normal;
    font-weight: 400;
    src: local('Oxygen'),url('http://themes.googleusercontent.com/static/fonts/oxygen/v1/↵
eAWT4YudGOotf3rlsJD6zOvvDin1pK8aKteLpeZ5cOA.woff') format('woff');
}
```

When we link to the Google provided CSS file, notice that the CSS syntax is essentially declaring a new font face rule for Oxygen so that the rest of the document can understand what Oxygen is when the font family property gets assigned to it. In the listing, font family, font style, font weight, and a source to the font file are set for the browser to use. This portion may seem confusing, but it's really just targeting a WOFF font file. The arbitrary characters are simply generated at serve time by Google, most likely to mask the file name on their server and count requests to the file. The WOFF font file is one of many formats in the fragmented web font space (which we'll cover in more detail in the following sections). What's nice about Google's service is that it detects what browser is requesting the font and serves up the appropriate format for that particular browser.

WOFF

Starting off with the one we've just discussed, the WOFF (web open font format) font file is a developing standard for serving web fonts to browsers. WOFF files are essentially TrueType files compressed for delivery over the Web and with additional metadata information. The overall goal of the WOFF format is to have one standard that's accepted across all browsers and light enough to serve to browsers and devices with minimal bandwidth (like mobile). At the time of writing the WOFF format has been supported by Mozilla's Firefox version 3.6 and up, Google's Chrome version 5 and up, and Opera; it is also supported by Microsoft's IE9. For Apple and Safari, starting at release 5.1, support is available only on Mac OS X Lion. Many assume that WOFF files will be the de facto standard for delivery of web fonts in the very near future. My hope is that it does so fragmentation in this space goes away.

TrueType Fonts

TrueType fonts (TTF) are the oldest font formats I'll be discussing. Developed back in the 1980s by Apple, TrueType fonts are used in Apple's Safari browser before OS X Lion (version 10.7) and Safari version 5.1. If you try validating this by viewing our Oxygen style sheet URL in a Safari browser, you get the following response from Google:

```
@font-face {
  font-family: 'Oxygen';
  font-style: normal;
  font-weight: 400;
  src: local('Oxygen'), url('http://themes.googleusercontent.com/static/fonts/oxygen/v1/
WNVARKadHCfwbQ2n3MQeIOvvDin1pK8aKteLpeZ5cOA.ttf') format('truetype');
}
```

Thankfully Google is doing the browser detection for you as you can see, the font space is already becoming pretty fragmented.

Embedded OpenType

Apropos web font fragmentation and our Google web font example for Oxygen (Listing 4-14), Embedded OpenType (EOT) font files are used in the Microsoft browser, Internet Explorer. Making the request to our stylesheet from an IE browser will yield the following response from Google:

```
@font-face {
  font-family: 'Oxygen';
  font-style: normal;
  font-weight: 400;
  src: url('http://themes.googleusercontent.com/static/fonts/oxygen/v1/⏎
RuRdwqUdkfYPOfpTfyGHiA.eot');
  src: local('Oxygen'), url('http://themes.googleusercontent.com/static/fonts/oxygen/v1/⏎
RuRdwqUdkfYPOfpTfyGHiA.eot') format('embedded-opentype'),
url('http://themes.googleusercontent.com/static/fonts/oxygen/v1/⏎
RzoNiRR1p2Mqyyz2RwqSMw.woff') format('woff');
}
```

Google is handling Internet Explorer browsers by supplying them with EOT files, as well as through the newly adopted WOFF format for later browsers. This is a great way to show you that you'll need to often supply multiple fonts depending on your target audience.

Using SVG with Fonts

Let's have a last look at SVG; specifically, at serving an SVG file as a font character sheet. We still rely on SVG fonts because older versions of mobile Safari (on the iPhone and iPad) accept only this file format. But SVG fonts aren't really a font format as you've just learned; they're just instructions for font glyph outlines represented as standard SVG elements and attributes. You may think that including all the glyphs is fine, but what if you need just 10 of them and not all 200? This is one of the biggest difficulties related to using SVG as a font for the Web. EOT and WOFF have compression built into the font format; it allows for quick transfer and download times. By the spec's very nature, however, SVG fonts are uncompressed and pretty large, especially for mobile use. Another issue with SVG is that certain font files contain information on how certain characters will be used together. This information gets lost when the font gets converted to SVG. Lost, too, are important metadata information about how to layout certain ligatures, special characters, leading, and kerning. Mobile Safari has adopted the soon-to-be standard WOFF format starting at mobile Safari version 5, however for Android user's you'll need to supply TTF or SVG formats.

Font Squirrel

You may be thinking, "It's pretty ridiculous that I have to remember the syntax for web fonts, not to mention how to generate the different file formats, as well as which browsers support which formats." We'll I'm here to tell you that a very good tool to bookmark is Font Squirrel for web font creation (fontsquirrel.com/fontface/generator) Font Squirrel allows developers to upload a font file to their user interface; the free service handles the conversion process to the other formats, as well as providing you with rock-solid CSS syntax for use within your creative. To get a detailed understanding of how Font Squirrel generates its code, look at Paul Irish's blog on the font face implementation syntax (paulirish.com/2009/bulletproof-font-face-implementation-syntax).

When using this free service, you'll find that some fonts you try to upload will be blacklisted to prohibit conversions. You need to have the licensing terms in place to perform this action; so consider exploring alternative avenues. This brings us to the topic of web font licensing.

Web Font Licensing

Though there are many free, open-source web font services on the Web, including Google's and Adobe's Typekit, you may be wondering how you can access licensed fonts from well-established font foundries—Helvetica Neue, Futura, and Myriad, to name a few. There are paid services on the Web for licensing fonts, such as some from Typekit's Monotype and WebType. These services, which provide many of the popular fonts most of your brands are or could be using, use a rental license business model. They either allow the developer to host or provide hosting, as well as easing a common problem by handling browser fragmentation. You shouldn't be shocked to learn that purchasing a font license to use a specific font in certain creatives doesn't mean you can also use it in web embedding, or @font-face. There are specific licenses for @font-face; they are typically sold separately from the specific foundry. Before starting a campaign you're your advertiser, find out if they've already purchased the font licensing for their site. If they have, you can more than likely use it for their ad campaigns. More information about web font EULAs (end-user license agreements) can be found at blog.themeforest.net/general/font-licensing-for-the-web.

Web Fonts in Advertising

It's pretty obvious that an advertiser's marketing team expects you to use the brand's identity and specific font family in any campaign you design. As Flash and the font-rendering engine it used recede into the past, you'll need to leverage web fonts using newer web standards. This definitely raises some concern for publishers, as k-weight limitations for additional font families will need to be revised. As you've seen, the Oxygen font family could add 100 kilobytes or so to the overall size of all file formats and supply the whole gamut of fonts for cross-browser ad serving. So take a tip from Google: detecting a user agent on request and serving the appropriate file makes the most sense, especially if users are on devices with cellular connections and limited bandwidth.

Since you'll want to support all the various formats to allow for a seamless cross-browser experience, another thing to mention is making sure your ad server's mime type can handle updated file formats before going live in a production environment. Also please don't use solutions like the JavaScript library called Cufon [http://cufon. shoqolate.com]. They can render web fonts, but they can cause accessibility and performance problems and take a long while to load due to the increased file size. Many discussions concern supplying web fonts for mobile visitors, as their download costs are higher and the wait to get to their content is much longer. Even so, I think advertisers and brands want a consistent experience, no matter what device or screen a user is on. So whether or not to provide special web fonts for mobile users is really an advertiser's call. However, you should outline the concerns of speed vs. visual continuity to your clients, then allow them to make the decision. In some cases publishers and content owners may not want to budge, may just say no to any web fonts in their mobile advertising inventory. Be sure to keep this in mind when you plan use of web fonts across publishers and ad networks.

Another common issue in non-Webkit browsers like Firefox and Opera is dealing with FOUT (flash of unstyled text). Chances are it will come up sooner rather than later. FOUT refers to content being rendered to the screen before the style on the type is set. A nice trick to get around this problem, found in Google's free web service, involves leveraging a JavaScript technique to detect when the style has loaded. If you're not using Google's service, you can hide all onscreen copy for 2 to 5 seconds and then toggle its visibility on. Hacky, for sure, but as Listing 4-15 shows, it works.

Listing 4-15. Paul Irish's FOUT Script

```
<script>
            (function(){
            // if firefox 3.5+, hide content till load (or 3 seconds) to prevent FOUT,
from paulirish.com
            var d = document, e = d.documentElement, s = d.createElement('style');
            if (e.style.MozTransform === ''  || e.style.OTransform === ''){
              s.textContent = 'body{visibility:hidden}';
              var r = document.getElementsByTagName('script')[0];
```

```
            r.parentNode.insertBefore(s, r);
            function f(){ s.parentNode && s.parentNode.removeChild(s); }
            addEventListener('load',f,false);
            setTimeout(f,3000);
        }
    })();
```

```
</script>
```

Keep in mind that there are also vendor-specific CSS properties to include, like Webkit font smoothing and legibility optimizing, that will render anti-alias your font and smooth any rough spots.

For more information on CSS3 web fonts, see `www.w3.org/TR/css3-webfonts`. At the risk of beating a dead horse, note yet again that it's still emerging, but adoption is growing quickly; so be sure to check `caniuse.com/#feat=fontface` to locate browsers currently supported.

Summary

This chapter, on working with the HTML5 canvas element, the SVG spec, and using web fonts, has covered a lot! I've set the stage for the power that HTML5 is bringing to the browser and for features that developers and designers can take advantage of right now. You've seen code samples that show you how to use the canvas element with graphics, images and animation, as well as how SVG and SMIL provide a similar experience. The differences between these approaches and how each can help in the advertising space have been discussed. You've also seen how to create native graphics within a browser without leveraging a third-party plug-in—a huge advance in web standards that HTML5 provides.

In the next chapter there'll be more discussion about graphics using JavaScript and CSS3 and about how to bring animations and presentations to your creatives using nothing but web standards. So take a break if you need to, because we're just getting started!

CHAPTER 5

■ ■ ■

Animations and Presentations

As you've seen, animation can be handled in many forms within the browser: via the new `canvas` element, animated GIFs, and even animation within SVG using SMIL. This section will cover building animations in the browser and creating them using CSS level 3 (or CSS3). In addition to CSS animations, transforms, and transitions, all the new presentations and styling that CSS3 brings will be covered in detail. Features, browser support, and important "gotchas" to remember will all be reviewed as the chapter digs deep into the world of CSS3. Once you've got your fill, we'll cover the important topics of sprite sheets (the huge impact they're making in web optimization for designers and developers) and, even more importantly, mobile devices that access the Web, a technology where optimizing file size is vital.

Please note that, from here on in this chapter and for the remainder of the book, I'll be referring to the CSS spec, level 3, as CSS3. Also, you should understand that HTML5 isn't CSS3 and vice versa, but you may know that HTML5 is becoming a blanket term for everything new and emerging in browser leveraging, new HTML markup, updated CSS specs, and new JavaScript and DOM APIs. So while it's not accurate, the terms are often used interchangeably, and typically, any HTML5-compliant browser will render most CSS level 3 features. Even though CSS3 isn't technically part of the HTML5 specification, it will still be beneficial to learn about *all* the new web technologies and how they complement each other. With all that said, get ready to learn what CSS3 is, how it will impact your web development, and most specifically, how CSS3 will help you construct advertising for the modern browsers that support it.

Note, too, that what follows assumes you are familiar with basic CSS and the styling of DOM elements and that you have an understanding of vendor prefixes, as they'll be used frequently in this chapter. If you need a refresher, head to `http://developer.mozilla.org/en-US/learn/cssCSS3`.

As I write, CSS3 is the latest working draft of the W3C's standard for cascading style sheets. The same spec that has always handled the style and layout of web pages has been updated with many new additions, which caused some developers to scratch their heads in the early days of release. Not only does CSS3 handle style and layout, but it now allows handling of animations, rich effects and content, and even 3D, all within the CSS arrangement. You can see CSS3's fresh, new (albeit still unofficial) logo in Figure 5-1.

Figure 5-1. CSS3's official new logo

CSS3 is bringing a world of new efficiencies to modern browsers, and you'll hear about them all in this chapter. However, since, as of late 2012, the final specification hadn't been yet decided upon, I can cover only what has been released to date. So be sure to check on the spec by visiting a very useful site, `http://css3clickchart.com`. In addition, you'll learn about the features being submitted to and included within the spec by companies like Adobe, Apple, and Google, which are doing some remarkable things.

First up, though, let's look at CSS3 animations where, for the first time ever, you can leverage keyframe data within the CSS of your page or, more importantly, your web advertisements. With this update the latest browsers can handle the animations natively, thus providing yet another way to animate within the browser. But don't get too overwhelmed—you'll discover its benefits and downsides and learn the ideal way to handle animations in many different scenarios.

Browser Support

First, though, let's cover the omnipresent issue of browser support when working with CSS3 animations. Currently, since CSS3 animations are still in a working-draft state, browsers are adopting features at different rates. For example, Microsoft just adopted them in the latest Internet Explorer browser, version 10, available on Windows 8. The chart in Figure 5-2, from `http://caniuse.com`, shows support for CSS3 animations as of November 2012.

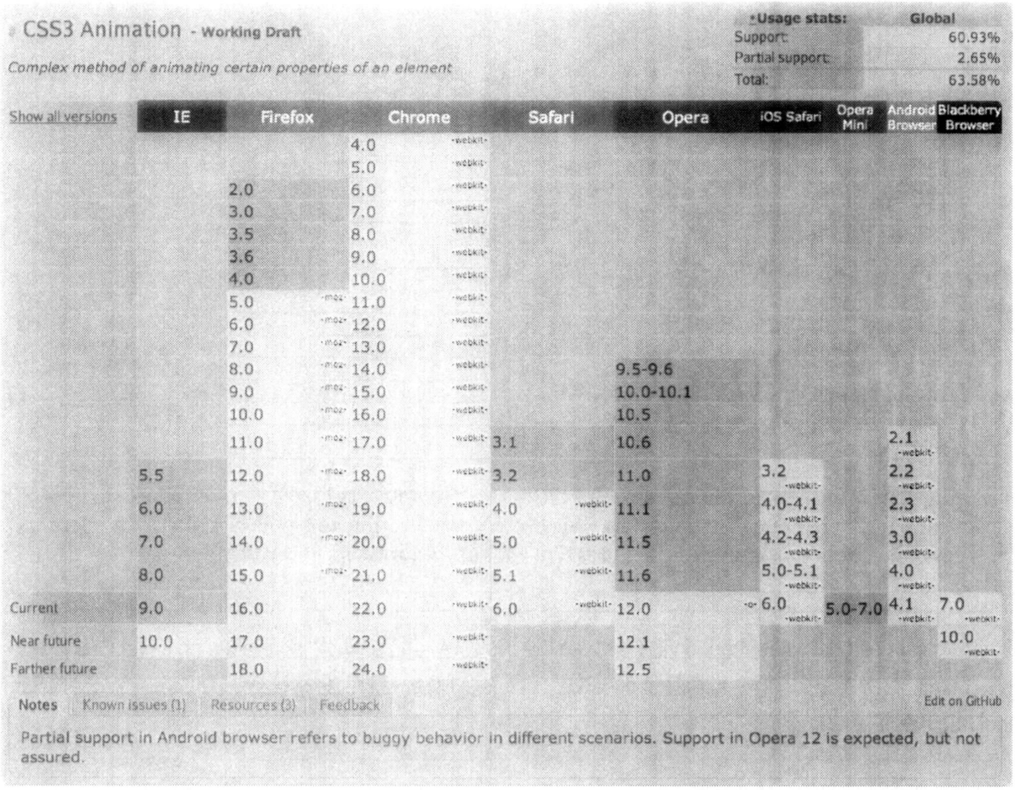

CSS3 Animation - Working Draft

Complex method of animating certain properties of an element

Usage stats:	Global
Support:	60.93%
Partial support:	2.65%
Total:	63.58%

Show all versions

IE	Firefox	Chrome	Safari	Opera	iOS Safari	Opera Mini	Android Browser	Blackberry Browser
		4.0 -webkit-						
		5.0 -webkit-						
	2.0	6.0 -webkit-						
	3.0	7.0 -webkit-						
	3.5	8.0 -webkit-						
	3.6	9.0 -webkit-						
	4.0	10.0 -webkit-						
	5.0 -moz-	11.0 -webkit-						
	6.0 -moz-	12.0 -webkit-						
	7.0 -moz-	13.0 -webkit-						
	8.0 -moz-	14.0 -webkit-		9.5-9.6				
	9.0 -moz-	15.0 -webkit-		10.0-10.1				
	10.0 -moz-	16.0 -webkit-		10.5				
	11.0 -moz-	17.0 -webkit-	3.1 -webkit-	10.6			2.1 -webkit-	
5.5	12.0 -moz-	18.0 -webkit-	3.2 -webkit-	11.0	3.2 -webkit-		2.2 -webkit-	
6.0	13.0 -moz-	19.0 -webkit-	4.0 -webkit-	11.1	4.0-4.1 -webkit-		2.3 -webkit-	
7.0	14.0 -moz-	20.0 -webkit-	5.0 -webkit-	11.5	4.2-4.3 -webkit-		3.0 -webkit-	
8.0	15.0 -moz-	21.0 -webkit-	5.1 -webkit-	11.6	5.0-5.1 -webkit-		4.0 -webkit-	
Current 9.0	16.0	22.0	6.0 -webkit-	12.0	6.0 -webkit-	5.0-7.0	4.1 -webkit-	7.0 -webkit-
Near future 10.0	17.0	23.0 -webkit-		12.1				10.0 -webkit-
Farther future	18.0	24.0 -webkit-		12.5				

Notes | Known issues (1) | Resources (3) | Feedback | Edit on GitHub

Partial support in Android browser refers to buggy behavior in different scenarios. Support in Opera 12 is expected, but not assured.

Figure 5-2. *Browser support for CSS3 animations (November 2012;* `http://caniuse.com`*)*

So when you run a campaign that uses animations via CSS3, keep in mind that your audiences on older IE or Opera Mini will need a graceful failover to another form of animation or perhaps even a static experience. Work with your ad server partner to target specific creative to specific browsers, browser versions, and devices so your user base still gets somewhat of an experience even if its not the most compelling one. Typically a first- or third-party ad server can do this.

When dealing with advertising and overall browser support, keep in mind that on the type of target audience that will be viewing your ads. This may include various browsers, browser versions, operating systems, and devices. With this in mind, a very good CSS3 generator called CSS3 Maker (`http://css3maker.com`) offers the ability to generate new CSS3 features for your ad content and check the current browser support for that given feature. Figure 5-3 shows some of what's supported in CSS3 as of November 2012.

BROWSER SUPPORT

						iOS		O Mini	O Mobile
CSS3 3D Transforms	12+	10+	4+	—	10	6+	3+	—	—
CSS3 Transforms	4+	4+	4+	11+	9+	6+	3+	—	11+
CSS3 Animation	4+	5+	4+	12+	10	6+	4+	—	12.1
CSS3 Transitions	4+	4+	4+	11+	10	6+	3+	—	10+

Data courtesy of caniuse.com and Chrome Platform Status

Figure 5-3. *Browser support for CSS3 features (November 2012;* `http://html5rocks.com/en/features/presentation`)

For the most up-to-date information, you can always go to `http://w3.org/Style/CSS/current-work` to view the W3C's latest work and working group discussions on CSS level 3's specification and as always, for quick reference bookmark `http://caniuse.com` before employing features that your users' browsers may not support.

■ **Note** If you absolutely need to target users on IE6 through IE9 browsers and a client is insisting on using CSS3 features, visit `http://css3pie.com`, or have the client download Google's Chrome Frame `www.google.com/chromeframe`. It will help you out in either scenario.

CSS3 Animations

As already stated, CSS3 animations are a completely new addition to the draft. With the most recent updates to the spec, browser vendors are supporting animations via CSS, and the W3C is even compliant to the updates (for the most part), making it a very soon-to-be standard amongst browsers.

This CSS module describes a way for authors to animate the values of CSS properties over time, using key frames. The behavior of these keyframe animations can be controlled by specifying their duration, number of repeats, and repeating behavior.

`w3.org/TR/css3-animations`

This is a pretty big deal. Prior to CSS3 animation, you needed to use animated GIFs, third-party plug-ins like Flash, or expensive JavaScript commands to pull off animation. This is obviously before what we've just covered in Canvas and SVG animations. In most cases, the more complex and robust the animation, the more taxing it was for the user to handle and render the animation. Now with CSS3, animations can be offloaded to the GPU of the user's machine or device, an approach that offers a much more fluid and seamless approach to animating in the browser. This is exciting!

Let's take a look at the new animation properties within CSS3 that you can take advantage of today (see Table 5-1).

Table 5-1. *CSS3 Animation Properties*

Property	Use
Animation-delay	defines when the animation will start.
Animation-direction	defines whether or not the animation should play in reverse on alternate cycles.
Animation-duration	defines how many seconds or milliseconds an animation takes to complete one cycle.
Animation-fill-mode	specifies how a CSS animation should apply styles to its target before and after it is executing.
Animation-iteration-count	defines how many times an animation should be played.
Animation-name	specifies a name for the @keyframes animation.
Animation-play-state	specifies whether the animation is running or paused.
Animation-timing-function	specifies the speed curve of the animation.

All of these properties when used in CSS3 compliant browsers make up the definitions of animation for the browser to handle. Let's take a look at an example that you may want to use in your next campaign or at some other time in the future. Let's call this animation "glow" and pay close attention to the vendor prefixes (see Listing 5-1).

Listing 5-1. CSS3 Glow Animation

```
<html>
<head>
<meta http-equiv="Content-Type" content="text/html; charset=UTF-8">
<style>
#square {
        -webkit-animation-name: glow;
        -moz-animation-name: glow;
        -ms-animation-name: glow;
        -o-animation-name: glow;
        animation-name: glow;
        -webkit-animation-duration: 1s;

        -webkit-animation-iteration-count: 15;
        -moz-animation-iteration-count: 15;
        -ms-animation-iteration-count: 15;
        -o-animation-iteration-count: 15;
        animation-iteration-count: 15;
        -webkit-animation-direction: alternate;

        -webkit-animation-timing-function: ease-in-out;
        -moz-animation-timing-function: ease-in-out;
        -ms-animation-timing-function: ease-in-out;
        -o-animation-timing-function: ease-in-out;
        animation-timing-function: ease-in-out;
```

```
        -webkit-animation-fill-mode: forwards;
        -moz-animation-fill-mode: forwards;
        -ms-animation-fill-mode: forwards;
        -o-animation-fill-mode: forwards;
        animation-fill-mode: forwards;

        -webkit-animation-delay: 2s;
        -moz-animation-delay: 2s;
        -ms-animation-delay: 2s;
        -o-animation-delay: 2s;
        animation-delay: 2s;
}

@keyframes "glow" {
 0% {
     -webkit-box-shadow: 0px 0px 0px #999999;
        box-shadow: 0px 0px 0px #999999;
 }
 50% {
     -webkit-box-shadow: 5px 5px 15px #ffffff;
        box-shadow: 5px 5px 15px #ffffff;
 }
 100% {
     -webkit-box-shadow: 0px 0px 0px #999999;
        box-shadow: 0px 0px 0px #999999;
 }

}

@-moz-keyframes glow {
 0% {
   box-shadow: 0px 0px 0px #999999;
 }
 50% {
   box-shadow: 5px 5px 15px #ffffff;
 }
 100% {
   box-shadow: 0px 0px 0px #999999;
 }

}

@-webkit-keyframes "glow" {
 0% {
   -webkit-box-shadow: 0px 0px 0px #999999;
   box-shadow: 0px 0px 0px #999999;
 }
 50% {
   -webkit-box-shadow: 5px 5px 15px #ffffff;
   box-shadow: 5px 5px 15px #ffffff;
 }
}
```

```
100% {
    -webkit-box-shadow: 0px 0px 0px #999999;
    box-shadow: 0px 0px 0px #999999;
  }


}

@-ms-keyframes "glow" {
 0% {
    box-shadow: 0px 0px 0px #999999;
  }
 50% {
    box-shadow: 5px 5px 15px #ffffff;
  }
 100% {
    box-shadow: 0px 0px 0px #999999;
  }


}

@-o-keyframes "glow" {
 0% {
    box-shadow: 0px 0px 0px #999999;
  }
 50% {
    box-shadow: 5px 5px 15px #ffffff;
  }
 100% {
    box-shadow: 0px 0px 0px #999999;
  }
}
</style>
</head>
<body>
      <div id=square></div>
</body>
</html>
```

If you're following along, don't get scared of the new keyframe block within CSS3. All this example does is apply a glow animation using the box-shadow property in CSS to the square element in the DOM by using the percent method of keyframing. The animation is even within publisher animation specs, since it's only 15 seconds long—you can see this by viewing the animation-iteration-count. As you can see this is pretty long winded just to accomplish something pretty simple so keep in mind that CSS also has a shorthand way of writing the properties for animation. Here's how you'd write that glow example using the shorthand technique.

```
#square {
      -webkit-animation: glow 1s 15s alternate forwards ease-in-out;
      -moz-animation: glow 1s 15s alternate forwards ease-in-out;
      -ms-animation: glow 1s 15s alternate forwards ease-in-out;
      -o-animation: glow 1s 15s alternate forwards ease-in-out;
      animation: glow 1s 15s alternate forwards ease-in-out;
}
```

I think you'll agree that this technique is much easier on the fingers. Obviously, you'll still need to define what "glow" is, using keyframes to animate the square element. Also, keep in mind that we are using all the necessary vendor prefixes to allow this effect to run across browsers. This may reduce depending on the needs of your campaign and what your target audience's browsers are.

■ **Note**   Including all of your animation keyframe definitions on a separate style sheet would be a good idea. That way, it won't clutter up your main style sheet and keeps style separated from core layout.

As for the animation properties, the direction takes two different values, normal and alternate. The timing function takes several different values of, ease, ease-out, ease-in, ease-in-out, linear, and cubic Bézier (x1, y1, x2, y2), which allows for custom timing functions (a very good web tool to use when using cubic Bézier is http:// cubic-bezier.com). The fill mode's values are forwards, backwards, both, or none. Delay is the offset of time before the animation begins and in the example above it would begin 2 seconds after the DOM loads. Finally, the play state property determines whether the animation is either running or paused, which is useful for detecting if an animation is running or not via JavaScript. Using all of these properties to your advantage, you'll be able to create a very believable and realistic animation that you may remember from using Flash in your advertisements.

■ **Note**   The shorthand order of properties doesn't matter except when using both duration and delay, they need to be in the order, first duration than delay.

Now that the basics of CSS-based animations are covered, let's take a look at working with the @keyframes rule within CSS and putting these new properties to use. As shown above, our first example involved percent. Listing 5-2 uses the words *from* and *to* declare our keyframing events.

Listing 5-2. CSS3 Keyframe Example

```
<!DOCTYPE HTML>
<html>
<head>
<meta http-equiv="Content-Type" content="text/html; charset=UTF-8">
<style>
#square {
 width:100px;
 height:100px;
 background:black;

 -webkit-animation:spin 5s; /* Safari and Chrome */
 -moz-animation:spin 5s; /* Firefox */
 -ms-animation:spin 5s; /* IE */
 -o-animation:spin 5s; /* Opera */
 animation:spin 5s;

 -webkit-animation-iteration-count: infinite;
 -moz-animation-iteration-count: infinite;
 -ms-animation-iteration-count: infinite;
 -o-animation-iteration-count: infinite;
 animation-iteration-count: infinite;
```

```
 -webkit-animation-timing-function: ease-in-out;
 -moz-animation-timing-function: ease-in-out;
 -ms-animation-timing-function: ease-in-out;
 -o-animation-timing-function: ease-in-out;
 animation-timing-function: ease-in-out;
}

@keyframes spin {
from {
  background:black;
  -webkit-transform: rotate(0deg);
  -moz-transform: rotate(0deg);
  -o-transform: rotate(0deg);
  -ms-transform: rotate(0deg);
  transform: rotate(0deg);
} to {
  background:yellow;
  -webkit-transform: rotate(360deg);
  -moz-transform: rotate(360deg);
  -o-transform: rotate(360deg);
  -ms-transform: rotate(360deg);
  transform: rotate(360deg);
  }
}

@-moz-keyframes spin {/* Firefox */
from {
  background:black;
  -webkit-transform: rotate(0deg);
  -moz-transform: rotate(0deg);
  -o-transform: rotate(0deg);
  -ms-transform: rotate(0deg);
  transform: rotate(0deg);
} to {
  background:yellow;
  -webkit-transform: rotate(360deg);
  -moz-transform: rotate(360deg);
  -o-transform: rotate(360deg);
  -ms-transform: rotate(360deg);
  transform: rotate(360deg);
  }
}

@-webkit-keyframes spin {/* Safari and Chrome */
from {
  background:black;
  -webkit-transform: rotate(0deg);
  -moz-transform: rotate(0deg);
  -o-transform: rotate(0deg);
  -ms-transform: rotate(0deg);
  transform: rotate(0deg);
} to {
```

```
  background:yellow;
  -webkit-transform: rotate(360deg);
  -moz-transform: rotate(360deg);
  -o-transform: rotate(360deg);
  -ms-transform: rotate(360deg);
  transform: rotate(360deg);
  }
}

@-o-keyframes spin {/* Opera */
from {
  background:black;
  -webkit-transform: rotate(0deg);
  -moz-transform: rotate(0deg);
  -o-transform: rotate(0deg);
  -ms-transform: rotate(0deg);
  transform: rotate(0deg);
} to {
  background:yellow;
  -webkit-transform: rotate(360deg);
  -moz-transform: rotate(360deg);
  -o-transform: rotate(360deg);
  -ms-transform: rotate(360deg);
  transform: rotatc(360dcg);
  }
}

</style>
</head>
<body>
    <div id='square'></div>
</body>
</html>
```

OK, let's break down this example. First, let's set up the HTML document, then include some CSS to target the div by the ID "square" by writing #square {. . .}; nothing new there. Now give the square a background color of black and a width and height of 50 pixels. Finally and most importantly, make an animation called "spin" with a duration of 15 seconds and a repetition of "infinite". Now, using CSS3, declare the spin animation by using the @keyframes rule. Inside the rule, define its start ("from") and end ("to") by animating the square and rotating it 360 degrees. (I am including the necessary prefixes since I am working across all browsers, but keep in mind that the final specification will not include the prefix. However, browsers may still support it for backwards compatibility so no code breaks in the future.) Finally, open this in your browser—that's it! This is pretty amazing stuff from just using straight CSS.

There are a few things to note when using CSS animations. For starters, they cannot stack—that is, you cannot have an animation called "wiggle" and apply an animation called "spin" and have them animate at the same time. Only the last-applied animation, in this case "spin", will get applied to the DOM object you're targeting (note that this could very well change as the spec finalizes, but at the time of writing, this was how it was in the browsers I've tested). Also, when using CSS3 animations, you may notice a slight flicker to your screen when the animation is applied and when it finishes. This is the browser leveraging on the machine's GPU for handling the animation. It's a bug, if you ask me, and it requires a hacky workaround. The hack that seems to work best is applying a z index to your transform, even if you don't intend to animate in the (3D) z space. Including the z-axis property enables hardware acceleration (GPU) initially and eliminates the screen flicker when animation occurs. (If you're into the seizure effect, this won't matter much to you, although your clients may ask for it to be removed.)

Finally, keep in mind that the W3C's spec will more than likely be much more limited than what the browser actually supports. Apple, Mozilla, Google, and other vendors support a variety of features that may not make it into the W3C's decision, but they're still fun to play with, especially in creating 3D and interesting parallax effects. However, I remind you to understand your user base—whom are you developing for and deploying toward with your campaigns? This ought to dictate what feature set you should and shouldn't use for your next campaign.

Vendor Prefixes

As was discussed in Chapter 3, in order to use the latest and greatest CSS3 features of the browser, vendor prefixes are your passport. Animation prefixes are no different: there still need to be clear ways to call a browser's rendering engine. Think of them as their own API to instruct the browser to animate—because that's what they are. Predictably, developers and designers have a love-hate connection with vendor prefixes. On the one hand, they allow use of up-to-date and emerging technologies; on the other hand, they come with the expense of long statements that will ultimately break if browser manufacturers drop their own prefixes for the final CSS specification. The Web could get really ugly if that happens! It can be challenging to understand if a vendor-prefixed property is part of the CSS specification or will eventually become part of it, since some vendors don't even submit all their (browser-specific) properties for W3C standardization. In some cases you'll find that sites use the `-webkit` prefixes alone, especially in mobile, even though Opera, IE, and Firefox have mobile builds of their browser. With all that said, let's review some of the vendor prefixes in Listing 5-3 and take a look at the prefixes for a radial gradient class in CSS.

Listing 5-3. CSS3 Vendor-Prefix Example

```html
<!DOCTYPE HTML>
<html>
<head>
<meta http-equiv="Content-Type" content="text/html; charset=UTF-8">
<style>
#square {
 width:500px;
 height:500px;
}

.radial-gradient {
  background: -webkit-radial-gradient(10% 10%, yellow, black);
  background: -moz-radial-gradient(10% 10%, yellow, black);
  background: -o-radial-gradient(10% 10%, yellow, black);
  background: -ms-radial-gradient(10% 10%, yellow, black);
  background: radial-gradient(10% 10%, yellow, black);
}

</style>
</head>
<body>
    <div id='square' class='radial-gradient'></div>
</body>
</html>
```

Holy repetition! If you're a developer or programmer, having to do anything over and over again is a clear sign that you can do it better. This example gives an idea of the operational load that designers and developers face when creating cross-browser experiences using emerging features—and in this case emerging is a requirement for penetration on devices like the iPhone and iPad. I usually laugh whenever I hear "operational scale" and "emerging" used in the same sentence. Now you can too!

A common predicament in the advertising industry involves the fact that many clients want to use the latest and greatest features available, but they don't understand what goes into developing them nor why it takes so long to accomplish something that seems to them rather simple. In the simple gradient example, it takes four times the amount of code it would if standardization were in place. More bytes are also eaten up to download from the server, as our code is now four times as large. Plus when an updates needs to be made, we now have to make it in five different places for the same effect. It gets exhausting quickly as your code grows.

This topic is raising some big concerns throughout the industry; there was even a discussion in April 2012, where the W3C and Opera questioned whether to add webkit prefixes as a standard. Essentially, Opera would adopt Webkit commands into its browser engine to adapt to the laziness of most programmers omitting their specific prefix. This, in my opinion, goes against everything that the W3C stands for—and in the CSS realm, that should be creating a vendor-agnostic standard to eliminate the need for any and all prefixes, thus creating true browser interoperability. Going with Webkit as a standard and having other browser manufacturers adopt it is not creating a standard at all; it's creating conformity to what's popular and is used most commonly due to developer laziness. A good article on this topic can be found at `http://www.sitepoint.com/opera-css3-webkit-prefix`.

Going Prefixless

The general consensus among developers seems to be that the way to head is having no prefixes at all. The ability to use these new features by calling upon them without any vendor specificity is something that needs and should happen across browsers as they become standardized in the open web. Some of the new features in the CSS3 spec are currently pretty much finalized and at a "candidate recommendation" level within the adoption process. This means some of these require no prefixes at all, since browsers are starting to support them prefix-less. Some of these properties are outlined in Table 5-2.

Table 5-2. *CSS Prefixless Properties*

Property	Use
Border-radius	Used for rounding borders of DOM objects.
Box-shadow	Used for adding shadow effect to DOM objects.
Colors (RGBA)	Allows colors to be defined via RGB along with an alpha (transparency) setting.
Colors (HSLA)	Allows colors to be defined in HSL (hue, saturation, and lightness) or HSLA format (hue, saturation, lightness, and alpha).
Media queries	Serve styles to a browser depending on media type (print, screen, etc.) and media condition (screen size, portrait, landscape, etc.).
Multiple backgrounds	Allows multiple background images to be placed on a single element.
Opacity	Allows application of a transparency setting to an element and all of its children.

It truly comes down to the very emerging features that need prefixes. However, the Web, as you know, moves very quickly; so keep checking up on the features that can be put to use today. There are also some pretty nice tools on web sites that any developer or designer can use to take the guesswork out of writing CSS3. One such tool is Prefix Free (`http://leaverou.github.com/prefixfree`). Prefix Free is a JavaScript file to be included in your document that adds the current browser's prefix to any CSS code but applies it only when it's required. Minimal code bloat! Its small file size (it comes in at only 8 kilobytes minified) makes it especially great for advertising. However, it has some limitations, so be sure to read up on at the site before implementing it in a production campaign. Another useful tool is Prefixr (`http://prefixr.com`). You paste in your CSS syntax, and with the press of a button, WHALAA! It allows you to update your CSS to include all the vendor prefixes you may require for cross browser deployment.

JavaScript Animation vs. CSS3 Animation

After learning a bit about JavaScript and animating on the canvas element in the previous chapter, you're most likely wondering what the difference is between JavaScript and CSS3 animations? Both have pros and cons, in truth; look at your campaign's end goals and requirements to determine which method to use. However, I can provide a few tidbits of information to start you off with. First, JavaScript is an interpreted language. JS animations rely on the JavaScript engine of the browser to interpret, parse, and execute instructions during runtime. On the other hand, browsers can implement CSS3 animations natively in the underlining code base of the browser (the engine). Usually written in C, C++, or something similar, this code gets compiled to machine language, so it's always present, shipped, and installed with a browser. This allows CSS3 to often be hardware-accelerated and offloaded to a machine's GPU for intensive operations like animation, which makes for better-performing experiences a user can notice on a mobile browser like iOS Safari or Android's native browser.

Between the two, many developers will argue that it comes down to some combination of ease of use, extensibility, support, and overall performance. If you need to target older browsers, JavaScript is the clear winner. If you care only about subjective ease of use, the modern Web, and hardware support, CSS3 is a viable solution. Also, remember that JavaScript is blazingly fast on newer browser engines! As a developer in the advertising world, where optimization and performance are everything, you should ultimately utilize both to your advantage while taking the requirements of the campaign and the target audience into consideration. At the end of the day, there are many ways to pull something off. Knowing one way of doing something doesn't mean it's always the best way at any moment and for any scenario. Understand who your target audience is and what primary browser they're running. This could involve some browser statistics investigation on the publisher's part to figure out what their users primary user base is.

I strongly recommend you get familiar with http://stackoverflow.com if you aren't using it yet. If you have questions regarding this or other topics, chances are you won't be the first one asking.

Finally, I can't perform every test known to man to figure out which animation technique is better in your specific scenario. I want to empower you to test on your own; in return, do a service to the developer community by recording your tests with a really great tool: http://jsperf.com. Get familiar with using this if you need to re-create bugs or test differences between multiple ways of doing something in your script.

requestAnimationFrame, setInterval, and setTimeout?

Let's talk a bit about the code that drives animation via JavaScript. Traditionally, before `requestAnimationFrame` was available in support of IE10, Firefox 4, Chrome 10, Safari 6, and other modern browsers, animation was achieved by calling either `setInterval` or `setTimeout`. By calling one of these JavaScript methods in repetition, the browser would execute the command over and over again, usually until a certain condition was met and stopped the animation. If for some reason it never stopped, the browser would execute the script forever and eventually crash or freeze (this still sometimes happens with poorly written scripts). However, since `requestAnimationFrame` was introduced by Mozilla and repeated by Webkit, the objective was simple: provide a native API for controlling animations in the browser entirely. Whether it's a DOM element, CSS, canvas-based, or even WebGL (there'll be more on WebGL in Chapter 12), the browser will handle and optimize any animations into a single animation phase, leading to higher animation quality overall. If you have animation looping in a tab that's not visible—say, your advertisement's animation and the user isn't viewing the ad—the browser won't keep it running and hogging system resources. Publishers should love this—it means fewer resources to allocate and much less memory usage, leading ultimately to much longer battery life, especially for mobile devices that support the new approach. I feel Microsoft's Developer Center explains it perfectly:

> *The msRequestAnimationFrame method provides smooth animations and optimal power efficiency by taking the visibility of the web application and the display's refresh rate into account to determine how many frames per second to allocate to the animation. msRequestAnimationFrame is a very efficient way to schedule non-declarative script animations and should be used instead of setTimeout and setInterval.*

msdn.microsoft.com/en-us/library/windows/apps/hh453391.aspx

So if you're animating for modern browsers, stop using `setInterval` or `setTimeout` in JavaScript and learn to take advantage of `requestAnimationFrame`. Otherwise, use CSS3 based animations when you can and where it's supported. Learning and using both will save time and headaches down the road, especially when you have to optimize or debug due to publisher kickback or get assets handed off from creative agencies.

CSS3 vs. Flash

All you have to do is read through web articles stating Flash is dead and it shouldn't be long until you get a sense of the complete madness on the Web. The mob screams, "Long live HTML5!" Coming back to reality for a moment, I'm not here to pick sides or even discuss in depth on that trivial topic. It's not what this book is about, nor do I want to waste your time on it. Simply put, both technologies have their pros and cons, but one thing is for certain: HTML5, CSS3, and JavaScript are here to stay, so whether you choose to use them or not, you should damn well learn them. Flash is still an amazing platform in my book and has many years on the latest web standard.

However, CSS3 particularly for its animation features to emerging browsers natively, demonstrate how web standards will soon be the standard going forward. A really good side-by-side comparison on Sencha's blog showcases how two identical ads, one created with CSS3 and one with Flash, pair up (`http://dev.sencha.com/deploy/css3-ads`). Improvements are necessary, but for an initial look, they are pretty darn close and it shows the plugin-free but rich web is right around the corner. What's not apparent is that this example also demonstrates something much broader: that CSS3 ads live in the same domain as Flash ads and my thought is that this is where web advertising will be for some time: a combination of Flash and web standards (HTML5/CSS3/JS) living side by side in harmony. (Cue inspirational music . . .)

One thing that comes to mind is file size. Having created web advertisements for quite some time and knowing that publishers keep tight control on the file size spec, I have a couple questions I'd like answered.

- How much k-weight should HTML/CSS/JavaScript ads have?

- Can loading of assets and external files be controlled in sequence?

- How are analytics and measurement affected?

- What happens to performance and user experience if multiple units are loaded onto the page at once?

These questions come up more and more often as clients want to use HTML5 for reach, and really, there is no silver bullet until the specifications are set, tested and adopted. Ads using the Flash Player weren't adopted overnight so what makes this any different? One thing is for certain, though: publishers, agencies, and ad-serving platforms, as well as the IAB, need to work out and agree on a set of standards to remedy these pressing issues before they become a very apparent and widespread problem throughout the industry. Luckily, there is an active working group dedicated to this initiative and many others that fuel our industry. You can learn more about these functions by heading over to. `http://iab.net/member_center/committees`.

CSS3 Presentations and Style

Now that I've covered a lot on CSS3 animations and how they play out in the space, this section reviews the new CSS3 presentation enhancements in the modern Web. Traditionally, CSS stood for layout and style, but with the latest features coming in to play—shadow, transforms, and gradients—more can be done with CSS than ever before. Having already covered some of the new selectors, pseudo classes, web fonts, and animation, let's dig in and take a look at some of the other enhancements to CSS's conventional approach to presentation and style.

Box Shadows

CSS3 box shadows are a new feature, one almost set for W3C finalization and supporting browser vendors. Box shadowing allows application of a slick drop shadow-type effect to such DOM objects as images and canvas or div elements. Listing 5-4 shows a box shadow working in advertising.

Listing 5-4. Box Shadow Ad Example

```
<style>
#ad {
  position: absolute;
  width: 300px;
  height: 250px;
  background-color: white;
  -webkit-box-shadow: 0px 0px 20px 0px rgba(0, 0, 0, 1);
  box-shadow: 0px 0px 20px 0px rgba(0, 0, 0, 1);
}</style>
```

As you can see, it's just the regular CSS syntax you're used to, with some updates to give access to new browser effects. Assuming our ad element has the ID of ad, this CSS block will apply a nice drop shadow to our ad on the publisher's page. This listing would produce the effect shown in Figure 5-4.

Figure 5-4. *An ad container with box-shadow using CSS3*

As you see, some pretty straightforward CSS can apply a nice drop shadow to where our ad inventory will live on the publisher's page. The box shadow property uses two required parameters, horizontal shadow position and vertical shadow position, followed by four optional parameters, blur (which we're setting to 20 pixels), spread, color, and inset.

Note   Color can use HEX, RGBA, or HSLA color values for the box-shadow property.

Multiple Backgrounds

Building on what you saw in Listing 5-4, multiple backgrounds are a new feature that allows designers to apply multiple background images to an element. This could be helpful if you want to create a complex ad background image from two independent image sources. In fact, let's attempt to do just that in building our ad's background (see Listing 5-5).

Listing 5-5. Multiple Background Example

```
<!DOCTYPE HTML>
<html>
<head>
<meta http-equiv="Content-Type" content="text/html; charset=UTF-8">
<style>
#ad {
 position: absolute;
 width: 300px;
 height: 250px;
 background-color: white;
 -webkit-box-shadow: 0px 0px 20px 0px rgba(0, 0, 0, 1);
 box-shadow: 0px 0px 20px 0px rgba(0, 0, 0, 1);

 /*
 top level icon (x,y,repeat)
 bottom level background (x,y,repeat)
 */
 background:
  url(logo.png) 20px 10px no-repeat,
  url(300x250Bg.jpg) 0px 0px no-repeat;
}
</style>

</head>
<body>
    <div id='ad'></div>
</body>
</html>
```

If you add the previous code and refresh the browser, you'll see that this example loads in two separate images to the background property of the div element ad (see Figure 5-5). Notice that the parameters are URL, X, Y and repeat.

Figure 5-5. *An ad background with multiple backgrounds using CSS3*

Calling the background property via CSS provides a comma-delimited list of image assets by URL location. The order of images matters, so add the top-level asset first and the bottom level last.

Text Shadows

Lets add some copy to our ad unit by adding a call to action (CTA). But let's also add a drop shadow to the CTA as well. Text shadowing is very similar to box shadowing, with the exception that text shadows can be applied only to fonts. Let's look at working with text shadows (see Listing 5-6).

Listing 5-6. Text Shadow Example

```
<!DOCTYPE HTML>
<html>
<head>
<meta http-equiv="Content-Type" content="text/html; charset=UTF-8">
<style>
#ad {
  position: absolute;
  width: 300px;
  height: 250px;
  background-color: white;
  -webkit-box-shadow: 0px 0px 20px 0px rgba(0, 0, 0, 1);
  box-shadow: 0px 0px 20px 0px rgba(0, 0, 0, 1);

  background:
   url(logo.png) 20px 10px no-repeat,
   url(300x250Bg.jpg) 0px 0px no-repeat;
}
```

```
#cta {
  position: absolute;
  top: 210px;
  left: 190px;
  color: white;
  font-family: Verdana;
  font-size: 16px;
  cursor: pointer;
  text-shadow: 0px 0px 5px #000000;
}
</style>
</head>

<body>
<div id=ad>
  <section>
    <div id=cta>Click Here</div>
  </section>
</div>
</body>
</html>
```

Add the updated code and refresh your browser, and you'll see an example of text shadow in action within our ad (see Figure 5-6).

Figure 5-6. *An ad with a CTA using the text-shadow property in CSS3*

While a drop shadow may be hard to see, adding it on the copy allows a user to view the important information much more clearly by separating it from the background. This is especially the case when using drop shadows on such an important copy feature of an ad as a CTA. The text shadow property's syntax is identical to that of the box-shadow property, but it applies only to fonts. It also allows the addition of this effect natively in the browser, without having to use images with the drop shadow effect applied.

Note   A text shadow can also be applied to web fonts (see Chapter 4).

Border Radius

Another almost finalized feature of the specification is border radius, probably one of the early CSS3 features that had all designers jumping for joy. They called for this effect for a long time, the reason being that before border radius, designers needed to export rounded images via Photoshop and load them into the page. This was time-consuming to develop, as well as costly to download to a user's machine. Now without the need of Photoshop, we can let the browser handle the heavy lifting. Let's add some rounded borders to our ad example (see Listing 5-7).

Listing 5-7. Border Radius Example

```
<!DOCTYPE HTML>
<html>
<head>
<meta http-equiv="Content-Type" content="text/html; charset=UTF-8">
<style>
#ad {
  position: absolute;
  width: 300px;
  height: 250px;
  background-color: white;
  -webkit-box-shadow: 0px 0px 20px 0px rgba(0, 0, 0, 1);
  box-shadow: 0px 0px 20px 0px rgba(0, 0, 0, 1);

  background:
   url(logo.png) 20px 10px no-repeat,
   url(300x250Bg.jpg) 0px 0px no-repeat;

  -webkit-border-radius: 10px;
  -moz-border-radius: 10px;
  border-radius: 10px;
}
#cta {
  position: absolute;
  top: 210px;
  left: 190px;
  color: white;
  font-family: Verdana;
  font-size: 16px;
  cursor: pointer;
  text-shadow: 0px 0px 5px #000000;
}
</style>
</head>

<body>
<div id=ad>
```

```
  <section>
    <div id=cta>Click Here</div>
  </section>
</div>
</body>
</html>
```

Adding the CSS properties for border radius (in boldface type in Listing 5-7) and refreshing your browser will add a 10-pixel rounded corner to our ad element. The border radius syntax is fairly simple: all you need do is pass it a value (in pixels) you want to round. You can see the effect in Figure 5-7.

Figure 5-7. *Our ad with rounded borders using CSS3*

Note Border radius can be adjusted independently instead of all four corners at the same time. This could be helpful if your client is, say, CVS Pharmacy (www.cvs.com).

Gradients

CSS3 now offers gradients, which are another feature of the spec that allows designers to lay off the images and take advantage of the browser's graphics natively. As you learned using gradients with the canvas element, it allows the definition of a linear or radial color gradient via JavaScript. Now with our CSS syntax, we can do similar things without touching our script files. Let's add a gradient to our ad example by making our CTA more of a button with style (see Listing 5-8).

Listing 5-8. Gradient CSS3 Example

```
<!DOCTYPE HTML>
<html>
<head>
<meta http-equiv="Content-Type" content="text/html; charset=UTF-8">
```

```
<style>
* {
  font-family: Verdana;
}
#ad {
  position: absolute;
  left: 30px;
  top: 30px;
  width: 300px;
  height: 250px;
  background-color: white;
  -webkit-box-shadow: 0px 0px 20px 0px rgba(0, 0, 0, 1);
  box-shadow: 0px 0px 20px 0px rgba(0, 0, 0, 1);

  background:
   url(logo.png) 20px 10px no-repeat,
   url(300x250Bg.jpg) 0px 0px no-repeat;

  -webkit-border-radius: 10px;
  -moz-border-radius: 10px;
  border-radius: 10px;
}
#cta {
  position: absolute;
  top: 190px;
  left: 160px;
  color: white;
  font-size: 16px;
  cursor: pointer;
  text-shadow: 0px 0px 5px #000000;
}

.button {
  font-size: 16px;
  color: white;
  padding: 10px 20px;
  background: -moz-linear-gradient(
    top,
    #e3e3e3 0%,
    #545454);
  background: -webkit-gradient(
    linear, left top, left bottom,
    from(#e3e3e3),
    to(#545454));
  -moz-border-radius: 0px;
  -webkit-border-radius: 0px;
  border-radius: 10px;
  border: 1px solid #000000;
  -moz-box-shadow:
    0px 1px 3px rgba(0,0,0,0.5),
    inset 0px 0px 2px rgba(255,255,255,0.7);
```

```
  -webkit-box-shadow:
    0px 1px 3px rgba(0,0,0,0.5),
    inset 0px 0px 2px rgba(255,255,255,0.7);
  box-shadow:
    0px 1px 3px rgba(0,0,0,0.5),
    inset 0px 0px 2px rgba(255,255,255,0.7);
  text-shadow:
    0px -1px 0px rgba(000,000,000,0.4),
    0px 1px 0px rgba(255,255,255,0.3);
}
</style>
</head>

<body>
<div id=ad>
  <section>
    <div id=cta class=button>Click Here</div>
  </section>
</div>
</body>
</html>
```

If you've followed along, refresh your browser, and you'll notice the outcome (see Figure 5-8).

Figure 5-8. *Our ad with a sexy CTA button using CSS gradients and rounded borders*

Adding gradients with CSS is a great way to leverage the browser to build a slick button or complex backgrounds instead of using the traditional image approach. It's also easier on the end user, since it won't eat up k-weight and tax a user for another download, both of which are huge gains in the advertising world. A tool I myself use quite often is at http://colorzilla.com/gradient-editor, specifically because it is easy to use, adds all the vendor prefixes, and offers older Microsoft browser support via the filter property.

Transitions

The CSS3 Transitions module offers a great way to add transitional properties to certain elements. Transitions can be applied to background, color, height, width, and other specific properties, or the special "all" keyword can be used to apply transitions to all properties on the element. Transitions allow the ad experience to expand and contract, creating an iconic rich media expansion effect. Listing 5-9 shows how to transition the ad container to expand 500 pixels when a user clicks the CTA (let's also add a bit of JavaScript).

Listing 5-9. CSS Transitions Example

```
<!DOCTYPE HTML>
<html>
<head>
<meta http-equiv="Content-Type" content="text/html; charset=UTF-8">
<style>
* {
  font-family: Verdana;
}
#ad {
  position: absolute;
  left: 30px;
  top: 30px;
  width: 300px;
  height: 250px;
  background-color: white;
  -webkit-box-shadow: 0px 0px 20px 0px rgba(0, 0, 0, 1);
  box-shadow: 0px 0px 20px 0px rgba(0, 0, 0, 1);

  background:
   url(logo.png) 20px 10px no-repeat,
   url(300x250Bg.jpg) 0px 0px repeat;

  -webkit-border-radius: 10px;
  -moz-border-radius: 10px;
  border-radius: 10px;

  -webkit-transition: all 1s ease-in-out;
  -moz-transition: all 1s ease-in-out;
  -ms-transition: all 1s ease-in-out;
  -o-transition: all 1s ease-in-out;
  transition: all 1s ease-in-out;
}
#cta {
  position: absolute;
  top: 190px;
  left: 160px;
  color: white;
  font-size: 16px;
  cursor: pointer;
  text-shadow: 0px 0px 5px #000000;
```

```
  -webkit-transition: all 1s ease-in-out;
  -moz-transition: all 1s ease-in-out;
  -ms-transition: all 1s ease-in-out;
  -o-transition: all 1s ease-in-out;
  transition: all 1s ease-in-out;
}

.button {
  font-size: 16px;
  color: white;
  padding: 10px 20px;
  background: -moz-linear-gradient(
    top,
    #e3e3e3 0%,
    #545454);
  background: -webkit-gradient(
    linear, left top, left bottom,
    from(#e3e3e3),
    to(#545454));
  -moz-border-radius: 0px;
  -webkit-border-radius: 0px;
  border-radius: 10px;
  border: 1px solid #000000;
  -moz-box-shadow:
    0px 1px 3px rgba(0,0,0,0.5),
    inset 0px 0px 2px rgba(255,255,255,0.7);
  -webkit-box-shadow:
    0px 1px 3px rgba(0,0,0,0.5),
    inset 0px 0px 2px rgba(255,255,255,0.7);
  box-shadow:
    0px 1px 3px rgba(0,0,0,0.5),
    inset 0px 0px 2px rgba(255,255,255,0.7);
  text-shadow:
    0px -1px 0px rgba(000,000,000,0.4),
    0px 1px 0px rgba(255,255,255,0.3);
}

#close {
  position: absolute;
  top: 10px;
  left: 480px;
  opacity: 0;
  cursor: pointer;
  color: white;

  -webkit-transition: all 1s ease-in-out;
  -moz-transition: all 1s ease-in-out;
  -ms-transition: all 1s ease-in-out;
  -o-transition: all 1s ease-in-out;
  transition: all 1s ease-in-out;
}
```

```
</style>
</head>

<body>
<div id=ad>
  <section>
    <div id=close>X</div>
    <div id=cta class=button>Click Here</div>
  </section>
</div>
</body>
</html>

<script>
var ad = document.querySelector('#ad');
var cta = document.querySelector('#cta');
var close = document.querySelector('#close');
cta.addEventListener('click', expandAd, false);
close.addEventListener('click', collapseAd, false);

function expandAd () {
  ad.style.width = '500px';
  cta.style.left = '360px';
  close.style.opacity = 1;
}

function collapseAd () {
  ad.style.width = '300px';
  cta.style.left = '160px';
  close.style.opacity = 0;
}
</script>
```

If you've followed along, keep a close eye on the boldface sections of the Listing 5-9 code. In its CSS, transition: all 1s ease-in-out; has been added to all the elements to be moved—in this case, our ad, our CTA, and our new Close icon. In the HTML markup, a new div element is added inside our section container by writing <div id=close>X</div>. This is what will close the expanded ad experience. Finally, take a look at the JavaScript toward the end of the listing's code. The minimal JavaScript code first declares variables to reference the objects in our DOM. In this case, it's our ad, the CTA button, and the new Close icon. Next, event listeners are added for the user's mouse click by writing cta.addEventListener('click', expandAd, false); and close.addEventListener('click', collapseAd, false);. Doing this allows handling the user's action appropriately and calls expandAd and collapseAd, respectively. Inside the expand method the ad's width is expanded to 500 pixels, the button is moved on its left property, and the Close icon's opacity is toggled by setting it to a value of 1. (The opacity property is another almost finalized feature in the CSS3 specification; it gives the ability to adjust the fill of an element or image between 0 and 1.) Conversely, the ad is reset to its original setting by calling the collapseAd function. Figure 5-9 shows what you'll get in the browser if you click on the CTA button.

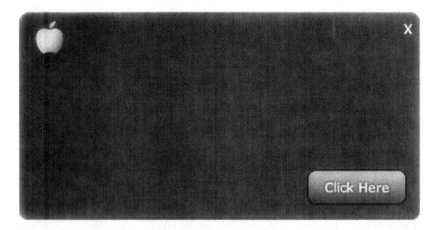

Figure 5-9. *Our ad expanding using CSS3 Transitions*

Hopefully you can see from Listing 5-9 that you can re-create an expanding ad unit fairly easily using CSS, with a little JavaScript for control. Also, keep in mind that you can use a transition for multiple CSS properties, including color, height, margins, and much more. Super helpful if you need ads to expand in a variety of directions and dimensions.

Note You can add a JavaScript event listener to the DOM's `transitionend` event by writing `element.addEventListener('transitionend', transitionEndHandler);`. This can be useful to control your ad content in a certain way when the transition is complete.

CSS3 Transforms

Let's wrap up the examples by discussing CSS3 Transforms, which allow elements to be manipulated and transformed in a relational space. The `transform` property applies a 2D or 3D transformation to an element, which allows you to rotate, scale, move, and skew to create some really interesting transformations. By default `transform` applies to the top left of an element, or (0,0), but you can adjust the `transform-origin` property on an element as well to re-orient the center point. There is also a property, currently supported in Webkit browsers, that allows nested items to preserve the space that the elements reside in (2D or 3D). The `transform-style` property identifies how nested elements are rendered in the desired space. Listing 5-10 adds a quick 3D flip to our expanding ad unit.

Listing 5-10. CSS3 Transforms Example

```
<!DOCTYPE HTML>
<html>
<head>
<meta http-equiv="Content-Type" content="text/html; charset=UTF-8">
<style>
* {
  font-family: Verdana;
}
#ad {
  position: absolute;
```

```
    left: 30px;
    top: 30px;
    width: 300px;
    height: 250px;
    background-color: white;
    -webkit-box-shadow: 0px 0px 20px 0px rgba(0, 0, 0, 1);
    box-shadow: 0px 0px 20px 0px rgba(0, 0, 0, 1);

    background:
     url(logo.png) 20px 10px no-repeat,
     url(300x250Bg.jpg) 0px 0px repeat;

    -webkit-border-radius: 10px;
    -moz-border-radius: 10px;
    border-radius: 10px;

    -webkit-transition: all 1s ease-in-out;
    -moz-transition: all 1s ease-in-out;
    -ms-transition: all 1s ease-in-out;
    -o-transition: all 1s ease-in-out;
    transition: all 1s ease-in-out;
}
#cta {
    position: absolute;
    top: 190px;
    left: 160px;
    color: white;
    font-size: 16px;
    cursor: pointer;
    text-shadow: 0px 0px 5px #000000;

    -webkit-transition: all 1s ease-in-out;
    -moz-transition: all 1s ease-in-out;
    -ms-transition: all 1s ease-in-out;
    -o-transition: all 1s ease-in-out;
    transition: all 1s ease-in-out;
}

.button {
    font-size: 16px;
    color: white;
    padding: 10px 20px;
    background: -moz-linear-gradient(
      top,
      #e3e3e3 0%,
      #545454);
    background: -webkit-gradient(
      linear, left top, left bottom,
      from(#e3e3e3),
      to(#545454));
    -moz-border-radius: 0px;
    -webkit-border-radius: 0px;
```

```
  border-radius: 10px;
  border: 1px solid #000000;
  -moz-box-shadow:
    0px 1px 3px rgba(0,0,0,0.5),
    inset 0px 0px 2px rgba(255,255,255,0.7);
  -webkit-box-shadow:
    0px 1px 3px rgba(0,0,0,0.5),
    inset 0px 0px 2px rgba(255,255,255,0.7);
  box-shadow:
    0px 1px 3px rgba(0,0,0,0.5),
    inset 0px 0px 2px rgba(255,255,255,0.7);
  text-shadow:
    0px -1px 0px rgba(000,000,000,0.4),
    0px 1px 0px rgba(255,255,255,0.3);
}

#close {
  position: absolute;
  top: 10px;
  left: 480px;
  opacity: 0;
  cursor: pointer;
  color: white;

  -webkit-transition: all 1s ease-in-out;
  -moz-transition: all 1s ease-in-out;
  -ms-transition: all 1s ease-in-out;
  -o-transition: all 1s ease-in-out;
  transition: all 1s ease-in-out;
}

.flip3D {
  -webkit-transform: rotateY(360deg);
  -moz-transform: rotateY(360deg);
  -o-transform: rotateY(360deg);
  -ms-transform: rotateY(360deg);
  transform: rotateY(360deg);
  -webkit-transform-style: preserve3d;
  -moz-transform-style: preserve3d;
  -ms-transform-style: preserve3d;
  transform-style: preserve3d;
}
</style>
</head>

<body>
<div id=ad>
  <section>
    <div id=close>X</div>
    <div id=cta class=button>Click Here</div>
  </section>
```

112

```
</div>
</body>
</html>

<script>
var ad = document.querySelector('#ad');
var cta = document.querySelector('#cta');
var close = document.querySelector('#close');
cta.addEventListener('click', expandAd, false);
close.addEventListener('click', collapseAd, false);

function expandAd () {
  ad.style.width = '500px';
  cta.style.left = '360px';
  close.style.opacity = 1;
  cta.style.opacity = 0;
  ad.classList.toggle("flip3D");
}

function collapseAd () {
  ad.style.width = '300px';
  cta.style.left = '160px';
  close.style.opacity = 0;
  cta.style.opacity = 1;
  ad.classList.toggle("flip3D");
}
</script>
```

Again, jopefully you've followed along and noticed the boldface sections of updated code. The first thing to do in our CSS is add a class of .flip3D and define its transform properties by writing rotateY(360deg) for all browser vendors. Second, add another transform property of style, which tells the browser to preserve-3D space when applying the transformation. Next, utilize a new feature in HTML5 browsers called the classList API; in our JavaScript, toggle the flip3D class by calling ad.classList.toggle('flip3D');. This instructs the browser to add or remove the class on expand and collapse (http://developer.mozilla.org/en-US/docs/DOM/element.classList has more information on the classList API).

Adding the code in Listing 5-10 and refreshing your browser should give an experience similar to the one shown in the snapshot in Figure 5-10.

Figure 5-10. *Our ad expanding with a 3D spin using CSS3 Transforms*

When using this new CSS3 feature, keep in mind that this spec is in the working-draft state and requires vendor prefixes. There is more on Transforms at `http://w3.org/TR/css3-2d-transforms`. Check for browser support at `http://caniuse.com`.

Note   CSS3 Transitions and Transforms are complicated to demonstrate on paper. There is more detailed information at `http://w3.org/TR/css3-transitions` and `http://w3.org/TR/2012/WD-css3-transforms-20120911`.

Some other features can be briefly discussed in wrapping up our examples of CSS3. One addition is text wrapping via the `text-overflow` property, a great new feature that lets you manipulate how a line of text will break as it gets close to the edge of the object's container element or browser window. This is very helpful in responsive ad techniques; as the ad manipulates size, you can specify how you want the lines of ad copy to break. This is also exceptionally helpful when working with dynamic data and web services, where character counts can vary widely depending on the amount of information the server returns. (There will be more on this topic in Chapter 11.) Let's take our ad example and add a CSS property of `text-overflow: ellipsis` and have the browser handle add "..." to copy that's larger than our desired ad area of 300 × 250. Listing 5-11 showcases this technique.

Listing 5-11. Text-overflow Example

```
<!DOCTYPE HTML>
<html>
<head>
<meta http-equiv="Content-Type" content="text/html; charset=UTF-8">
<style>
* {
 font-family: Verdana;
}
.adContainer{
 position: absolute;
 width: 300px;
 height: 250px;
}
```

```css
#ad {
  position: relative;
  width: 100%;
  height: 100%;
  background-color: white;
  -webkit-box-shadow: 0px 0px 20px 0px rgba(0, 0, 0, 1);
  box-shadow: 0px 0px 20px 0px rgba(0, 0, 0, 1);

  -webkit-border-radius: 10px;
  -moz-border-radius: 10px;
  border-radius: 10px;

  -webkit-transition: all 1s ease-in-out;
  -moz-transition: all 1s ease-in-out;
  -ms-transition: all 1s ease-in-out;
  -o-transition: all 1s ease-in-out;
  transition: all 1s ease-in-out;

  white-space:nowrap;
  overflow:hidden;
  text-overflow: ellipsis;
}
</style>
</head>

<body>
  <div class='adContainer'>
    <div id='ad'>

Lorem Ipsum is simply dummy text of the printing and typesetting industry. Lorem Ipsum has been
the industry's standard dummy text ever since the 1500s, when an unknown printer took a galley of
type and scrambled it to make a type specimen book. It has survived not only five centuries, but
also the leap into electronic typesetting, remaining essentially unchanged. It was popularised in
the 1960s with the release of Letraset sheets containing Lorem Ipsum passages, and more recently
with desktop publishing software like Aldus PageMaker including versions of Lorem Ipsum.

    </div>
  </div>
</body>
</html>
```

There are quite a few CSS3 features. I'll review many more emerging CSS3 submissions from vendors like Adobe and Google, including shaders, filters, regions, and exclusions, in Chapter 12. But start playing with them today—if for no other reason than just to test their performance and add some pizzazz to your ads. A good place to start digging deeper is http://css3clickchart.com, which outlines both common and emerging CSS features. If you're interested in learning more about CSS3 animations, Dan Eden's Animate.css (http://daneden.me/animate) is a great tool for getting started quickly—but as always have a graceful failback because it may not work everywhere.

If you've followed along, you'll see it's fairly simple to create a straightforward advertisement that looks pretty good by just adding some simple CSS. You saw everything from adding multiple background images, rounding corners, adding gradients, and even transitions and transforms leveraging a bit of JavaScript for control. Use all of these tools to your advantage, and you'll be able to come up with some really amazing ads to wow your clients.

CSS3 in Advertising

So CSS3 animations and how they're affecting the advertising space is HUGE! Seriously, when was the last time you didn't see an ad animate or utilize some presentation features just covered? Usually it's "Make my logo bigger" and "Can we add a little animation here?" Advertisers are all fighting for users' attention, so keeping the ad moving is very important to them. A couple of examples that can be extremely helpful for CSS3 animations, especially if they're leveraging the GPU, are particle generators (or systems) and loader icons. A prime example of when they're used is the holiday season, when ads need that falling snow effect.

Handling the snow animation via CSS3 and utilizing the z space will have the animation running super smooth on top of the GPU (even for mobile). Obviously, this could also be done in JavaScript, but depending on the number of other animations occurring, CSS3 will most likely come out on top.

Loader icons are huge in advertisements where a user opts for more content and the ad pulls in more than it could on its initial load. Spinners, loaders, and other icons of the sort can all be offloaded to the browser instead of making an additional HTTP request to grab an animated GIF. Again, this is helpful for additional subsequent loads based on user interaction. Often, ads will load an initial k-weight limit of 70-100 kilobytes; after a user interaction, they'll load additional weight up to 100 or even 200 kilobytes more (depending on pub spec).

In short, I have three simple rules to follow if you use (or plan on using) any emerging CSS3 features in your next advertising campaign.

1. Understand your target audience, and learn from what the publisher is currently taking advantage of with regard to features. Chances are it sells the media inventory that aligns with its content. If its content is aimed at a more tech-savvy audience and the publisher isn't too concerned with users on IE6 through IE8, you should be able to use more cutting-edge features.

2. If you need to appease the masses, work with your publisher to include a polyfill. More than likely, you'll need that extra k-weight allowance if it's not already baked into the site.

3. Use a CSS Reset for your ad. Eric Meyer's Reset for HTML5 is one of the better ones out there (`http://html5doctor.com/html-5-reset-stylesheet`). Keep in mind that you should only be resetting ad contents and not the page the ad is living on. So be sure to namespace your CSS rules appropriately. There is no sense working to make a creative experience consistent across multiple browsers if the underlying browser technology is rendering creative differently. It will be a mess to debug if you don't reset and start from ground zero.

Since the CSS3 spec is evolving and many submissions from vendors are already in working order, some browsers can't wait for the W3C to adopt, and so we get division. It's really important to understand what you can and can't do with CSS3 in modern browsers. Defining your campaign's reach will dictate what features you can take advantage of, both today and in future campaigns. Don't rely just yet solely on core CSS3 features. Start with features that are standard in all browsers by referencing `http://caniuse.com`, and add progressive enhancements to your ads in browsers that can support the richer feature set.

Sprite Sheets

Last but not least in this huge discussion of CSS3 is file size and keeping image use under control, especially on devices with limited bandwidth. Sometimes you can't get away from using images, and sometimes you'll have a campaign with a lot of them, so now's a great time to discuss sprite sheets. A perfect use case is a character animation in a game. You can't usually get around working with images when you need specific frames of bitmap data redrawn to the screen in a sequence. To optimize this use case, we can use a sprite sheet, which includes every frame of animation in a large image sheet. Sprite sheets are ideal due to the fact that there is only one request made to the server hosting the image asset. Once the file is stored in browser cache, the developer can move the sprite sheet, via

CSS and/or JavaScript, to the specific region to show a specific frame of animation at any given point in time. This is extremely powerful in animation but should also be best practice when delivering ads with imagery to a publisher's page. A sprite sheet provides huge image optimization benefits, as all images in it can share pixel data. That is, the JPEG, GIF, or PNG image codec doesn't need to write that information multiple times for different images; once written, its shared by all other images on the sheet that share the same values. If you notice you're often compressing images to get under k-weight limitations, try bundling all your images in one file, as closely as possible (with enough whole pixel padding), and compress it. Chances are you'll save much more k-weight than by compressing individual files, plus you'll eliminate multiple HTTP request overhead.

So how do you work with sprite sheets? CSS can offset the top and left properties of a background element or elements at given points in time to create seamless transitions from one region to another. Figure 5-11 shows a mashup of six popular web icons that, individually tallied, amount to 84 kilobytes. However, using the sprite sheet method gets it down to 66 kilobytes. (It can even be squashed, using a great free tool called ImageOptim (http://imageoptim.com), all the way down to 55 kilobytes.)

Figure 5-11. *An example of a sprite sheet saved as a PNG file at 55 kilobytes*

Now that you have the final image asset, just adjust the CSS of this sprite sheet by using the CSS code shown in Listing 5-12.

Listing 5-12. Sprite Sheet CSS

```
.linkedin, .twitter, .yahoo, .yelp, .youtube, .rss{
        background: url(sprites.png) no-repeat;
}
.linkedin{
        background-position: -7px 0;
        width: 256px;
        height: 256px;
}
```

```
.twitter{
        background-position: -269px 0;
        width: 256px;
        height: 256px;
}
.yahoo{
        background-position: -8px -252px ;
        width: 256px;
        height: 256px;
}
.yelp{
        background-position: -269px -252px ;
        width: 256px;
        height: 256px;
}
.youtube{
        background-position: -531px 0;
        width: 256px;
        height: 256px;
}
.rss{
        background-position: -531px -253px ;
        width: 256px;
        height: 256px;
}
```

As you can see from our example, we initially set a background image to our social icon classes by writing background: url(sprites.png) no-repeat; Then based on the class assigned, we simply offset the background image at a specific X,Y location in order to just show the portion of the image were looking for. Sprite sheets are all over the Web. In fact, even the popular Apple.com navigation bar consists of a sprite sheet. (If you view the source, you'll find that one single request goes to http://images.apple.com/global/nav/images/globalnavbg.png.) So get creative, experiment with them, and keep optimization in mind, along with fewer requests to the server. Animated GIF sprite sheets anyone?

Last, a very good tool for creating sprite sheets is straight-up Adobe Flash CS6, but it comes at a steep price point. So if you don't have Flash available, I recommend you download the AIR application Zoe, by Grant Skinner and his team (http://easeljs.com/zoe.html) or use a few free online-based tools called SpritePad (http://spritepad. wearekiss.com a personal favorite) and SpriteCow (http://spritecow.com). Go to http://css-tricks.com/css-sprites for more detailed information on sprite sheet uses.

Sprite Sheets on Mobile

In mobile development, where we all often try to save on HTTP requests to a server due to the possibility of inconsistent network connections, sprite sheets are a huge advance in ad optimization. Ideally, the goal is to use as little imagery as possible in mobile and go the route of SVG, canvas, or font-based icons rather than bitmaps due to higher pixel density screens and increased file size, but sometimes there's no way around it. Understandably, there are many different views on this situation, whether it be animated GIFs or sprite sheets using CSS and JavaScript. Either way, just make sure you understand the needs and goals of the campaign as well as your users experience. It's far less work to make updates to one sprite sheet as a Photoshop (PSD) file rather than thirty independent images needing to be reedited and reexported. If you're interested in learning more about this topic and enjoy listening to people talk about these topics, I suggest you check out the *5by5* talk show *Hypercritical*, specifically episode 61, http://5by5.tv/hypercritical/61.

Summary

In closing out this chapter, let's review what's been discussed so far. CSS3 is not final, but it provides developers and designers many astounding features to play around with. It also can be used in production campaigns where browsers support it. You've seen some key factors in determining when to use JavaScript or CSS3 for animations; performance and ease of use have been discussed, as well as tools that make designing and developing easier. All of the presentation updates in the submitted spec and working drafts have been reviewed in great detail, and I've provided code samples you can take advantage of in your next advertising campaign. Last of all, I've covered sprite sheets, a very important topic—how they're used, what they're used for, and the performance gains that come from using them, specifically on mobile devices.

Being that optimization is crucial for advertising and for the Web as a whole, I encourage you to take the time to build these practices into your workflow so that the Web operates faster for everyone. Get excited about using some of these new features, and be prepared to learn new techniques as they are finalized. CSS3 is no longer solely about layout and style. It's much more than that. Combined with GPU support, rich graphics, and JavaScript, CSS level 3 is a great addition to a designer's tool belt.

In Chapter 6, the focus shifts back to HTML5 land, especially on new JavaScript APIs to take advantage of. We'll discuss in more detail some of the updated markup and elements available, including HTML5 inputs, as well as the Drag-and-Drop API and web workers.

▩ ▩ ▩

HTML5 APIs

Many people use a translator or tour guide when visiting a new country. They lean on someone who knows the land and the people inside and out, someone who can also show you what to do and what not to do when you arrive. In this case, think of the new country as all the modern browser technologies and that translator as the Application Programming Interfaces (APIs) used to communicate with those technologies. To get things done in this or any new country, you need to "talk the talk"—and that's basically what APIs do. They are a communication layer that gives access to a specific form of technology by communicating through code.

In this chapter, we'll cover a lot on HTML5 APIs. Since you've already learned a bit about them so far, consider yourself having a nice head start. The canvas, CSS3, even SVG—all are APIs in their own way, and this chapter will review some of the new APIs that emerging HTML5 browsers have brought to us. However, we will not be covering all of them as there are way too many to do that within the scope of this book. However, you can see most of them at http://platform.html5.org. Also, keep in mind that most of the APIs aren't part of the actual HTML5 specification. Several did start in the HTML5 spec and later were moved into their own standard and thus adopted the blanket term of HTML5 by default. While most of these APIs require some level of JavaScript to operate with, they all do different things and behave in different ways. Moreover, studying them will entirely change how you work inside the browser using standards. Trust me! So let's start digging into the real muscle of HTML5. Be sure to get your coding hat on because HTML5 APIs rely heavily on JavaScript.

Drag-and-Drop

Up first, let's chat about the drag-and-drop (DnD) API, a relatively new addition to the HTML5 spec. This API provides a very simple approach to dragging and dropping elements on a page or piece of content, like an ad unit. Moreover, it requires a minimal amount of code to implement. Originally created by Microsoft in version 5 of the Internet Explorer browser, it has experienced some developer backlash (to say the least) due to bugs in the API spec, implementations in browsers, and uses around drag events. See http://quirksmode.org/blog/archives/2009/09/the_html5_drag.html for more information.

After some improvements and since IE, Opera, Firefox, Safari, and Chrome support it in some way or another, this API now brings native drag-and-drop support to the modern browser environment without a third-party plug-in or JavaScript library. Simply by adding a "draggable=true" attribute on any DOM element you wish the user to drag (while including some basic event listeners/handlers via JavaScript on a "drop zone"), you can instruct the browser where elements can be dropped.

▩ **Note** The elements img and a (with an href) are draggable by default, but keep in mind that not all elements (e.g., images) can be drop areas.

The drag-and-drop API has come a long way. Before using the native features of the browser, developers and designers would need to use an external library like jQuery or a plugin like Flash. Thanks to the HTML5 spec, it's now a major component in modern browsers by default. Just about anything can be dragged: images, links, text—any DOM node, really. Note, too, that native browser support makes for a faster and much more responsive Web or, in our case, ad creatives. Anytime you can leverage a browser's native APIs, do it! After all, standardizing and constructing user-friendly APIs that are hardwired into the browser environment are what HTML5 and this book are all about. Listing 6-1 outlines how DnD can be used in a very simple ad, one where the publisher is a product manufacturer and the ad is a drop zone for products to be saved with drag-and-drop.

Listing 6-1. Drag-and-Drop Example

```
<!DOCTYPE HTML>
<html>
<head>
<style type="text/css">
* {
  margin:0px;
  padding:0px;
}
#ad {
  width:300px;
  height:250px;
  border:1px solid #000;
  overflow: hidden;
}
#logo {
  position: absolute;
  top: 5px;
  left: 1px;
  width: 300px;
  height: 250px;
  font-family: Arial, "MS Trebuchet", sans-serif;
  font-size: 40px;
  text-align: center;
  color: #fff;
  z-index: 3;
}
#cta {
  position: absolute;
  top: 220px;
  left: 1px;
  width: 300px;
  height: 250px;
  font-family: Arial, "MS Trebuchet", sans-serif;
  font-size: larger;
  text-align: center;
  color: #fff;
  z-index: 2;
}
#dropper {
  position: relative;
  top: 25px;
```

```
    left: 80px;
    z-index: 101;
}
#dropArea {
    position: absolute;
    top: 60px;
    left: 10px;
    width: 280px;
    height: 150px;
    background: #f2f5f6; /* Old browsers */
    background: -moz-linear-gradient(top,  #f2f5f6 0%, #e3eaed 37%, #c8d7dc 100%); /* FF3.6+ */
    background: -webkit-gradient(linear, left top, left bottom, color-stop(0%,#f2f5f6), color-
stop(37%,#e3eaed), color-stop(100%,#c8d7dc)); /* Chrome,Safari4+ */
    background: -webkit-linear-gradient(top,  #f2f5f6 0%,#e3eaed 37%,#c8d7dc 100%); /*
Chrome10+,Safari5.1+ */
    background: -o-linear-gradient(top,  #f2f5f6 0%,#e3eaed 37%,#c8d7dc 100%); /* Opera 11.10+ */
    background: -ms-linear-gradient(top,  #f2f5f6 0%,#e3eaed 37%,#c8d7dc 100%); /* IE10+ */
    background: linear-gradient(to bottom,  #f2f5f6 0%,#e3eaed 37%,#c8d7dc 100%); /* W3C */
    filter: progid:DXImageTransform.Microsoft.gradient( startColorstr='#f2f5f6', endColorstr='#c8d7dc',
GradientType=0 ); /* IE6-9 */

    border: 1px dashed;
    border-radius:10px;

    z-index: 81;
}
#background {
    position: absolute;
    top: 1px;
    left: 1px;
    width: 300px;
    height: 250px;
    background: #c0c5d6; /* Old browsers */
    background: -moz-linear-gradient(top,  #c0c5d6 0%, #3f4c6b 100%); /* FF3.6+ */
    background: -webkit-gradient(linear, left top, left bottom, color-stop(0%,#c0c5d6), color-
stop(100%,#3f4c6b)); /* Chrome,Safari4+ */
    background: -webkit-linear-gradient(top,  #c0c5d6 0%,#3f4c6b 100%); /* Chrome10+,Safari5.1+ */
    background: -o-linear-gradient(top,  #c0c5d6 0%,#3f4c6b 100%); /* Opera 11.10+ */
    background: -ms-linear-gradient(top,  #c0c5d6 0%,#3f4c6b 100%); /* IE10+ */
    background: linear-gradient(to bottom,  #c0c5d6 0%,#3f4c6b 100%); /* W3C */
    filter: progid:DXImageTransform.Microsoft.gradient( startColorstr='#c0c5d6', endColorstr='#3f4c6b',
GradientType=0 ); /* IE6-9 */

    z-index: 0;
}


/******Mock Publisher Content********/
#publisherContent {
    position: absolute;
    top: 300px;
    left: 100px;
}
```

```
#pubProduct {
  position: absolute;
  top: 0px;
  left: 0px;
  width:100px;
  height:100px;
  background: url(hammer.png) no-repeat;

  z-index: 90;
}

</style>
<script type="text/javascript">
//fires when product is over the drop area
function allowDrop(event) {
  //cancel default for drop event to fire
  event.preventDefault();
  console.log("YOU'RE OVER THE DROP AREA!!!")
}

function dropArea(event){
  var data = event.dataTransfer.getData("Text");
  var dropArea = document.getElementById('dropper');
  var element = document.getElementById(data);
  dropArea.appendChild(element);

  console.log(element)
}

//initial drag when product is selected
function drag(event) {
  var dropImg = document.createElement("img");
  dropImg.src = "add.png";
  dropImg.width = "48px";
  dropImg.height = "48px";
  dropImg.style.opacity = "0.5";

  event.dataTransfer.effectAllowed='all';
  event.dataTransfer.setData("Text", event.target.getAttribute('id'));
  event.dataTransfer.setDragImage(dropImg, 25, 25);
}

function adInit(event) {
  console.log(event.type)
}

window.addEventListener('DOMContentLoaded', adInit, false);
</script>
</head>
```

```
<body>
<div id="publisherContent">
  <div id="pubProduct" draggable="true" ondragstart="drag(event)"></div>
</div>

<div id="ad">
  <div id="logo">Shopping Cart</div>
  <div id="cta"> Drag Products To Drop Area! </div>
  <div id="dropArea" ondrop=dropArea(event) ondragover=allowDrop(event)>
    <div id="dropper"></div>
  </div>
  <div id="background"></div>
</div>
</body>
</html>
```

Hopefully you're following along in your favorite text editor. Now let's take a look at the code. First, we do some basic ad set up and design using the CSS in the listing. Second, in the HTML we mimic having publisher content (publisherContent) and dropping the mock products in our publisher page onto the ad area (ad). Next in our publisherContent div, there is a sample product, pubProduct, which has its attribute of draggable set to true and has an event, ondragstart, to be handled with the function called **drag(event)**.

■ **Note**   You must pass in the "event" argument; otherwise the code will not function correctly.

Next, we put some more event handlers in the ad by leveraging the ondrop and ondragover events. These events attach dropArea(event) and allowDrop(event), respectively. Next, our functions get written using JavaScript. For drag we use a drag image with the method from the dataTransfer object by calling the method setDragImage() and pass it three arguments. The first argument is the image asset, the second and third are the image's x and y coordinate location—the place where the mouse will start the drag. This could be helpful if you want to create a custom image for the element when the user is dragging.

Next, we tackle the allowDrop method, which signifies when the product can be dropped onto a content area. In this case, we're using the entire ad as a drop zone.

■ **Note**   By default, the dragOver and dragEnter events are not able to drop the element. You must explicitly cancel these default browser actions by calling event.preventDefault(); to drop an element.

Last, once you know you're allowed to drop the product and once the user lets go of the mouse, that action can be handled with the dropArea handler. Inside the dropArea method we grab the product's data by calling the dataTransfer object again—but this time we retrieve the data by writing var data = event.dataTransfer. getData("Text"). Having the data object, we can then inject the data into the ad's real estate. The user now sees the element inside the ad area, as Figure 6-1 demonstrates.

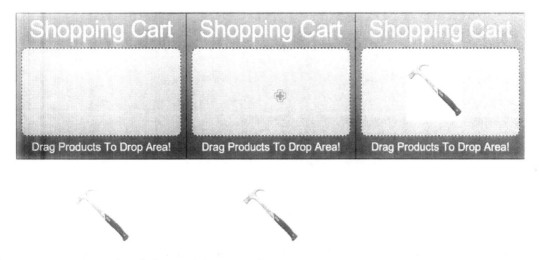

Figure 6-1. *Shows the ad's drag-and-drop example*

I hope you got all that; I know it's a lot. If you didn't, you can read through the previous code again and for follow up learning's visit http://html5laboratory.com/drag-and-drop.php. DnD is a bit of a hidden gem to some users, especially in the ad environment, so if it's a specific function in the ad experience, be sure to include a relevant and clear call to action to ensure that your users take the appropriate action.

Drag-and-Drop in Advertising

With some basic DnD primer under your belt, let's think about how the drag-and-drop (DnD) API can apply to us folks in the advertising space. At first thought, I believe the DnD API can bring new ways to play interactive games. For example, it allows a user to play the game of chess more accurately as it resembles the users' native behavior. It can re-create an interactive shopping cart experience, where users drag products to a checkout cart which could fill depending on the amount of products getting dropped into it. I think once you start playing around with this API, the possibilities when using this standard are limitless.

It can drag elements into a to-do list so a user can print at a later time or even be used for functionality on a mix up puzzle game, where the user needs to assemble the puzzle for a hidden offer. I also see DnD bringing the ability to handle a complex publisher integration—for instance, where a user drops select content from the publisher's page onto the ad's drop space (as was just covered). This could be sort of an Easter egg hunt, where the end user finds relevant content within the site and gets special deals with the discovery of these "eggs."

Granted, DnD still has its fair share of quirky issues, but if you're interested in an in-depth look at the DnD API, go to http://html5rocks.com/en/tutorials/dnd/basics. You can view the current spec at http://dev.w3.org/html5/spec/dnd.html#dnd and http://whatwg.org/specs/web-apps/current-work/multipage/dnd.html#dnd.

File

The updated File API in HTML5 allows web content to prompt users to select local files on their machine and then read the contents of those files within the browser itself, with no need of server-side help or a plugin. This selection can be done either by using an HTML input element or with the just-learned DnD API. If you use Gmail (Google's mail service) and a modern browser, chances are you're using the File API without knowing it when you attach files to mail. You may think, "Well sure, I've added attachments to e-mail before," but did you know you can drag those attachments into Gmail from the operating system of your computer? DnD lets you do data transfer of files to Gmail's application, but the reading of the file in your browser takes full advantage of the File API.

The DnD and File API, when used together, provide an experience identical to working with native applications on your operating system or desktop. This new addition to HTML5 essentially allows users to treat the web application as if it's an extension of their native operating system (OS). This can be a tremendous help if you're asking users to upload an image of themselves into your ad unit. All they'll need do is drag it from the desktop into their browser's defined drop zone - in our case it could be the ad.

Traditionally, the File API gave users a basic input using `<input type='file'>` that allowed for a native OS file picker window and also allowed an HTML document to refer to a file located on the users file system—but that was pretty much it.

Nowadays, the File API allows users to read the file in various file formats directly inside the browser, without server-side technologies. A file can be read as a string, an array buffer, or even a BLOB (binary large object) input using the new FileReader API. With this information native to the browser, binary information on a file can be read, interpreted, displayed, even manipulated, and then saved in an updated and modified version. Through JavaScript, the File API provides a native mechanism to read the data of a file and write it as you wish. As the Web becomes more application-focused (as HTML5 intends to), the native file system of the user's computer and the application on the web will become more interwoven. The lines between Web and native OS will be blurred for many normal everyday users. For instance, instead of having users retrieve an asset called `someimage.jpg` saved on their machine, the File API and FileReader API can be bolted onto the DnD API to seamlessly integrate operating system and web application or even allow access to a user's built-in camera and capture bitmap image information and save it to the web page or advertisement—again, all within the browser's native architecture.

This approach is much more advanced than just asking a user for a previously saved image asset, wouldn't you say? Moreover, you can even use an `XMLHttpRequest` (AJAX) method to retrieve information from another data source and import it as a `BLOB`, `Array`, or `String` object for the FileReader API to interpret and perhaps later ask the user to manipulate. Using the AJAX method, this process can occur by not triggering a page refresh, which again, makes the integration seamless to the end user.

With this in mind, lets take a look at working with the File API within JavaScript. Listing 6-2 asks the user to drag an image of themself into the ad experience.

Listing 6-2. File API Example

```
<!DOCTYPE html>
<style type="text/css">
* {
  margin: 0px;
  padding: 0px;
}
#drop_zone {
    width:300px;
    height: 250px;
    background-color:#999;
    border: 1px dashed #000;
}
p {
    width: 300px;
}
</style>
<head>
    <meta charset=utf-8>
    <body>
        <div class="percent">0%</div>
        <input type=file>
```

```
        <div id="drop_zone">Drop Zone</div>
        <p>Select an image from your machine or drop onto the drop zone to read the contents of the
file without using a server</p>
        <script>
            function adInit(event) {
                event.preventDefault();
                var upload = document.getElementsByTagName('input')[0];
                var progress = document.querySelector('.percent');
                var dropZone = document.getElementById('drop_zone');
                dropZone.addEventListener('drop', handleFileSelect, false);

                // Check for the various File API support.
                if (window.File && window.FileReader && window.FileList && window.Blob) {
                    var reader = new FileReader();
                    console.log('Sweet! All File APIs supported');

                    upload.onchange = function (event) {
                        var file = upload.files[0];
                        var img = new Image();
                        reader.onload = function (event) {
                            console.log(event.type);
                        };
                        reader.onprogress = function (event) {
                            console.log(event.type);
                            var percentLoaded = Math.round((event.loaded / event.total) * 100);
                            progress.textContent = percentLoaded + '%';
                            console.log(percentLoaded)
                        };
                        reader.onloadend = function (event) {
                            if (!file.type.match('image.*')) {
                                alert("Not an image!!");
                            } else {
                                img.src = event.target.result;
                                if (img.width >= 300) {
                                    img.width = 300;
                                }
                            }
                            console.log(event.type);
                            dropZone.innerHTML = '';
                            dropZone.appendChild(img);
                        };
                        reader.onerror = function (event) {
                            console.log(event.type);
                        };

                        reader.readAsDataURL(file);
                        console.log(reader);
                        return false;
                    };
                    function handleFileSelect(event) {
                        event.stopPropagation();
                        event.preventDefault();
```

```
                    //event.dataTransfer.dropEffect = 'copy'; // Explicitly show this is a copy.
                    var files = event.dataTransfer.files; // FileList object.
                    var file = files[0];

                    reader.onloadend = function (event) {
                        console.log(event.target);
                        dropZone.style.width = "300px";
                        dropZone.style.height = "300px";
                        dropZone.style.background = 'url(' + event.target.result + ')
no-repeat center';
                    };

                    reader.readAsDataURL(file);
                    return false;

                    console.log(file)
                }
            } else {
                alert('The File APIs are not fully supported in this browser.');
            }
        }

        window.addEventListener('DOMContentLoaded', adInit, false);
    </script>
  </body>
</html>
```

As this code shows, users are first allowed to select image files on their local machine or drag images onto an ad's drop zone by defining an area in the markup as drop_zone. Once the ad initiates after the DOM is loaded, the adInit function is fired; it kicks things off by grabbing a variable reference to the DOM objects. (You can see I'm using various ways of getting a reference by calling getElementsByTagName, getElementById, and the new querySelector.) Once the user drags-and-drops an image onto the drop area, we run through a few methods after creating a file reader reference, first called upload.onchange, which handles grabbing the user's image file once the input element changes state. Second, we use the file reader—let's call it reader—and attach specific methods to the object—onload, onprogress, onloadend, onerror and readAsDataURL—all of which handle specific commands when the user drops the image on the drop area. Last, let's focus on the onloadend method, which writes the user's image into the drop_zone element via CSS by writing dropZone.style.background = 'url(' + event.target.result + ') no-repeat center';. Once this occurs, the image is presented in the browser without a round trip to a server. This is shown in Figure 6-2 using an example image from my desktop.

Drop Zone

Select an image from your machine or drop
onto the drop zone to read the contents of the
file without using a server

Figure 6-2. *An example of an image file upload*

Note   With the `multiple` attribute, the user can select several files at once.

File Access in Advertising

Now that we've enabled users to upload an image, they can do the same with a text file, PDF, PSD—you name it—and have the browser parse, manipulate, and render the information to the screen. With this information in mind, let's allow users to drag-and-drop an image onto the ad's real estate from the desktop and have them use the HTML5 canvas element to paint on the image. From that, let's also allow the user to save that manipulated file locally. Listing 6-3 gives an example.

Listing 6-3. File API Example with Canvas

```
<!DOCTYPE html>
<style type="text/css">
    * {
        margin: 0px;
        padding: 0px;
        position: relative;
    }
    canvas {
```

```
            position: absolute;
            top: 20px;
            left: 0px;
            width: 300px;
            height: 250px;
            border: 1px solid #000;
        }
        .percent {
            position: absolute;
            top: 0px;
            left: 0px;
            width: 100%;
        }
        button {
            position: absolute;
            top: 300px;
            width: 200px;
            height: 50px;
            visibility: hidden;
        }
    </style>
<head>
    <meta charset=utf-8>

    <body>
        <div class="percent">Loader: 0%</div>
        <canvas width=300 height=250>
            <p>No Canvas Support</p>
        </canvas>
        <button></button>
        <script>
            function adInit(event) {
                event.preventDefault();

                var canvas = document.getElementsByTagName('canvas')[0],
                    context = canvas.getContext('2d'),
                    progress = document.querySelector('.percent'),
                    img = document.createElement("img"),
                    saveBtn = document.querySelector("button"),
                    mouseIsDown = false,
                    hasText = true,
                    clearCanvas = function () {
                        if (hasText) {
                            context.clearRect(0, 0, canvas.width, canvas.height);
                            hasText = false;
                        }
                    };

                // GENERIC CTA
                context.fillText("Drop an image onto the ad!", 50, 50);
```

```
        // Image for loading
        img.addEventListener("load", function () {
            clearCanvas();
            context.drawImage(img, 0, 0, 300, 250);
        }, false);

        // To enable drag and drop
        canvas.addEventListener("dragover", function (evt) {
            evt.preventDefault();
        }, false);

        canvas.addEventListener("drop", function (event) {
            var files = event.dataTransfer.files;

            if (files.length > 0) {
                var file = files[0];

                if (typeof FileReader !== "undefined") {
                    var reader = new FileReader();

                    reader.onload = function (event) {
                        console.log(event.type);
                    };
                    reader.onprogress = function (event) {
                        console.log(event.type);
                        var percentLoaded = Math.round((event.loaded / event.total) * 100);
                        progress.textContent = "Loader: " + percentLoaded + '%';
                        console.log(percentLoaded)
                    };
                    reader.onloadend = function (event) {
                        console.log(event.type);
                        if (!file.type.match('image.*')) {
                            alert("Not an image!!");
                        } else {
                            img.src = event.target.result;
                        }

                        beginCanvasDrawing();
                    };
                    reader.onerror = function (event) {
                        console.log(event.type);
                    };

                    reader.readAsDataURL(file);
                }
            }
            event.stopPropagation();
            event.preventDefault();
        }, false);
```

```
            function beginCanvasDrawing() {
                var brush = "rgba(200, 34, 2, .5)";

                canvas.addEventListener("mousedown", function (event) {
                    mouseIsDown = true;
                    clearCanvas();
                    context.beginPath();//starts the drawing once users mouse is down
                }, false);

                canvas.addEventListener("mousemove", function (event) {
                    if (mouseIsDown) {
                        canvas.style.cursor = "pointer";
                        context.strokeStyle = brush;

                        context.shadowOffsetX = 0;
                        context.shadowOffsetY = 0;
                        context.shadowBlur    = 15;
                        context.shadowColor   = brush;

                        context.lineWidth = 5;
                        context.lineJoin = "round";
                        context.lineTo(event.layerX, event.layerY);
                        context.stroke();
                    } else {
                        console.log("hold mouse button down")
                    }
                }, false);

                canvas.addEventListener("mouseup", function (event) {
                    mouseIsDown = false;
                    var colors = context.getImageData(event.layerX, event.layerY, 10, 10).data;
                    console.log(colors);
                    brush = "rgba(" + colors[0] + ", " + colors[1] + ", " + colors[2] + ",
" + colors[3] + ")";
                    console.log(brush);
                }, false);

                saveBtn.style.visibility = "visible";
                saveBtn.innerHTML = "Save Your Creation";
                saveBtn.addEventListener("click", function (event) {
                    var newImg = new Image();
                    newImg.src = canvas.toDataURL();
                    window.location.href = newImg.src.replace('image/png',
'image/octet-stream');
                }, false);
            }
        }

        window.addEventListener('DOMContentLoaded', adInit, false);
    </script>
  </body>
</html>
```

133

As you can see from the code, the user is asked to drag-and-drop an image onto the ad's canvas element, where the DND API and the File API render the image to the screen. From there, we'll call a method, beginCanvasDrawing, that will call up our specific canvas drawing functions allowing the user to "draw" once the user has inserted an image into the browser.

Inside beginCanvasDrawing, we'll detect whether a user is drawing with the mouse and present a button for the user to save the new image composition. Once the user selects the button, a new image is created, and the canvas's new bitmap information is applied to the image's source. From there the image is saved to their file system by using a replace on the image's file type to image/octet-stream, which allows the user to save the image information as a binary file. Figure 6-3 shows what the browser should render.

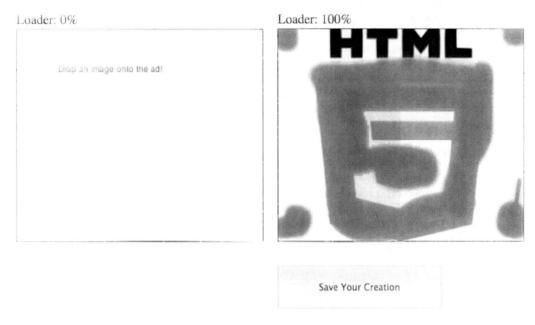

Figure 6-3. *The image file upload example with File and canvas*

Note   You can detect whether the browser supports the File Writer API and save information locally that way. Otherwise you can use server-side code to take the binary information and save the asset by its proper file name.

In addition, HTML5 is set to support a download attribute to <a> elements. This approach signifies that the browser should locally download the URL it points to rather than navigate to the URL. (See http://html5-demos.appspot.com/static/a.download.html for an example of this. Also, look at http://nihilogic.dk/labs/canvas2image; it's a useful and lightweight library that can save different image types from the canvas element.)

I myself still remember how excited I got when Flash Player 10 let ad developers gain file access to create user-generated content (with user permission). Now, within the browser natively, we can do the same thing—grab local files, access video or audio from the user's machine. It's all pretty amazing stuff if you ask me!

Note   Keep in mind that this API, which is not actually a part of the HTML5 specification, is in a working-draft state. Thus, features may be altered or changed as work on the specification continues. See www.w3.org/TR/FileAPI for more information on the File API.

Page Visibility

The Page Visibility API is something I've waited a long time for! I'm really eager to start taking advantage of this feature, as it provides huge performance benefits to end users and developers. The Page Visibility API allows the browser to handle or "toggle" content and system resources based on the visibility of the page. Simply put, if you aren't looking at something—say, if its on another tab—the browser will stop allocating resources to that content, freeing up more system resources for the content that the user is currently viewing. Let's take a look at working with the Page Visibility API in an ad example (see Listing 6-4).

Listing 6-4. Page Visibility API Example

```
<!DOCTYPE html>
<head>
    <meta charset=utf-8>
    <body>
    </body>
        <script>
            var isHidden,
              state,
              visibilityChangeEvent;

        function adInit(event) {
            console.log(event.type)

                if (typeof document.hidden !== "undefined") {
                    isHidden = "hidden";
                    visibilityChangeEvent = "visibilitychange";
                    state = "visibilityState";
                } else if (typeof document.mozHidden !== "undefined") {
                    isHidden = "mozHidden";
                    visibilityChangeEvent = "mozvisibilitychange";
                    state = "mozVisibilityState";
                } else if (typeof document.msHidden !== "undefined") {
                    isHidden = "msHidden";
                    visibilityChangeEvent = "msvisibilitychange";
                    state = "msVisibilityState";
                } else if (typeof document.webkitHidden !== "undefined") {
                    isHidden = "webkitHidden";
                    visibilityChangeEvent = "webkitvisibilitychange";
                    state = "webkitVisibilityState";
                }

        document.addEventListener(visibilityChangeEvent, function (event) {
            if (document[state] == "hidden") {
                        pauseAd();
                        } else {
                        startAd();
                        }
        }, false);
    }
```

```
        function pauseAd () {
          console.log("pauseAd");
          //code to pause ad animation or video
        }

        function startAd () {
          console.log("startAd");
          //code to resume ad animation or video
        }

        window.addEventListener('DOMContentLoaded', adInit, false);
    </script>
</html>
```

As the code shows, you can listen for a state change on the document's visibility and fire the method pauseAd or startAd, which will, respectively, pause or start an ad's animation or video playback should the creative leverage these features.

Page Visibility in Advertising

I think you'll agree that in the advertising space, that this could be a huge benefit for providing the best experience to the user. We can halt animation, video playback, even external requests that are on hidden browser tabs. I'd go as far as to say that this should be an absolute standard in the future of digital advertising (as browsers adopt this feature).

For even more granularity there's also a plug-in for JQuery to detect elements' visibility on the page. This plug-in could be even more beneficial when counting true visible ad impressions vs. served impressions or even when eliminating resources to an ad unit on the page that the user is not currently viewing. Think about it—why initialize creative content when no one is viewing? "If an ad is served to the page but no one is there to view it, does it still count as an impression?" Traditionally yes, but with measures like this in place, not for long—and that will give advertisers a better return for their ad dollars.

___

■ **Note** To detect element visibility, take a look at the
`http://inview` plug-in `https://github.com/protonet/jquery.inview`.

___

At the time of writing, this spec is still in a working-draft state, and so support for the Page Visibility API is pretty minimal. As I write, it's supported only in Chrome 13+, Firefox 10+, and Internet Explorer 10+. As adoption in the vendor market and user base grows, I'd like to see wider implementation and possibly even an IAB standard around this. See `http://dvcs.w3.org/hg/webperf/raw-file/tip/specs/PageVisibility/Overview.html` for the current working draft.

History

Now let's discuss the history API. Every Internet browser has it, and pretty much every Internet user hits the browser's Back button frequently in order to go back in the browser's time. It's undoubtedly the most popular button in the browser's overall interface. What the history API brings is a way to add and remove records in the user's browser history where the data to restore a page's state can be retained and the URL updated without refreshing the page's content. This approach is much different from selecting the Back button because in doing so, the page will always fire a reload, effectively causing the browser to rerender the content, make a request to the servers, and fire any ad impressions again.

The history API has a bunch of useful features, and it can also be fun to use in your next advertising campaign. For example, you could build a creative that pretends to know where the user visited last. Yes, kind of creepy; it may frighten a few users and even get some backlash, but it's really harmless, since you're not gathering any personally identifiable information. You'd simply be calling upon the history records in the browser's stored memory.

The API can get a bit tricky for ad developers. Let's say users are browsing around the ad content, perhaps searching for different products in a dynamic product feed and the developer has each user interaction logged to the history of the browser. Now, if the user uses the back button of the browser, it would just return to the state previously viewed in the ad content instead of going back to the previous page content. While this is all very new and emerging, we'll have to see where digital advertising fits within its use of the history API; it could conflict with many things and may even be off-limits to digital advertising all together. However things play out, the history API is worth familiarizing yourself with; I've even seen interesting examples that replicate the old marquee of scrolling text but, in this case, in the URL bar.

It's interesting how publishers and content makers will implement the history API in their pages. For example, when working with the API and adjusting the user's browser state, if no page reload happens, the ad content on the screen doesn't reload; thus no impression will fire. However, someone has seen the content again and it could even be someone entirely new, which should account for a new impression, right?

For more information on the History API, check out Opera's dev channel by visiting `http://dev.opera.com/articles/view/introducing-the-html5-history-api/`

Web Storage

Saving data is a pretty common task in any application, and with HTML5 it's becoming even more important on the Web. Sometimes you'll want to store data to reference at a later time; other times you can use the data saved with the HTML5 history API about users' browsing history. You can even save data for offline viewing, as you'll learn in Chapter 10. No matter which way you look at it, storage is a huge feature in software development so let's take a look at working with the web storage API in HTML5.

There are two types of web storage you need to remember.

- `localStorage`: saves data without an expiration date
- `sessionStorage`: saves data for one browsing session

Data in *localStorage* persists past browser restarts, whereas *sessionStorage* sticks around only when the page is refreshed. This specification is an API for data storage of a name/value pair of data in the browser. This is pretty revolutionary because you do not have to request the saved information via a server request; everything is saved client-side. Modern browsers typically allow up to 5 megabytes of client-side storage, whereas in HTML4, a cookie was used to store small amounts of information about a user's session, up to 4 kilobytes of storage, and it traveled with every HTTP request. Now you can save images into a string of text via *Base64* encoding and save that within the browser's 5 megabytes of storage per domain (approximately). Another nice feature is that if you attempt to exceed the default storage amounts set by the browser, the browser will ask the user to allow or deny the storage of more information.

sessionStorage

Now `sessionStorage` is a method of storing client-side data (name/value pairs) locally—much like cookies but it has many more advantages. Through `sessionStorage`, you can now save data from a user's browsing session in memory for retrieval at a later time in the ad experience, all without multiple round trips to a server. The real power in using `sessionStorage` is that it's supported across all major browsers, even down to IE8! Again, it's action is similar to that of cookies, but unlike cookies, web storage data are not sent with every server request and do not have the same data storage size limitations of cookies at 4 kilobytes. The data stored is domain-restricted; which means the browser's `sessionStorage` object information is only readable to the domain that initially placed that data.

Note   If the user has multiple windows opened at the same site, each one will have its own `sessionStorage` object.

---

localStorage

Since I am a Mac user, I use Command+Tab like crazy; for Windows users, it would be Ctrl+Tab. It provides an easy way to switch between multiple windows/applications on my machine, and if you're like me, you'll more than likely hit Command+Q or Ctrl+Q, which quits the application, by mistake a few times. (There's almost nothing more frustrating than having your finger slip and selecting Q instead of Tab as you're filling out a large form on the Web!

Now with `localStorage`, developers can help out users by saving the entries they made to text fields on the form. In this case, if I quit, which I inadvertently do pretty often, I can go back to the site after I restart my browser and pick up where I left off. This is hugely beneficial to a user's experience. The driving technology behind this is `localStorage`, which allows developers to save data that are persistent to the browser, enough so that if the user closes and reopens the browser, that data will remain, and a developer can retrieve the data at a later time.

As noted, `localStorage` is saved with no browser expiration date applied. That is, it's there forever, unless the developer clears or modifies it or the user deletes the browser application entirely or clears all the browser memory.

Whether you're using `sessionStorage` or `localStorage`, the syntax is identical for storing and retrieving values—as is shown in the following example, where the user's name is stored.

```
localStorage.setItem("userName", "John");
```

   or

```
sessionStorage.setItem("userName", "John");
```

Let's look at working with `localStorage` in an ad unit. In Listing 6-5, the user is prompted to enter his or her name; then the name value goes into the `localStorage` object, which allows the ad to use the name in the ad's text even if the user sees the ad at a later time and on another publisher site.

Listing 6-5. LocalStorage API Example

```
<!DOCTYPE HTML>
<html>
<head>
</head>
<style>
    * {
        margin: 0px;
        padding: 0px;
        position: relative;
        font-family: Verdana;
    }
    #ad {
      position: relative;
      top: 0px;
      left: 0px;
      width: 300px;
      height: 250px;
```

```
    border: 1px solid black;
    text-align: center;
  }
  #name {
    font-size: 60px;
    z-index: 20;
    color: white;
  }
  #usersName {
    font-size: 50px;
    z-index: 20;
    font-weight: bold;
  }
  #cta {
    z-index: 10;
    -moz-box-shadow: 0px 0px 0px 0px #caefab;
    -webkit-box-shadow: 0px 0px 0px 0px #caefab;
    box-shadow: 0px 0px 0px 0px #caefab;
    background:-webkit-gradient( linear, left top, left bottom, color-stop(0.05, #77d42a),
color-stop(1, #5cb811) );
    background:-moz-linear-gradient( center top, #77d42a 5%, #5cb811 100% );
    filter:progid:DXImageTransform.Microsoft.gradient(startColorstr='#77d42a',
endColorstr='#5cb811');
    background-color:#77d42a;
    -moz-border-radius:42px;
    -webkit-border-radius:42px;
    border-radius:42px;
    border:3px solid #268a16;
    display:inline-block;
    color:#306108;
    font-family:arial;
    font-size:28px;
    font-weight:bold;
    padding:20px;
    text-decoration:none;
    text-shadow:1px 1px 0px #aade7c;
  }
  #cta:hover {
    background:-webkit-gradient( linear, left top, left bottom, color-stop(0.05, #5cb811),
color-stop(1, #77d42a) );
    background:-moz-linear-gradient( center top, #5cb811 5%, #77d42a 100% );
    filter:progid:DXImageTransform.Microsoft.gradient(startColorstr='#5cb811',
endColorstr='#77d42a');
    background-color:#5cb811;
  }
  #cta:active {
    position:relative;
    top:1px;
  }
  #background {
    z-index: 0;
```

```
        width: 300px;
        height: 250px;
        position: absolute;
        top: 0px;
        left: 0px;
        background: rgb(201,222,150); /* Old browsers */
        background: -moz-linear-gradient(top,  rgba(201,222,150,1) 0%, rgba(138,182,107,1) 44%,
rgba(57,130,53,1) 100%); /* FF3.6+ */
        background: -webkit-gradient(linear, left top, left bottom, color-
stop(0%,rgba(201,222,150,1)), color-stop(44%,rgba(138,182,107,1)), color-
stop(100%,rgba(57,130,53,1))); /* Chrome,Safari4+ */
        background: -webkit-linear-gradient(top,  rgba(201,222,150,1) 0%,rgba(138,182,107,1)
44%,rgba(57,130,53,1) 100%); /* Chrome10+,Safari5.1+ */
        background: -o-linear-gradient(top,  rgba(201,222,150,1) 0%,rgba(138,182,107,1)
44%,rgba(57,130,53,1) 100%); /* Opera 11.10+ */
        background: -ms-linear-gradient(top,  rgba(201,222,150,1) 0%,rgba(138,182,107,1)
44%,rgba(57,130,53,1) 100%); /* IE10+ */
        background: linear-gradient(to bottom,  rgba(201,222,150,1) 0%,rgba(138,182,107,1)
44%,rgba(57,130,53,1) 100%); /* W3C */
      }
</style>
<body>
<div id='ad'>
  <div id='name'>Hello!<span id-'usersName'></span></div>
  <a id='cta'>Click Here</a>
  <div id='background'></div>
</div>
</body>
</html>
<script>

function adInit () {
  if(localStorage) {
    if (localStorage.getItem('userName') === '' || localStorage.getItem('userName') === null) {
      var uname = prompt('Enter Your Name');
      localStorage.setItem('userName', uname);
      document.getElementById('usersName').innerHTML = uname;
    } else {
      document.getElementById('usersName').innerHTML = '<br>' + localStorage.getItem('userName');
    }
  } else {
    alert('Browser not supported!');
  }
}
window.addEventListener('load', adInit, false);
</script>
```

Let's review the code and feel free to follow along in your favorite text editor. By adding an event listener for the document to load and attaching a handler function called adInit, which kicks things off. That function detects first if the browser supports localStorage. If it does, the function proceeds to detect if a value's been entered for the item called username. If not, a prompt appears for the user to enter his or her name and render it into the ad unit. Now if the user refreshes the page, views the ad on another site, or even closes the browser, the name will show in the ad unit again until the data is cleared or modified.

By refreshing the browser, you should see something similar to the image in Figure 6-4.

Figure 6-4. A localStorage ad example with a user's name

If you see something similar to what's in the figure, great work! If not, rereview the code and give it another shot. Modern web browsers even have tools to help you. By using the web inspector and heading to the Resources tab, you can take a look at all the storage items being held by the browser. Figure 6-5 shows what this looks like using Google's Chrome browser. (There will be more on data storage and measurement in Chapter 10.)

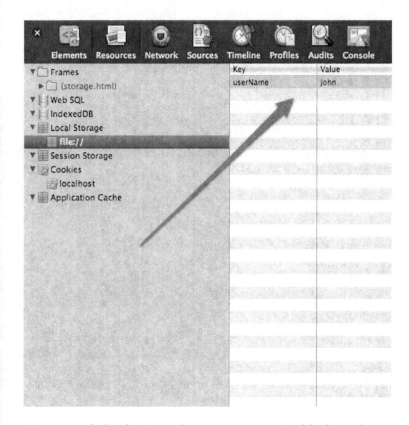

Figure 6-5. The localStorage web inspector view on Google's Chrome browser

---

Note   Using the web inspector, you can also view local databases, web storage items, cookies, and HTML5 application cache entries.

User Privacy

Privacy concerns connected with data storage always constitutes a huge topic for discussion among all parties involved in digital advertising. Currently, many startup companies attempt to utilize a device and user "fingerprinting" approach; it stores unique, trackable IDs on a user's machine through various forms of web storage for measurement across sites, ad networks, or both. Lawsuits have also involved such companies as Bluecava and Ringleader for their tricky user-detection techniques, which leverage HTML5 storage and databases to target and track unknowing users. Developers have even developed techniques known as a "Zombie Cookie", which persists through pretty much everything as it stores values in various areas including web storage, cookies and databases.

In the end, HTML5 storage is promising, but privacy is a bit concerning. If you need to support earlier browsers, you can leverage some great polyfills on the Web; try these at storejs: `http://github.com/marcuswestin/store.js` and `http://github.com/jensarps/IDBWrapper`. You can learn more about web storage APIs at `http://dev.w3.org/html5/webstorage` and discover more about user privacy within third-party ad networks at `http://dev.w3.org/html5/webstorage#privacy`.

Web Workers

Chances are you've seen browser notifications (see Figure 6-6) when browsing web pages.

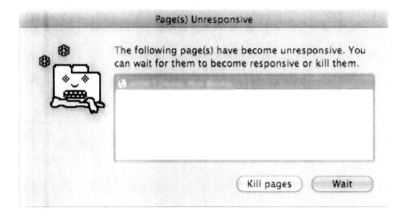

Figure 6-6. The "browser is unresponsive" screen

I use Chrome, but other browsers have similar messages showing you (as a user) that the page content has become unresponsive and asking you to stop and clear the code execution. Whatever the message, you get the idea that the browser has failed you. Don't fret; here comes an amazing new feature in new browsers from the team at Google called web workers.

When executing intense scripts, a browser can become unresponsive until the code on the page (or ad) finally finishes executing. In some cases this could take a while and worst cases, it would never stop executing. This could lock a user out of the user interface (UI) elements, pause animations, halt video playback, or worst of all, crash the browser.

What's going on here is that the browser is attempting to finish interpreting and running the scripts in question, and it will draw upon all available system resources to do so. To remedy this issue in the new modern browser market, a web worker can be used.

Essentially, a web worker is JavaScript that is interpreted in the background by the browser, independently of the other scripts and the DOM, without ultimately affecting overall performance. This is really awesome; you can continue to do whatever you want within the UI of the ad creative: clicking, tapping, hovering, scrolling—you get the idea—all while the worker script runs in parallel "helping" the other scripts and the functionality within your content. Web workers provide a much needed multithreaded approach to creative development using JavaScript, as Figure 6-7 illustrates.

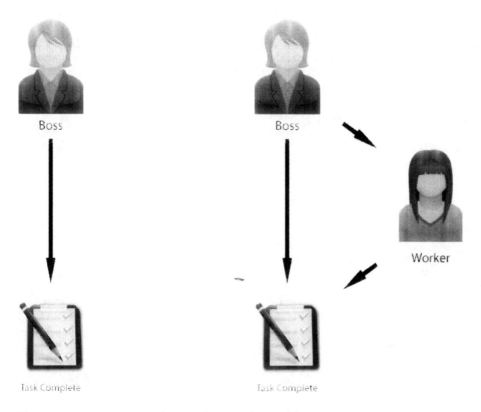

Figure 6-7. *Demonstration of a typical web worker workflow*

Hopefully, after looking at Figure 6-7, you'll agree that delegating another worker to do your work is much more efficient than taking on all the work yourself. This is what web workers strive to accomplish. They split up tasks for heavy JavaScript executions by separating them into multiple worker threads.

Before web workers, developers needed to be crafty and break apart their code so that the browser could interpret smaller "chunks" of code at a time. This amounted to a shoddy approach to multithreading in a single-threaded browser universe. Obviously, this never really worked too well, since it required the script to be heavily reliant on timers and intervals, all of which slowed the experience significantly, depending on the user's machine resources. It often created an undesirable "chugging," or staggered loading, effect for the user as well.

Initially a concept by Google with the Gears project, web workers have finally gained enough acceptance from other browser vendors and the W3C to produce its own specification. It can really speed up text filtering on search inputs, math computation, and even complex animations by offloading the physics or math onto a separate thread. Did someone say particle generators?

Web workers are a great way to modularize the code in your project or creative as well. If you have UI code, allow it to be a part of the markup, and load it independently of the worker script, which could be handling a random number generator or something else not directly tied to the UI.

■ **Note**   Web workers need to be hosted on a local or remote server in order to operate.

Web Workers in Advertising

In advertising, web workers can enhance user experience immensely. We finally have an API for running JavaScript in the background independent of anything else on the page, which will allow long-running tasks to be completed without making the page unresponsive. If you're doing any sort of calculation or complex algorithms with JavaScript, you should absolutely opt to use a web worker if they're available in the browsers you're targeting. The result is both a better and faster experience for end users. Let's take a look at working with a simple worker that returns the user's information from the `Navigator` object in their browser (see Listing 6-6).

Listing 6-6. Web Workers Ad Example (Main Script)

```
<!DOCTYPE HTML>
<head>
<script>
if (!!window.Worker) {
        var worker = new Worker('worker.js');

        // Receive the message from the worker thread
        worker.onmessage = function (event) {
                var workerMsg = event.data;
                document.write(workerMsg);
        };
} else {
        console.log('No Worker Support')
}
</script>
</head>
<body>
</body>
</html>


//Code in worker.js file
for (property in navigator) {
        postMessage("<b>" + property+"</b>: "+navigator[property]+"<br>");
}
```

From our example, you can see that, instead of setting up the `worker.js` script file by writing `<script src=worker.js></script>`, we create a new worker object and pass it the location of the script file by writing `var worker = new Worker('worker.js');`.

Next, the worker script will run through its `for` loop, which will return all the properties of the user's `Navigator` object through the `postMessage` call. Back at the main script, we handle the `postMessage` call by writing `worker.onmessage;` and through the event, we call a new variable, `workerMsg`, which we set to `event.data`.

Last, we simply output the results to the DOM for you to see, but in reality, this information could be used for other purposes more specifically tied to an ad server, such as for detecting a user's user agent, platform, app name, and version number.

There are many ways to leverage a worker. Perhaps you want do some complicated math or a repeating animation function; either way keep in mind that performance is ultimately everything, and providing a snappy experience goes a long way in ads, as well as on the Web in general.

▒ **Note**   Web workers do not have access to the following JavaScript objects: DOM, Window, Document, and Parent Objects.

CORS

Have you ever introduced people from two different crowds to each other? Rather than have them chat for the first time without you, you'd typically facilitate the introduction and conversation to ensure that the parties get to feel comfortable with each other. The same principal applies with resource sharing on the Web. Cross-origin resource sharing (CORS) defines how browsers (clients) and servers (hosts) can and should communicate with each other when accessing resources from different origins using normal HTTP requests.

CORS allows both the browser and the server to comprehend enough information about each other to determine if the request or response should happen or not. This means some configuration is needed at the server or host level as well as at that of the client. CORS is a specification that permits open-access resource sharing across domain requests without limitations of the "same-domain" policy, which authorizes scripts running on pages originating from the same site to access each other's methods and properties.

Let's face it, we often need to request data from a resource that doesn't have the same domain as the one we are requesting from. For this, there are workarounds, such as using JSON-P or a custom proxy service, but this takes more operational time to develop—plus wouldn't it be nice to just request what you need, when you need it, and know that the source can be trusted by the client and you're allowed to do so? To go back to the example above, since our two friends met, they should feel comfortable enough to call upon each other in the future.

▒ **Note**   There is more information on JSON-P at `http://json-p.org`.

CORS in Advertising

Let's say an ad hosted from DoubleClick wants to access some information on the site `www.nytimes.com`. This type of integrated publisher operation is typically a roadblock ad experience, one that would take a lot of time for both the creative agency, publisher and ad server to develop and pull off. Since the publisher and ad server reside on different domains, any scripts or access to scripts between the two traditionally wouldn't be allowed under the browser's same-origin policy, covered earlier.

However, by supporting CORS on the server and client, the `www.nytimes.com` domain can add a few special response headers that allow DoubleClick to access the site's data respectfully. This could mean the ad served by DoubleClick, a third party ad server, could rely on scripts hosted by the *New York Times* or even parse data from its site—essentially, becoming "whitelisted" for all future data transfers or just for the life of the campaign. Think back to our `canvas` examples in Chapter 4, where we couldn't reference images from an external domain. Now with CORS, we can! We can pull images from an external domain cleanly, without any errors thrown into the browser with CORS enabled. This gets really interesting when ad servers become "whitelisted," with certain data providers and publishers allowing them to pull information from various trusted sources. Let's look at Listing 6-7, where we use CORS to request data from one domain in order to display the response information.

Listing 6-7. CORS API Example

```
<!DOCTYPE HTML>
<head>
<script>
var call = new XMLHttpRequest();
var url = 'http://free.worldweatheronline.com/feed/weather.ashx?q=19043&format=json&num_of_
days=3&key=XXXXXXXXXXXXX';

function callOtherDomain() {
  if(call) {
    call.open('GET', url, true);
    call.withCredentials = true;
    call.onreadystatechange = gotThatData;
    call.send();
  }
}

function gotThatData (data) {
      console.log(data)
}

callOtherDomain()
</script>
</head>
<body>
</body>
</html>
```

From the listing, you can see we're using the XMLHttpRequest objectXMLHttpRequest object by writing var call = new XMLHttpRequest();. From there, we set up another variable, url, which will point to the free weather service, where we're trying to access the information. Next, we set up a function, callOtherDomain(), which will handle making the request to the domain and providing a callback to the function gotThatData(), where we simply log out the response (if there is one).

If you're following along in your browser and make that request, first, you'll need your free API key for the requestrequest to www.worldweatheronline.com, but after that, you should see something pretty interesting in the browser's console—something like what you see in Figure 6-8.

Figure 6-8. *Demonstration of a failed CORS request*

This message is pretty much telling you that the domain of the weather service is not set up, with CORS using the origin of my localhost domain. If this weren't the case, you'd be able to see the response data in our browser.

For leveraging APIs where ads will need to pull in information from other domains, this means the server's response headers will need to include some basic access by having Access-Control-Allow-Origin: * (for public) or Access-Control-Allow-Origin: http://example.com (for protected). In the first example, it's a wildcard, thus allowing any domain to access the information. In the latter, the URL will match whichever domain you're making requests from with the ad content. If that domain doesn't match the **access-control header, the response to the ad will fail.**

Another interesting concern involves users' personal and private data. This is **an important topic in any form of advertising, especially when sharing data between domains, so be sure to check with the publisher and data provider to ensure their terms of services (TOS) comply with the features you intend to use in your advertisements. There are plenty of web services out there that you can "technically" use, but the last thing you want to worry about is a lawsuit!**

Also, be sure, when you are working with the publisher for these kinds of rich integrations, to obtain a test page, but ensure that the test page is hosted on the same domain as the live page and represents the experience as closely as possible on the day of launch. If you're going to be posting and requesting data between the ad server and the publisher's and data provider's domains, they'll all need CORS access privileges to do so. I've seen many campaigns get "whitelisted" to a sandbox or test account just to have the thing go belly up once it went live because the content was hosted on a different domain.

Finally, keep in mind that CORS is in a working draft spec, but it's quickly showing adoption in all of the major browsers, as outlined by Caniuse (`http://caniuse.com/#feat=cors`). There's more information on the CORS spec at `www.w3.org/TR/cors`. While you're at it, take a deep dive into enabling CORS on your server by visiting `http://enable-cors.org`.

Microdata

Just in case you wanted to extend HTML5 a bit more, the microdata API adds a supplementary layer of semantics to your HTML markup. With this added information, search engines, browsers, and machine readers can mine through all the metadata in your markup and ultimately provide a richer and more adaptable experience for different devices, including those that can assist special-needs individuals, if this information is made available by the developer. Microdata uses simple name/value pairs in markup attributes to define items. It can be really helpful in dynamic advertising or asset tagging to learn semantically when a value was last updated—or even to simply keep track of changes to a creative. In the following example, using the `itemprop=date`, you can timestamp directly into the ad's markup and have specific information to parse or filter at a later time. Let's take a look at some sample markup (see Listing 6-8) that may be included in a dynamic retail ad selling drink products.

Listing 6-8. Microdata Example

```
<!DOCTYPE html>
<html lang="en">
<head>
<meta charset=utf-8>
<body>
<span itemprop=products>
<span itemprop=name><a itemprop=url href="http://www.retailer.com/soda">Soda</a></span>
<time itemprop=date datetime="2012-06-04">Last Updated</time><span itemprop=name><a itemprop=url
href="http://www.retailer.com/juice">Juice</a></span>
<time itemprop=date datetime="2012-06-14">Last Updated</time><span itemprop=name><a itemprop=url
href="http://www.retailer.com/milk">Milk</a></span>
<time itemprop=date datetime="2012-06-05">Last Updated</time><span itemprop=name><a itemprop=url
href="http://www.retailer.com/beer">Beer</a></span>
<time itemprop=date datetime="2012-06-10">Last Updated</time>
</span>
</body>
</html>
```

Now you can parse through all the `itemprop=products` nodes in the markup while referencing the `itemprop=date` and `datetime` attributes. Anywhere you see a dated product different from the current date, you know that the product hasn't been updated. This is also good practice for accessible rich Internet application (ARIA); though it's not (at least not yet, as of late 2012) a standard for web advertising, it's still great practice for content development on the web. For more information on the microdata API or ARIA, see www.w3.org/TR/microdata/#using-the-microdata-dom-api and www.w3.org/TR/wai-aria.

Summary

In this chapter, we only scratched the large surface of each of these useful and powerful APIs. In order to find out more and get under the hood of each, go dig into the code and experiment with what's possible. All of these APIs and similar technologies still to come can be classified as the modern Web and they will affect how advertising is created in the future.

There were a lot of APIs covered in this chapter, and honestly, if I were to list all the other APIs that are closely related to HTML5, this chapter alone could be a very big book. Just know that browsers are developing very quickly, and the competition in the market is enormous. It will take a while before these emerging features acquire a standard from groups in the W3C and WHATWG, and it's often hard for these committees to keep up! That being said, bookmark as much useful information as you can, and use online tools like http://html5please.com to ease your development woes.

As this chapter closes, you should know that there is one other API we haven't yet discussed, an API so large and groundbreaking that it is justified in having its own chapter. The media API is that API, and it's a large part of the true HTML5 specification. This API alone has caused many arguments, so-called Flash vs. HTML5 wars, and overall confusion on the Web over the past couple of years. The next chapter will focus on arguably the most prevalent feature in HTML5: native audio and video support inside the browser.

CHAPTER 7

■ ■ ■

HTML5 Media

In this chapter, you will learn how to deploy video within your ads across browsers using the new HTML5 video element. I'll also cover failover support to a plug-in when browsers do not recognize the new video element. There are a lot of things to take notice of when working with video, including browser support, transcoding, compression, delivery, and much more. This chapter will not make you an expert, but it will give you the platform to educate yourself so you can make smarter decisions when dealing with video alongside web standards.

Back in the day, Flash was used for beautiful cross-browser video experiences, independent of operating system. Regardless if you were deploying video to Mac users who supported QuickTime or Windows users who supported Windows Media Player, Flash was a ubiquitous option for deploying the video once and reaching everyone with one universally accepted format, FLV. Because the Flash Player was ubiquitous across all desktop screens, this created a video solution that would run flawlessly across the ecosystem. However, with the emerging phone and tablet markets, marketers and creative developers are now faced with building a "browser-only" solution using HTML5's new video element. With HTML5, video is now a first-class member of the browser's architecture. That means video is now part of the HTML specification, just like paragraphs and divs are.

Prior to my development endeavors, I was heavily involved with video production and postproduction, so I know the great lengths that content creators go to in order to achieve great quality within their productions. The knowledge of formats, codecs, and math needed when dealing with video online can get exhausting, so I'll cover the formats that browsers can decode as well as offer useful tips along the way. If you're confused about which video formats work in which browsers, what codecs are and how they're used to obtain the best quality, or how to follow publisher and device specifications accurately, this chapter will quickly make sense of it all with a focus on industry terminology. This chapter will explain in detail how to develop, design, and optimize digital media content for HTML5 browsers and devices. Let's begin!

HTML5 Video

In this section, I'll discuss the new APIs for controlling and handling video playback in HTML5, which undoubtedly is one of the biggest enhancements of the new specification. The HTML5 Video API has spawned a large "Flash is dead" debate, causing much turmoil and confusion in the Web and advertising industries. As you've learned, Flash (specifically video, with its rich feature set and player ubiquity, such as GPU acceleration video playback, adaptive bitrate streaming, and digital rights management protection for content creators) has long been the king of web advertising. However, with HTML5 now allowing for native video support, do you need to rely on Flash anymore?

When HTML5 video burst on the scene in 2007/2008 with the introduction of the Apple iPhone and later the iPad, publishers and content owners panicked to figure out how to make their video content available and accessible on the new devices; currently, if you want to reach people with your video content, you need to be thinking about HTML5 video as well as Flash. This is especially true when you're targeting people with older operating systems and browsers (such as IE8) as well as those on mobile and tablet devices.

You most likely know that having a video presence in your next digital marketing campaign is very important. The current digital video market is huge, about $4+ billion in 2012, and showing no signs of slowing up anytime soon. But how can you provide video content across screens, devices, and browsers in this new modern Web? HTML5 video is big news for any content producer, publisher, and designer because by implementing a simple video tag in your HTML markup, you can now create a video playback controller with the upmost of ease. Before I showcase the simplicity, I'll review with you how it was achieved using Flash. Listing 7-1 shows a sample video using this method.

Listing 7-1. Flash Video Playback Example

```
<div id="flashContent">
<object classid="clsid:d27cdb6e-ae6d-11cf-96b8-444553540000" width="640" height="360" id="VideoTest"
align="middle">
<param name="movie" value=" VideoTest.swf" />
<param name="quality" value="high" />
<param name="bgcolor" value="#ffffff" />
<param name="play" value="true" />
<param name="loop" value="true" />
<param name="wmode" value="window" />
<param name="scale" value="showall" />
<param name="menu" value="true" />
<param name="devicefont" value="false" />
<param name="salign" value="" />
<param name="allowScriptAccess" value="sameDomain" />
<!--[if !IE]>-->
<object type="application/x-shockwave-flash" data="VideoTest.swf" width="640" height="360">
        <param name="movie" value="VideoTest.swf" />
        <param name="quality" value="high" />
        <param name="bgcolor" value="#ffffff" />
        <param name="play" value="true" />
        <param name="loop" value="true" />
        <param name="wmode" value="window" />
        <param name="scale" value="showall" />
        <param name="menu" value="true" />
        <param name="devicefont" value="false" />
        <param name="salign" value="" />
        <param name="allowScriptAccess" value="sameDomain" />
        <!--<![endif]-->
                <a href="http://www.adobe.com/go/getflash">
                <img src="http://www.adobe.com/images/shared/download_buttons/get_flash_player.gif"
        alt="Get Adobe Flash player" /></a>
        <!--[if !IE]>-->
</object>
<!--<![endif]-->
</object>
</div>
```

I think you'd agree that's a lot of code to just show a video on the screen! Now, to implement an HTML5 video element within your ad creative, you simply create the video element within the DOM by writing the following:

```
<video></video>
```

Next, you'll need to include some attributes to customize the video experience for your particular use case. In the following example, I've included a source, a height attribute, and a width attribute:

```
<video src='yourVideoFile.mp4' height='640' width='360'></video>
```

By writing this, I've instructed the browser to render an HTML5 video element to play back the file yourVideoFile.mp4 at the dimensions 640x360. If you want to include video controls, you simply add another attribute by writing the following:

```
<video controls src='yourVideoFile.mp4' height='640' width='360'></video>
```

The browser will now render the player's controls. Otherwise, you can keep the controls hidden and create your own. You can do this by using CSS to style the control elements and by using JavaScript to handle the video's behavior. Obviously, this method is much more streamlined than the Flash-based example.

Let's first take a look at the markup that drives HTML5 video and deconstruct its syntax, and then I'll get into the nitty-gritty of development. Consider the code in Listing 7-2.

Listing 7-2. HTML5 Video Playback Example

```
<html>
<head></head>
<body>
<video>
        <source src="sample.mp4" type='video/mp4; codecs="avc1.42E01E, mp4a.40.2"' />
        <source src=" sample.webm" type='video/webm; codecs="vp8, vorbis"' />
</video>
</body>
</html>
```

The preceding code uses the new HTML5 video tag along with the necessary source tags, which allows the browser to call on the supported video file. Ideally, there would be one supported file format that every browser can handle. If this were the case, having the video's source inline would work as well, as demonstrated in the following example:

```
<video src="sample.mp4"></video>
```

It's important to make sure that the server hosting and delivering your files has the correct MIME type set to deliver the file format for each video file. Also, be sure to specify the type attribute so the user's browser doesn't download files it cannot play. Essentially, dictating a type with a MIME type and codec allows the browser to effectively choose which file it needs.

So, you may be asking, "What happens if my advertising campaign needs to reach the widest audience possible? Including support for older IE versions?" Simply, you really have two options: either use Google's Chrome frame or have a Flash failback.

Google's Chrome frame injects a Webkit rendering engine inside IE browsers, which gives you the ability to render HTML5 content inside the older IE environments. Alternatively, having a Flash failback will allow your users to have HTML5 video first, and in the event the video tag isn't supported, the previous method will be used via the object tag for a SWF file.

HTML5 video is a great advancement to the browser. The video element supports an array of features and attributes, and support within the current browser market is almost stable. However, as with all emerging things, it can have a few inconsistencies, and it doesn't stop at the video element itself for its fragmentation. Support across browsers, screens, and devices requires a multitude of source video files to actually play back the video asset from within the HTML5 video tag. As you may have guessed, it takes some time and money to create, size, transcode, and host all of the different asset versions, and if you're talking about multibitrate streaming, you have even more to create (more on these topics later). A great link to visit is http://caniuse.com/video, which can better help you develop video across browsers.

Content Creation

Creative agencies are shooting video exclusively for the various screens. No longer do you see repurposed broadcast television spots in online ad units. They'll typically do a roadblock that takes over a good portion of the user's screen with full interactive video and sound. Others specifically produce the spot for the desktop and shoot their actors in an environment that would seamlessly work on the various screens. In any event, digital advertising is all about making an impact creatively, and most impactful ads have video in their arsenal. Now that you have an idea of what goes into building an HTML5 video element, the really awesome part comes when you integrate the video element alongside other emerging web technologies like the canvas, SVG, and CSS3. Keeping this thought in mind, you can create some amazingly rich features and graphics in your next online campaign. However, before you head down that path, there are a few things you'll want to use with the video element as well as a few you'll want to avoid. Let's take a look at each, starting with the things you should use.

What You Should Use

A poster image is the static image (or an animated GIF) that is initially viewable before video playback begins. I like to think of this as your CTA message to entice the user to click and play your video content. The poster image isn't a required attribute, but in terms of advertising, you should use it so that if your user never clicks your video, they'll still get a static (or animated) image or message.

Next are controls; controls are the play/pause controls, mute/unmute, the scrubber bar, the current time indicator (CTI), and full-screen icons that your browser natively uses with the video tag. Adding controls to your video is simple, as follows:

```
<video src="sample.mp4" controls></video>
```

If you are using video for anything other than animation purposes, you should make sure your controls are turned on. Don't worry if you dislike the native controls the browser uses; you can always skin them via CSS and add their functionality via JavaScript to control the video. However, in the event you choose to use CSS and JavaScript for your controls, be sure to remove the controls attribute in the video tag. Because video is now a first-class citizen and part of the DOM, you can also style it with the latest CSS3 properties such as reflections, masks, gradients, transforms, transitions, and animations (assuming your browser supports them). You can even use SVG and SMIL for animations on top of the video element. Perhaps you want to blur the video using SVG filters while it's animating across the screen or have the video element swing open like a gate door on a fence. There are so many tips and tricks you can implement to have your video perform better and more uniquely in your next campaign.

What You Shouldn't Use

When using video in your next campaign, you should almost never use the loop attribute, which plays your video over and over again. This would create a poor user experience and have the publisher or ad-serving company red flag it before the campaign ever going live.

Second is the use and reliance on autoplay. Autoplay is a great feature for in-banner forced video that acts like animation, but some mobile devices that leverage a cell network or data plan, such as the Apple iPad and iPhone, restrict the autoplay attribute from working in order to protect customers' data plans from exceeding the limits for content they didn't even choose to view. If you do in fact use autoplay video within your desktop advertisements, be sure to have the audio off by default. No one wants to go to a site to read or watch content and have advertising blasting with full sound. That's a poor experience for every user!

Another thing to be mindful of is removing small type in video. If you don't do this, your video's copy (depending on browser zoom level) can look pretty poor and create unwanted text aliasing.

Also, if you're animating the `video` element, make every attempt to keep the video player on a whole pixel. This will again eliminate any unwanted aliasing to the video player.

Finally, keep a close eye on CPU and GPU loads for larger data rate videos. In fact, if you're noticing the browser slugging during playback, chances are the system resources are being taxed too much for the video you're playing back. My suggestion with this is to optimize your video further (more on that later).

In the end, it's really up to the tools you use when creating your online video content. Keep in mind that HTML5 video is just a way of playing the video content inside the browser without a plug-in. How you create that creative content is entirely up to you and the requirements of the campaign. I suggest using some of the following tools. For high-end motion graphics and keying out footage shot on a green/blue-screen, I like Adobe's After Effects (`http://adobe.com/products/aftereffects.html`). For 3D needs, I use Maxon's Cinema 4D (`http://maxon.net/products/cinema-4d-studio`). Using both together can create amazing videos that can be deployed to any screen. Using tools like Adobe's Media Encoder (`http://adobe.com/products/mediaencoder.html`), Apple's QuickTime Pro (`http://apple.com/us/product/D3380Z/A/quicktime-7-pro-for-mac-os-x`), and others gives designers and developers robust features, including setting compression, size, frame rate, and others, for tweaking their video content to their liking as well as publisher requirements.

Encoding and Transcoding

Now that you understand the content creation part of the video asset as well as the basic building blocks for the HTML5 `video` tag, you can move into the complex world of video encoding and transcoding. In short, *encoding* is the initial compression technique used for video, usually from a postproduction video house, and *transcoding* is transferring a video from one format to another.

Encoding

In the Flash days of online advertising, it was pretty common to take a raw MOV or AVI file and transcode it to an FLV video, suitable for playback within a SWF. For initial encoding tasks, this will often be a *lossless* compression, which means the core fidelity of the file is preserved within the output file. This *lossless* technique is more or less for transferring the file when bandwidth limitations are not a concern, and the output is ideal for archiving or playback truest to the source video.

Transcoding

Transcoding, on the other hand, is commonly a *lossy* compression technique. Lossy is typically used when you are generating a video file for playback over the Web, usually for transferring over the HTTP or RTMP protocol. Lossy does not maintain the quality that the original source video file had; it sacrifices some of the overall video quality for a much smaller file size. Really good compression techniques can be used to maintain a really great-quality picture at a very small footprint as well, and I'll discuss some of them in the following sections.

Encoding and transcoding video are where most of the time is spent with video on the Web, and you'll learn quickly that video on the Web is only as good as the source file you use for the transcode. We call this the "garbage in, garbage out" rule. Basically, you cannot enhance the quality and playback of video that has been severely compressed or altered poorly. Video compression is much like image compression; once the data is lost in the file, it's gone for good! Encoding/transcoding video for web delivery is a science as much as it is an art. Seriously, a full book could be written just on the techniques, theory, and practice behind them (and many have been). This section is not geared to make you a compression expert but to give you a high-level strategy when working with video in your next HTML5 campaign. Let's take a look at some of the settings you can tweak to your advantage when working with your videos.

Multipass

Multipass encoding, also known as *two-pass* or even *three-pass*, is a technique for encoding and transcoding video into another format using multiple passes to maintain the best quality. Basically, the video encoder/transcoder initially examines the video before it applies any compression: that's one-pass. Next, the subsequent video passes happen two or three times from start to finish, and every frame in between, to apply the compression after the first pass has given some guidance to the encoder on how to do so. While examining the file, the encoder creates information about the source video and writes that information to a log file; once that information is written, the encoder can then look up the information and determine the optimal way to adjust the video quality within the predetermined limits the user has set for the process.

Multipass encoding is used only in variable bitrate encoding (VBRs) jobs, since constant bitrate (CBR) encoding doesn't offer any "bend or give" for the encoder to regulate the available bitrate for each frame. I like to think of this process as the difference between a "talking head" video and an "action sequence." The talking head video typically has little movement, so bitrate can be consistent across the frames, and typically a one-pass job will suffice. An action sequence needs to adjust its available bitrate as the frames in the scene become more complex with different color values, blends, and/or heavy motion blurs. This sequence will typically need a two- or even three-pass to get the desired quality and size within the specified video bitrate. This multipass technique creates better overall quality for variable scene differences that some videos may have.

Bitrate

Bitrate is typically one of those predetermined user settings developers adjust when transcoding video for the Web. Bitrate is really the amount of information stored in the video, and in most cases, the higher the bitrate, the sharper the video quality is. This is of course not true if you take a heavily compressed video asset like an FLV and transcode it to an uncompressed codec. The compression algorithm will write more data to the overall video without increasing the picture fidelity, but it's essentially overkill because the picture information was already lost prior to the compression job. This practice will give you a significantly higher bitrate in a video that has already been compromised. Bitrate plays a huge factor in the delivery of HTML5 video, as I'll discuss later with adaptive bitrate streaming.

Deinterlace

In traditional broadcast television, the moving picture was transported from a station head-end in an interlaced picture format. This means the picture would actually be made up of multiple individual scan lines where every two or three frames of video would be a blend of the previous and next frame, thus creating an *interlaced* image. With newer televisions and computer monitor technologies, the video picture on the Web is transported in a progressive matter, which means every frame is an individual picture delivered to the screen at one time. Confusing? Figure 7-1 explains. By looking at the image on the left, you can see that there is a blurring or ghosting effect. This effect is the interlaced picture. On the right, you see the image *deinterlaced*, or progressive, which creates no blurring effect, because the image is full-frame for one second. For delivery on the Web, it's best to use the progressive approach.

Figure 7-1. The visual differences between interlaced video footage (left) and progressive (right)

FPS

Frames per second (FPS) are the individual frames of video that make up the entire video sequence. Think of this as a group of images that make up one second of video. Did you ever make a flipbook when you were a kid, where you draw the same picture on every sheet of paper with slight adjustments so that when you flip through, it creates a seamless animation? This is essentially what video is doing. If you remember the discussion on CSS sprite sheets in Chapter 5, the same principal applies here. For the deinterlaced video, the typical FPS is 23.976 or 29.97 because of the blended frame occurrence, whereas the typical FPS of progressive video is 24 or 30 because of full individual images being rendered without the blend. Video with lots of fast-moving action will generally need a higher frame rate to combat the unwanted shuddering effect, and the same rule applies if you are looking for super-crisp slow-motion video. Some high-end cameras shoot frames of video upwards to a few thousand frames per second, which can create really amazing slow-motion footage to be used in a creative. Again, for web playback, you'll typically want to use 24 or 30 FPS.

Aspect Ratio

Much like images, videos have a width property and a height property. In video, much like images, it's important to maintain the proportion of the original dimensions. In videos, *aspect ratios* are the proportional relationship between its width and its height. Most common aspect ratios in web video are 16:9 for wide-screen format and 4:3 for standard format. This proportional relationship is directly tied to the size of the pixels within the video, because they can be square or rectangle. You will often hear this being referenced as "sixteen by nine" or "four by three." It's important to preserve the aspect ratio of the video you are transcoding because this keeps a one-to-one relationship between the source video asset and the transcoded file. However, in some cases, your creative will require you to serve your video asset into size not designed in 16:9 or 4:3. In this case, you will use a technique called *letterboxing* or *pillarboxing*, which adds black bars where there is empty space within the allotted video space. Figure 7-2 showcases a proportionally correct video with letterboxing and pillarboxing applied for 16:9 and 4:3 aspect ratios.

Figure 7-2. *The differences between letterbox video and pillarbox*

The most common scenario for this is when you serve video into an ad unit of varying sizes or a publisher's video player. If the advertiser's video asset is 16:9 and the player environment is 4:3, you'll notice black bars or letterboxing on the top and bottom of the video to preserve the proportion of the video.

Tools

Before I dig into the big topic of video codecs, you may be wondering why you should learn all of this video-related information when working with HTML5. Well, video is by far the most prevalent medium in online advertising, and ensuring optimal video playback will win your clients over. So, I'll cover the different video properties to be aware of as well as the different codec/formats to be on the lookout for in the space. It all boils down to developing and delivering optimal HTML5 video for the fragmented browser space. Let's look at some of the tools for creating HTML5 video before getting into the implementation.

Why are there all of these different video settings, variations, and fragmented browser and device support? Well, the patents, royalties (i.e., money), and compression quality are what keeps something from being open source and free to use. I like to think of it like this: whenever you have a really great product, you'd typically charge for the use of it even though there are free alternatives. For instance, you pay for cable television because it's a better quality and provides more channels, as opposed to standard over-the-air antenna broadcast where you get limited channels and the broadcast is of poor quality. Currently, these fragmented codecs and video formats are something you need to tolerate in the HTML5 space if you want to deploy your video content to the widest user base. There are many tools to help you do this for serving online video. Many of them are used to convert videos into their appropriate formats using free or purchased programs on your computer. This includes but is not limited to open source FFMPEG (http://ffmpeg.org), FireOgg (http://firefogg.org), QuickTime Pro (http://apple.com/quicktime), and Adobe Media Encoder (http://adobe.com/products/mediaencoder.html), and even more robust video applications such as Adobe After Effects (http://adobe.com/products/aftereffects.html), Avid (http://avid.com), and Apple Final Cut Pro (http://apple.com/finalcutpro).

FFMpeg is by far the most robust, and it's open source, which means you can universally transcode/encode into various different formats easily and freely. This tool can pretty much convert any video and audio format into anything suitable for various screens. If you're comfortable with the command line, I strongly suggest using FFMpeg. It's quite possibly the most robust video conversion tool available. Plus, there are many plug-ins and libraries for converting to different formats. Always check with your publishers because they'll require certain-sized video assets for their players, and be sure to check out their specs frequently and adapt correctly.

Video Codecs

Now that you understand what goes into video encoding and transcoding, I'll talk about the video codecs you have at your disposable and what you will be using when leveraging HTML5 video. Codecs can be a bit confusing because there are so many to choose from and all come with certain variations and browser support. A *video codec* is software that compresses the video for your desired needs, and as you've just learned with all of the previous video properties, all of them are configurable using video certain codecs.

This section is not intended to make you an expert in video codecs, but it will give you an idea of what to look out for the next time you want to include HTML5 video in your campaigns and when you come across video assets from various creative agencies. Codecs have specific browser and device support and require a time-consuming process to deliver video correctly to multiple users. Figure 7-3 demonstrates the proliferation of video codecs throughout the last 12 years.

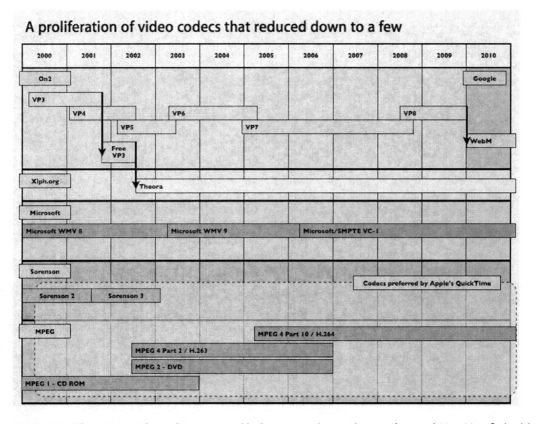

Figure 7-3. The various video codecs supported by browser and manufacturer (source: http://appleinsider.com)

This may look confusing, but as you can see, most codecs have come and gone, much like many other technologies, and for the remainder of this section, I'll discuss only the codec technologies that remain apparent in today's market of HTML5 video, which are MP4 (H.264), WebM (VP8), and OGV (Theora). I'll exclude VC-1 because at the time of this writing, no browser supports this codec/wrapper variation.

H.264

I'll now discuss probably the most popular video codec on the modern Web, MPEG's H.264. The H.264 codec is a highly optimized codec that offers supreme compression with little quality loss to the overall video. H.264 can provide great lossy quality at relatively low bitrates. H.264 comes with many adjustable parameters and features—so many in fact that if you look up H.264, you will be amazed at what this codec is capable of doing. However, you need to be specifically aware of its profiles, which are baseline, main, and high. Certain devices such as older iPhones and iPod touches can support only a baseline profile, where other high-end devices, such as your desktop computer and Blu-ray players, support main to high profiles. The profile's level is measured in a scale between 1 and currently 5.2, and as the profile level increases, the bitrate and usually the quality do as well.

Note   To learn more about H.264 video, I suggest reading the works of Fabio Sonnati at
`http://sonnati.wordpress.com`.

H.264 is pushed hard by Apple, Microsoft, and various other large companies, and it's currently supported by Apple, Microsoft, and Google in their respective browsers, although Google has mentioned that it will stop the support for the codec in support for its VP8 alternative (more on this in the following section). However, as of this writing, Google still supports it in releases of Chrome. In addition, Mozilla has even discussed supporting H.264 because of the lack of support for its supported open source codec, Ogg Theora (more on this in the following section). H.264 also has royalty-free open source variations on its sophisticated encoding algorithms called X264 (`http://x264.nl`).

Apple, which is a major supporter of the H.264 codec because, it's the only codec supported in its Safari browser, recommends the encoding settings shown in Figure 7-4 for serving to iDevices via Safari.

HTTP Streaming Encode Recommendations

16:9 Aspect Ratio

	Dimensions	Total Bit Rate	Video Bit Rate	Keyframe	Restrict Profile to:	iPod Touch Gens 2, 3, 4 iPhone 3G 3GS	iPhone 4 iPad 1, 2	Apple TV 2
						WORKS ON		
CELL	480x320	64	na	na	na	*	*	*
CELL	416x234	150	110	30	Baseline, 3.0	*	*	*
CELL	416x234	240	200	45	Baseline, 3.0	*	*	*
CELL	416x234	440	400	90	Baseline, 3.0	*	*	*
WIFI	640x360	640	600	90	Baseline, 3.0	*	*	*
WIFI	640x360	1240	1200	90	Main, 3.1		*	*
WIFI	960x540	1840	1800	90	Main, 3.1		*	*
WIFI	1280x720	2540	2500	90	Main, 3.1		*	*
WIFI	1280x720	4540	4500	90	Main, 3.1		*	*

4:3 Aspect Ratio

	Dimensions	Total Bit Rate	Video Bit Rate	Keyframe	Restrict Profile to:			
CELL	480x320	64	na	na	na	*	*	*
CELL	400x300	150	110	30	Baseline, 3.0	*	*	*
CELL	400x300	240	200	45	Baseline, 3.0	*	*	*
CELL	400x300	440	400	90	Baseline, 3.0	*	*	*
WIFI	640x480	640	600	90	Baseline, 3.0	*	*	*
WIFI	640x480	1240	1200	90	Main, 3.1		*	*
WIFI	960x720	1840	1800	90	Main, 3.1		*	*
WIFI	960x720	2540	2500	90	Main, 3.1		*	*
WIFI	1280x960	4540	4500	90	Main, 3.1		*	*

* Frame Rate: Assumes current frame rate is 29.97. For other frame rates see below:

For	For 150k Use	For 240k Use	For All Else Use
30	10	12 to 15	30
60	10	12 to 15	30
29.97	10	12 to 15	29.97
59.94	10	12 to 15	29.97
24	8	10 to 12	24
23.98	8	10 to 12	23.98
25	8	10 to 12	25
50	8	10 to 12	25

***Figure 7-4.** Apple's encoding recommendations for iOS devices*

This chart is incredibly important to keep an eye on when you deploy your video to mobile iOS devices. Because just as the overall video landscape is fragmented among codecs, Apple's own devices require specific adjustments to compensate for its older devices such as iPhone 3G, not to mention WiFi versus cell network connection. This only bloats the time to develop video that deploys across screens and devices.

Keep in mind also that H.264 is not free software; it's owned and patented by many different companies, including Microsoft, and it's managed by a consortium called MPEG-LA. Apple pays a license for every computer, device, camera, and accessory that it produces that can encode and decode H.264 video. Think about this the next time you purchase an Apple product, because a bit of what you're paying for is the ability to use the H.264 technology.

VP8

Another popular codec in the HTML5 video space is VP8. Once a technology from On2 and later acquired by Google, it was renamed to the WebM codec. Google has been pushing this as the de facto codec to use when delivering video using HTML5 in modern browsers. However, for it to take full shape, browser vendors need to adopt this as the standard for their video requirements. As you've just learned, Apple and Microsoft haven't taken much to WebM because of their longtime support for H.264. VP8/WebM is comparable to H.264 in its encoding algorithms and quality, but more importantly it comes with no license costs, which is a huge win for open web standards and the browsers such as Firefox, Chrome, and Opera that support it.

Theora

Although H.264 is an open standard, it is not free. It is based upon a pool of video compression and related technology patents contributed by various companies in exchange for "fair, reasonable, and nondiscriminatory" licensing fees. Mozilla, Opera, and other free and open source advocates opposed the use of any technology that might require licensing fees to produce or distribute web content because doing otherwise would go against their support for the open Web. Because of this, they've relied on an open source video compression technology in addition to VP8, called Theora from the Xiph foundation. The Ogg Theora war on H.264 ended when HTML5 working group members agreed that rather than defining Ogg Theora or H.264 or anything else as the "baseline" codec for video served via the HTML5 video tag, the decision should be left to the market and to the votes of web users and Internet broadcasters (this obviously created fragmentation). Theora is the old VP3 codec that was used in early versions of Flash Video (FLV). They've taken the older version of that and improved on it; it's not as efficient as H.264, but it's open source.

Historically, HTML has always worked with every other type of media file for images; there is no baseline graphic format. For example, developers decided for themselves whether to use the GIF, JPEG, or PNG format. Modern browsers support them all, and in my eyes video should follow suit.

GOP and Keyframes

In compression techniques, you have what is known as a group of pictures (GOP). This group is dictated by keyframe intervals. If you've ever done any Flash animation or any timeline-based animation work, you know that keyframes are significant or key points in time where something important happens. In video compression, these are the points in video playback in which the encoding/transcoding engine gets a chance to rest and reanalyze the video content to make sure it's on track with the rest of its encoding process. Some codecs support different compression algorithms such as I, P, and B frames.

- *I-frames*: This is the least compressible frame but does not require other frames to decode.

- *P-frames*: This uses information from previous frames to decompress.

- *B-frames*: This uses previous and forward frames of video to obtain a reference and get the highest amount of intelligent compression.

Figure 7-5 shows the video keyframes for different frame types. Keep this information in the back of your mind if your client asks you to optimize their video content for various screens using the HTML5 video element. However, note that certain codecs allow only for specific keyframe settings.

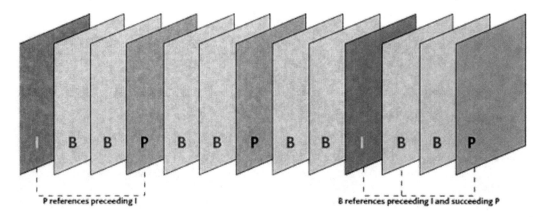

Figure 7-5. I, P, and B frames of compression

It's interesting that compression technology dictates the overall quality and size of the encoded file; people often get concerned about the size of the video, but really it's the size plus the duration. For example, if you have a 6MB file and the duration of the video is 1 minute, that means you have 1MB of data per every 10 seconds of video. If you have a 60MB file for 1 minute of video, you'd have 10MB of data per every 10 seconds, or 1MB per second. So, you need to find a good trade-off between size and duration of your video. Some machines and decoders are simply not fast enough to decode the videos frames at such a quick rate. Often you will see a machine choke on playback if the data rate is too high to process; others with enough power will handle it no problem and provide amazing playback quality. This is also why higher-end graphics cards are used for professional video-editing bays in order to handle the heavy data rate. However, for the Web and HTML5 video, keep a good relationship between size and duration, especially when delivering to devices such as phones and tablets with slower system resources than desktop machines.

The Rule of 16

One last note to touch on in regard to video transcoding is what is known at the "rule of 16." If you haven't already, you'll find a lot of your time when creating video for the Web dealing with different-sized video assets and needing to transcode to different sizes. I mentioned before that there is a certain science to the world of video encoding, and no one is better at that science than video expert Robert Reinhardt. Reinhardt was first to my knowledge to coin the name of this rule. Basically, at a high level, it breaks down the optimal sizes that videos should be converted to when a transcoding job is performed and when a video is decoded by a machine for playback. If you take a look at Figure 7-6, you'll notice that video encoding is best done in multiples of 16 with a decrease in quality going to 8 (better) and 4 (good).

4:3 aspect ratio sizes			16:9 aspect ratio sizes		
Best (16)	Better (8)	Good (4)	Best (16)	Better (8)	Good (4)
640 × 480	608 × 456	624 × 468	1280 × 720	1152 × 648	1216 × 684
576 × 432	544 × 408	592 × 444	1024 × 576	896 × 504	1088 × 612
512 × 384	480 × 360	560 × 420	768 × 432	640 × 360	960 × 540
448 × 336	416 × 312	528 × 396	512 × 288	384 × 216	832 × 468
384 × 288	352 × 264	496 × 372	256 × 144	128 × 72	704 × 396
320 × 240	288 × 216	464 × 348			576 × 324
256 × 192	224 × 168	432 × 324			448 × 252
192 × 144	160 × 120	400 × 300			320 × 180
128 × 96		368 × 276			192 × 108

Figure 7-6. *Robert Reinhardt's chart for optimally sizing video*

Reinhardt's findings reveal that video performs best when the frame width and height use multiples of 16. Keep this in mind when you transcode your next video, and while you can use any width, nonoptimal dimensions can result in reduced quality and dropped frames and can tax the decoding playback more than necessary. To maintain the best output, you should always use a width and height in a multiple of 16, 8, or at the very least 4. The lower your multiple gets, the more that the quality and performance get impacted. A very good tool to bookmark is Reinhardt's video sizer at `http://videorx.com/video-sizer`. This tool allows you to plug in your numbers and get instant feedback on how good or poor your conversion job will end up when using the desired settings. If you're interested in learning more about encoding, transcoding, and compression techniques, I strongly recommend visiting his site (`http://videorx.com/`).

Wrappers

You just learned what you need to know about the codecs for video, so now I will cover the file formats that support each of these flavors. Container formats, or *wrappers*, are the file format that video information gets stored into. This would be your typical MOV, AVI, and FLV file formats. These containers all house encoded video information along with essential metadata information about the file. Wrappers for video are much like PNG, JPEG, and GIF files for images. In fact, they're so identical in HTML markup that it's pretty simple to include video in your browser if you know how to use an `img` tag.

MP4

MP4 is a common web video format for most HTML5 browsers like Apple's Safari, Microsoft's Internet Explorer, and, currently, Google's Chrome. It is essentially the container format that houses the AVC/H.264 codec, as discussed in the previous sections. The file extensions can vary for this container type and can include M4P, M4V, and even Adobe's F4V. Figure 7-7 shows the current browser support at the time of this writing.

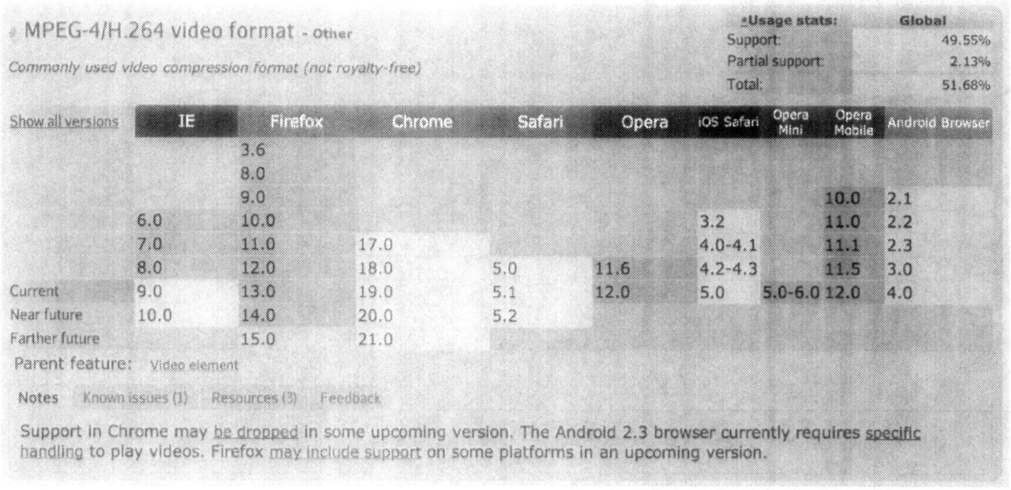

MPEG-4/H.264 video format - Other

Commonly used video compression format (not royalty-free)

Usage stats:	Global
Support:	49.55%
Partial support:	2.13%
Total:	51.68%

Show all versions	IE	Firefox	Chrome	Safari	Opera	iOS Safari	Opera Mini	Opera Mobile	Android Browser
		3.6							
		8.0							
		9.0						10.0	2.1
	6.0	10.0				3.2		11.0	2.2
	7.0	11.0	17.0			4.0-4.1		11.1	2.3
	8.0	12.0	18.0	5.0	11.6	4.2-4.3		11.5	3.0
Current	9.0	13.0	19.0	5.1	12.0	5.0	5.0-6.0	12.0	4.0
Near future	10.0	14.0	20.0	5.2					
Farther future		15.0	21.0						

Parent feature: Video element

Notes   Known issues (1)   Resources (3)   Feedback

Support in Chrome may be dropped in some upcoming version. The Android 2.3 browser currently requires specific handling to play videos. Firefox may include support on some platforms in an upcoming version.

Figure 7-7. *The current browser support for H.264/MP4 videos (source: `http://caniuse.com`)*

MP4 is a common format when working with HTML5 video. In fact, and from my experience, it's the most common format you'll end up dealing with, especially within advertising campaigns running across mobile devices. Advertisers will want to target the growing number of Apple iPhones and iPads in the market, and using MP4 with H.264 is the only way to make that happen.

Note Mobile video typically plays within the device's native video player, not the browser.

WebM

Another video container format is WebM, which, as you learned, houses the open source VP8 codec from Google. Simply put, WebM can provide the same quality as MP4 videos without the penetration on Microsoft and Apple browsers. Moreover, if you are concerned with paying royalties or licensing fees, the WebM format is your best choice since it isn't patent encumbered. WebM is intended for the Web and geared toward easing the video problems on the open Web. Google attempts to provide a high-quality and efficient encoding tool that is free for anyone to use for their web content, and Google is actively working on making WebM the open source standard for delivering audio and video online via the HTML5 `video` tag. At the time of this writing, `http://caniuse.com` outlines support for the WebM format, as represented in Figure 7-8.

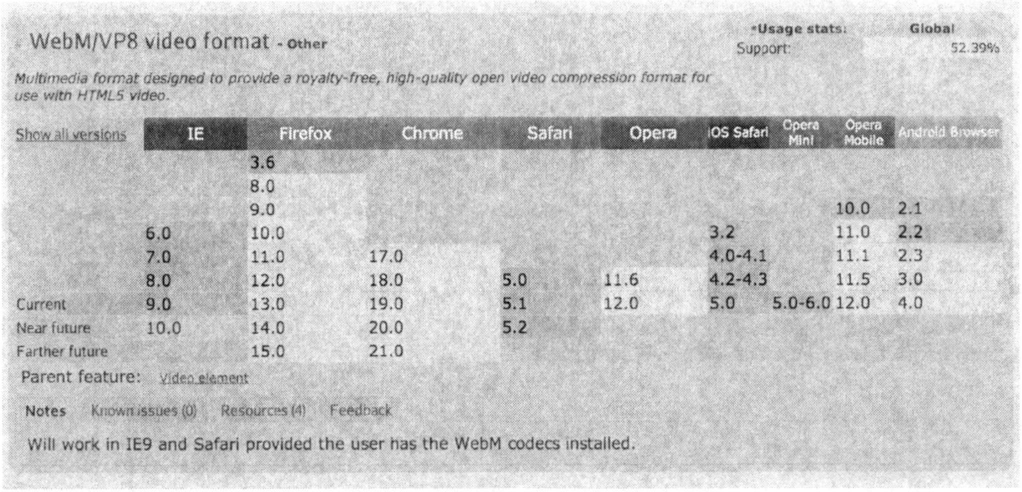

Figure 7-8. The current browser support for VP8/WebM videos (source: `http://caniuse.com`)

If you're interested in learning more about the WebM video container format, I suggest visiting Google's WebM site at `http://webmproject.org/docs/container`. Keep in mind that any video advertisements being served to users of Chrome, Firefox, and Opera can rely on this format safely.

■ **Note**   Users with the VP8/WebM codec installed will be able to view the video on Safari and IE.

OGG

Lastly, there is the OGG video format. OGG is an open container format managed by the open source foundation Xiph. OGG's container formats include OGG, OGV, and OGA, to name a few. Based on the video compression algorithms of Theora and audio compression of Vorbis, OGG aims to create a truly open source video codec/wrapper for anyone to use regardless of royalties or licensing rights. Much like the previous examples, Figure 7-9 outlines the browser support for the OGG video format.

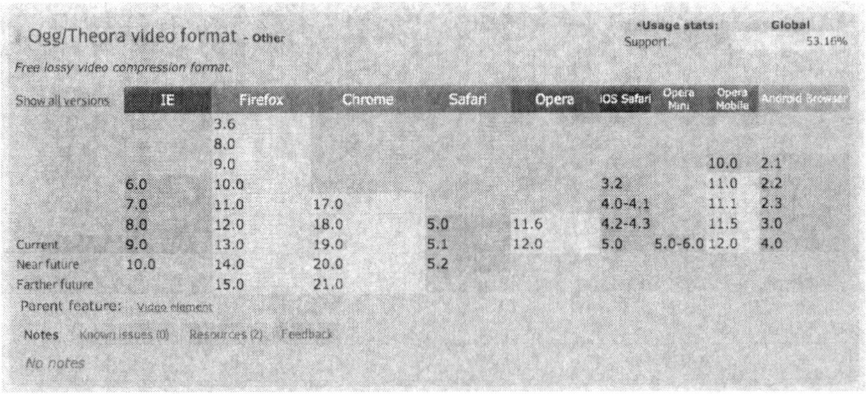

Figure 7-9. The current browser support for Theora/OGG videos (source: `http://caniuse.com`)

From these graphs, I think you can clearly see that Google Chrome is the most robust feature-rich browser when it comes to HTML5 video codec support. However, most of your clients will want to reach across all browsers when using HTML5 video, and while the support for the HTML5 video element is almost 100 percent, the video codec/format that fills that element is still quite fragmented, which requires you to develop to all of those formats for cross-browser penetration. Yes, it's a very time-consuming process indeed.

To support both HTML5-compliant browsers and older ones, it's recommended that you use browser and device detection and degrade gracefully to an alternative video experience, such as a Flash failover by including either an embed or object tag within your video element, as outlined here:

```
<video controls height='640' width='360'>
<source src='yourVideo.mp4' type='video/mp4' />
    <source src='yourVideo.webm' type='video/webm' />
    <! -- Flash Code Here -->
    <embed src='yourVideo.flv' width='640' height='360' quality='high' type='application/x-
shockwave-flash'></embed>
</video>
```

By including the Flash failover code in the video tag, the browser will omit the video tag if it does not recognize it and use the Flash code. Conversely, browsers that support the video element will not render the portion within the video tag, in this case the Flash embed code.

Alpha Support

Alpha video is the transparent portion of the video. Typically a video will be shot on top of a green or blue screen and later *keyed* in postproduction, which is the removal of the green or blue background elements. After the key is done, the video is then exported to a video codec and format that supports the alpha transparency information. This is common in video that overlays page content or provides a seamless integration between ad video content and publisher page content. Figure 7-10 shows the codec "animation" in Apple's QuickTime (QT) 7 Pro and the setting of millions+, which stands for millions of colors; plus, the alpha information is preserved in the video. If you're getting a video file from your client or agency, it's best to test your video by opening it using Apple's QuickTime and press Command+I for Mac or Control+I for Windows, which will open the QT inspector panel.

Figure 7-10. *The millions+ information in Apple's QuickTime Player*

This keying technique knocks out all of the pixels with the color value in question, which is something you see every day and may not even notice. In fact, did you happen to catch last night's weather report on the news? Well, chances are that the meteorologist was standing in front of a green-screen and not an actual map. The big thing to understand here is that this is a huge functional part of video in any medium and, of course, online media. Having video, interactive or not, overtop a publisher page is a necessity in cutting-edge advertising campaigns. Some of the most innovative home-screen takeovers have achieved great results by using alpha video.

However, in HTML5 video support, there are currently no cross-browser codecs/wrappers that support the alpha channel—not H.264, VP8, or even Vorbis. Only VP8 shows promise that it can handle the support in its future, but it's limited to work in certain browsers, and on top of that, Apple's Safari shows no signs of supporting it, which is a huge miss in the whole market share on mobile. It's pretty obvious that this is a huge problem and one that will soon be fixed, but in the interim, designers and developers will need to leverage HTML5's `canvas` element and write the bitmap data from the video onto the `canvas` element during playback and key the pixels there. You can find a really great example of this at `http://jakearchibald.com/scratch/alphavid` or `http://github.com/m90/jquery-seeThru`. While no true HTML5 video codec supports the alpha information, the effect to the end user is essentially the same; however, keep performance in mind because you're essentially doubling the load for the browser by combining two elements for writing the video information to the canvas element. In the interim and until HTML5 video natively supports a codec that handles the alpha information; you can always fail back to use Flash Player because it has supported this feature since 2005 with the VP6 codec.

Video Delivery

So, you now know how much work it takes to encode and transcode videos on the Web; I'll now talk about actual delivering video on the Web. One of the biggest concerns with HTML5 video is around its delivery. Traditionally, Flash ads would pull video off a streaming server to avoid incurring any of the video's file size in the ad's overall k-weight. However, for HTML5, we are currently limited with a standard streaming solution, and because of this, most HTML5 video delivered over desktop and mobile still use progressive download over HTTP as the primary delivery method. While this method is widely supported across all browsers, it does not avoid that this will undoubtedly increase the ad's weight and impact a user's experience with longer "wait" times. This also gets increasingly worse when video bitrates increase for larger dimension and higher-quality video assets (HD).

In the massive world of video creation and delivery, it's ultimately about defining the target user base that you want to reach (and in advertising it's typically everyone), the resources you have at your disposable, and client turnaround times. Operationally, converting all the different flavors of video can be a very time-consuming task since browsers and devices require different codecs and formats. The following sections will help you understand the current problems in the space, how to work around them, and how to effectively deliver your content in HTML5-compliant video players.

Delivery specifications through video ad networks and publishers can be tricky. Every publisher and network will have their own specifications as far as what they expect, which adds to the confusion in the space. These specifications are typically in place to ensure a light footprint to their end users and to ensure video content has the furthest reach while also matching the publisher's video content as closely as possible. The following sections cover the two ways video is delivered on the Web today.

Progressive

Progressive video delivery is when a file comes down from one server and is stored on the client for playback. Progressive delivery is a pretty common form of video transfer because it's accepted across all browsers and devices, and even major sites like YouTube use this method daily. Progressive can allow a user to begin watching a video before it fully downloads, so the wait time is significantly reduced, but it also comes at a significant cost since the actual file is cached on the client. Progressive is typically served over the HTTP protocol, and since the actual asset is stored on the client machine, the user could in theory save that asset for viewing at a later time. For advertising, this is not a concern, but for premium long-form content, there is little to no protection in this matter, which makes this form of delivery less than ideal for content owners. Listing 7-3 shows an example HTML5 video tag; pointing to a video asset such as MP4, WebM, or OGG, you see that the video will be progressively downloaded.

Listing 7-3. HTML5 Progressive Video Example

```
<video autoplay src='http://cdn.someSite.com/someVideo.mp4'></video>
```

As you can see, I'm pulling an MP4 video asset off the server at someSite.com through the HTML5 video's source. If you were to insert this line of code into your text editor, save it as an .html file, and open it in a browser, you'd be able to see the video autoplay. (Keep in mind that you'll need to update your video src attribute to point to where an actual video is present.). While this approach is less than ideal in advertising situations for keeping a light footprint, the specification set by the IAB is 2.2MB for video file size. For more information on the rich media guidelines, visit www.iab.net/displayguidelines.

Streaming

Next I'll talk about the second form of video delivery over the Web. *Streaming* delivery is when the video asset is served off a streaming server and the video is presented to the user in real time upon user request. Since there is no storing of the asset on the client's machine, streaming is ideal for premium content protection as well as getting around publisher file size limitations. Publishers and ad servers may require the use of streaming video since it will not impact the overall file size of the ad unit like it would for progressive downloads. A common streaming server protocol is the Real-Time Messaging Protocol (RTMP). Originally developed by Macromedia and later acquired by Adobe, this server protocol supports encryption for content protection and HTTP tunneling to pass through firewall limitations. Many other streaming servers exist as well, such as the Apple QuickTime streaming server, but they're all pretty expensive to run and operate unless you're a large company with a strong focus on video delivery. If you're a major content provider like Hulu or Netflix, a streaming server is more or less a requirement for protecting your content from download and piracy as well as providing a good user experience.

Clients may ask you to do a live streaming broadcast in real time, for instance taking the video and compressing the video while transporting over the Web at the same time. This is popular for major events that are publically broadcasted such as sports, politics, and news. Companies such as Influxis (`http://influxis.com`) make this pretty simple using technologies that sit on top of Adobe Media Server (formally called Flash Media Server), which supports streaming video to Flash Player as well as HTML5- video players. However, keep in mind that there are also free alternatives like UStream, JustinTV, and others, but they do not offer the same support, quality, and service as paid services.

Streaming is also pretty tough on a user experience level because users cannot scrub through the timeline accurately like a progressive file can. This is because the player needs to ping the streaming server with the update that the user wants, and because the information is not present on the client side (like progressive), the request needs to be made at the time the user drops the video playhead, which creates some unwanted video buffering.

There is also what is called *adaptive streaming* over HTTP that basically transfers small chunks of video information over standard HTTP protocols, but I'll touch on that in more detail in the following sections.

Adaptive Streaming

Bandwidth is a crucial issue on the Web, and you need to be cognizant about how much of it you use for your video delivery with HTML5. More and more devices than ever before are accessing information, and we as developers and designers need to spare the bandwidth whenever possible, especially when serving larger files over various network connections. As an advertiser, you need to respect that a user may be viewing content on a wireless device on a poor cellular network connection or, worse, offline. Luckily, using sophisticated programming techniques; developers can take advantage of bandwidth detection and serve appropriate video files to an end user at request time while throttling the playback if there are hiccups in the user's connection.

I'll now introduce *adaptive bitrate streaming*. This technology is hardly new, but it's more important than ever to provide quality video experiences under various conditions by detecting and, well, adapting to them. In adaptive bitrate streaming, the server pings the user requesting the content and understands to what level the user can handle the playback and bitrate quality of the video. Earlier I discussed the bitrate of a video file and how the bitrate is holding all of the information of the video asset. Once the information is gathered about the user's ability to handle the video content, the appropriate bitrate video is delivered as described by a description or manifest file. This process happens throughout the video's playback and adapts or changes as bandwidth increases or decreases. This provides a seamless playback to the end user regardless of connection quality, and it's a feature that is incredibly important for long-form content, especially on mobile devices. Typical use cases start with a lower bitrate video and ramp up as bandwidth becomes detected and is found to be more plentiful. This ramp-up time could take a few seconds to happen, so short-form content may not see the effect take place.

Now that you understand the basics of adaptive bitrate, let's dig into the various technologies that support it and how to leverage each of the technologies in HTML5 video workflows. Keep in mind that there may not be a standard in video streaming just yet, but these are the technologies you are encouraged to use when you know your ads will target specific browsers and devices.

HLS

HTTP Live Streaming (HLS) is Apple's specification for delivering segments of a video file (transport streams) over HTTP by way of an M3U8 file. Apple's Developers Tools include a media segmenter, which is a command-line tool for Mac users to segment and create a manifest file of the video asset they want to use. Listing 7-4 instructs the media file segmenter (http://developer.apple.com/library/ios/#documentation/networkinginternet/conceptual/ streamingmediaguide/UsingHTTPLiveStreaming/UsingHTTPLiveStreaming.html) to take an H.264 file at your location and segment the output to an M3U8. The M3U8 file is simply a description file instructing the HTML5 video player on how to play back the video segments along with specific video metadata. In the example, save the segments and M3U8 file in your desired destination, with a target duration of each chunk at roughly 17 seconds.

Listing 7-4. Media Segmenter Example

```
mediafilesegmenter Your/File/Location.mov -t 17 -f Your/File/Destination.m3u8
```

Since the media file is segmented into smaller "chunks," or segments, the delivery of the video asset comes in spurts rather than one large progressive download, which improves the overall playback experience. What this means to you in HTML5 advertising is that instead of locating a source asset, you now target the M3U8 file in your video source attribute. Based on the previous command, Listing 7-5 demonstrates the output from a manifest file, which is known as an M3U8 file.

Listing 7-5. M3U8 Example

```
M3U8 File:
#EXTM3U
#EXT-X-TARGETDURATION:18
#EXT-X-VERSION:3
#EXT-X-MEDIA-SEQUENCE:0
#EXT-X-PLAYLIST-TYPE:VOD
#EXTINF:16.984,
fileSequence0.ts
#EXTINF:17.017,
fileSequence1.ts
#EXTINF:16.95,
fileSequence2.ts
#EXTINF:17.017,
fileSequence3.ts
#EXTINF:16.95,
fileSequence4.ts
#EXTINF:17.017,
fileSequence5.ts
#EXTINF:16.95,
fileSequence6.ts
#EXTINF:17.017,
fileSequence7.ts
#EXTINF:16.984,
fileSequence8.ts
#EXTINF:16.316,
fileSequence9.ts
#EXT-X-ENDLIST

HTML5:
<video src=index.m3u8></video>
```

As you can see, the M3U8 file describes all of the video transport streams in sequential order and the relative path to the transport stream (TS) asset. Note that these could be absolute paths to another location, even remotely on another server altogether. This is important to take notice of because you can do some dynamic insertion of video ads within the M3U8 manifest.

Being that it's a definition by Apple and not an open web standard, adoption is limited to certain devices and browsers; however, in relatively recent news, Adobe showcased support for HLS within Flash Player 10.1, so if you're targeting HTML5 with a Flash Player failback, you could use the same delivery mechanism. To see a good example of HLS, visit Wowza's example at `http://wowza.com/html/iphone.html`.

Note   At the time of writing, HTML5 HLS support is only in iOS, Safari, and Android 3.0+.

HDS

Speaking of Adobe supporting HLS, Adobe also supports a specification of its own for delivering video over HTTP. Adobe's solution is called HTTP Dynamic Streaming (HDS). Adobe has its own manifest specification for serving packets of video over HTTP to its Open Source Media Framework (OSMF). Much like HLS, HDS requires a video asset (MP4) and a manifest file, which is known as an F4M file.

Here's an example of the F4M manifest file; take notice that the file is just straight XML schema where there is a base file node with a single piece of media and different media URLs for the various videos with different bit rate.

```
<?xml version="1.0" encoding="utf-8"?>
<manifest xmlns="http://ns.adobe.com/f4m/1.0">
    <id>videoRx.com :: Adaptive Bitrate Video Player</id>
    <mimeType>video/mp4</mimeType>
    <baseURL>rtmp://hosted.videorx.com/vods3</baseURL>
    <media url="vid1.mp4" bitrate="385" width="364" height="156" />
    <media url="vid2.mp4" bitrate="508" width="436" height="184" />
    <media url="vid3.mp4" bitrate="651" width="506" height="214" />
    <media url="vid4.mp4" bitrate="1030" width="646" height="274" />
    <media url="vid5.mp4" bitrate="1487" width="858" height="364" />
</manifest>
```

Note   Only the Windows and Linux operating systems support the Adobe file packager for HDS at the time of this writing.

Smooth Streaming

Now that you've seen both Apple's and Adobe's specifications for delivering video content over HTTP, let's take a look at Microsoft's smooth streaming spec. Listing 7-6 demonstrates the manifest file for producing adaptive streaming to Silverlight, Windows Media Player and other devices capable of smooth streaming delivery.

Listing 7-6. Microsoft's Smooth Streaming Example (Source: `Silverlight.net`)

```
<SmoothStreamingMedia
  MajorVersion="2"
  MinorVersion="0"
  Duration="5964800000">
  <StreamIndex
    Type="video"
    Chunks="299"
```

```
      QualityLevels="3"
      MaxWidth="368"
      MaxHeight="208"
      DisplayWidth="368"
      DisplayHeight="208"
      Url="QualityLevels({bitrate})/Fragments(video={start time})">
      <QualityLevel
        Index="0"
        Bitrate="477000"
        FourCC="WVC1"
        MaxWidth="368"
        MaxHeight="208"
        CodecPrivateData="250000010FC38E0B70678A0B7819E80450808E8E7474400000010E5A67F840" />
      <QualityLevel
        Index="1"
        Bitrate="331000"
        FourCC="WVC1"
        MaxWidth="284"
        MaxHeight="160"
        CodecPrivateData="250000010FC38A08D04F8A08D813E80450808A1950CF400000010E5A67F840" />
      <QualityLevel
        Index="2"
        Bitrate="230000"
        FourCC="WVC1"
        MaxWidth="224"
        MaxHeight="128"
        CodecPrivateData="250000010FC38606F03F8A06F80FE80450800704704DC00000010E5A67F840" />
      <c n="0" d="19999968" />
      <c n="298" d="4166661" />
    </StreamIndex>
    <StreamIndex
      Type="audio"
      Index="0"
      FourCC="WMAP"
      Chunks="299"
      QualityLevels="1"
      Url="QualityLevels({bitrate})/Fragments(audio={start time})">
      <QualityLevel
        Bitrate="64000"
        SamplingRate="44100"
        Channels="2"
        BitsPerSample="16"
        PacketSize="2973"
        AudioTag="354"
        CodecPrivateData="1000030000000000000000000000E00042C0" />
      <c n="0" d="22755555" />
      <c n="298" d="4992290" />
    </StreamIndex>
  </SmoothStreamingMedia>
```

To save space, I removed the segments between 0 and 298, but you can see in this example that this format separates the media into stream indices where the type is either video or audio. Again, you should be seeing a trend here between the different delivery specifications because all of them rely on some form of instruction or manifest file.

░ **Note**   Some campaigns may require smooth streaming to be used. It's normally a requirement for Microsoft video advertising to Silverlight players, Windows Phone 7, and Xbox gaming consoles.

MPEG-DASH

As you can see from the previous examples, the fragmentation for delivering video over HTTP is growing pretty diverse and competition is strong. As the open web world searches for a one-stop HTTP delivery solution that will appease all platforms and browsers from Adobe, Microsoft, and Apple, the DASH promoters group (http://dashpg.com) is out to do just that. Currently, the group is working on a standard in hopes of gaining adoption in the market and become a ubiquitous solution across browsers and devices while using HTML5 video.

Meet MPEG-DASH. DASH stands for Dynamic Adaptive Streaming over HTTP. The group's work on this spec started in 2010 in order to provide an agnostic delivery mechanism for audio and video that requires a standard manifest file to deploy across firewalls and over straight HTTP. Adoption in the industry is growing strong from companies such as Adobe, Akamai, Microsoft, and even device manufacturers such as Cisco and Samsung.

In 2012, Adobe and Akamai released an example of DASH working in the latest Flash Player at the NAB conference, which gained a lot of interest from the industry, especially with intentions for HTML5 support. DASH uses what is called a *media presentation description*, or an MPD manifest, to define its transport streams, much like the earlier example manifest in HLS. The promise is that the DASH presentation file (MPD) will become the all-encompassing solution for delivering all video in HTML5 browsers and devices, not just Flash Player. Listing 7-7 shows an example of the DASH manifest file.

Listing 7-7. MPEG-DASH Example

```
<MPD type="static" xmlns="urn:mpeg:DASH:schema:MPD:2011" profiles="urn:mpeg:dash:profile:full:2011"
minBufferTime="PT1.2S" mediaPresentationDuration="PT0H2M59.23S">
  <Title>MPEG-DASH Example</Title>
 </ProgramInformation>
 <Period start="PT0S" duration="PT0H2M59.23S">
  <AdaptationSet>
   <ContentComponent id="1" contentType="video"/>
   <SegmentTemplate initialization="vid.mp4"/>
   <Representation id="1" mimeType="video/mp4" codecs="avc1.64001f" width="1280" height="720"
startWithSAP="1" bandwidth="534520">
    <SegmentTemplate timescale="1000" duration="9750" media="vid.mp4." startNumber="1"/>
   </Representation>
   <Representation id="2" mimeType="video/mp4" codecs="avc1.64001f" width="1280" height="720"
startWithSAP="1" bandwidth="812797">
    <SegmentTemplate timescale="1000" duration="9750" media="vid.mp4" startNumber="1"/>
   </Representation>
   <Representation id="3" mimeType="video/mp4" codecs="avc1.64001f" width="1280" height="720"
startWithSAP="1" bandwidth="1607936">
    <SegmentTemplate timescale="1000" duration="9750" media="vid.mp4" startNumber="1"/>
   </Representation>
   <Representation id="4" mimeType="video/mp4" codecs="avc1.64001f" width="1280" height="720"
startWithSAP="1" bandwidth="3088816">
```

```
        <SegmentTemplate timescale="1000" duration="9750" media="vid.mp4" startNumber="1"/>
      </Representation>
      <Representation id="5" mimeType="video/mp4" codecs="avc1.64001f" width="1280" height="720"
startWithSAP="1" bandwidth="3861547">
        <SegmentTemplate timescale="1000" duration="9750" media="vid.mp4" startNumber="1"/>
      </Representation>
    </AdaptationSet>
    <AdaptationSet>
      <ContentComponent id="1" contentType="audio" lang="en"/>
      <SegmentTemplate initialization="vid.mp4"/>
      <Representation id="1" mimeType="audio/mp4" codecs="mp4a.40.02" sampleRate="44100"
numChannels="2" lang="en" startWithSAP="1" bandwidth="257141">
        <SegmentTemplate timescale="1000" duration="9980" media="audio.m4s" startNumber="1"/>
      </Representation>
    </AdaptationSet>
  </Period>
</MPD>
```

In the previous example, you can see that the MPD file is really just straight XML outlining the instructions for the video player to ingest. You'll notice in the XML that certain nodes outline the representation of instructions for the DASH player to interpret. DASH is video codec agnostic, and ideally through browser and device adoption, MPEG-DASH will become the de facto standard for delivering HTML5 video over HTTP. If this adoption takes, as I believe it will, you will see very good uses of dynamic video advertising handled completely on the client side. Basically, the manifest files are really just a playlist or description file; as a viewer begins to view the first few segments, the later segments in the description could be reserved for targeted advertising. This will eliminate the need for rendering hundreds upon thousands of custom video permutations on a server in order to target them to the correct audience. With DASH, truly addressable video content can be achieved rather simply.

▦ **Note**   You'll learn more about dynamic advertising in Chapter 11.

Cloud Services

You may be asking, "With all the talk about encoding, transcoding, and delivery issues with video, how can an organization make sense of it all operationally and turn a profit?"

Fear not, there are a lot of cloud encoding services such as Encoding.com (Vid.ly), Wowza, Zencoder, Akamai, and others that are aiming to ease this video fragmentation for businesses and content owners. These services allow you to upload your source media asset to their cloud-based services; then you select what devices and browsers you want to target, and they handle the transcoding and delivery process. You can even open up the "hood," so to speak, and really customize the video encoding parameters that you've learned in this chapter, that is, if you feel comfortable enough to do so. These cloud services typically sit on top of an Amazon cloud server where, as more requests come in, they spin up more servers to process the transcoding jobs. This greatly reduces the overhead of running and maintaining several servers that could or could not be working at that given moment. If you're building a content site for a major media network or are a content owner looking to deploy across all screens, you'll want to take a look at one of these white-label solutions. Having an external service handle your video conversions into all the correct formats is a blessing; it allows you to "pass the buck" to your clients and spares you from the operational nightmare of managing, converting, and hosting all of your video assets. This process works with YouTube, Vimeo, Ooyala, Brightcove, and others. I believe as more solutions like open source WebM encoding and player-agnostic MPEG-DASH delivery become available, we as an industry will work our way out of the fragmentation woes. I hope we all reflect on this a few years from now and shake our heads at the crazy hoops we had to jump through to deploy video across.

Content Delivery Networks

If you're looking to host your assets instead of having a third party do so, most of these cloud services will automatically transfer the transcoded video files onto your hosting server and allow for caching to a content delivery network (CDN). Storing assets (video, JavaScript files, CSS files, images, and so on) on a CDN allows the asset to be stored on multiple server locations on a shared network. Caching these assets on multiple servers is known as *edge caching*. Essentially, you are placing the asset on the very edge of the network so the user requesting it does not have to make an HTTP request to a location too far from them. I like the definition given by Wikipedia for CDNs:

> *A CDN is a system of computers containing copies of data, placed at various points in a network so as to maximize bandwidth for access to the data from clients throughout the network. A client accesses a copy of the data near to the client, as opposed to all clients accessing the same central server, so as to avoid bottleneck near that server.*
> *Source: Wikipedia*

You can see the visual of this process in Figure 7-11.

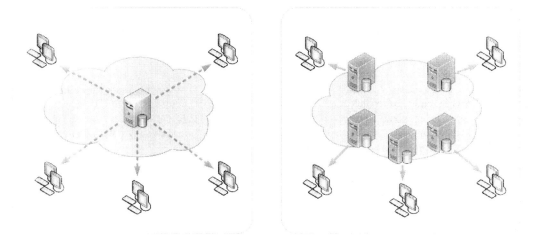

Figure 7-11. *The process of a single server and multiple servers on a network (CDN)*

Figure 7-11 demonstrates on the left how one server contains the data, whereas the image on the right (CDN) has multiple copies of the data to support multiple users requesting the content. In fact, if you're building any large enterprise video network like a YouTube, Netflix, or Vimeo, a CDN will be a requirement for your users, because it will speed up the response times of video playback to your users' machines.

HTML5 Video Developments

HTML5 video is still a relatively new feature for many browsers, and there are certain things that technologies have done for a long time really well, such as Flash, that the browsers will need to take time to implement into the spec and gain adoption among users. It's obvious that it's a fragmented space when it comes to video codecs and delivery, but it's even more so for full-screen support and subtitles.

Fullscreen API

The Fullscreen API is a feature that plug-ins such as Flash and Silverlight have had for some time, and it's becoming a feature of the browser as well. Currently, most of the full-screen options in the browser just scale the `video` object to the height and width of the browser window, unlike the intended method of taking over the full screen of the display. This is another feature that advertisers offering games in ads and especially entertainment clients love because it allows users to get fully immersed in the content whether it be interactive games or high-definition video trailers. The Fullscreen API is pretty divided among browser vendors, to say the least, so be sure to check out `http://caniuse.com/#search=fullsc` for the latest information.

What's interesting with the Fullscreen API is that when it becomes supported, it should have an included pseudo class in CSS. Here's an example:

```
<style>
        video:-webkit-full-screen {...}
        video:-moz-full-screen {...}
        video:fullscreen {...}
</style>
```

The previous code allows developers and designers to customize the layout for their video and ad content in its full-screen mode. Currently, if you want to use the Fullscreen API for your `video` or `canvas` element, you will need to use the vendor prefixes for Webkit and Mozilla to call the JavaScript methods, as follows:

```
<script>
someElement.requestFullscreen(); //go fullscreen
someElement.exitFullscreen(); //exit fullscreen
</script>
```

Note that you don't have to do this in newer versions of Opera where support is native!

Subtitles and Captions

Another developing feature of HTML5 video is what's known as the text track API, which would allow video content to be accessible to a global audience. For example, advertising and advertisers may want to include their content's voice-over as subtitles and use creative elements universally, meaning have a single video asset run in multiple locations so long as the subtitles are in a correct language. Figure 7-12 from a Google I/O presentation shows that this could be a very beneficial feature.

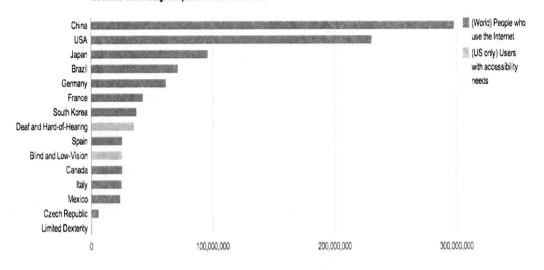

Sources: World Bank (WDI, 2008) and CDC.gov (NHI Survey, 2008)

Figure 7-12. *Internet usage compared with U.S. access needs*

While it's a small portion of the overall market, we shouldn't leave these users out from online experiences. The Web should be for everyone! Another possible way you can leverage the subtitles is to include relevant data as the video is playing. Think about gearing offers based on location and adding localized directions via the subtitle text. A benefit of using subtitles and captions is that they're searchable, so content providers and publishers will benefit from the SEO increases as well. The WebVTT file outlines a description file for a video to parse and gathers the information that it should preset on-screen as playback is happening. Listing 7-8 demonstrates the WebVTT file format.

Listing 7-8. WebVTT Example

```
WEBVTT FILE
0:00:00.000 --> 0:00:02.000
<b>Hello, World!</b>
0:00:03.040 --> 0:00:06.920 T:60% A:middle
Just <i>dropping</i> by to say <i>HELLO!</i>
```

In this code, a sample WebVTT file shows on-screen text while video playback is occurring. As you can see, between the times of 0 seconds and 2 seconds, the words "Hello, World" will appear in bold text. Using some basic HTML tags for bolding, italicizing, and underlining as well as using a positioning of middle, you can really add some flavor to the subtitle content. The current specification allows for horizontal text position, alignment, and vertical line position. You can even use CSS to style the captions to your liking using a new pseudo element called cue. See Listing 7-9 to learn more about how to implement the cue element in CSS.

Listing 7-9. WebVTT Cue Example

WEBVTT

```
1
0:00:00.000 --> 0:00:05.000
<b>Hello, World</b>

2
0:00:05.000 --> 0:00:10.000
How <i>are</i> you <i>,<c.green>Today?!</c></i>
```

CSS

```
<style>
       .green {
           color: green;
           text-transform: uppercase;
       }
</style>
```

HTML

```
<video width="640" height="360">
  <source src="someVideo.mp4" type="video/mp4" />
  <source src=" someVideo.webm" type="video/webm" />
  <source src=" someVideo.ogg" type="video/ogg" />
  <track src="helloWorld.vtt" kind="subtitles" srclang="en" label="English" />
</video>
```

■ **Note**   Be sure your server's .htaccess or http.conf file is configured to support the MIME type VTT.
Use AddType text/vtt .vtt.

Using the track tag in an HTML5 video, you can show captions, subtitles, and/or metadata about the video content, and using the previous example, you can see that you can even target specific CSS rules to the subtitle information. The file format for the track element uses a WebVTT file, and browser support is currently limited, but it's coming! Using the previous code, you should be seeing an example similar to Figure 7-13.

Figure 7-13. *WebVTT video subtitles*

If you're not seeing this, make sure your browser supports WebVTT and the HTML5 video `track` element; if your browser does not support either, I suggest using a great JavaScript polyfill called `captionatorjs.com`.

This could potentially be a huge advancement in dynamic video advertising going forward using web standards. What's really exciting is if the WebVTT formats start to support some more CSS features, and even features of CSS3 including transforms and animations, you'll have the ability to do some very real dynamic insertions of content over video. Until then, we'll have to wait and find out. For more information on the WebVTT specification, I encourage you to visit `http://dev.w3.org/html5/webvtt`, and if you're interested in understanding whether your WebVTT is valid, you can bookmark the useful link `http://quuz.org/webvtt`.

Note   I'll discuss other emerging HTML5 video capabilities like Web Cam and Mic access in Chapter 12.

Video Measurement

As you are aware, a big portion of video is measurement for advertisers so they can see how their campaign worked for them. They'll often want to know how well a video performed at the time a viewer watched it. Measurement also includes such things as video starts, completions, quartiles, plays, pauses, replays, sounds on/off, and so on. Pretty much any toggle, button, or switch a user operates, the ad server will report on it. The HTML5 Video API exposes all of these video properties via JavaScript, so attaching events and tracking calls is straightforward. For more information on all the video properties, visit `www.w3.org/2010/05/video/mediaevents.html`.

QOS

In addition to the normal ad server reports, advertisers can also bake analytics engines into their video content and video players to report on the quality of service (QOS) a video has in real time. Companies such as Akamai make use of its Media Analytics tool, which is an API that can get bundled into video players so real-time technical analysis can be performed on the video. This analysis can include highest bitrate served, bandwidth and network connections, frames per second, and even playback frame rate. From these measurements, companies can dial into the media files that could possibly be inefficient and re-optimize for a better user experience. A lot of this QOS is tied directly to the "garbage in, garbage out" rule of video where you can only preserve quality of transcoded video files; you cannot add to them after they've been manipulated for the worse. These analytics allow advertisers, content owners, and ad servers to test real-world examples of how their content is performing.

Video Players

Various video players are becoming more and more HTML5 compliant as more of the browser market and their respective user base supports the HTML5 video tag. Companies such as YouTube, Vimeo, Brightcove, and others do this by offering the HTML5 video while failing gracefully to a Flash or Silverlight experience as needed. Also, companies such as Netflix and Hulu needing DRM protection rely on these plug-in technologies since there is no streaming protection standard in the HTML5 video specification, but one is in the works. Some delivery formats I've discussed such as HLS can use a token/key exchange from server to client to offer some sort of protection, but this feature is supported only in Safari browsers as of yet.

As advertisers need to deploy ads to various video players, the IAB along with industry working groups have developed a standard specification for delivering ad tags to publisher and network video players that is universal. The specification is called VAST.

VAST

Video Ad Serving Template (VAST) is the universal tag delivery format for a video players. Currently in release 2.0 and moving quickly into 3.0, VAST aims to ease the ad delivery requirements to all the various video players by creating a universal definition for which all players can and should adhere. VAST allows for easy ad insertion in between video content, also known as *video preroll or in-stream video*. The video player will reach out to the ad server via a URL request, and the ad server will respond with valid XML markup. Listing 7-10 shows an example VAST response from a dummy ad server.

Listing 7-10. VAST Example

```
<VAST version="2.0">
<Ad id="12345">
<InLine>
<AdSystem>Acudeo Compatible</AdSystem>
<AdTitle>VAST 2.0 Instream Test</AdTitle>
<Description>VAST 2.0 Instream Test</Description>
<Error>http://url/error</Error>
<Impression>http://tracking/impression</Impression>
<Creatives>
<Creative AdID="12345">
<Linear>
<Duration>00:00:30</Duration>
<TrackingEvents>
<Tracking event="creativeView">http://tracking/creativeView</Tracking>
<Tracking event="start">http://tracking/start</Tracking>
<Tracking event="midpoint">http://tracking/midpoint</Tracking>
<Tracking event="firstQuartile">http://tracking/firstQuartile</Tracking>
<Tracking event="thirdQuartile">http://tracking/thirdQuartile</Tracking>
<Tracking event="complete">http://tracking/complete</Tracking>
</TrackingEvents>
<VideoClicks>
```

```
<ClickThrough>http://www.somedomain.com</ClickThrough>
<ClickTracking>http://tracking/click</ClickTracking>
</VideoClicks>
<MediaFiles>
<MediaFile delivery="progressive" type="video/x-flv" bitrate="800" width="640" height="360"
scalable="true" maintainAspectRatio="true">
http://cdn.somedomain.com/video</MediaFile>
</MediaFiles>
</Linear>
</Creative>
<Creative AdID="12345Companion">
<CompanionAds>
<Companion width="300" height="250">
<StaticResource creativeType="image/jpeg">http://cdn.somedomain.com/some.jpg</StaticResource>
<TrackingEvents>
<Tracking event="creativeView">http://tracking </Tracking>
</TrackingEvents>
<CompanionClickThrough>http://www.somedomain.com</CompanionClickThrough>
</Companion>
</CompanionAds>
</Creative>
</Creatives>
</InLine>
</Ad>
</VAST>
```

As you can see from the example, the XML outlines many useful values for the video player to handle including various ad server IDs, creative and media URLs, tracking nodes, and sizes of the creative. From this information, the video player will have everything it needs to deploy the ad.

■ **Note** There are different versions of the ad that can be served: linear and nonlinear. *Linear* means it happens before the video content, whereas *nonlinear* happens in the middle of the content, usually as an overlay.

If you were to test the previous VAST ad tag, it would fail because it's just a mock; however, you can see how some of these sample tags work by heading over to the IAB's site and downloading some samples at http://iab.net/guidelines/508676/digitalvideo/vsuite/vast/vast_copy/vast_xml_samples. Once you get a sample, swing on over to Google's VAST Inspector located at http://developers.google.com/interactive-media-ads/docs/vastinspector_dual and paste in the ad tag. You should see some example content, as shown in Figure 7-14.

Video Suite Inspector

Verify Your VAST Ad Response

To check whether your video ad response is VAST compliant, paste your VAST ad tag or VAST ad response into the field below and then click the "Test Ad" button. Our video player will verify and display the VAST ad response, and the tracking URLs.

Input Type: ◉ VAST tag (Sample) ◯ VAST XML

http://demo.tremormedia.com/proddev/vast/vast_inline_linear.xml

Preferred Ad Type: ◉ Linear ◯ Non-linear

(Test Ad)

Master Ad

00:12 / 00:31

Switch to HTML 5 player

Events

(06:31:55 PM) Ads requested
(06:31:55 PM) adsManagerLoaded
(06:31:56 PM) adMetadata
(06:31:56 PM) loaded
(06:31:57 PM) contentPauseRequested
(06:31:57 PM) started
(06:31:57 PM) impression
(06:32:05 PM) firstQuartile

Figure 7-14. *A typical in-stream VAST ad*

Keep in mind many publishers and ad networks rely on publisher-side platforms like Adobe's Auditude (http://adobe.com/products/auditude.html) or the Platform (http://theplatform.com) to handle their media content and to traffic their ads. These tools can encode video assets to a desired specification so they can run across platforms and devices. Using this platform is equally beneficial to advertisers and ad servers because they can tap into the publisher's delivery specifications and serve up video ads at just as good quality as the content they're producing. This gives a broadcast-like experience when content cuts to ads, and vice versa.

VPAID

Now that you have an idea of how to serve the video ad to a video player via VAST, you may be wondering, "How do I make it interactive? Won't that conflict with the video playback?" This is where VPAID comes into play. Video Player-Ad Interface Definition (VPAID) is fundamentally an API to communicate to the video player from within the ad unit through various exposed API calls.

The VPAID API is baked into the JavaScript of the creative to give certain commands to the publisher video player such as "Pause your video; the user wants to expand the ad" or "You can resume playback; the user has closed the ad." These instructions allow for a seamless integration between the player content and ad experience. Moreover, it's an adopted standard in the industry backed by the IAB and others. Ads that leverage VPAID work in conjunction with VAST; VPAID handles the interactivity, and VAST handles the delivery. Using both to your advantage will allow your ad tag to run across multiple video players with ease, but make sure you reach out to the certain publishers to ensure that their player is VAST compliant and can handle the VPAID API before developing your creative execution.

Using VPAID, it could get very interesting if advertisers wanted to do out-of-player video ads that interact with the surrounding elements of the page. Obviously, this would be pretty complex to pull off across a media plan because publishers would more than likely all need a specific creative version, but one-off solutions can be done much more easily. For more information on VPAID and the JavaScript API documentation, visit `http://iab.net/media/file/VPAID_2.0_Final_04-10-2012.pdf`; note that version 3.0 will be out soon.

VMAP

Video Multiple Ad Playlist (VMAP) is a new protocol that allows content owners to describe where ad slots or breaks should be placed within their video content when they do not control the video player or the content distribution outlet. Video ad enhancements include support for a "skippable" video ad, which allows publishers and content owners to price differently, based on ads that can play to completion or offer the skippable functionality. In addition, there is also support for "pods" or multiple ads to be displayed in a single ad break. This allows for the creation of similar experiences to broadcast television where you'll often see two 15-second ads back-to-back in a 30-second ad slot. For more information on the IAB's VMAP specification, visit `http://iab.net/guidelines/508676/digitalvideo/vsuite/vmap`.

Mobile Video

Mobile video content is increasing at a rapid pace, and as more and more people place their eyeballs on the smaller screen, advertisers are soon to follow. Currently, the fragmentation in the technology proves hard to deploy a mobile ad campaign, but using VAST and VPAID, advertisers can get into the mobile video realm much easier. To get an idea of the current mobile video landscape, take a look at the graph from eMarketer in Figure 7-15.

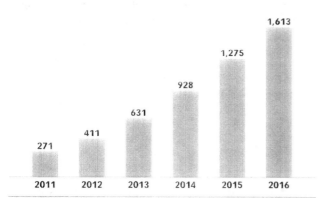

Mobile Video Viewers Worldwide, 2011-2016
millions

Note: includes on-demand video content downloaded or streamed to a
mobile handset
Source: Cisco Systems, "Visual Networking Index: Service Adoption
Forecast, 2011–2016," May 30, 2012
141000   www.eMarketer.com

Figure 7-15. Projected mobile video viewers worldwide from 2011 to 2016 (source: eMarketer.com)

This shows pretty amazing growth, and using the IAB's standard delivery formats like VAST, advertisers can deliver cross-screen video to every video player that supports the VAST tag format. This currently includes YouTube, VEVO, Tremor, and Adap.tv, among others, and adoption is quickly growing. This works in both desktop and mobile, and since iOS doesn't support Flash, you absolutely need to start using HTML5 video if you're deploying to mobile.

It should also be noted that all video is played in the native player of the phone device. The use of CSS and JavaScript to style and control player controls cannot happen in mobile, unless it's played inline on tablet devices. The following should give you a good idea for video specifications when deploying for mobile devices:

- Format: H.264/MP4

- Resolution: 480x360 or 640x360

- Video duration: 15 to 30 seconds

- Video bit rate: 600k to 1024 kbps or faster

- Audio: 64k to128k @ 44.1kHz or faster

- Frame rate: 24 or 30 FPS

- File size: 2.2MB or smaller unless streaming is used

HTML5 Audio

I just reviewed the HTML5 video landscape in exhaustive detail, outlining many of the features to take advantage of but also reviewing some of the issues. As you know, video is nothing without audio, and finally with HTML5, audio is now a native feature of the browser. For a long time, you needed to rely on plug-ins or applications to play back audio within the browser environment, much like video. In the following sections, I'll review how to load and interact with audio using HTML5 and JavaScript; I'll also discuss failovers in case browsers aren't HTML5 capable and the current support in the market. I'll focus on the different audio formats needed to appease all browsers. After reading the previous sections, understanding the audio in HTML5 will be a lot easier. Aren't you glad I covered the hard part first?

The audio Tag

New to HTML5 is the audio tag, much like video, audio becomes a first-class citizen in HTML5-compliant browsers with many great features to take advantage of. Let's dig right into the new audio element in HTML5 by looking at some of the code to get it to work (see Listing 7-11). Be sure to take notice of the source tags to satisfy the various browser environments.

Listing 7-11. HTML5 Audio Example

```
<!doctype html>
<html>
  <head>
    <meta charset="UTF-8"/>
  </head>
    <body>
    <audio controls>
<source src="sampleAudioFile.mp3" type="audio/mpeg" />
<source src=" sampleAudioFile.ogg" type="audio/ogg" /> <!-Support Old FireFox -->
<object type="application/x-shockwave-flash" width="250" height="50">
<param name="movie" value="sampleAudioPlayer.swf" />
<param name="FlashVars" value="mp3=sampleAudioFile.mp3" />
<embed href="sampleAudioPlayer.swf" width="200" height="20" name="movie" type="application/x-
shockwave-flash" flashvars="sampleAudioFile.mp3"></embed>
</object>
</audio>
</html>
```

Let's take a look at the previous code. First you add the attribute *controls*, which as you've learned from the video section allow the user to see the browser's native controls for the element. For audio, it would look something like Figure 7-16.

Figure 7-16. *The audio element with controls in HTML5*

Keep in mind you have the same ability to skin the controls as you have for the video tags. In the example, I'm sure you can agree it looks very similar to the video implementation, providing a Flash failback for older browsers as well as including multiple audio files to support all browsers that need varying audio codecs and formats.

Audio Formats and Codecs

Let's talk a little bit about the different codecs you'll most likely come across when developing ads that leverage audio. Audio is a bit less complicated than video in that there is much less to be concerned about as far as visual integrity goes; however, audio still must be clear and compressed correctly for the Web. Most browsers that you'll target in your next campaign will be fine supporting one of the formats outlined in Table 7-1.

Table 7-1. *HTML5 Audio Formats and Browser Support*

Browser	Version	Codec
Internet Explorer	9+	MP3, AAC
Chrome	9+	OGG, MP3, WAV
Firefox	4+	OGG, WAV
Safari	5+	MP3, AAC, WAV
Opera	10+	OGG, WAV
Android	2.3+	Device dependent
Mobile Safari	3+	MP3, AAC
BlackBerry	6+	MP3, AAC

As you can see from Table 7-1, audio support is pretty fragmented, so be sure to include multiple audio sources if you intend to target multiple browsers for your campaign. You may also want to stream audio into your ad, and you would need to lean on one of the adaptive streaming techniques discussed earlier. The only difference is instead of using an MP4 or another video file, you would include your audio file and adjust the bitrate settings accordingly. The last thing to note is that it's important to provide a failback for browsers that don't support the audio tag, so leverage plug-ins like Flash or Silverlight to handle this.

> ■ **Note** I'll discuss more emerging features with HTML5 audio including the Web Audio API in Chapter 12.

Audio Tools

There are many free services on the Web if you need to convert your audio files into the previous formats for multibrowser support. For example, if you intend to convert to all the previous audio flavors (OGG, WAV, AAC, and MP3), I suggest visiting http://audio.online-convert.com where you can convert to those formats and many others.

Audio JavaScript API

As you may have guessed, you can use JavaScript much like in video to control the audio playback. This is exceptionally helpful if you're customizing your own controls for the browser's internal player. Since you'll likely be re-creating custom buttons for play/pause and audio on/off, you'll need to leverage the JavaScript API to add events and check formats. Listing 7-12 shows the previous example, where instead of using the default controls by the browser, I'll show how to build them using JavaScript.

Listing 7-12. HTML5 Audio JavaScript Example

```
<!doctype html>
<html>
<head>
<meta charset="UTF-8"/>
</head>
<body>
<button onClick="handleEvent(this);">Play Audio</button>
```

```
<button onClick="handleEvent(this);">Pause Audio</button>
<button onClick="handleEvent(this);">Audio On</button>
<button onClick="handleEvent(this);">Audio Off</button>
</body>

<script>
var player = new Audio ();
if (document.createElement('audio').canPlayType('audio/ogg')) {
    //play ogg file
    player.src = 'someAudioFile.ogg';
} else if (document.createElement('audio').canPlayType('audio/mpeg')) {
    //play mp3 file
    player.src = 'someAudioFile.mp3';
} else if (document.createElement('audio').canPlayType('audio/mp4')) {
    //play aac file
    player.src = 'someAudioFile.aac';
} else {
    //Flash or Silverlight failover
}

function handleEvent (event) {
    var t = event.textContent;
    switch (t) {
        case 'Play Audio' :
            player.play();
            break;
        case 'Pause Audio' :
            player.pause();
            break;
        case 'Audio On' :
            player.volume=1;
            break;
        case 'Audio Off' :
            player.volume=0;
            break;
    }
    console.log(t);
}
</script>
</html>
```

As you can see from the example, you remove the audio element from the HTML markup and instead add it to the JavaScript. The first thing you do is create the buttons to toggle your audio play/pause and sound on/off. Next you head into the JavaScript where you create a new audio object by writing the lines var player = new Audio ();. From there, you check to see which audio format the browser can play back. In this conditional check, you use the canPlayType method to determine whether it's OGG, MP3, or AAC. Once you determine what the browser can play, you assign the specific audio format that you converted to the player's source attribute by writing player.src = 'someAudioFile'. From there you can kick things off by clicking the Play Audio button, which runs through the case statement called handleEvent. Lastly, you handle all the specific events by attaching the play() or pause() method to the player object, as well as adjusting the volume to 1 or 0. Give it a shot for yourself! Also, keep on top of the emerging browsers and their support for the audio tag by visiting http://caniuse.com/#feat=audio.

Terminology Review

I've covered a lot of new terminology and acronyms this chapter. To better provide you with a quick reference, I'll outline some of the ones I've touched on in detail; see Table 7-2.

Table 7-2. *HTML5 Media Terminology Review*

Word	Definition or Meaning
Encoding	This is the preparation of a video project for output according to different playback specifications.
Transcoding	This is the conversion process from one format into another according to different playback specifications.
CBR	This is the rate at which a codec's output bitrate data should be set, and it's a constant value.
VBR	This varies the amount of output data to be consumed per time segment. VBR allows for higher bitrate in complex scenes and lower in less complex.
Bitrate	This is the number of bits used per unit of playback time to represent audio or video.
FPS	This is the number of frames of video rendered to the screen within one second.
Aspect ratio	This is the proportional relationship between a video or image's width and its height; typically this is 16:9 or 4:3, but other ratios exist.
Codec	This is a device or software capable of encoding or decoding digital data.
GOP	This is a group of successive pictures within an encoded video file.
Alpha channel	This is a pixel's data that is reserved for transparency information. This is typically used for overlaying or compositing graphics on top of each other.

Summary

We're at a huge turning point in the industry in that online audio and video delivery is more confusing and important than ever. Clients expect to have their produced video spots delivered to every screen with optimal quality and clear audio, and users expect quick-starting video with great quality and no hiccups in playback. However, with only certain video formats playing nicely in certain browsers, operating systems, and devices, creating a ubiquitous and high-quality cross-screen experience is challenging and often very time-consuming.

This chapter covered a lot, but it's important to understand the large landscape and digest all the moving parts that go into creating, delivering, and optimizing video and audio for the Web, especially for online advertising using HTML5. Your potential customers won't give you the time of day if you're using poor-quality video assets and delivery mechanisms that the user can't even play. I suggest reviewing this chapter if your next campaign requires some form of media so you can make sure you understand the overall process that goes into video creation, compression, and delivery. But even more so, make sure your clients understand. Video, like a lot of things on the Web currently, is super-fragmented, but the process is getting easier to work with, and you'll have a firm grasp on the competition because you were working through it now. Don't be afraid to start using HTML5 video with your next advertising campaign and look for integration points with VAST and VPAID to help speed up your campaign needs. This will ensure that your video will work across media buys, while the technology I covered will ensure that it will work across browsers and devices. Play around with different compression techniques and start getting familiar with working with the JavaScript APIs. Also, be sure to test your creatives and video on different devices including mobile devices, tablets, and operating systems under varying network conditions. And if it's too hard to take it all into consideration under compressed timelines, remember the online services I've covered to help you get started quickly.

The next few chapters in this book are geared toward working with mobile, and I'll talk more about video in those chapters. Take what you've learned here and apply it going forward.

CHAPTER 8

███

Mobile Web Advertising

I think it's safe to state that the mobile and tablet market rushed the emergence of HTML5 onto the scene. With Apple's release of the iPhone and iPad paired with the sole reason that both of them would never support a Flash player, made HTML5 something of a household name and the required technology that would fuel the mobile landscape. This chapter will focus on HTML5 advertising as it relates to the constantly growing, ever changing, and slightly fragmented mobile landscape. As I write, the mobile market is chock full of various browsers, devices, and operating systems, let alone several versions of each browser and operating system with varying HTML5 support. The market's actually pretty fragmented, to say the least but fear not, I'll be sure to navigate you through it all.

So far the focus has been on HTML5 features as they pertain more or less to desktops, but the features of mobile devices allow HTML5's strengths to stand out more fully. Through use of APIs, you can leverage native device features like touch, orientation, compass, accelerometer, and battery status, not to mention all of the new features HTML5 brought to desktop browsers that filter down into the mobile realm as well. Let's face it, we live in a mobile world now. Because of smart devices with web access, people can use a phone for boarding passes on flights, to make payments electronically, even, with a service like Uber, to hail a cab. So let's talk about how mobile development takes HTML5 a step further and talk specifically about device features, how they're used, what is supported currently, and what will be available very soon. Since mobile devices and desktop browsers use HTML5 much differently, this chapter will outline current device features that HTML5 can access, as well as focus on how to use those features to create really amazing advertisements for our clients. If advertisers are looking to reach their audience on phones and tablets, they'll most certainly need to rely on HTML5 going forward. The mobile market gives entry to many innovative things; so let's dig in and find out exactly what.

The Mobile World

Let's get one thing straight: mobile is here and, trust me, it's here to stay! More and more people are equipped with smart phones and tablets with network connections. The hardware is cheaper than ever to make, and with Apple, Samsung, LG, and other OEMs (original equipment manufacturers) creating very sophisticated and connected devices with a relatively small price tag, the barrier of entry has been lowered for everyday consumers, which makes it a highly profitable channel for advertising. These devices are sophisticated in many ways, but one to focus on is modern browsers' support for HTML5. Because it's easier than ever to socialize, work, e-mail, or just play a game on the go and with so many eyeballs shifting from the traditional desktop and television to the smaller screen, advertisers, having taken notice of the trend and are hungry to be in this emerging market. Many analysts predict that the mobile market will pass the standard desktop market in the next two or three years. Look, for instance, at Figure 8-1 from Morgan Stanley Research.

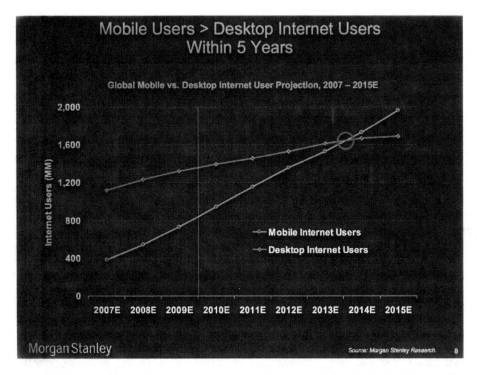

Figure 8-1. *Projections for mobile Internet users and desktop users, 2013–2015 (source: Morgan Stanley Research)*

As you can see, for anyone in the mobile space, this is an exciting trend with an opportunity for a long and prosperous future. One thing is for certain: HTML5 will be very prominent in this market, as it's currently the only ubiquitous technology that can span all the mobile platforms. No other technology can deploy to all the browsers and devices natively—not Flash or Silverlight. You certainly can't build applications for major mobile operating systems unless you know Objective-C or Java or use Adobe AIR for iOS or a similar packager. Not only does HTML5 allow you to build amazing web apps; it even enables the creation of native mobile apps with the help of a framework like PhoneGap (http://phonegap.com) built on Apache Cordova (http://incubator.apache.org/cordova). Using the same tools and syntax that work in the modern web browser, can now be used across devices, browsers, and various operating systems to ensure compatibility when compiling to a native app. This is the main reason that HTML5 is becoming so attractive on mobile devices. You build have the ability to build once and deploy everywhere-(well everywhere its currently supported for now). Now that you know why HTML5 is so important, let's look at the various devices on the market before digging into the code and practice of each.

Mobile Devices, Browsers, and OSs

Desktop browsers are fragmented in their HTML5 support, and mobile devices are no different. There are many different device manufacturers, each with its own variation and adoption of the HTML5 specification in its browser. There are so many different devices in the space currently that it's nearly impossible to keep track of what is supported where and what the latest features of the device are that we have access to.

Note   For very good information around the fragmented mobile ecosystem, I strongly suggest checking out
http://www.quirksmode.org/mobile/.

The following few sections will deal with the top devices in the market at the time of writing and we'll review some of the emerging competition that could be here at any time. There are various screen sizes and operating systems, tons of browser versions, and hundreds of device models that ad units will all have to be displayed on. The next sections are geared to help you navigate the landscape and make sense of it all.

Apple iOS

Once Apple launched the iPhone back in 2007, the smart phone market really took off. Phones have never looked the same since, and users have become accustomed to rich, touch-enabled features on their handheld devices. Through the years Apple's had multiple hardware and software iterations; developers and users have benefited greatly from faster hardware, more device APIs, and overall performance gains. For example, with the recent release of iOS 6, users can access the camera and photo library from web browsers and utilize a new feature called the Web Audio API (More on that in Chapter 12). For developers, iOS provides a great developing environment, with rich tools and simulators for testing native application and web content. Apple pretty much reigns as king in the smart phone market, as far as developers and advertising spending goes, even though its main competitor, Google, has a larger overall user base worldwide. JiWire (www.jiwire.com/insights) outlines the number of ad requests per device in the United Kingdom and the United States. The 2012 results show that iOS has the largest market share in advertising.

This information demonstrates a few things, one of them being that advertisers seem to have taken a liking to the iOS market for developing content since it's such a structured environment, whereas Android, for one, is much more fragmented because of its openness. A second thing is that it could mean that many more people are viewing online content and applications with advertising-supported models on iOS devices. Whichever way you view it, the numbers don't lie.

Google Android

Google firmly believes in open source, and it holds fast to that belief with its mobile operating system, Android. Android is by far the largest OS within the mobile landscape, with installs on a wide variety of devices. Openness in this case is both a good and bad thing though. It creates a lot of innovation and competition but also, conversely, a lot of frustration for developers who need to build in this landscape. Being that there are upward of 2,000 different Android products in the wild (and growing), developers are faced with various levels of HTML5 compliance in their browsers, different screen resolutions, varying pixel densities, and even legacy Flash Player support. But the Flash Player support will offically be gone with full Android 4.1 adoption. Visit http://opensignalmaps.com/reports/fragmentation.php, and you'll get an idea how fragmented and confusing developing for Android is. You might find the results of this study shocking! As the study states, it makes the most sense to test and develop content with Samsung or HTC devices, as they're the most prominent in the market today. Yet if you're a developer, you cannot escape developing for Android devices. Since most of the phone and tablet market uses versions of this OS, advertisers have all the more reason to want to be on their screens.

Others

Some of the other devices in the market are Galaxy Tablets, Blackberry Playbooks, Nooks, and Kindles, all of which support various blends of the Android operating system—with the exception of the Playbook, which uses Blackberry's own Tablet OS. Amazon's Kindle Fire is said to have 54.4 percent of US Android tablets as of April 2012, a fact that justifies creating content that displays and works correctly for the device. Most of these devices offer very HTML5-compliant browsers, with most OSs getting frequent updates. (You can view these results at http://html5test.com.) Other open source browsers and platforms are being developed, among them Tizen (http://tizen.org), said to have one of the best HTML5-compliant browsers at the time of this research (http://itworld.com/mobile-wireless/262120/tizen-pops-html5-winner). In the end, the world of mobile may really be fragmented, but it's still necessary to support advertising on these devices so be sure to discuss with your client which OS platforms they wish to target within the allotted time and budget for the campaign. This could save you hours if not days of development and debugging if you know out of the gate that your client wishes to target.

Mobile Advertising

You've seen that HTML5 is a standard for structuring and delivering advertising in desktop-compliant browsers; now let's dig in deeper to understand how this affects the mobile landscape. Advertising with HTML5 provides a seamless integration between ad content and page content especially where support for iFrames in mobile are non-existent. With ads truly a part of the page, web and ad developers have the ability to do some amazing things. But it also can get pretty disruptive for them, and so they'll need to work together closely to pull off complex rich media executions. Because of HTML5's current state of acceptance, there's no guarantee that an HTML5-built ad will render equally on all browsers and operating systems in the mobile ecosystem. The same issues and testing that web designers and developers go through to ensure that every pixel and function is correct across browsers applies here as well. In the next sections, let's review how mobile advertising is bought, sold, created, served, and analyzed.

It's no secret that the mobile advertising industry is booming and shows no time of slowing down anytime soon. If you're new to mobile advertising you'll soon see that mobile is a beast of its own kind; developers and designers transitioning from desktop have their work cut out for them. Mobile is an emerging and lucrative industry, but there is still much to learn and work out before we are as comfortable in it as we are in desktop creation. In fact, an entire book could be focused specifically on this topic. All the ways that ads are bought, sold, created, served, and analyzed are still in a developing state, but with so many phones and tablets within the market, advertisers want their campaigns to have the broadest reach. Often the big sacrifice comes with operational scale and turnaround times, as development entails writing many conditionals and feature detections so ads can deploy across screens effectively and properly while also failing gracefully. Mobile advertising is a market still in its infancy but it's growing rapidly. For proof, take a look at Figure 8-2, with data from eMarketer regarding online ad spending worldwide by format.

Online Ad Spending Worldwide, by Format, 2011-2016
billions and % change

	2011	2012	2013	2014	2015	2016
Paid search	$39.03	$45.13	$51.40	$58.15	$65.66	$74.00
—% change	24.3%	15.6%	13.9%	13.1%	12.9%	12.7%
Display and other internet	$38.44	$40.25	$42.78	$44.45	$45.95	$47.67
—% change	12.4%	4.7%	6.3%	3.9%	3.4%	3.7%
Mobile	$4.22	$6.31	$8.41	$10.89	$14.06	$17.20
—% change	53.1%	49.7%	33.3%	29.5%	29.1%	22.3%
Online video	$4.30	$5.94	$7.40	$9.16	$11.14	$13.47
—% change	45.7%	38.2%	24.5%	23.8%	21.6%	20.9%
Total	$85.99	$97.64	$109.99	$122.65	$136.81	$152.34
—% change	20.6%	13.5%	12.7%	11.5%	11.5%	11.4%

Source: MAGNAGLOBAL as cited by Barclays Capital, "Facebook," June 27, 2012

142185   www.eMarketer.com

Figure 8-2. Total online ad spending worldwide by format (source: eMarketer.com)

If you're looking for a career change or even just a new hobby, this is a great industry to be in! Mobile is projected to have the largest percentage growth in ad spending worldwide going into 2016. However, there are many things to cover before you can think of it as all fun and profit. Let's start off with mobile advertising pricing.

Mobile Pricing

Mobile ad pricing is very similar to desktop in that ads are typically billed off impressions; that is, the number of times an ad is rendered to the page or requested. Traditionally, mobile rich media are billed on a CPM basis (that is, on the basis of every thousand impressions). This can also be joined with viewable impressions—that's when an ad is actually within view on a user's machine. Typically, this metric aids ads that render "below the fold," the area not in initial view when a user visits a page. Taps, or clicks, are the number of times a user touches a banner to expand it, and CTR (click-through rate)—it should be known in mobile as TTR (tap-through rate)—is the total number of times an ad is tapped divided by the number of served ad impressions. For example, if an ad shown 1,000 times receives 10 taps, it has a CTR of 1.0 percent. Finally, the cost is factored by the total amount paid for the reported time period and possibly a bill based on the total number of impressions served. There is a nice, really detailed breakdown of mobile ad pricing at `http://mymobileagency.co.uk/blog/mobile-advertising-pricing-explained.html`.

Ad Creation

Now that you understand mobile ad pricing, let's dig into the bigger topic at hand, which is the creative design and development of the ad. For mobile, it's best to include all the ad's style sheets in the head of the publisher's page or in iFrame's head, if it's being served that way (your publisher will inform you of the way your ad will be rendered to the page).

▓ **Note** iFrame ads in older device browsers can cause system memory issues, especially when nested inside one another. It's becoming less of a concern with newer devices but keep this in mind when you define your campaign's reach.

Styles shouldn't be included anywhere else, as applying them after an element is created causes reflow, repaints, and unwanted (and unnecessary) flashes of unstyled content. When including the CSS specific to your ad, be sure to bundle all the CSS files into one file while minifying and compressing it. In mobile, the fewer requests the better, because network conditions can vary tremendously. I recommend using CSSCompressor, `http://csscompressor.com` and JSCompress (`http://jscompress.com`), as minifying or compressing the code will reduce the overall file size—which is SUPER important for mobile devices. For scripts dependent on elements, have them execute after the DOM is "ready" or "loaded"—this is done by using the `DOMContentLoaded` or "load" event.

Also, if you need to rely on image assets, you should be preloading whenever possible; preloading provides the complete ad experience before rendering any ad content to the screen. While images are pretty heavy in the mobile universe, you can't always get away from using them so definitely employ the learning's of sprite sheets as we've learned in Chapter 5. This way, you're positive that the content will be operational and visible when the user finally sees it. Listing 8-1 presents a common technique to preload image assets.

Listing 8-1. JavaScript Image Preloader

```
<!DOCTYPE html>
<html lang="en">
<head>
<script>
    var images = new Array();
    var numImages = '3';
    var count;
    function preloading () {
        for (i = 0; i < preloading.arguments.length; i++){
            images[i] = new Image();
```

```
            images[i].src = preloading.arguments[i];
            count = i+1;

            if(count.toString() === numImages) {
                //initialize ad
                console.log('adInit');
            }
        }
    }
}
preloading(
    "image1.gif",
    "image2.gif",
    "image3.gif"
);
</script>
</head>
<body>
</body>
</html>
```

As you can see, an array object called `images` is being set up. Next, let's create a function called `preloading` that will get passed a bunch of image assets and will loop through and create new image objects out of them and assign their source attribute to the file path that's provided in the function. Last, anything else needed, such as an `init` function to kick things off in the ad, can be called when the images are loaded.

In addition to preloading external content, you should also prioritize specific assets to load before others. Sequencing is mandatory if you're leveraging external JavaScript libraries that your script will rely on. Luckily, you can leverage two new script tag properties, `Async` and `Defer`, to better assist publishers with this code sequencing. `Defer` scripts are scripts that are dependent on other scripts, such as external libraries. Thus, you should defer on jQuery and other dependent scripts if you absolutely must need to use them in your mobile campaigns.

Note   `Defer` scripts execute just before the `DOMContentLoaded` event.

The ad server's JavaScript ad tag should use the `async` property so that the publisher page loads much more quickly. Async is for scripts that execute as soon as they're loaded and require no dependencies on other scripts—they're perfect for ads tags, social networking widgets, and other third-party content on sites not tied specifically to the site's content. The real benefits in both of these new attributes are that they don't block the HTML parser, which could block vital UI (user-interface) elements to a user otherwise. Let's look at Listing 8-2, which outlines the use of the `defer` and `async` attributes.

Listing 8-2. JavaScript Defer Example

```
<html>
<head>
<script defer src='jquery.js'></script>
<script defer src='mainSiteScript.js'></script>
<script async src='adTag.js'></script>
</head>
</html>
```

You can see that the jquery.js script is being loaded first, using a defer setting, then the mainSiteScript.js, which has dependencies on the JQuery library. Last, call in the third-party JavaScript tag for our ad content, which has no dependencies on the publisher content. Since parsing JavaScript on mobile can take many milliseconds longer, depending on the network connection, it's important to maintain the site's functionality to the user and load the ads after the main content has loaded.

Before starting an HTML5 campaign and before starting creative development, always ask your ad ops or campaign manager where the tag will run. What device, browser, and so on. Define your reach; this will dictate the overall functionality, as support is limited for certain features. The functionality of the creative required will dictate the amount of time to develop for cross-browser/device builds. There is a very comprehensive outline on mobile ad development in HTML5 at http://media.admob.com.

With this in mind, let's first discuss the *viewport* in mobile. The viewport is really the virtual window for the browser to render the content on mobile devices. By using meta tags in the head of your document page, you can specify width, scale, and user scalability and even set minimum and maximum values for the browser window to interpret. Since this is very important for formatting content correctly for mobile devices, let's look at Listing 8-3, which shows the browser window being set to the size of the screen on the device that's accessing its content.

Listing 8-3. Viewport Meta Tags for Mobile

```
<!DOCTYPE HTML>
<html>
<head>
<meta name = "viewport" content = "width=device-width">
</head>
```

When you open this document in your mobile browser, you'll notice that any content in your browser has been set to the device's width. For an Apple iPhone, this would be 320 CSS pixels wide; it would be 600 CSS pixels for a Kindle Fire. This variable width is a great feature. Since it makes the browser seem like a native application for the device, it's something ads should take into consideration, as most publisher pages will include these meta tags. Listing 8-4 shows a more elaborate viewport example by setting scale values as well as user input.

Listing 8-4. Setting Scale with Viewport Meta Tags

```
<!DOCTYPE HTML>
<html>
<head>
<meta name = "viewport" content = "initial-scale = 1.0, minimum-scale=1.0, maximum-scale=1.0,
user-scalable=no, width=device-width">
</head>
```

This can also be achieved using the JavaScript method included in your JavaScript file (see Listing 8-5).

Listing 8-5. Setting Viewport Width and Scale with JavaScript

```
var viewMeta=document.createElement('meta');
viewMeta.name='viewport';appleMeta.content='width=device-width, initial-scale=1, maximum-scale=1,
minimum-scale=1, user-scalable=0';
document.getElementsByTagName('head')[0].appendChild(viewMeta);
```

Either of these code examples when viewed in a browser will set the page content's width to the device's screen width, set the initial, min, and max scale level to 100 percent, and not allow the user to zoom in on the page content using a pinch gesture. This information is vital to content owners looking to achieve the best possible presentation for mobile visitors, especially those wanting to mimic native applications built for the Web. Regarding advertisers, agencies, and ad servers—again, this is something to be aware of when delivering ads to pages that have this viewport set specifically, as your creative could be affected. The creative elements could scale up or down depending on the scale set, which could create copy or images that are illegible or worse or make an unwanted change to the ad's width if the publisher makes the content narrower than the ad intends to be.

Media Query and Pixel Density

When adjusting the viewport, you'll more than likely want to make use of CSS media queries for your mobile ad creative. Chances are you won't know every device that will be accessing your ad content on a media sheet, so you'll have to build an ad that is responsive and that adapts to the device viewing it. Responsive ad design takes a lot of work and a lot of planning for clear execution, but if done correctly, a lot of time can be saved down the road. Since many devices come at different screen sizes and pixel densities, it's increasingly hard for ad designers to handle all the variances in the creative builds. Because this is such an issue for designers developing for mobile devices of various sizes and densities, the folks at Teehan+Lax developed a nifty graphic and chart (`http://teehanlax.com/blog/density-converter`) to help you design content for screens of various pixel density (see Figure 8-3).

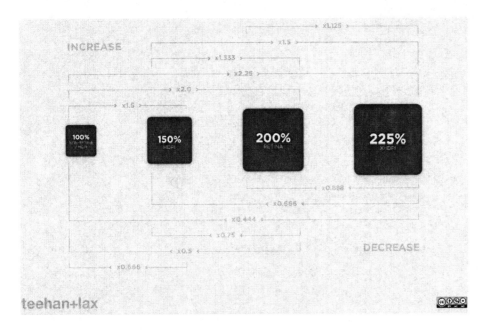

Figure 8-3. *Scaling content for screens of various pixel density*

At the time of writing, Apple devices had a pixel density of 1.0 and 2.0; Android had various others, including 1.4, 1.75, and 2.3. For example, iPhone 4 and above supports a higher pixel density—what Apple calls Retina Display. On these devices, the width is still 320 in CSS pixels, but the device's pixels double every pixel to create higher image fidelity. For example, an image at 300 × 250 would need a 600 × 500 image to look sharp on these higher pixel density displays (see `http://quirksmode.org/blog/archives/2010/04/a_pixel_is_not.html` for more on this topic). By reading over the post, you'll understand that the moral of the story is that CSS pixels have little or nothing to do with actual physical device pixels. Thus, they should be used whenever possible, as they are interpreted consistently across browsers regardless of device's underlying resolution. Listing 8-6 takes a look at working with higher pixel density images using CSS. (Don't feel uncomfortable writing something like this.)

Listing 8-6. Double Pixel Density in CSS Example

```
<style>
.adContainer {
    background-image: url(bg_600x500.jpg);
    width: 300px;
    height: 250px;
}
</style>
```

As you can see, the code example doubled the background image's size to make up for the extra device pixels. This can get very confusing, I know! However, there are specifications being developed and even specific vendor-prefixed features you can use today. For more information, read up on the Image-Set property in CSS (`http://blog.cloudfour.com/safari-6-and-chrome-21-add-image-set-to-support-retina-images`) and the highly anticipated and emerging Picture element spec (`http://github.com/scottjehl/picturefill`).

Mobile Tips

Now that you're all set with viewport and CSS, let's discuss some important "gotchas" around working with various mobile devices. The following sections will be geared to help you deal with some common pit falls of mobile ad development. Oftentimes clients will request that the devices' gray outline be removed. This outline looks like a gray click region on mobile Safari and an amber or green region on Android devices. See Figure 8-4 for an illustration of the issue.

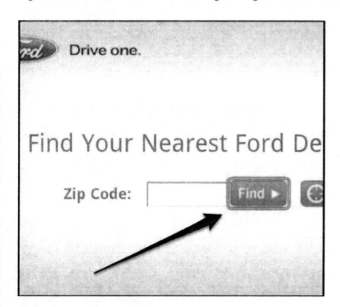

Figure 8-4. *The touch outline on certain mobile devices*

If you're looking to get rid of this outline, here's some code that demonstrates how to do just that using CSS.

```
button {
    -webkit-tap-highlight-color: rgba(0,0,0,0);
    -webkit-tap-highlight-color: transparent;
    outline: none;
}
```

Notice how we're setting the prefixed `webkit-tap-highlight-color` to 0 on its RGBA scale as well as calling it transparent. Finally, for safe measure, we're disabling the outline by setting it to none.

Another useful feature with CSS and mobile is the disabling of selections. If you or your client wants to disable the cutting, copying, and pasting actions from within the ad unit, you can use CSS to make that happen. Figure 8-5 outlines how the copy-and-paste process looks on mobile.

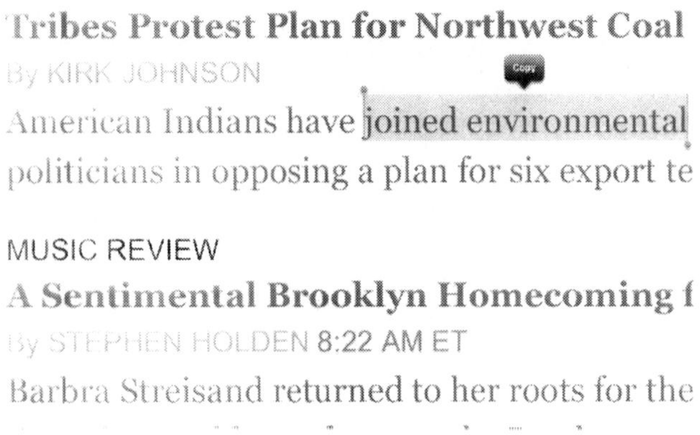

Tribes Protest Plan for Northwest Coal

By KIRK JOHNSON

American Indians have joined environmental
politicians in opposing a plan for six export te

MUSIC REVIEW

A Sentimental Brooklyn Homecoming f

By STEPHEN HOLDEN 8:22 AM ET

Barbra Streisand returned to her roots for the

Figure 8-5. *Copy-and-paste technique on mobile devices*

Disabling this feature could be useful if you want to prohibit users from taking information from the ad unit with them. Maybe it's timely and dynamic data or a one-time coupon deal. Either way, just be sure you really want to disable this setting for your user base. Here's a CSS snippet that can achieve this result.

```
p {
    -webkit-user-select: none;
}
```

Sometimes you may get a request to disable the callout window on iOS devices when a user taps on an image and holds it or holds a link within your content. Figure 8-6 better illustrates what I'm talking about.

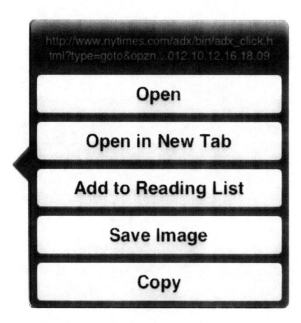

Figure 8-6. *The callout balloon on iOS*

This feature happens by default when a user taps an image or URL and presses it for some length of time—the OS will provide a list of menu items for the user to choose from. If this isn't a desired part of your ad experience, CSS can remove that native callout window.

```
img, a {
    -webkit-touch-callout: none;
}
```

In the preceding code, simply setting a Webkit property called touch-callout to none disables this OS callout feature.

Often, you want the user to be presented with a specific entry input instead of a traditional keyboard for text entry. This could be useful for inputting numerical data—a phone number, a ZIP code—into your form. In order to change these keyboard displays on your form inputs, specify the input-type attribute on your input tags. For example, in Figure 8-7 I have the input field set to tel with a pattern of [0-9]* because I want the user to input a ZIP code. A bit confusing, but it works, because there is no input type for a ZIP (at least, not yet), and all I'm concerned about are the number entries for this specific input.

Figure 8-7. *The "tel" keyboard input on mobile devices*

As you can see, when a user gives focus to the input field, the device's numerical keyboard is presetnted. Here is some code that can be used to switch the keyboard for a better user experience.

■ **Note**   If the input types aren't supported, the browser will default to a generic input of type "text."

```
<!-- display a standard keyboard -->
<input type="text" />

<!-- display a telephone keypad -->
<input type="tel" />

<!-- display a URL keyboard -->
<input type="url" />
```

```
<!-- display an email keyboard -->
<input type="email" />

<!-- display a numeric keyboard on iOS -->
<input type="tel" pattern="[0-9]*" />
```

With these code snippets, you can display all types of input fields for your users depending on your creative goals. What makes this really easy and helpful is that the browser takes care of it all for you. You don't need to build and customize specific input fields.

Another interesting thing to note is the font-smooth property. You'll often have some sort of animation in your creative, and sometimes it will involve animation of copy elements. Figure 8-8 showcases what font smoothing looks like on the "o" character.

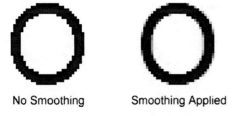

No Smoothing   Smoothing Applied

Figure 8-8. *The effect of the CSS font-smooth property*

Some of that animation may involve copy or text elements, and there is a great CSS snippet to prevent jaggedness or ridged animations on fonts. Here's some code to provide anti-aliasing on copy elements.

```
.smoothCopy {
    font-smooth:always;
}
```

■ **Note**   At the time of writing, font-smoothing was available only in Webkit browsers. It was not a part of any web standard spec.

Further to this topic, mobile advertising and CSS-based web fonts pose a potentially large problem. On the one hand, advertisers and brands will want to use their actual fonts, as they are usually at the core of their branding identity—think of Coca-Cola or Budweiser—and the only way to do that is to increase the k-weight for either CSS fonts or transparent PNG images. On the other hand, the load experienced with CSS3 fonts leads to much longer download times for end users, and more HTTP requests are needed for the various formats. There is no silver bullet for this scenario; some clients will absolutely request that you use their branded fonts. The best thing to do is to show the client that doing what it wants will come at a cost to users. Their experience may suffer, especially on lower bandwidth connections. If the client insists, there are some very good optimized font libraries to use: Google's Web Font Library (http://www.google.com/webfonts), Adobe's Typekit (https://typekit.com/), and WebType (http://www.webtype.com/), which as you've learned in Chapter 5, only bring in the format required for the device. Weigh the pros and cons of using or not using, and consider transparent PNG files, too. However, when copy needs to change or be dynamic, PNGs are not an option. For default font support on iOS devices, check out http://iosfonts.com. Android users have much more limited options for default fonts—Droid Sans, Droid Sans Mono, Droid Serif, and Roboto—but hopefully more will come with future updates of the OS.

Note   These are just a few gotchas and workarounds. Many more are out there, but given all the devices and browsers in use, listing them all would be beyond this book's scope. See `http://css-infos.net` for more mobile CSS adjustments.

As you might have guessed, a lot of mobile advertising comes from what's been learned from desktop advertising. Such ad features as surveys, "send to a friend," coupon downloads, customer data collections, animations, direct links to app stores, mapping, video, polling, interactivity, in-ad purchasing, and location-based deals are all possible, but they may take a bit more understanding to implement flawlessly and across device. These features can really benefit advertisers; they can use what they've learned from their desktop campaigns and apply it to what works in mobile or reposition their campaign for features that work better on mobile devices altogether. It's by far not the same medium, but featurewise, a lot of the same things and more can be accomplished. A large question in the industry is how to handle assets now that they're not just SWF files. This applies to mobile as much as to HTML5 advertisements in general. Here's what to look for when handling or handing-off creative assets between team members both internal and external.

- HTML
- CSS
- JavaScript
- layered PSDs and/or images with sprite sheets
- Illustrator files
- storyboards
- fonts
- media files (video/audio) if needed
- A README text file, which outlines instructions of the assets.

All of these assets may come your way in a ZIP file, which ensures that all the assets remain together throughout the transfer. Confirming that all of these files are present when assets need to be handed off avoids confusion down the line. This confusion often eats up valuable time and could potentially derail a campaign's launch.

A campaign often requires you to ping data to a third-party server, especially when other vendors give you 1 × 1's in order to validate tracking metrics. This can be done by creating a new `Image` object in JavaScript and applying the image's `source` attribute to point to the third-party destination you wish (see Listing 8-7).

Listing 8-7. Pixel Tracking Example

```
<!DOCTYPE HTML>
<html>
<head>
</head>
<body>
    <div id='icon' style='background-color:black; width:50px; height:50px;'></div>
</body>
<script>
var someElement = document.querySelector('#icon');
someElement.addEventListener('touchstart', activityHandler, false);
```

```
function activityHandler () {
   var img = new Image ();
   img.src = 'http://www.tracker.com/ping';
}
</script>

</html>
```

You can see that an event listener has been added to the element of your choice and when tapped, we call the activityHandler function. From within that function a new image object, img, is created and sourced to the destination to be called. Now the browser will make a request to that source, and the receiving end will log an interaction metric. (Just be sure to do this on the user's activity you wish to track; otherwise your reporting metrics will be skewed.) Also, keep in mind that using this for mobile means another HTTP call, which could be skewed, based on bandwidth constraints. If there isn't enough bandwidth, the request could fail to the third party, but the action will still have taken place from within the creative.

Last, with mobile as in display advertising, the same "in/out" rule applies. If users are clicking or tapping to engage with the ad in order to expand it, they'll more than likely need to click or tap to close the experience. This is more or less set by publisher requirements, but keep this in mind in considering the overall user experience.

Optimization

Optimization is a crucial part of mobile development. Keeping a lightweight ad in the mobile ecosystem should be a primary focus for any developer or designer, as it is extremely important for the varying network connections an end user may face. As images and scripts are heavy over 3G connections, detect these constraints and offer users alternative experiences. On Android devices 2.2 and higher, check the navigator.connection.type property; it allows detection of WiFi from Ethernet, 2G, or 3G connections and adapts your ad accordingly. For Blackberry devices, check blackberry. network to get similar information; on iOS ,unless the first-party ad server can provide it, wait until the API on network information comes to that browser. See http://w3.org/TR/netinfo-api for more information on the network API.

In an ideal world, the best scenario would be to detect the current bandwidth of a user and provide alternative information or graceful failovers. For example, if the user is not on WiFi or has a poor connection, offer a reduced creative version with little to no imagery and dynamic content that relies on various HTTP requests. Connection information will let ads really adapt to the user's device and viewing condition. Pair this with a responsive creative design for the ad content, and you'll have an ad that can run on any screen in any condition—no problem! It's essentially the holy grail of ad serving.

In addition, with mobile it's best to remove all heavy, unneeded external libraries ; use straight native JavaScript whenever possible. Libraries provide great ease of use, but for this reason too many developers rely on them. Their inclusion may not be warranted if the content is being targeted only to one operating system or device. A library like jQuery gives amazingly consistent cross-browser experiences, but if you're using it just for its animation and syntactical ease of use, you're killing end users with that extra weight. In fact, in one of its 2012 versions, jQuery sits around 93 kilobytes minified and 34 kilobytes minified and gzipped. That's pretty large for a mobile user, especially just for ad content. Always try to use naked JavaScript, minimize k-weight, reduce network downloads, and never forget the normal methods you should be taking advantage of, such as minification of scripts and CSS files, as well as gzipping your assets for the smallest transfer size.

Finally, try to keep your browser repaints very low. Repainting the layout of the DOM is a pretty expensive task for mobile devices. As more animations and DOM manipulations occur, repaints could drastically decrease your user's battery life.

Code Execution

On the heels of optimization, another important practice is code execution. For mobile ads, code execution can be a nightmare to work with, especially when waiting for page content to load, first, various network conditions and non-mobile-optimized web content on mobile devices. It's really a game of sequence, checks, and playing traffic cop. A coworker and friend of mine always calls this "the Dance." Whether you're checking if DOM elements exist before calling actions on them or waiting for JavaScript platforms and libraries to download, it's always a debugging process when your ad tag goes into the live environment. Indeed, this statement really sums up the frustration one can have when dealing with interpreted code execution in the browser, especially code you have no control over on the publisher's side. Much as with a new dancing partner, you don't know whether they'll step on your toes.

In the advertising realm, the publisher's page content first has to load, usually as an onload event; then the page makes a request to the ad server to request the ad content. At this point the ad populates the publisher's page or designated iFrame. The ad code still has to load all of its ad-dependent files—in this case it could be CSS, JavaScript, any images, web fonts, and whatever else. Finally, having gotten the go-ahead, our ad experience can than start up. I've seen this done a number of ways, but no matter how it gets done, there are a lot of steps, especially for ad content that has to execute quickly! Remember, no one goes online to look at ads, so you have to render quickly and grab a user's attention while you can. You'll learn that the best sites provide callbacks for ads to begin loading or even load their ad scripts asynchronously. Listing 8-8 shows my own method of ensuring that all elements have been written to the page.

Listing 8-8. DOM Element Checker Example

```
<script>
function adChecker () {
    if (document.querySelector("#yourLastDOMElement")) {
        initAd();
    } else {
        setTimeout(adChecker,100);
    }
}

function initAd () {
    //Ad content starts here
}

adChecker();
</script>
```

You can see from the code that a function called adChecker is being used. It runs through a conditional to check whether the ad code's last element is rendered to the page. Once it returns true, the function called initAd is executed. It will kick things off in our creative. Otherwise, set a timeout function of 100 milliseconds and call the adChecker function again. This will occur over and over until the ad's markup is fully rendered to the document. This looping over and over again can be a costly operation, which is why I say the best sites provide callbacks for ads to hook onto. They are a lot more efficient than this repeating function, especially on mobile.

Mobile Site Events

A common request from clients will be to have the ability to track site events on mobile devices. Site events are tracking tags placed on an advertiser's web site. When a user views or interacts with an ad and later visits the advertiser's site, a site event metric is fired, thus showing the ROI that the ad could potentially have made the user go to the advertiser's URL after taking notice of the ad. Site events traditionally operate on the cookie model for tracking;

in some mobile browsers this is perfectly fine. However, on iOS and mobile Safari, where third-party cookies are disabled by default, these devices and browsers are prohibited from tracking site events using the cookie approach. To better illustrate this setting, look at Figure 8-9, which exhibits the default settings on iOS.

Figure 8-9. Default cookie settings on iOS Safari

This state of affairs can be a big limitation if you're relying on the cookie model in mobile ads. Instead, leverage HTML5's localStorage property to place that information, rather than a cookie, on the client's browser. Listing 8-9 shows how this can be achieved in ad code using JavaScript.

Listing 8-9. A localStorage Site Event Example (Ad)

```
<script>
//iOS Site Events - local storage technique - platform.
function setiOSiteEvent (ad, placement, campaign, publisher) {
    var m = new Date().getMonth()
    var d = new Date().getDate();
    var y = new Date().getFullYear();
    var dom = window.location.href;
```

```
        var timeLoc = m + '/' + d + '/' + y + '&' + dom;
        var se = ad + '-' + placement + '-' + campaign + '-' + publisher + timeLoc;
                    localStorage.setItem('SiteEvent', se);
}
setiOSiteEvent('advertiser', 'placement', 'campaign' , 'publisher');
</script>
```

As Listing 8-9 shows, you can make a function called setiOSiteEvent, which gets a few parameters that will eventually be passed in by the ad server at ad-serve time. These could be the advertiser's name, placement identifier, campaign identifier, and the publisher where the ad is running. Next, inside our function, declare a few variables—m, d, y—they accurately timestamp when the site event occurs. Next, grab a reference to the URL location by writing var dom = window.location.href;—this will give the exact page location where the viewer saw the ad. Next, call another var, timeLoc, which stands for time/location and gets a concatenated value of the time values and the location, or the URL address. Next, create our final var, called se, which gets all of the ad server values, as well as our timestamp and location values. Finally, call up our localStorage object and assign se to it by storing the value through a setItem call. This localStorage.setItem call will store all of the site event (se) information to the user's browser so the advertiser's page can later reference it. Listing 8-10 showcases how this could be performed on the advertiser's page.

Listing 8-10. A localStorage Site Event Example (Advertiser's page)

```
function getiOSiteEvent () {
                    if(localStorage == '' || localStorage == null) {
                                return;
                    } else {

                                //Grab iOS Site Event
                                console.log(localStorage.getItem('SiteEvent'));
                                var seCall = new Image();
                                seCall.src = 'http://tracking.adserver.com?siteevent=' +
localStorage.getItem('SiteEvent');

                                setTimeout(localStorage.clear(), 500);//Clear the information
once the metric is reported
                    }
}

getiOSiteEvent ();
```

When a user visits the advertiser's page, the function getiOSiteEvent will fire. In the function, check whether the user has any location storage information. If the user doesn't, just back out of the function; if the user does, create a new Image (much like our third-party tracking example) and set its source attribute to the tracking location. Finally, once the ad server gets the metric, set a time-out and clear the localStorage in the user's browser so we never track this value again. There are many ways, other than the dated cookie approach, to do this; generally, the choice will depend on the ad server you're using and the browser adoption of client-side storage techniques.

Mobile Video Advertising

At the time of writing, the biggest mobile advertising market is video—traditional in-stream or pre-roll video with VAST. As the last chapter demonstrated, VAST is the IAB's industry-wide specification for delivery of video ads to video players—and mobile is no different. Mobile video being one of the fastest-growing markets in our industry, advertisers started looking to use pre-roll ads to get the attention of all the eyeballs in the small screen space. Figure 8-10 (from eMarketer) estimates worldwide mobile video use going into 2016.

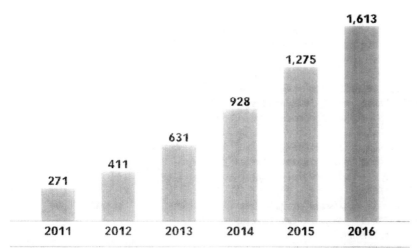

Mobile Video Viewers Worldwide, 2011-2016
millions

Note: includes on-demand video content downloaded or streamed to a
mobile handset
Source: Cisco Systems, "Visual Networking Index: Service Adoption
Forecast, 2011–2016," May 30, 2012

141000   www.eMarketer.com

Figure 8-10. *Estimated mobile video viewers worldwide, 2011–2016*

Many networks and publishers implement HTML5 support with their video players, and as I write, they've made different degrees of progress. But expect implementation to grow over time. One technical concern, loading external assets from an ad server, brings with it certain same domain security restrictions in native JavaScript. This is why using a CORS method, as discussed in Chapter 6, is highly important for resource sharing. Let's take a look at working with a mobile VAST tag with reference to an HTML5-compliant video asset (see Listing 8-11).

Listing 8-11. Mobile VAST Example

```
<VAST version="2.0">
    <Ad id="12345">
        <InLine>
            <AdSystem>HTML5 Compatible</AdSystem>
            <AdTitle>VAST 2.0 Instream Test</AdTitle>
            <Description>VAST 2.0 Instream Test</Description>
            <Error>http://url/error</Error>
            <Impression>http://tracking/impression</Impression>
            <Creatives>
                <Creative AdID="12345">
                    <Linear>
                        <Duration>00:00:30</Duration>
                        <TrackingEvents>
                            <Tracking event="creativeView">http://tracking/creativeView</Tracking>
                            <Tracking event="start">http://tracking/start</Tracking>
```

```
                    <Tracking event="midpoint">http://tracking/midpoint</Tracking>
                    <Tracking event="firstQuartile">http://tracking/firstQuartile</Tracking>
                    <Tracking event="thirdQuartile">http://tracking/thirdQuartile</Tracking>
                    <Tracking event="complete">http://tracking/complete</Tracking>
                </TrackingEvents>
                <VideoClicks>
                    <ClickThrough>http://www.somedomain.com</ClickThrough>
                    <ClickTracking>http://tracking/click</ClickTracking>
                </VideoClicks>
                <MediaFiles>
                    <MediaFile delivery="progressive" type="video/mp4" bitrate="1000"
width="640" height="360" scalable="true" maintainAspectRatio="true">
                        http://cdn.somedomain.com/video.mp4
                    </MediaFile>
                    <MediaFile delivery="progressive" type="video/ogg" bitrate="1000"
width="640" height="360" scalable="true" maintainAspectRatio="true">
                        http://cdn.somedomain.com/video.ogg
                    </MediaFile>
                    <MediaFile delivery="progressive" type="video/webm" bitrate="1000"
width="640" height="360" scalable="true" maintainAspectRatio="true">
                        http://cdn.somedomain.com/video.webm
                    </MediaFile>
                </MediaFiles>
            </Linear>
        </Creative>
        <Creative AdID="12345Companion">
            <CompanionAds></CompanionAds>
        </Creative>
    </Creatives>
  </InLine>
 </Ad>
</VAST>
```

It's just regular VAST markup—however, look for the mediafile nodes (bolded) and the specific video asset used. Can you see it? Three different video types (MP4, OGG, WebM) are being used in order to appease all the HTML5 browsers and their different format requirements. Also, keep in mind that some HTML5 video players may require JSON code as opposed to XML. Again, this information will come from the specific publisher and their video player requirements.

Native Device Features

This section will review some of the native features that mobile can access and the various APIs that give mobile developers permission. Mobile browsers and devices have many features: phone calling, GPS location, deep linking into app stores, accelerometers, gyroscopes, and compasses, to name a few. All these device features can be used to better enhance your creative, as you'll learn in the following sections. Some emerging devices even have support for NFC (near field communication), barometers for detecting climate, and magnetometers for inspecting magnetics, all of which can help your ad get really relevant information—like how humid it is when a user is viewing your ad. Let's review how you can use these amazing APIs and JavaScript to access these features and provide highly rich advertising experiences for mobile with graceful failovers where they're not supported. Before digging in, see http://mobilehtml5.org to learn which APIs and features can be used to target specific devices and browsers.

Touch

Let's start with touch, probably the most popular mobile device feature. You're surely aware that most phones and tablets in today's market offer a capacitive touch screen interface, allowing users to interact with their fingers as opposed to the traditional point-and-click mouse interface. This is a huge shift in the way web content is developed, as the industry so accustomed to working with mouse clicks and mouseovers as a form of interaction and measurement. Now developers can take advantage of taps, swipes, pinches, and other gestures to add interactivity to creatives and thus open up a whole new world of immersive creativity for advertisers and creative agencies to work inside. Instead of using traditional "click to expand" CTA, you'll notice "tap to expand," "tap to call," "tap to map," and so on. These CTAs are ever more widely used in this, the dawn of touch devices, and specifically mobile advertising.

Touch Events

The following events are used when working with touch API on mobile and tablet: touchstart, which is triggered when a finger is placed on any DOM element; touchmove, triggered when a finger is dragged along any DOM element; and touchend, triggered when a finger is removed or picked up from any DOM element. Remember our viewport settings? Mobile browsers natively have default touch settings. If you think about it, this won't work so well if your browser has its own set of swipe and gesture behaviors and your ad creative does, too. To work around this, set the viewport so the user cannot scale using user-scalable=no. By following in your code editor and using the JavaScript touch API, you can use the code to touch and drag an element onscreen and instruct the browser to prevent its default behavior, which would be to move the window as a whole (see Listing 8-12).

Listing 8-12. Preventing the Browser's Default Touch Behavior

```
<!DOCTYPE HTML>
<html>
<head>
<meta name="viewport" content="initial-scale=1, user-scalable=no">
</head>
<body>
    <div id="element" style="position:absolute; background-color:black; width:50px;
height:50px;"></div>
</body>
<html>
<script>
var element = document.getElementById("element");

element.addEventListener('touchmove', function(event) {
    event.preventDefault();

    if (event.targetTouches.length === 1) {
        console.log(event)
        var touch = event.targetTouches[0];
        // Place element where the finger is
        element.style.left = touch.pageX + 'px';
        element.style.top = touch.pageY + 'px';
    }
}, false);
</script>
</html>
```

If you refresh your page on a touch-capable browser, you can touch and drag the *element* all around the browser using your finger. Wherever your finger goes, the element follows. This could be a great method for achieving a drag-and-drop type of effect on touch-enabled browsers.

If you use touch a lot—and I hope you do when developing for mobile—a really good JavaScript framework, called HammerJS (http://eightmedia.github.com/hammer.js), can speed up your development. This framework allows you to rapidly develop with touch in mind and only costs around 2 kilobytes when compressed, which is enough to use freely within a mobile ad unit.

Note When applying CSS3 transforms on input fields in touch-enabled browsers, some Android devices have lost focus on input. It's best not to apply CSS transforms until such issues are fixed in future versions.

Orientation

Orientation is another interesting feature of mobile devices (most of them have these sensors). Orientation simply refers to how the user physically holds the actual phone or tablet. In either portrait or landscape mode, you can use the orientation API to detect the screens layout and react accordingly. This is important to note, as you'll more than likely need to develop two variations of your ads for both versions or use a "safe area" that can fit comfortably within both. Sometimes publishers will request delivery of two separate ad tags, but that will hopefully phase out soon, as another HTTP call shouldn't be made for a device-level feature. Ideally, a responsive ad layout, which can adapt to the device's screen, should be the goal. The typical case uses JavaScript and CSS to rework the creative to the new dimensions and adjust the creative layout accordingly. Listing 8-13 can be used to detect orientation within your creative.

Listing 8-13. Orientation Example (HTML)

```
<html>
<head>
<link rel="stylesheet" media="screen and (orientation:portrait)" href="portrait.css"><link
rel="stylesheet" media="screen and (orientation:landscape)" href="landscape.css">
</head>
<body>
</body>
</html>
```

From this code you can see that in the head of the document there are two style sheet references—one to handle portrait layout and the other, landscape (notice the media query). This way, the ad creative can adjust its layout accordingly, depending on the user's orientation. There is also a way to achieve this effect by using straight CSS (see Listing 8-14).

Listing 8-14. Orientation Example (CSS)

```
@media only screen and (orientation: landscape) {
                /* rules for device in landscape orientation */
                #ad {...};
}

@media only screen and (orientation: portrait) {
                /* rules for device in portrait orientation */
                #ad {...};
}
```

As you can see, CSS rules can include media queries specifically inside the CSS style sheet. To learn more about other media queries you can target in addition to orientation, see `http://w3.org/TR/css3-mediaqueries`.

Note At the time of writing, the orientation property in media queries did not work on Apple's iPhone and some other phone devices.

Still the best technique ,in my opinion, is to know the screen dimensions of the devices you're serving for and cater to each using CSS media queries and the `orientationchange` event in JavaScript. Listing 8-15 shows how to detect the change event.

Listing 8-15. Orientation Example (JavaScript)

```
<!DOCTYPE HTML>
<html>
<head>
</head>
<body>
</body>
<script>
window.addEventListener("orientationchange", function() {
    if (window.orientation === 0 || window.orientation === 180) {
    //portrait
    showPortrait();
    } else {
        //landscape
      showLandscape();
    }
}, false);

function showPortrait () {
   document.body.style.backgroundColor = 'yellow';
}
function showLandscape () {
   document.body.style.backgroundColor = 'black';
}
</script>

</html>
```

Notice that an event listener is being added to the window object for the `orientationchange` event. If a device changes orientation, it will broadcast this event, which can be adjusted for. Inside our function, notice that `window.orientation`, a native property of the window object, is being checked for. If you find that it returns a 0 or 180, you know that the device is in portrait, as shown in Figure 8-11.

Figure 8-11. *A device in portrait orientation*

Otherwise, it's either 90 or –90, which means the device is in landscape orientation, as in Figure 8-12.

Figure 8-12. A device in landscape orientation

Since in advertising you mostly have to get things out the door pretty quickly, developing two creative layouts simply isn't an option. For this scenario, I typically instruct clients to develop for whichever orientation makes the most sense for the ad layout and toggle an instruction card for users when or if they switch orientation. Figure 8-13 shows a recent iPad campaign that does just that. On the left you'll see the instruction card for portrait layout, and on the right you'll notice the full ad experience.

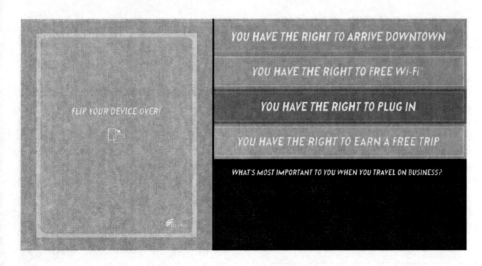

Figure 8-13. Here's how a mobile ad can have two different designs per orientation

In some cases, this is a better technique altogether, especially if the creative is a video that looks better in landscape or if it's a game that works better in portrait. Again, most of this will be dealt with on a case-by-case basis, so be sure to take your own creative in consideration and instruct your clients before development.

Gyroscope, Compass, and Accelerometer

Since you've just learned about the orientation of mobile devices, let's take it a step further and discuss the gyroscope, compass, and accelerometer. Each of these APIs can give your ad creative rich enhancements by tying directly into device features. A good example of how this API can be used in an ad experience is found at `http://bit.ly/OAf8BX`, where it takes advantage of the accelerometer API as well as the Canvas to provide the user a mazelike experience.

In order to take advantage of these cool features, you'll need to learn a bit about the `deviceorientation` spec. The device orientation API outlines how the DOM will listen for specific events—such as `deviceorientation`, `compassneedscalibration`, and `devicemotion`—to tap into via our ad's JavaScript. Look at the code in Listing 8-16 to see how to work with this API.

Listing 8-16. Accelerometer/Gyroscope Example

```
<script>
var ad = document.querySelector('#ad');
window.addEventListener("deviceorientation", function(event) {
        // process
        var a = event.alpha;
        var b = event.beta;
        var g = event.gamma;

        console.log('Alpha : ' + a + ' Beta : ' + b + ' Gamma : ' + g);
        ad.style.webkitTransform = 'translate3d(' + Math.round(a) + 'px, ' + Math.round(b) + 'px,
 ' + Math.round(g) + 'px)';
}, true);
</script>
```

You can see that we're adding an event listener for the device orientation event, which will return an `alpha`, `beta`, and gamma on the window's orientation state. So what are `alpha`, `beta`, and gamma? They're actually the measurement of the rotation the device has from top to bottom, left to right, and rotating in a circular fashion (there is a more detailed explanation in the orientation spec). Finally, take our ad element and apply a CSS3 transform on the ad unit by calling a `translate3d` function and applying the `alpha`, `beta`, and gamma values to the x, y, and z properties of the ad. If you're following along, you should be able to see your ad element move about the screen based on how you change the orientation. A pretty subtle but slick effect if you ask me!

Using the accelerometer also gives access to a "shake" gesture, but since some coding is required, be sure to check out `http://github.com/alexgibson/shake.js` for quick implementations. For more information on the device orientation specification, see `http://dev.w3.org/geo/api/spec-source-orientation.html`. For more on iOS and compass use, see `developer.apple.com/library/safari/#documentation/SafariDOMAdditions/Reference/DeviceOrientationEventClassRef/DeviceOrientationEvent/DeviceOrientationEvent.html`.

■ **Note** There is a great example using the Webkit compass at `http://help.arcgis.com/EN/webapi/javascript/arcgis/help/jssamples_start.htm#jssamples/mobile_compass.html`.

Protocols

Another great feature to take advantage of in mobile advertising is calling and texting from directly within the ad experience. Specific protocols can be used for TEL and SMS, among others in mobile devices. TEL and SMS can let a user open the native phone or text-messaging client on the device. This example demonstrates how to do it.

```
<a href="tel:18005551212">Call!</a>
<a href="sms:18005551212">Text!</a>
```

This simple interaction provides a great user experience; users don't have to copy and paste text and toggle between applications. All they need to do is tap on the link CTA and get prompted with the notification to call or text. This is really great if you want to have someone contact customer service or even schedule a test drive for a vehicle at a local car dealership. In addition to these built-in protocols, native applications can assign their own protocols to open up themselves from the browser when a user interacts on specific links. Here is a code snippet that shows how Apple's Facetime and Microsoft's Skype use their own protocols.

```
<a href="facetime://18005551212">Facetime me!</a>
<a href="skype:youUserID?call">Skype!</a>
```

Keep in mind that many applications have their own protocols, but in the mobile space, this could be very advantageous for an advertiser. This isn't specific to phone or communication applications either; content providers and publishers—including the *Wall Street Journal*, which uses `wsj://`—use protocols to open specific user interactions inside an application from a link. This is a very nice feature when seamless communication between a web page or ad and the native application. You can give users a taste of information from within the ad unit and ask them to read more by digging deeper within the application environment.

MMA and the IAB

You may be asking yourself a question about standards and mobile advertising guidelines while reviewing all of this information. Luckily much as in desktop advertising; there is a set of emerging standards and guidelines to adhere to in mobile as well. The Mobile Marketing Association (MMA) (`http://mmaglobal.com`) and the Interactive Advertising Bureau (IAB; `http://iab.net`) are the standards organizations for mobile online advertising. The MMA traditionally focuses on static advertising, whereas the IAB focuses more on rich advertising within the mobile landscape. Here are some of the common mobile ad unit sizes for rich and static as set by the IAB and the MMA.

- typical mobile rich media banner sizes: 300 × 50, 320 × 50
- typical mobile rich media panel sizes: 300 × 300, 320 × 320 or Full-Screen (320 × 480)
- requires a Close button on panel
- static MMA sizes
- XL (300 × 50)
- large (216 × 36)
- medium (168 × 28)
- small (120 × 20)

The IAB also focuses on mobile rich media formats called "rising stars," formats that are much more engaging f or ad publishers and ad servers to adopt. Such formats include Full Screen units, Sliders, and the Filmstrip creative ad units. Each offers a unique experience; they go well beyond the static banner real estate. See `http://iab.net/risingstarsmobile` to learn more.

Device Testing

As this chapter closes out, I want to touch on the tools you can use when dealing with mobile development—it can get overwhelming, I know! Testing on all of these mobile devices can be a pain. There are just too many devices out there in the wild to control how your content will look and behave on every screen. There are many services out there to do virtual device and browser testing: Device Anywhere, BrowserStack, Opera's Mobile Emulator, and others. They are very good, but nothing is as accurate as testing on real thing, so be sure to reach out to the online community to initiate some testing on devices they may have readily available to them. There are also various free tools on the Web to relieve your mobile development woes: `http://jsconsole.com`, `http://remote-tilt.com`, and mobile "view source" tool, `http://snoopy.allmarkedup.com`, all have really great free feature sets. In addition, there are free remote debugging tools: Adobe Edge Inspect (formally Adobe Shadow) [`http://html.adobe.com/edge/inspect`], Weinre [`http://people.apache.org/~pmuellr/weinre/docs/latest`], and Safari's new developer tool set for iOS 6 are worth checking out. In the end, sometimes you'll absolutely need to test on the actual device, so if you need to drive to your local electronics store to check up on the latest devices, do so—especially if your client will be on the devices not available to you. Chances are you'll have at least one client who will view your creative on a "one in a million" device, and it could potentially cost you the entire campaign if you're not testing for it.

Summary

This chapter has covered a lot on mobile advertising and the mobile web. The landscape is wide, and the fragmentation is pretty apparent. Certain technologies work only in some browsers, devices, and operating system versions. Mobile advertising and HTML5 go hand in hand, and mobile has specific takes on how it works with the evolving HTML5 spec and what its various API developers can gain access to. We had a review of the mobile world we live in and how to build for it, and there was even discussion of various native device features you can tap into for building rich ad creatives. Hopefully, after reading this chapter, you'll feel confident in answering a client's question like "Can JavaScript be used along with HTML5 to develop an interactive ad for the iPad?" The next chapter focuses on the vast world of mobile in-application advertising. This is where things get trickier and the fragmentation in the space becomes noticeably thicker. But it's also where mobile advertisements have much more complexity and more engaging features available to them. If you're ready, let's dig into the world of in-application advertising.

CHAPTER 9

In-Application Advertising

After reviewing Chapter 8 about mobile web advertising, it's time to jump in and understand how advertisers get their advertisements into the budding world of applications. These applications can be anything from apps on a phone that users download from an app store to apps on game consoles or smart TVs. I'll discuss the different environments per device and OS and discuss use cases for all. I'll review software development kits (SDKs) and how they're involved in serving ads as well as how ads can have much more feature-rich capabilities when served into an app than a mobile web environment. I'll talk about SDK providers such as AdMarvel, Medialets, and Millennial Media, which provide in-app advertising, and I'll focus on the IAB's solution and standard with the ORMMA and MRAID API.

Note   Keep in mind while reviewing this chapter that SDKs and applications change. This chapter covers what to do currently, but the information may change as SDK vendors and content owners update their SDKs or use other vendors to traffic their ads.

Mobile Applications

Mobile applications are native applications that run on your mobile device. Think of them as applications like Microsoft Office or Adobe Photoshop that run natively on your desktop computer but are on your phone or tablet instead. Mobile applications are used instead of forcing a user to visit a URL in a browser; in addition, by offering an application, the content owner has full control over their application because it lives outside the walls of the device's browser. Application developers create these "apps" by using the low-level code that the operating system relies on. In the case of Apple iOS, it is Objective-C, and for Android, it is Java. Developers with these skills can create a very lucrative career for themselves developing applications for productivity, entertainment, or even gaming. The market for applications is booming, to say the least, because in-application purchases accounted for $970 million in sales in 2011. By 2015, that figure is anticipated to grow to $5.6 billion. Juniper Research reported in 2012 that in-app advertising will hit $2.4 billion by the end of the year. By 2015, that figure will soar to $7.1 billion. These applications get a lot of views because people can download them to their devices at any time for a very small fee, or even free. This, of course, brings a lot of attention to the application market and how easy it is for users to grab them up.

There are close to a million different applications to choose from in the various app stores such as Apple's App Store, Google's Play marketplace, and BlackBerry's App World; each app varies in function and price, all the way down to free with the possibility of making in-application purchases. In the following sections, I'll cover some of the leading application marketplaces.

Apple

Apple is no stranger to the mobile application market. With iOS and the Apple App Store, users can browse for more than half a million applications, and most of the apps are free with the inclusion of advertising. Developers used to be able to grab a user's unique device identifier (UDID) in their apps, but Apple removed this feature because it posed threats to privacy concerns among users. Basically, having a UDID for a user allows app developers to better target an advertiser's message to the right customer through their application. Tying information such as location, time, and interest all to a unique device ID or hash means an advertiser can better understand who is viewing their ad content and when. Although UDIDs are now not accessible for applications to access for advertising in iOS, there is another advertising identifier as of iOS 6 that allows for apps to better target by similar means. In addition, there is even an initiative for an open UDID called OpenUDID, which would be accessible by all devices, but it has yet to really take off (http://github.com/ylechelle/OpenUDID).

Apple pretty much reigns supreme in the app market with the number of quality apps offered in such a controlled developer environment. This coupled with the explosive growth of Apple's iDevices means that applications are a very fruitful market to be in. Figure 9-1 shows what eMarketer projects for U.S. iPad users over the next three years.

US iPad Users and Penetration, 2010-2015						
	2010	**2011**	**2012**	**2013**	**2014**	**2015**
iPad users (millions)	**11.5**	**28.0**	**53.2**	**70.5**	**81.1**	**90.8**
—% change	-	143.9%	90.1%	32.6%	15.1%	11.9%
—% of total population	3.7%	8.9%	16.8%	22.1%	25.2%	27.9%
—% of internet users	5.1%	12.1%	22.2%	28.7%	32.3%	35.3%
—% of tablet users	88.0%	83.0%	76.4%	71.2%	68.0%	68.0%

Note: individuals of any age who use an iPad at least once per month
Source: eMarketer, June 2012

140849   www.eMarketer.com

Figure 9-1. *U.S. iPad users 2010 to 2015 (Source: eMarketer.com)*

Figure 9-1 says by 2015 about 90 million U.S. users will be touching and interacting with iPad tablets. With this many people making the switch to tablet-based experiences as opposed to traditional desktop apps, expect to see more applications and advertisers moving into this space.

Android

Google's Android is the other main competing application operating system. Google, as of last year, has the most OS installs per device worldwide, and many believe it's because it provides a stable and open operating system that can be installed across many manufacturer's devices such as Samsung, LG, Motorola, and others (http://canalys.com/newsroom/smart-phones-overtake-client-pcs-2011). Google provides a very similar experience as the Apple App Store to download and install applications on Android devices; Google's store is called Google Play (http://play.google.com/store/apps). From an Android device, users can navigate through close to a million apps, both free and paid. Much like its competitor, Apple, since many of these apps are offered for free, Google apps generally are fueled by an advertising-based model.

One important thing to note about Android is that its operating system versions vary tremendously among its user base, which is why for Android you often hear about *fragmentation*. This fragmentation arises because of all the different OS versions and the users' inability or lack of interest to adopt the latest versions. I state "inability" because many devices are not capable of updating to the latest versions of Android, which makes its user base very diverse. This, in turn, creates a lot of extra work for developers and designers creating native apps and HTML5-based advertisements. This is one of the main reasons that iOS remains very attractive to developers; its user base adopts (and is capable) of installing the latest OS very quickly, which gives developers an even playing field to deploy content toward. To better understand this fragmentation, visit http://allthingsd.com/20120920/usage-of-apples-ios-6-hits-staggering-levels-on-first-day-of-availability, where you'll find that Android's OS adoption rates fails in comparison to Apple's iOS.

Android still remains a top competitor in the mobile OS landscape, and if you're interested in building applications for the world's largest mobile operating system, visit http://developer.android.com/sdk/index.html.

Others

Many other mobile operating systems are in the market, including BlackBerry with its App World (http://appworld. blackberry.com) and Windows Phone with its store (http://windowsphone.com/store), but all currently have a very small slice of the global OS pie compared to iOS and Android. BlackBerry is expected to release its latest and greatest OS called BlackBerry 10 by 2013, which could be the push that the company so desperately needs. Read more of the features at http://blackberry.com/BlackBerry-10.

Windows Phone has also had a slow start with Windows Phone 7, according to research firm Nielsen (http:// blog.seattlepi.com/microsoft/2011/06/30/windows-phone-7-has-thin-sliver-of-u-s-share-nielsen-says), but expect big changes because Windows should be taking off with its Windows 8 update, which released in conjunction with Microsoft's first tablet, called Surface. Windows first coined this new operating system's UI as "Metro" but has since removed that branding for Windows 8 UI. BlackBerry and Windows remain competitive in the mobile landscape, and if you're building advertisements that need to deploy across various applications on these OSs, you'll need to read on to understand how to take advantage of the vastly fragmented mobile market.

In-Application Advertising

You may have guessed that with all of these app stores, the number of users on these devices, and the number of free applications, it's only a matter of time until advertisers take notice and move some of their ad spend to this emerging digital outlet. Well, you're exactly correct. In-app advertising is becoming a huge market for developers' revenue stream when developing native applications for devices. Many content providers and developers are offering their apps for free with an ad-supported model. Take the very popular game *Word with Friends*, which runs on any OS and comes in free and paid versions for users to download. Both games offer very similar experiences to the end user, with the exception of ads in the free version and no ads in the paid. With millions upon millions of downloads of these popular games, advertisers are taking notice that the eyes aren't all on desktop or TV any longer, so they're shifting ad dollars over to where the eyeballs are.

In-application advertising is not really new; in fact, ever since the tablet market was "invented" by the Apple iPad in 2010, advertising was there, in applications, from day one. For example, the ad server PointRoll served the ad units shown in Figure 9-2, the first day the iPad was released to users. Figure 9-2 showcases a rich media Lincoln ad that was deployed through the TextPlus (http://textplus.com) application using the SDK provider AdMarvel on the iPad.

Figure 9-2. One of the first rich iPad ads

The Lincoln ad was pretty groundbreaking when it comes to first-to-market and innovative tablet advertising. A user's experience was to tap the static banner within the application, where they were taken to a full-screen immersive environment with video, high-resolution images, and multiple layouts depending on the orientation of the device. This experience paved the way for even more innovative ad experiences including gaming, interactivity, and live polling. Soon advertisers learned that anything you can do on the desktop, you can pretty much bring to the mobile and tablet environments as well.

With advertisers dipping into this medium more and more, it's anticipated that additional dollars will pump into this market for years to come. In fact, eMarketer and Juniper Research state that the in-application advertising spend will reach more than 7 billion dollars in 2015 (see Figure 9-3).

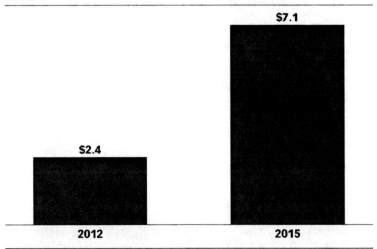

Figure 9-3. *Mobile in-app ad spending worldwide 2012 to 2015 (Source: eMarketer.com)*

With in-app ad spending on the rise for the next few years to come, now is a perfect time to learn how to deploy rich advertisements to these new distribution channels. But it's not all fun and profit just yet; there are some key technological points you'll need to grasp before you can develop across OSs. You may think that all the bugs are ironed out by now and that this landscape is much less fragmented than what you learned initially with HTML5 and other mobile devices in general. Sadly, this is far from the case, and in the next section, you'll learn about the additional fragmentation that needs to be considered when working with in-application ads.

SDKs

Fragmentation in HTML5 is pretty apparent, as you've learned in previous chapters. It's even more so in the mobile web space, with all the different operating systems, version numbers, and various levels of HTML5 compliance. For the in-application world of mobile, it gets even trickier because now developers have to understand which applications support which ad platform SDKs and versions of the SDK. Software development kits (SDKs) are used by many publisher and application ad servers to handle the trafficking and scheduling of various ad tags in many different application environments. Think of SDKs as the mediatory level between the ad management system and the application living on a user's device. Since SDKs are really just a bit of code to include in the native application, the developer needs the foresight to see that their application should or will include advertising at some point. For example, currently some applications such as Facebook, Instagram, and even Twitter do not have ads, so no third-party ad SDKs would be needed in the development of their applications. However, applications like the *Wall Street Journal*, *USA Today*, and Pandora Radio offer advertising to a user in exchange for free content, whether it be music, sports, or news. These ads are typically trafficked through a publisher-side ad server and application SDK. On one side of things, you have the ad server's campaign management tool, which allows users to schedule and target their tags as well as set up basic delivery rules. On the other side of things, you have an SDK that communicates with that campaign management tool in order to receive the specific ads scheduled. Figure 9-4 better illustrates the connection between the two ends.

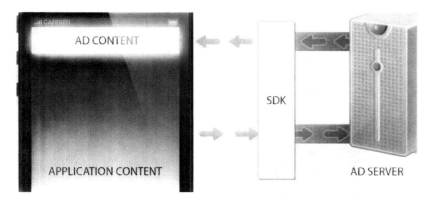

Figure 9-4. *The communication between application and ad server through an SDK*

In Figure 9-4, you can see that the application content will make a request to the ad server through the SDK. Once the ad server understands what application is making the ad request, it returns the appropriate ad content through the SDK. So, you may be thinking that there has to be a standard way of doing this, right? Well, to answer your question, the answer is both yes and no. Currently, there are many different publisher ad servers as well as SDKs in the mobile in-app landscape, and in the following sections, you'll take a closer look at some of the more popular ones that you'll deal with when developing for in-app campaigns.

Apple's iAd

One of the more popular in-application ad networks is Apple's own iAd platform (http://advertising.apple.com). The Apple iAd platform allows developers to obtain revenue through banner and rich full-screen advertisements, where Apple sells the advertising space within your application and delivers the ads via its network to fill the ad slots. Application developers can then earn income when users view (*impressions*) or interact (*activities*) with the ads that are displayed in the application.

Introduced to iOS developers and advertisers in version 4.0 of the OS, the Apple iAd platform used to come with an extremely large price tag of $1 million per advertising campaign but has since come down significantly because of the lack of initial participants. To use Apple's iAd platform, you must become an Apple developer and iAd Network member, and only then can the application publisher or developer control the ads that get served into the apps. With iAd, developers can use free tools from Apple such as the iAd Producer, which allows for a clean interface for building iOS ads quickly. In addition, since the ads are built for iOS and Apple devices such as the iPhone and iPad, developers can take advantage of some really amazing in-app features such as the following:

- Download an app or iTunes content in the background

- Add a reminder directly to the calendar app

- Compose and send branded e-mails from within an ad, using their contact list

- Experience immersive 3D graphics with WebGL support (more on WebGL in Chapter 12)

- View in-line audio and video in a custom frame

- Save coupons, barcodes, recipes, or branded wallpaper

- Find nearby stores using geolocation

In addition to the rich features available to iAd users, valuable **metrics and analytics** are also available via the platform such as the following:

- Impressions

- Taps and tap-through rate

- Unique visits

- Average time spent

- Views and views per visit

- Interactions (videos viewed, games played, and so on)

- Conversions and downloads

Finally, iAd also provides some rich audience and device targeting features such as the following:

- Demographics

- Application preferences

- Music, movie, TV, and audiobook genre interests

- Location

- Device (iPhone, iPad, iPod touch)

- Network (WiFi, 3G)

If you're a publisher or content owner and looking to utilize the iAd platform within your application, I strongly recommend visiting `http://developer.apple.com/library/ios/#DOCUMENTATION/UserExperience/Conceptual/ iAd_Guide/Introduction/Introduction.html`.

Google's AdMob*

As you've may have guessed, Google is in this space as well with its large mobile advertising platform called AdMob (`http://google.com/ads/admob`). Google acquired the company in 2009 for a cool $750 million dollars, and currently AdMob runs billions of banner and text-based ad impressions a year. Its SDK operates across Android, iOS, and Window Phone 7 applications and manages multiple ad networks into a single interface. AdMob provides a huge ad network mediation by working with networks like Adfonic, BrightRoll, HUNT, iAD, InMobi, Jumptap, Millennial Media, MobFox, and many others to provide a single interface for ad management. Application developers install the SDK code base into their app and can earn revenue by serving Rich Media advertising within the environment. In addition to the SDK, AdMob interfaces directly with DoubleClick for publishers (DFP), which allows users to fill ad inventory directly through the AdMob advertising network. AdMob allows for rich media, offers advanced creative formats leveraging HTML5, and offers audience targeting to specific demographics and locations. To download the latest AdMob SDK, visit `http://developers.google.com/mobile-ads-sdk/download`. For example, for applications using the AdMob SDK, visit `http://code.google.com/p/google-mobile-dev`.

Opera's AdMarvel*

Another mobile ad server and SDK provider is AdMarvel `http://admarvel.com`. Owned by the browser manufacturer Opera, AdMarvel is a powerful publisher-side ad server, optimization/mediator (mobile ad exchange), and rich media SDK provider. Much like AdMob, it provides an iOS and Android SDK as well as a BlackBerry SDK. As such, app developers/publishers can have the best of services and have access to other rich media providers while reducing the SDK clutter within their applications. Through the AdMarvel interface, standard targeting includes the following:

- Time

- Region

- Devices

- Operating system

- Network carrier

Note that custom targeting is also available (to AdMarvel specifically). This means that campaign managers and developers can set rules for certain ad tags to render to a user's device based on the previous inputs. This is very helpful when you want to offer customized messaging or creative to a specific device, time of day, or even cell network status.

Medialets*

Another popular mobile rich media ad server and SDK provider is Medialets (http://medialets.com). Specializing in mobile rich media specifically, Medialets has a large penetration in the market for both online publishers and digital publications like e-magazines. Medialets offers its own SDK for integration into iOS, Android, and BlackBerry applications and provides a suite of analytics to measure the effectiveness of your campaign. Because Medialets is an SDK provider working within the application environment, it can offer great targeting including time of day, geolocation, app content, device type, and connection status.

Millennial Media

Millennial Media (http://millennialmedia.com) is the self-proclaimed largest independent mobile ad network, competing with the big players of Google's AdMob and Apple's iAd. Millennial Media also brings to the table a full SDK (MMSDK) where it can serve rich media mobile ads into various applications on various devices. You can download the MMSDK for a variety of device operating systems including iOS, Android, BlackBerry, Windows Phone, PSP, and WebOS, to name a few. Through Millennial Media's tools, developers can support interactive mobile video ads, mobile rich media, and traditional banner ads all with real-time results and analytics. Millennial Media also offers targeting, including demographic, behavioral, geolocation, and contextual, among others. You can learn more about its tool set at http://tools.mmedia.com (be sure to register first).

Others

The list goes on for mobile ad networks and SDK providers offering HTML5-driven rich media. There are too many to name for the scope of this book, and it's an ecosystem that is constantly changing. But to outline a few others so you're aware of them, you may also need to traffic your ad tags into networks like Jumptap (http://jumptap.com), Greystripe (http://greystripe.com), and InMobi (http://inmobi.com); note that they may rely on an SDK that wasn't mentioned here. In fact, certain applications have their own "homebrewed" SDKs for ad serving, like the Pandora Music app, and when serving into applications like these, the app provider, the SDK vendor, and the creative agency together need to determine what calls need to be made to the platform to recognize certain rich features of the ad such as whether the ad is expanding or closing. Pandora is not amateur to the mobile space, but for some reason it choose not to go with providers like iAd, Millennial Media, and AdMeld, perhaps because of security issues (http://cnnmoneytech.tumblr.com/post/4588292154/pandora-boots-its-outside-ad-platforms).

The point of all this SDK vendor information is that these SDKs need to be referenced by the HTML5 ad creative you deliver. This communication between the ad and the SDK vendor happens by way of an API, and it typically communicates through the ad's JavaScript code. For mobile rich media ads that expand, close, and offer video and gaming, the application housing the ad needs to understand what state the ad is in based on user interaction. This may seem familiar because I discussed working with the VPAID API inside the publisher's video player in Chapter 7. Basically, same rules apply here, the ad needs to communicate to the publisher's app so the experience isn't jarring to the end user. The problem is that with all of these different vendors in the space, it's hard to understand what API works across all of them, if one even exists. This is where the fragmentation occurs within the mobile in-application space. This can vary tremendously across networks and devices, which makes it very tough for an advertiser to secure a media buy that will run flawlessly everywhere.

For example of working with a "home brew" solution, when working with the Pandora application, you can use the code snippet shown in Listing 9-1 to run a basic expand/collapse rich media ad within its mobile application.

Listing 9-1. Pandora App API Example

```
<!DOCTYPE HTML>
<html>
<head>
<meta name = "viewport" content = "width=device-width">
</head>
<body>
  <button onclick=expandPandora()>Open Panel</button>
  <button onclick=closePandora()>Close Panel</button>
</body>
<script>
document.addEventListener('DOMContentLoaded', function() {


}, false)

function expandPandora() {
    try {
        PandoraApp.setViewportHeight(300)
    } catch (e) {
        console.log (e + " No PandoraApp Reference")
    };

    initExpand();
}

function initExpand () {
    console.log('initExpand')
}

function closePandora () {
    try {
        PandoraApp.setViewportHeight(50);
    } catch (e) {
        console.log(e + " No PandoraApp Reference")
    };
```

```
    closeExpand();
}

function closeExpand () {
    console.log('closeExpand')
}
</script>
</html>
```

As you can see from the previous example, working with Pandora's SDK via JavaScript calls is fairly straightforward, but it works only for Pandora. An advertiser running ads across other publishers will need to have a customized ad for each one, and operationally this does not make sense for scale and quick turnaround times because you could be tasked with creating a large conditional statement inside your script to interface with all the vendor's APIs.

Note   The Pandora code in Listing 9-1 works at the time of this writing, but please note all of this is subject to change at the discretion of the publisher and application provider.

For the purposes of thinking that this ad could be trafficked to publishers outside of Pandora, I like to wrap my calls in a `try`/`catch` method. While not the best coding practice, it ensures that if the Pandora object does not exist, the code would just log a message and continue running without any breaks. For now, this is a good practice when you want one ad to run across multiple sites and networks. Again, this specific use case is just for Pandora, but you can easily see how this can get out of hand quickly! Having a developer add numerous `try`/`catch` statements or conditionals is a lot of added work and testing, and between what features you can use in what browser, on what device, on what operating system version, adding this SDK fragmentation to the puzzle can really make your head hurt! (Remember how advertisers want scale?) There has to be something better, right?!

ORMMA and MRAID

So, with all of these applications, you may be asking yourself, "What gives? Why do I need to worry about this additional SDK fragmentation on top of everything else I need to worry about in this already diverse landscape with HTML5 ad development?" Well, for some time (and even as I write this), this is the way it has been because vendors thought they could tie their clients into using their own proprietary SDK code base, thus resulting in the clients being "stuck" with them for ad serving. While a pretty clever business model because it makes it hard for developers to make the switch, the reality is that it's not a long-standing one, and with that, I introduce to you ORMMA (`http://ormma.org`) and MRAID (`http://iab.net/mraid`).

Open Rich Media Mobile Advertising (ORMMA) was an industry-wide initiative for advertisers to have one common set of rules for displaying rich media ads across various mobile application platforms. ORMMA was an SDK and an API for allowing ad designers to use a common way to interface with ORMMA-compliant applications. Application developers would have needed to follow the ORMMA specification to allow ad designers to add compelling rich media ads into their apps. While ORMMA started the building blocks for executing mobile rich media at scale, it is a thing of the past now with the release of the IAB's MRAID.

Mobile Rich Media Ad Interface Definition (MRAID) is essentially what VPAID is to publisher video players except for mobile applications. Founded on many of the principals that ORMMA addressed, its sole purpose is to ease fragmentation across devices, applications, and ad servers so mobile rich media can be a profitable industry. MRAID is backed firmly by the IAB and has a dedicated working group committed to its development. The IAB believes that MRAID should be the de facto standard for having mobile rich media ad units communicate with application environments. Currently on its second version, MRAID allows mobile ad developers to utilize a set of standard functions to communicate between the ad and application's SDK, for instance telling the application the ad will expand, close, or even play a video. MRAID isn't meant to trample HTML5 or the current APIs; instead, it's there to aid in the development for ad designers where certain HTML5 fragmentation may still exist.

MRAID is meant to be simplistic and implemented easily and has no dependency on various SDKs. In fact, the only requirement for MRAID is that the SDK the application chooses should be MRAID compliant and recognize the API calls from within the ad code. This information would come only from the publisher or possibly the IAB who keeps tabs on who is MRAID certified and not. However, most SDK vendors I mentioned earlier are working toward MRAID compliance, so working within their platforms should be fine going forward.

So, now that you know a little bit about why MRAID is important to ad designers, let's review some basic MRAID code in the following section and in Listing 9-2.

Note   At the time of writing, the SDK sections marked with * are said to be compliant supporting the IAB's MRAID.

MRAID Code

Being that all SDKs going forward should be MRAID compliant, it's worth reviewing the MRAID code for interfacing with compliant SDKs in applications. Listing 9-2 outlines a rudimentary expandable ad using basic MRAID API functions.

Listing 9-2. MRAID JavaScript API Example

```
<!DOCTYPE HTML>
<html>
<head>
<meta name = "viewport" content = "width=device-width">
</head>
<body>
  <div id='cta' hidden data='http://johnpercival.org'>Click Here</button></div>
  <section id='banner'><button onclick=expandMRAID()>Open Panel</button></section>
  <section id='panel'><button onclick=closeMRAID()>Close Panel</button></section>
</body>
<script>
function checkMRAID (){
    if (mraid.getState() != 'ready') {
        console.log("MRAID Ad: adding event listener for ready");
        /* mraid still loading, registering for ready event */
        mraid.addEventListener('ready', init);
    } else if (mraid.getState() === 'ready') {
        console.log("MRAID Ad: already ready, calling init");
        init();
    } else {
        console.log("MRAID Ad: I think its ready, calling init");
        init();
    }
}

function init () {
    mraid.removeEventListener('ready', init);
```

```
        console.log("Mraid Version = " + mraid.getVersion());
        console.log("Mraid Placement Type = " + getPlacementType());

        mraid.setExpandProperties({
            width : 320,
            height : 480,
            useCustomClose : true
        });

        mraid.addEventListener('error', handleErrorEvent);
            mraid.addEventListener('stateChange', handleStateChangeEvent);

        document.getElementById('cta').removeAttribute('hidden');
        document.getElementById('cta').addEventListener('click', function() {
            var url = document.getElementById('cta').getAttribute('data');
            openBrowser(url);
        });
}

function expandMRAID () {
    try {
        mraid.expand();
    } catch (e) {
      console.log(e + " No MRAID Reference")
    };
}

function closeMRAID () {
    try {
        mraid.close();
      } catch (e) {
        console.log(e + " No MRAID Reference")
    };
}

function handleStateChangeEvent(state){
    switch (state) {
        case "default":
            document.getElementById('banner').style.display = 'block';
            document.getElementById('expandable').style.display = 'none';
            break;
        case "expanded":
            document.getElementById('banner').style.display = 'none';
            document.getElementById('expandable').style.display = 'block';
            break;
    }
    console.log("State - " + state + " at handleStateChangeEvent");
}
```

```
function openBrowser(href) {
    try {
        mraid.open(href);
    } catch (e) {
        console.error(e);
    } finally {
        window.setTimeout('location.href="' + href + '"', 150);
    }
}

function handleErrorEvent (message, action){
  var msg = "MRAID ERROR ";
  if (action != null) {
     msg += "caused by action '" + action + "', ";
  }
  msg += "Message: " + message;
  console.error(msg);
}

window.addEventListener("DOMContentLoaded", function() {
    try {
        var head = document.getElementsByTagName('head')[0];
        var js = document.createElement('Script');
        js.setAttribute('type', 'text/javascript');
        js.setAttribute('src', 'mraid.js');
        head.appendChild(js);
    } catch (e) {
        console.log("Error injecting mraid.js");
    }
    console.log('DOM Loaded');

    checkMRAID();
});
</script>
</html>
```

The code outlines how to interface with the MRAID API in the most simplistic of senses. The first thing you need to do as an ad developer is to signify that you are an MRAID ad by adding the mraid.js script to your ad tag. You do this by listening for the DOMContentLoaded event because this will fire before your DOM load event. It's crucial that you present this information to the SDK as soon as you are able because this is the sole signifier that you are working with an MRAID ad. If you don't have the ability to listen and handle for the DOM events, your ad script tag should include the mraid.js file as the first script tag within its markup by writing <script defer src='mraid.js'>.

■ **Note** DomContentLoaded is supported in Chrome, Firefox, Opera, Safari, and IE9+. If you're targeting IE8, be sure to use onload or DOM ready if using jQuery.

Back to the code: next you listen for the MRAID ready event by adding an event listener in the method checkMRAID();. Sometimes the event fires before you can call your listener to handle it, so in that case, you can just assume MRAID is present and loaded and can safely call init();. Inside of init you remove the event listener, check what MRAID version the SDK is supporting, and check what placement type you are. This information can be very important to an ad developer so they can adapt the ad experience if certain features aren't supported in earlier versions of the MRAID API. You also set your expand properties by setting a width of 320, setting a height of 480, and telling the SDK that you are using your own custom close button so you do not need to have the SDK supply one for you when you are expanded. Lastly, you add two more event listeners for errors on MRAID as well as state changes on the ad. Finally, when the ad calls `expandMRAID()` and `closeMRAID()`,you can call the `mraid.expand()` and `mraid.close()` methods to instruct the application that the ad is opening and closing, respectively, and this function should pause any content in the application environment.

The example is fairly straightforward but may take some getting used to as far as the syntax goes. MRAID doesn't end there; there is much more to add if the creative or SDK requires it, including methods for saving pictures, playing videos, and even saving reminders to the calendar app of the mobile device. In version 2.0 of the API, open these feature sets, which offer great benefits to an ad developer where those standards aren't quite finalized and adopted in HTML5 or other specifications just yet. That said, MRAID isn't intended to conflict with HTML5 and DOM APIs or new features of browsers. It's there to act as a layer of communication between the ad and the application, as well as provide feature detection to the ad creative if it needs it and allow the ad to degrade gracefully. The IAB describes MRAID 2.0 as follows:

> *MRAID v.2 provides a standard way to query a rich media SDK regarding certain device capabilities, offers consistent handling of video creative, and addresses two native device capabilities not well implemented by HTML5 at present: adding an entry to the device calendar and storing an image in the device photo roll.*

MRAID is a blessing for anyone developing ad creative to applications, and if you find an application not supporting it but offering advertising, I strongly recommend contacting the developers and getting them to adopt it. In fact, push very hard for it; you'll be doing a service to them, yourself and everyone else that will need to run campaigns in the future. For more information on the MRAID documentation, visit `http://iab.net/mraid`.

Testing

In the world of in-application advertising, nothing works better than testing creative on the device in the application it's intended to run in. However, in many cases this is far from the actual reality. Publishers and content owners of the applications often do not have the ability to allow every ad developer access to a "test build" of their application, either because they're unaware of how to do so or because they've reached their limit of devices that they can hand out.

Note   A great app testing service called TestFlightApp (`http://testflightapp.com`) can aid with this problem.

Whatever maybe the case, just know that most times it's a luxury to get a test build of the publisher's application, so debugging your ad code can be a hell of a challenge. The catch here is that testing on a device in the application provides the most accurate results, much like testing in multiple browsers for desktop campaigns. Think back to when publishers would offer up test pages so ad servers could traffic their ad tag to an environment that resembles accurately what will be live the day the ads launch. It's the same concept here, just much harder to get!

Always ask the publisher and/or app provider you're working with at the very beginning if they can support this and, if not, in what other ways they can support testing. Find out whether they can provision a build of their application so you can run your ads without just testing in the browser or taking someone's word for it. Personally,

I like to break my ad testing down into the following four tiers. I always try to shoot for the first one, but again sometimes it's out of reach for various reasons outlined earlier.

1. Use a test build of the application on the device it's intended to run on.

2. Test using the native web browser on the device it's intended to run on.

3. Test using a device simulator of the device it's intended to run on.

4. Use the desktop browser with a similar rendering engine as the mobile web browser such as Webkit for Mobile Safari.

In the case of MRAID, you can view compliant ads in the MRAID web tester located at `http://webtester.mraid.org`, but you can also download the source code and run your own web tester on your own domain. There you'll be able to simulate an application environment using the MRAID API and validate whether your ad's functions are working correctly.

I think you'd agree that testing is a challenge for in-application advertising, but I predict this getting much easier as time moves on and as more ad spend moves into this market. In fact, Apple's iOS 6 and Mac OS X Safari allow for testing and inspecting on devices such as iPhones and iPads through desktop Safari using the Safari's Developer tools. Designers and developers can now view their applications, web content, and advertisements as they render in real time on the actual device.

At the end of the day, testing on a device within the application is ideal. But if you need to settle for what you can get access to, use simulators for iOS, Android, and other mobile OSs, and if you need to, drive to your nearest electronics store and test on the floor models (seriously, I've done this). Remember, it's tablets and phones today, but next it will be TVs and other appliances and vehicles. We can't be expected to own and test on every refrigerator, can we? Fight for getting that testing application from the publisher, especially if you plan on doing more than a one-off campaign with them. Building, testing, and debugging will go much more smoothly when you do, and if you're an application maker or publisher, use tools like TestFlightApp (`http://testflightapp.com`), which allows you to pass around your apps to various team members over the air (OTA). This is especially helpful if your production and development team is stretched all over the globe!

MRAID Adoption

MRAID is still fairly new in some regard, but the promise is that this will be the standard going forward when working with advertising inside applications. Publishers take a while to adopt new practices, but MRAID support is a huge push in the industry and even a bigger one by the IAB. As I write this, the IAB is currently going through many tests and discussions for future versions of MRAID and releasing certification tags to publishers and ad servers that state they are MRAID compliant. While I personally wish they'd police this a bit better so publishers and ad servers had to prove that they're MRAID compliant, I guess it'll do that they state that they are. Hell, we can always call them out if they aren't.

The truth is if you have a campaign coming up that requires you to serve into an application because it's outlined in the media buy, first make sure that the publisher's SDK is MRAID compliant. Second, perform a test flight to ensure everything is ironed out before running an actual campaign. This will allow you to comfortably scale across many publishers and applications with ease and with the certainty that your ad will be functioning correctly in any and all applications that support the API. There is no longer a need to handle the SDK fragmentation in this space. We all know developers have much bigger things to worry about, especially with the fragmentation in other areas in the industry. If you do in fact run into an issue with a publisher or application stating it's MRAID compliant but your tests prove otherwise, tell the IAB about so it can enforce compliance (`http://iab.net/guidelines/508676/compliance/2153679`). Again, this is for the betterment of the industry as a whole, not to point fingers.

Creative Features

Working inside application environments allows ads to have much more deeply integrated tie-ins with the device and native device features. You can have much more rich functionality than typical mobile web ad delivery. The creative can use features such as detecting network connections, device hardware, and special file access to add to calendars or photo albums, as you've just learned. This should all be taken into account when you dream up your next advertising campaign because the creative can take all of these amazing features into account and really wow a user. Be sure to bring in the right developers and technologists for the creative brainstorming sessions. They'll be able to inform you if something is not possible before any development occurs.

Summary

This chapter covered a lot about mobile applications, including the landscape and profitability of being part of it. Moreover, it covered the vast world of advertising in applications on various mobile devices. Specifically, I covered the complex world of application SDKs and their integral role in delivering cutting-edge rich media inside the application environment and how it differs from a mobile web environment. I reviewed the fragmented role of SDKs and how technologies like MRAID are out to ease the fragmentation from an application developer and ad developer standpoint. I went over some of the nuances between SDKs and even reviewed some code samples so you can start working with them today in your campaigns. I stressed that it's important to ensure that applications become MRAID compliant, because it's the standard that will make everyone's lives much easier.

In the next chapter, I'll discuss how ads can be taken offline and still reported on when a user regains a network connection. Mobile is a tricky world to successfully navigate through, but knowing the basics will help you as you head into the next chapters. See you in Chapter 10!

CHAPTER 10

Offline Storage, Tracking, Debugging, and Optimization

This chapter is focused on the increasingly important offline support for ads on mobile and tablet devices, on mandatory tracking, and on the tedious and often very time-consuming process of debugging in a browser and on a device. Offline support is becoming a requirement for many web apps, and advertising is quickly following suit. In this chapter, I'll review how to handle offline events, detect when a user comes back online, and even discuss APIs that will detect when a user has a poor network connection. I'll cover how to cache assets to client browsers and devices using HTML5's AppCache API. I'll also discuss tracking users' interactions within advertising via tracking pixels and JavaScript, and I'll use the methods to handle tracking calls and store calls in a client-side database using HTML5's APIs. In addition, I'll discuss the differences and browser support between the IndexDB API and the WebSQL API. I'll also discuss APIs such as Lawnchair JS and how to handle cross-browser storing and caching as well as how to fire off tracking calls when a user is offline. Lastly, I'll cover the detailed realm of debugging and optimization on desktop browsers and mobile devices. It's a lot, so let's get started.

Offline Support

For as long as I can remember, I've always recognized the Web in terms of of network access. Starting in the old days, we had dial-up modems, then DSL, then cable lines, and then the present-day fiber optics. However, in today's world, we also have to focus on wireless cell networks such as 2G, 3G, and even 4G LTE connections and how more and more devices are mobile such as smartphones, e-readers, and tablets. With these devices able to go into areas typical computers can't, like planes, trains, and automobiles, network connections can come and go quickly and suddenly. Luckily, developers can use a useful new feature of browsers that detects whether a user has network access or not. Listing 10-1 outlines how to detect for this in compliant browsers.

Listing 10-1. Detecting Offline Example

```
<!DOCTYPE HTML>
<html>
<head>
<script>
function networkIndicator() {
document.getElementById('status').textContent = navigator.onLine ? 'online' : 'offline';
}
</script>
</head>
<body onload="networkIndicator()" ononline=" networkIndicator ()" onoffline=" networkIndicator ()">
```

```
<p>The network is: <span id="status"></span></p>
</body>
</html>
```

From the previous code, you can see I'm creating a function called networkIndicator, which will update the text inside the status element to online or offline. Then on the onload method of the body element, I call the networkIndicator function on the handlers ononline and onoffline. This simple detection can determine whether there is a network connection. In addition, the previous code, when the user's network access changes to connected or disconnected, it will also dispatch the following events that you can handle via JavaScript:

```
<script>
window.addEventListener("offline", function(e) {
        alert("offline");
});

window.addEventListener("online", function(e) {
    alert("online");
});
</script>
```

Checking the browser's navigator.onLine property and providing alternate experiences when a network connection is not present is a must-have in any HTML5 web application, and as more advertising moves into the world of web standards, you'll need to take this into account for publisher's that require it. Personally, it makes the most sense to factor offline support into branding campaigns where gaming, video, or some form of heavy user interaction is at the forefront of the campaign's success. Having offline support for direct-response ads may not make the most sense because if users can't connect to any network, they won't be able to click/tap to the destination and landing pages. However, having elements of a game cached to a device or even a smaller teaser video for offline use allows a user to interact and spend valuable time within an ad experience. All of this can be tracked when a connection is regained for the brand or advertiser to analyze after the campaign. Basically, if a user has network access, you can serve them up the full experience; for example, it could be a feature-rich game or a long-form video ad. In addition, you can cache vital or even alternate assets to a user's browser so they can still interact with the ad at some level when they're offline.

Note   Publishers may request that nothing be cached for offline use or that certain k-weight limitations be in place for offline content. Consult with your publisher or application developer before developing the ad.

Offline support within advertising is anything but a standard practice. In fact, the whole industry is working toward a solid standard because there are holes in using navigator.onLine when checking for a reliable connection status. For example, what's to happen if your ISP is down but your wireless router is up and running? The browser may say the user is online but they're in fact not. A better way to test is to make small checks by requesting a small asset from your server via an XMLHttpRequest (Ajax request) so it's transparent to the end user and they won't incur any bandwidth bottlenecks nor refresh the page. Using the code shown in Listing 10-2, you can confidently recognize whether the user is connected or not.

Listing 10-2. Detecting Offline Using Ajax Example

```
<script>
function testConnection (fileToPing) {
  var xhr;
  if (window.XMLHttpRequest) {
    xhr = new XMLHttpRequest();
```

```
  } else {
    //For IE6, IE5
    xhr = new ActiveXObject("Microsoft.XMLHTTP");
  }

  xhr.onreadystatechange=function() {
    if (xhr.readyState==4 && xhr.status==200) {
      console.log("Online")
    } else {
      console.log("Offline")
    }
  }

  xhr.open("GET",fileToPing,true);
  xhr.send();
}

testConnection("http://www.yourdomain.org/1x1.gif");
</script>
```

Listing 10-2 creates a method called `testConnection`, which takes an argument of `fileToPing`, which is a string value of the URI you want to ping to check the connection. The function creates an `XMLHttpRequest` and checks whether the status is 200 from the server's headers. If so, you know your request to that asset has resolved correctly, and therefore the user is connected. If you didn't get your 200 response from the server, you'll confidently know the user is offline.

Note   You must allow `Access-Control-Allow-Origin` on your server for the domain you want to request. For example, use `Access-Control-Allow-Origin: http://yourdomain.com` or `*`, which will allow any origin to access the asset.

The best situation is to use both techniques to get the most information about the user's connection. Also, be sure to ask whether offline is a mandatory requirement from the publisher and/or advertiser. Whether you use HTML5 or specific "hooks" from API calls to the application's SDK, just be sure to understand the full scope of work up front. This is crucial information so designers and developers can factor in the added time (if any) that there will be to develop and design the ad in this manner.

Sometimes files get cached to a browser/device, and you do not want them to be. This could be if you are firing off third- or fourth-party tracking calls in order to validate metrics. In the event you don't want to allow the caching of your files, you can use the "cache-bust" method when making those specific HTTP requests to those file locations. Listing 10-3 showcases how you would do that for firing off a third-party impression 1x1.

Listing 10-3. Cache Busting Example

```
<!DOCTYPE HTML>
<html>
<head>
<script>
function fireImpression () {
    var beacon = new Image ();
    beacon.src = "http://tracking.somedomain.com?r=" + cacheBust();
}
```

```
function cacheBust () {
    var num = Math.random();
    return num;
}
</script>
</head>
<body onload=fireImpression()>
</body>
</html>
```

When using the previous code snippet, you create a new image and set the source of that image to the URI you want to hit, but you concatenate a cache-busting method to the string. This cache-busting method, called cacheBust, tells the browser to generate a random number and adds it to the r param in the query string. This will yield something similar to http://tracking.somedomain.com?r=0.123456, and this practice can be used with any HTTP request; just keep in mind that caching assets is a good thing in most cases such as heavier k-weight JavaScript libraries, images, or CSS files that won't change. However, for reporting and analytics, cache busting is pretty mandatory for accurate results.

When working with in-app, some SDKs require that the ads be cached to the device for offline use. For example, if you were to view the *Wall Street Journal* iPad application, the content and ads get cached to the device so a user can view the content in offline mode. This is super-helpful if a user is about to board a plane where a connection is nonexistent. In this case, the current SDK provider AdMarvel caches the application content and all ads to the device by way of a cache file. Listing 10-4 shows how this is implemented using the AdMarvel SDK.

Listing 10-4. AdMarvel Cache File Example

```
ADMARVEL-CACHE
assets/style.css       http://cdn.domain.com/assets/style.css
assets/script.js       http://cdn.domain.com/assets/script.js
assets/logo.png        http://cdn.domain.com/assets/logo.png
```

The cache file is saved as a tab-delimitated .txt (plain text) file that locates all the assets that make up the ad experience by relative and absolute locations (local/remote) and is delivered to AdMarvel with the ad creative.

■ **Note** Every SDK will have its own way of implementing cached ad assets. Be sure to check with them before campaign launch.

Network Connection API

This section covers the Network Connection API, which allows developers to query the strength and type of the network connection the user is currently using. The API, at the time of this writing, is currently not supported in any of modern browsers, but its API documentation is being revised and will offer many useful features when this emerging standard becomes available in modern browsers. The API as it stands now allows for a developer to detect whether a user is on Ethernet, WiFi, 2G, 3G, 4G, none, or an unknown connection. With this sort of information combined with Navigator.onLine and the Ajax test, developers can cater their ad experiences for sophisticated offline use. If you can't wait for the spec to finalize or browsers to implement this into their architecture, you can take advantage of this from within in-application advertising by way of the SDKs. In fact, in MRAID, ad developers and designers are able to query the MRAID-compliant SDK for information about users' connectivity by calling the method getNetwork. In addition, they can add an event listener for the networkChange event when network connections change. Currently, the possible connection types in MRAID are offline, WiFi, cell, and unknown. Ideally, we'll see these APIs take shape rather quickly and be implemented immediately so that adoption takes rapidly. Only then will you be able to offer accurate network connection detection and provide rich offline experiences.

■ **Note**   If your ad requires offline availability, make sure to remove any CTAs around `tap` because there will be no network when viewing ads offline, so users will not be able to view pages.

Application Cache

In this section, I'll cover an offline web application specification and how to work with application caching. This section is geared toward publishers and content owners looking to bring offline support to their web applications. In HTML5, application caching is supported by creating a simple manifest file, which lists the assets to be used for the application offline. These assets are the files needed to be stored to the users' browser in order to render correctly without any Internet access. Before we dig in deeper, keep in mind that caching all the assets to a user's browser could result in very long caching times as well as a bloated manifest document, so choose your storing wisely.

When a user views the document without network access, the browser switches to use the local cached assets in its place. So, in theory, the user should be able to finish interacting with that game or watching that video spot while on the subway or on a plane with no in-flight WiFi, assuming the application cache stored the files to the device correctly. With strong browser support, especially in the mobile realm, this is something you can start taking advantage of immediately. Figure 10-1 outlines the tremendous support for the application cache as of November 2012.

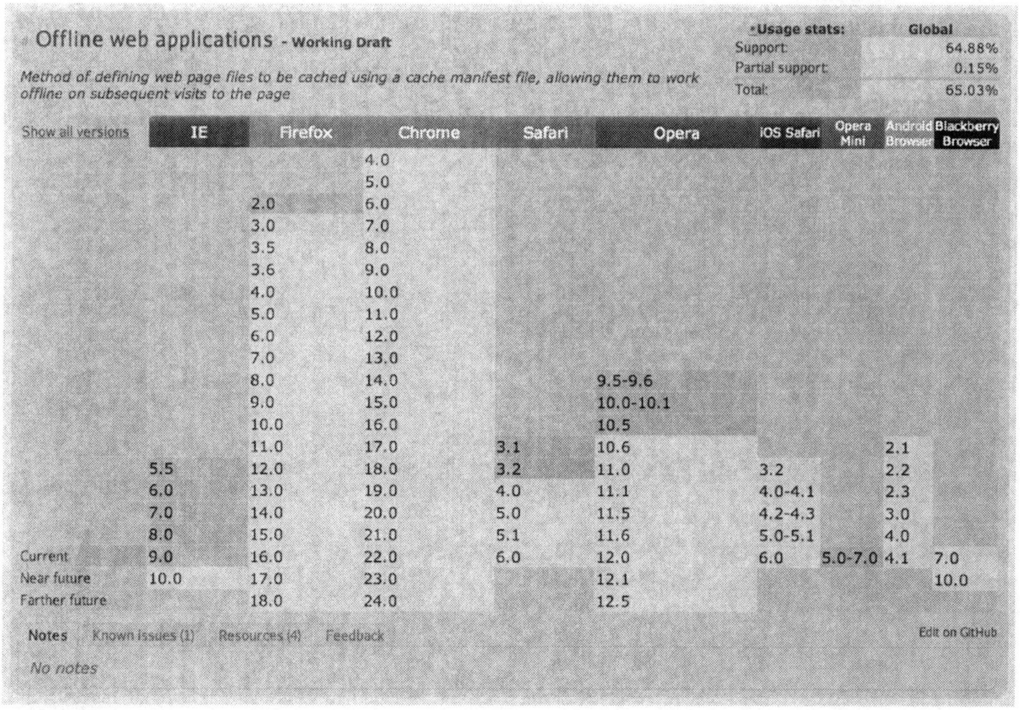

Figure 10-1. Demonstrates the browser support for HTML5 app cache (Source: `caniuse.com`)

Using the HTML5 application cache, publishers can offer speedier and more responsive web apps, which is a better user experience for the end user all around. Also, if you're a Chrome user, I suggest using `chrome://appcache-internals`, which can help in detecting what domains are storing assets in your browser.

App Cache Example

Since I just covered why you should take advantage of offline asset caching, I'll show how to put the theory into practice. While the HTML5 AppCache API is typically used for caching specific assets in web applications, you can use similar caching mechanisms for caching your ad content offline. Sure, this will certainly mean that if you're on the publisher end, this will increase your workload since you'll need to update the cache manifest every time news ads are updated. This is increasingly important when your publisher's content is meant to be viewed offline such as magazines, newspapers, and other content that's completely cached to the user's device. Check out the following code snippet to understand how to use AppCache. In the HTML markup, it's very simple to add a reference to the `.appcache` file by writing the following:

```
<!DOCTYPE HTML>
<html manifest="cache.appcache">
...
</html>
```

In the previous example, you add an attribute to the HTML node in the HTML file called `manifest`, and you set that equal to `cache.appcache`, which is your manifest file located in the same directory as your HTML file.

Next, let's take a look at building the manifest file. You can use the following sample manifest structure to build your offline ad, but note that the assets will need to change for your own specific use case depending on publisher and ad content. The first thing to do before building the manifest cache file is to set your server to accept the MIME type of `.appcache`. I do this by simply writing `AddType text/cache-manifest .appcache` to my `.htaccess` file on my server's root directory. Keep in mind that some servers may not have this file, or it may be hidden at first, so be sure to view hidden files to find it. Otherwise, just create one.

Note   For more information on `.htaccess`, I recommend visiting `http://htaccesstools.com`.

Once you have your server configured to accept the file type of appcache, you can build a manifest text file with your caching assets and save it as `yourfile.appcache`. Let's review the manifest now (see Listing 10-5).

Listing 10-5. Building an HTML5 AppCache File

```
CACHE MANIFEST
# 2012-12-13:v1 - Keep the version to purge the cache when updates are needed

# Explicitly cached entries
CACHE:
index.html
css/style.css
ad/adstyle.css
js/script.js
ad/adscript.js
ad/bg.jpg
images/button.png
images/bg.jpg
```

```
fonts/webfont.otf
fonts/webfont.ttf
fonts/webfont.woff
fonts/webfont.svg
media/audio.mp3
media/video.mp4
media/video.webm

# offline.html will be served if the user is offline and request new "non-cached" assetsFALLBACK:
index.html offline.html

# Resources that require the user to be online.
NETWORK:
submit.aspx
http://api.twitter.com
etc...
```

Note   You can add comments to the manifest file by beginning a line with #. Also, if one asset fails to download, the entire cache fails.

Let's review the manifest. The first thing you do is define the cache manifest and set a comment with the date of the last update as well as a version number of 1. The second thing you do is list all the assets and files you need cached to the user's browser for offline use, including the ad's assets, by writing ad/style.css, ad/adscript.js, and ad/bg.jpg. Remember, this does not need to be all of your assets, just enough to provide an acceptable offline experience. In this example, I've included the CSS, JS, images, fonts, media, and ad assets, but this could very well be overkill depending on the creative requirements of your web app and advertisements. Also, be careful with what you cache in the ad. Once an asset such as a JavaScript file is cached, the browser will continue to use the cached version even if you change the file on the server. The only way to ensure that the browser updates the cached asset is to change the .appcache file, which is why you add a date and version in the comments section by writing . # 2012-12-13:v1. The next step in the manifest file is that you provide an alternate offline.html file for your index.html file under the FALLBACK section of the manifest, which will get served when a user is offline and attempting to access information that isn't cached. The is great to have in the event the user accesses information that they can't view; in that case, they'll get served a default cached asset instead of something that wasn't cached while they were online.

Publishers may see the real benefit from HTML5's AppCache API because they can effectively create a very rich offline experience for their customers and visitors while still offering them the content their users are after. Ads will more or less find their own way for caching assets to a user, but be sure to have conversations with your publisher, ad server, and agency before heading down any specific path.

Now that you have your cache file set up and assigned in your HTML document, let's use some of the JavaScript to detect the loading and caching of your assets (see Listing 10-6).

Listing 10-6. HTML5 AppCache JavaScript Example

```
<script>
var cache = window.applicationCache;

cache.addEventListener('cached', handleCacheEvent, false);
cache.addEventListener('checking', handleCacheEvent, false);
cache.addEventListener('downloading', handleCacheEvent, false);
cache.addEventListener('error', handleCacheError, false);//Good to use if the manifest is moved or
```

```
if the user is offline
cache.addEventListener('noupdate', handleCacheEvent, false);
cache.addEventListener('obsolete', handleCacheEvent, false);
cache.addEventListener('progress', handleCacheEvent, false);

// When a new manifest is downloaded, swap the new cache assets and reload.
cache.addEventListener('updateready', reloadAssets, false);

function reloadAssets (){
    if (cache.status == cache.UPDATEREADY) {
        cache.swapCache();
        if (confirm('A new version is available')) {
            window.location.reload();
        }
    }
};

function handleCacheEvent () {
...
}
</script>
```

Using the previous JavaScript, you can add event listeners to applicationCache and handle when your assets are in different stages of the caching process, when they're downloading, and when they're ready to be used, among other events. This is super-helpful when determining whether the user has the latest and greatest assets for offline use and when doing general debugging of your cache manifest files.

So, you may be wondering why to cache assets locally. Don't browsers have native caching? Well, true, they do, but it's often unreliable because users and browsers often clear their cache after the cache pools fills too much or it could be a default browser setting to clear the cache after each and every browser session.

Caching resources creates faster web content, which is an overall improvement regardless of network connections. This could be hugely beneficial when you get into dynamic ads where a user will perhaps see a variety of ad versions throughout the campaign's life cycle. Since only certain portions of the ad will be dynamic (copy, images, and so on), why not just pull down the dynamic assets on subsequent views and leave the other assets untouched? This will allow for a faster load time and the ability to pull only the assets you need from the server, thus reducing the number of requests that need to occur. These practices are being used in many web apps today, including Google's Gmail for iOS and Android. A very good article on caching and its impact on the web can be found at http://www.stevesouders.com/blog/2012/10/11/cache-is-king

---

■ **Note**   For more information and facts on AppCache, visit http://appcachefacts.info.

Tracking

Tracking for advertising is a crucial part of any campaign. Analytics teams crave the metrics gathered by ad-serving companies so they can better adjust their media spend and better educate their clients on what's working and not working in their online advertising campaigns. To do this, tracking has to be included throughout the ad so that when a user interacts with the ad content, the reporting companies can learn about the interactions taking place. One important topic in tracking requirements is the ability to track users when network access is not present. This sort of offline tracking is big in mobile devices where users are more prone to interact with phone and tablet applications in offline scenarios.

As you are aware from previous sections in the book, cookie dropping on mobile Apple devices is accepted only if the user has visited the cookie-dropping domain or has toggled their browser setting to accept all. While this eliminates a huge portion of the market advertisers are looking to target, other browsers are gaining popularity on iOS like Google's Chrome browser, which accepts cookies by default regardless of domain, and at the time of this writing, Chrome for iOS has roughly 20,000 user ratings. While not a true measure of installs, it's still a promising number, but with no ability to make Chrome a user's default mobile web browser (unless you "jailbreak" your iOS device), you're sure to see more mobile Safari traffic overall than Chrome. Other browsers in the mobile landscape such as Opera Mini handle tracking differently. For a large portion of the market share in developing countries like Africa, wired networks are few and far between and phones with Opera Mini are the majority. However, with Opera Mini, JavaScript is not on by default, or is nonexistent, so in these scenarios, the only form of tracking is called *pixel tracking*, or using 1x1 images, where a user clicks a tags in the HTML markup and the request goes through a redirect URL. In most cases, though, JavaScript is the most common, and many analytics platforms like Google's Analytics use the tracking approach shown in Listing 10-7.

Listing 10-7. Google Analytics Tracking Example

```
<script type="text/javascript">
  var _gaq = _gaq || [];
  _gaq.push(['_setAccount', 'UA-25177661-1']);
  _gaq.push(['_trackPageview']);

  (function() {
    var ga = document.createElement('script');
    ga.type = 'text/javascript'; ga.async = true;
    ga.src = ('https:' == document.location.protocol ? 'https://ssl' : 'http://www') + '.google-
analytics.com/ga.js';
    var s = document.getElementsByTagName('script')[0]; s.parentNode.insertBefore(ga, s);
  })();
</script>
```

Now within HTML-based ads, you can use web analytics platforms such as the one outlined from Google to handle your metrics. However, if JavaScript is disabled in the browser, so is JavaScript-based tracking. A good workaround is to use image *beacons*, which are a 1x1 GIF images that ping a server, usually with specific query parameters indicating session IDs or creative IDs along with activity type and a random number to cache bust. To work one way or another, it's best to understand who your audience is. If you're targeting a bunch of mobile devices, keep in mind that some mobile browsers do not have JavaScript on by default in some phones, such as BlackBerry's OS5 and older and most Nokia feature phones.

Storing and Firing Offline Tracking

While there is no standard definition in offline ad tracking , there is a need for a standard, and ideally through practice and adoption, we'll have a clean way of implementing offline in future campaigns. The vice president of development at Crisp Media and a cofounding member of the ORMMA initiative, Nathan Carver, states the following:

> *"This does depend a little bit on the ad. If it is a direct response, for example, then offline doesn't make sense. Really only brand ads benefit from offline. Ultimately, this is a space for the SDKs to differentiate for now. A store-and-forward, or keeper/share technology could really help, but there is no definition about the offline market right now."*

Nathan Carver

First users interact online with an ad; throughout the interaction, the network connection gets so poor that the user is unavoidably offline for a few moments. Since the ad has been cached to the user's device (using ad-serving device detection), the user doesn't notice that they're actually offline because all the features of the ad are still intact. The important change here is that every interaction in the ad is trackable; those tracking activities won't find their way back to the server if the user is offline. That said, you'd need to capture those interactions on the client side before they're lost forever and you lose out on valuable brand insight. You have a variety of new technologies to leverage for achieving this using HTML5 and various other APIs, including local storage/session storage or even client-side databases like WebSQL and IndexedDB, as you'll learn a bit in the following sections. Let's take a look at how you can attempt to handle offline click tracking with Listing 10-8 using HTML5's localStorage technique.

Listing 10-8. LocalStorage Offline Click Tracking Example

```
<script>
var NetworkAccess = navigator.onLine;
var trackingCalls = {
    "clicks" : [{
        "name": "clickButton1",
        "online": "1023-online",
    }, {
        "name": "clickButton2",
        "online": "1024-online",
    }]
}

function trackClick(name) {
    if (!NetworkAccess) {
        //No network - clicks won't fire
        return false;
    } else {
        var trackingID;
        var clickName;
    }

    for (var n = 0; n < trackingCalls.clicks.length; n++) {
        if (name == trackingCalls.clicks[n].name) {
            clickName = trackingCalls.clicks[n].name;
            trackingID = trackingCalls.clicks[n].online;
        }
    }

    if (trackingID){
        location.href = "http://clicks.someurl.com?clickName=" + clickName + "&trackingID=" +
trackingID + "&r=" + cacheBust();
    }
}

function cacheBust () {
    var num = Math.random();
    return num;
}
```

```
function buttonClick (event) {
    var type = event.target.attributes.value.value;
    switch (type) {
        case "buttonOne" :
            trackClick("clickButton1");
            break;
        case "buttonTwo" :
            trackClick("clickButton2");
            break;
    }
    console.log(type)
}

function AdInit () {
    console.log("AdInit : NetworkAccess " + NetworkAccess)
    document.removeEventListener("DOMContentLoaded", AdInit);

    //set up Ad UI here

    document.getElementById('buttonOne').addEventListener('click', buttonClick, false);
    document.getElementById('buttonTwo').addEventListener('click', buttonClick, false);
}

document.addEventListener("DOMContentLoaded", AdInit, false);
</script>
```

Let's review this code. The first thing you do is set up your tracking variables at the top of the script by checking for NetworkAccess and the important trackingCalls JavaScript object, which stores all the clicks for online use. Next, at the bottom of the script, you start listening for your DOMContentLoaded event and fire off the adInit function, which will kick things off; there's nothing new there. Next, if a user clicks buttonOne or buttonTwo within the ad environment, it will channel through a function called buttonClick, which will take the event parameter and perform a switch/ case for determining which button was clicked. Depending on which event fired, you'll call the function trackClick and pass in the string value for your button; in this case, it would be either trackClick("clickButton1"); or trackClick("clickButton2");. Now if you head up to the trackClick function, you'll notice that the first thing you do is detect whether the user has network access. If they don't, you simply return the user out of the function. However, if they do, you set up two new variables called trackingID and clickName, which will house the values for tracking for which you want to save. When the for loop loops through all the tracking clicks as defined in your JavaScript object, you can track and send the user to the appropriate URL (if connected) based on their actions.

Now that you understand how to handle offline clicks, let's take a look at user activities from within the ad experience. Again, this is something local to the ad that you want to report on that doesn't navigate the user away from the ad experience. It is important to understand interactions such as swipes, touches, video plays, gaming, and whatever else is important to an advertiser's branding awareness campaign. Take a look at the revised code in Listing 10-9.

Listing 10-9. LocalStorage Offline Activity Tracking Example

```
<script>
var NetworkAccess = navigator.onLine;
var trackingCalls = {
    'pings': [{
        'name': 'touchstart',
        'online': '1011-online',
```

```
                'offline': '1011-offline'
        }, {
            'name': 'touchmove',
            'online': '1012-online',
            'offline': '1012-offline'
        }]
}

function trackPing (name) {
    var activityName;
    var onlineTrackingID;
    var offlineTrackingID;

    for (var n = 0; n < trackingCalls.pings.length; n++) {
        if (name == trackingCalls.pings[n].name) {
            activityName = trackingCalls.pings[n].name;
            onlineTrackingID = trackingCalls.pings[n].online;
            offlineTrackingID = trackingCalls.pings[n].offline;
        }
    }

    if (NetworkAccess) {
        fire('http://tracking.someurl.com?trackingName=' + activityName + '&trackingID=' +
onlineTrackingID + '&r=' + cacheBust(), false);
    } else {
        var t = new Date().getTime();
        var m = new Date().getMonth()
        var d = new Date().getDate();
        var y = new Date().getFullYear();
        var timeStampedName = activityName+t+m+d+y;
        //No network - storing offline tracking
        storeOffline(timeStampedName, offlineTrackingID);
    }
}

function storeOffline (name, id) {
    //store client side and add listeners for network events
    console.log('Storing Offline : ' + name + ' + ' + id)
    localStorage.setItem(name, id);
}

 //on reconnect fire off all the cached pings
function checkOfflineStorage () {
    if(NetworkAccess) {
        if (localStorage.length >= 1) {
            for (var i = 0; i < localStorage.length; i++) {
                var key = localStorage.key(i);
                var value = localStorage[key];
                var offlineCall = 'http://tracking.someurl.com?trackingID=' + value + '&r=' +
cacheBust();
                fire(offlineCall, true);
            }
```

```javascript
        } else {
            console.log('No offline metrics stored')
        }
    }
    console.log('NetworkAccess ' + NetworkAccess)
}

//Tracking Utils
function fire(url, clear) {
    var trackingImg;
    if (clear === true) {
        trackingImg = new Image ().src = url;
        console.log(trackingImg);
        setTimeout(clearStorage, 3000);
    } else {
        trackingImg = new Image ().src = url;
    }
}

function clearStorage() {
    console.log('clearing storage');
    localStorage.clear();
}

function cacheBust () {
    var num = Math.random();
    return num;
}

function userAction (event) {
    var type = event.type;
    switch (type) {
        case 'touchstart' :
            trackPing('touchstart');
            break;
        case 'touchmove' :
            trackPing('touchmove');
            break;
    }
    console.log(type)
}

function AdInit () {
    console.log('AdInit')
    document.removeEventListener('DOMContentLoaded', AdInit);

    //set up Ad UI here
    window.addEventListener('touchstart', userAction, false);
    window.addEventListener('touchmove', userAction, false);

    checkOfflineStorage();
}
```

```
window.addEventListener('online', checkOfflineStorage);
window.addEventListener('offline', checkOfflineStorage);

document.addEventListener('DOMContentLoaded', AdInit, false);
</script>
```

Let's review the code example. Again, it's very similar in setup as the click tracking example, but now once you're inside the adInit function, you set up your touch event listeners for the ad environment and also an event listener for the online/offline state by calling window.addEventListener("online", checkOfflineStorage, false);. Next you call the checkOfflineStorage function to determine whether there has been any stored offline activities. Inside checkOfflineStorage, you initially check whether the user has a network connection and whether there are items stored in the localStorage object. If there's network but no storage, you simply log to the console by writing console.log('No offline metrics stored'). However, if there are items that are stored in localStorage, you loop through them all by grabbing their key/value and passing them to a function called fire. Now, inside of the fire function, you check to see whether you need to clear the storage after you fire off the tracking calls, by writing if (clear === true). Now, you'll create image objects and add the URL request to the tracking server by setting that value to the Image's source attribute. Lastly, once you've fired off all the calls, you set a timeout to call the function clearStorage, which will clear the user's browser of all localStorage tracking calls. Now there is a lot going on in the code, so I suggest following along in your favorite text editor and checking all the logs in your favorite browser's web inspector. Keep in mind that this technique is becoming increasingly important for digital magazines and publications where everything gets cached to a user's device. Using HTML5's offline detection through JavaScript, you can handle metrics accordingly; in addition to the previous XMLHTTPRequest method, you can ensure the user is truly connected or not.

For mobile folks working with SDK vendors such as AdMarvel or Medialets, there's a good chance they can provide the caching of offline metrics for you. As an ad designer, you'll most likely just need to call specific SDK methods, and the SDK will handle that for you. In addition to that, the MRAID working group has tossed around the idea of including a standard way for implementing offline tracking, but the reality is that the space is too young to be standardized just yet. Just take a look at the quote from the MRAID API documentation:

> Rich Media Ads that can work while the device is without network connectivity need the ability to store and later forward metrics about how and when users interact with the ad. MRAID has the potential to provide common APIs to facilitate storing and forwarding of ad impression delivery, view, and other metrics from the SDK back to the ad server. However, until measurement methodologies and the metrics themselves are standardized (for example by the ongoing IAB/MMA/ MRC In-App Ad Measurement Guidelines project), adding measurement functionality to MRAID would be premature. The MRAID working group expects that this capability will be evaluated and potentially added to MRAID as part of a future version 3.0 release.

MRAID Working Group

MRAID's working group has a good approach, and I think it's often better to see all the proposed solutions before setting a single solution in stone and calling it a standard. Will it be HTML5 and the various JavaScript APIs that allow for standardized offline tracking? Or will it be something else with SDK involvement only? Perhaps a mixture of both? In the meantime, clients will ask you for this, and it will eventually become a standard operating procedure in the online advertising space. For now, you'll have to come up with your own homebrewed solutions like the one outlined previous, or you can even look to lightweight JavaScript libraries such as Lawnchair (http://brian.io/lawnchair) for what you need.

Lawnchair is seemingly a possible answer to client database storage because it uses a simple name/value pair assignment through JavaScript and retrieves values through JSON. It also can be equipped with many adapters to fail gracefully to other client-side storage technologies if some browsers don't accept others. This means it will use blackberry-persistent-store, DOM storage, WebSQL, and IndexDB, to name a few. Lawnchair eases the fragmentation between the storage technologies as well as gives developers an easy approach for saving values. Plus, it comes at a very small 6KB when minified and even smaller when gzipped. This could be very beneficial for creating an offline archive of user interactions and eventually iterating over the interactions and firing off the user activities as the user regains network connection.

■ **Note** Tracking can get skewed for offline use if a majority of users interact with an ad and never regain network access to push out the metrics to the reporting server. It should be communicated to all teams that this will never be 100 percent accurate.

IndexDB

When discussing the topic of offline caching and offline metrics, I have to touch on a new and emerging API in HTML5 called IndexDB. IndexDB is an API for storing significant amounts of data on the client side in a very structured matter. Using IndexDB generally means you have lots of data to work with and much more than your typical DOM storage using `sessionStorage` or `localStorage`, which could be faced with browser limits on the amount of data you'll store to the client. While both of these APIs provide a great way of handling large amounts of data to the client browser, when you are dealing with very large data pools and a need to handle data at scale in a structured matter, IndexDB will be your go-to choice. Developed by the Mozilla group, using this type of elaborate web storage, you could possibly allow the user to customize a detailed vehicle within the ad experience and pick up where they left off the next time they visit the ad on another site.

IndexDB is now the current specification being worked on by the HTML5 working groups. Previously WebSQL API was the main way of storing large amounts of data offline, but that specification has since ended in development, according to the W3C. (However, it's still in use in some browsers.) The industry is said to be transitioning to IndexDB in the foreseeable future. *Origin*, or the domain of the site that creates the database, scopes each IndexDB database, and this could be a good solution of handling offline data for your advertisement, but be warned that it may not work in all browsers just yet. Be sure to keep tabs on `http://caniuse.com/#feat=indexeddb` to determine support.

Web Inspector

Arguably the most popular web development tool is Web Inspector, and it comes built into all of the modern browsers. If you use Chrome, Opera, Firefox, or IE 10, you can simply right-click your browser window and choose Inspect Element. This will open Web Inspector in your browser and give you an array of tools to use for actions such as inspecting elements in your DOM, viewing loaded scripts, analyzing network traffic, finding out about offline storage, and executing commands in real time. If you're using Safari, you will need to go into the browser preferences first and enable the Develop menu in your menu bar. Once this is enabled, you will be able to right-click and inspect elements like the others. Figure 10-2 shows what to look for in Apple's Safari browser.

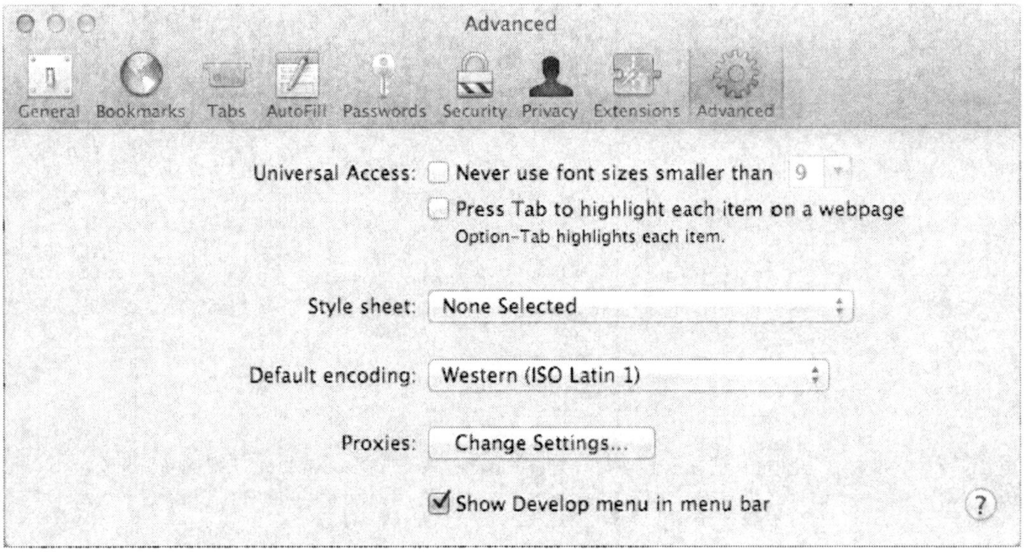

Figure 10-2. Safari's Develop menu setting

In addition to the popular Web Inspector, there is also a browser extension called Firebug that essentially does similar things and provides developers with similar tools for debugging web content on various browsers. To learn more about Firebug, visit http://getfirebug.com. Firefox also has recently updated its Web Inspector to view content in 3D. This is incredible helpful if you need to understand the stacking order of elements and determine whether certain elements lay on top of others

Development Tools

If you've been a developer for any amount of time in your life, you know how much time can be dedicated to the art and process of debugging code. If you're new to development, trust me when I say, "Get used to things not working and start learning to figure them out." Patience is a key trait in debugging, along with having the right tools, workflow, and techniques. In this section, I'll review some really great tools to use that are free and some amazing techniques that will give you the edge over your competition when debugging for multiple platforms and devices.

Developer tools are plentiful on the Web. Just Google any web development tool, and you'll see many results. A few of my favorite online tools are JSConsole (http://jsconsole.com) for debugging JavaScript on mobile devices, JSBin (http://jsbin.com) for quickly mocking up and sharing code with friends and collegues, JSBeautifier (http://jsbeautifier.org) for cleanly unminifying libraries and code for readability, and RemoteTilt (http://remote-tilt.com) for working with motion events outside of the native device. Remy Sharp, developer extra-ordinaire, has created all of these tools except for JSBeautifer, and I've personally used them all on countless campaigns while debugging my ad content. Other very useful tools include DomMonster (http://mir.aculo.us/dom-monster), YSlow (http://yslow.org), and PageSpeed (http://developers.google.com/speed/pagespeed), all of which allow for debugging and optimizing your web content.

One of my absolute favorites is an HTTP monitoring tool. These types of tools capture and log all the HTTP traffic that happens in your browser. For example, if you have an ad that's making many HTTP requests and calling external services, this tool can be very valuable to give you a view into what's really going on under the "hood." Some of these tools are Charles (for Mac) (http://charlesproxy.com) and Fiddler (for PC) (http://fiddler2.com/fiddler2), and they can even be proxied to your mobile devices for capturing web traffic on smartphones, tablets, and TVs. What's really great about these HTTP monitoring tools is the ability to validate tracking, reporting, and redirect calls made from advertisements. It is crucial to do testing to ensure reporting is accurate after a campaign has launched. For those of you who use Firefox, there is also a free browser plug-in called HTTPFox (`http://addons.mozilla.org/en-us/firefox/addon/httpfox`), which essentially does the same thing as Charles and Fiddler but from directly inside the browser. Another one is the Firefox add-on called Live HTTP Headers (`http://addons.mozilla.org/en-US/firefox/addon/live-http-headers`), which allows a user to view the HTTP headers of a page while browsing. HTTP monitoring can be extremely helpful for mobile debugging since mobile devices currently lack in their native development tools. For tethering to your device using Charles, take a look at the following steps.

For iDevices, connect to a shared network between your computer and wireless device and go to the settings on the iDevice. Under HTTP Proxy, select Manual, and enter your computer's IP address into the server spot; then enter any unused port like *8888*. Next, begin to access mobile Safari or an application (anything with network traffic), and you'll eventually be prompted by Charles that another service is requesting to use this network as a proxy. Select Allow, and start using your device while viewing the network traffic on your computer.

Debugging on mobile can be even more problematic when you need to debug advertisements inside of applications where you don't have native features of browsers such as console logs. When debugging in mobile applications, you can leverage the power of HTTP requests to trick the calls into being tracing statements to understand what's happening inside your ad code. A good example of this is creating a dummy image file and assigning its source to a faux tracking call with some URL parameters for your log statement. The following example outlines what I'm discussing:

```
<script>
function adInit() {
        var traceImage = new Image();
        traceImage.src = "http://yourdomain.com?trace=statement";
}
</script>
```

Now when the function `adInit` is called, you'll see a request to a dummy URL in your HTTP monitor with the query param of `trace` equal to whatever statement you want to output. In this case, this may be the function that kicks things off in the ad experience, so it could look like the following code snippet (and Figure 10-3):

```
<script>
function adInit() {
        var traceImage = new Image();
        traceImage.src = "http://yourdomain.com?trace=AD-STARTED";
}
</script>
```

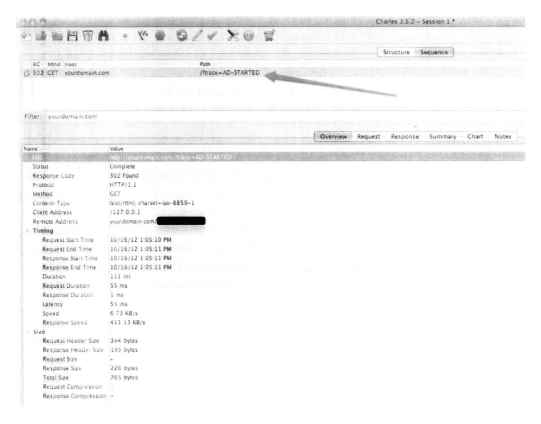

Figure 10-3. *Network monitoring in Charles (Mac)*

As you can see from the examples, this is very helpful when debugging the network traffic in browsers and on mobile devices. Using these tricks, developers can get insight into how their code is executing even if they cannot test on the physical device.

Mobile Development Tools

Mobile development tools are a growing business. It was once a complete headache to manage because the tools weren't available and advertising on mobile has skyrocketed as a business, so demand is plentiful. Tools like Adobe Edge Inspect (http://html.adobe.com/edge/inspect) and Weinre (http://pmuellr.github.com/weinre) offer remote debugging and development for mobile and tablets from directly on your desktop machine. Some other really great development tools are the ability to test on mobile emulators and simulators right on your personal computer. This would be using Apple's Xcode and iOS simulator found on the Mac AppStore, Google's Android developer tools (http://developer.android.com/tools/index.html), Blackberry 10 (http://developer.blackberry.com/platforms/bb10), Windows Phone (http://microsoft.com/en-us/download/details.aspx?id=27570), and Opera's Mobile Emulator (http://opera.com/developer/tools/mobile). Each of these tools offers a very similar experience to what you'd expect when viewing your content on the device itself. However, testing on the device itself is by far the best testing you can do as a developer. As I said, if you need to go to your local electronics store to test some ads, do it!

Now there are also many services you can use to test how your content will render and function on a variety of devices. One such service is called DeviceAnywhere (`http://keynotedeviceanywhere.com`), which effectively allows for a virtual view into your content on any specific device. You want to know how your ad looks on a first-generation Apple iPad running iOS 3.1? It's got you covered. How about an HTC running Android 2.3? Yep, that one too! DeviceAnywhere is a great tool to leverage for the arsenal of devices it has access to, but it still lacks in the hands-on debugging experience in my opinion. If you're a publisher wanting to test your web content on mobile devices but have limited at your disposal, check out MobiTest by Akamai (`http://mobitest.akamai.com/m/index.cgi`). This tool allows users to test page content on various devices from different locations, and you can even video capture the results to share with other colleagues. Again, most of these tools are virtual windows into the environment you're attempting to test for and for skeptics like myself; you may just need to test on the real thing.

Optimization

Optimization is an ongoing process when crafting web content or advertisements. Every single addition to the DOM or any additional asset being loaded into your ad will eventually need to be optimized, if not for the sake of performance for the sake of the publisher's requirements. Also, bandwidth is a limited resource and user experience is prime, so be sure to compress images using proper settings with programs such as Adobe's Photoshop or Fireworks. If you're a Mac user, check out the great image optimization applications called ImageOptim (`http://imageoptim.com`) and ImageAlpha (`http://pngmini.com`) for transparent PNG optimizations.

For the script side of things, make sure you clean up after yourself by doing your own garbage collection; if you have event listeners, make sure you remove them when you're done handling the event. Also, be sure to remove animation loops or iteration processes when they're not needed. Timers like `setInterval` and `setTimeout` can become expensive and taxing quickly, so be sure to clear them when not in use.

Be sure to always minify text-based files like HTML, CSS, and JavaScript for production ads and keep a copy of a more verbose version to go back and make edits so you don't have to work off the minified version. In conjunction with minification, be sure to use GZIP compression whenever you can. By gzipping your text-based files, you create a `.gz` version of your file, which is significantly smaller than the minified version alone. Compressing via GZIP allows for the smallest file transfer size, which will minimize bandwidth constraints and provide an overall faster web experience. Just be sure your hosting server or CDN has the appropriate configurations for serving GZIP files. If the users requesting browser cannot decompress or unzip the file before it renders it, the user will just be served the minified version of the asset although most browser now days support compressed content. To test whether your server is supplying gzipped files, visit `http://gidnetwork.com/tools/gzip-test.php`. Also, it may be best to use an automated build system that takes your source file, minifies it, GZIP compresses it, and places it in a desired location on your hosting server. Tools such as Ant [`http://ant.apache.org/`], Maven [`http://maven.apache.org/`], and others can help you do this automatically.

Avoid reflows and repaints to the DOM by inspecting the "timeline" tab in your favorite web inspector. By using this tool, you'll be able to see what the browser is actually tasked with doing when a user is requesting your content. By handling all of your DOM setup before it needs to reflow and/or repaint, this will eat up fewer processes and provide a better overall user experience. Figure 10-4 illustrates how the timeline section in your web inspector may look when requesting the page at `CNN.com`.

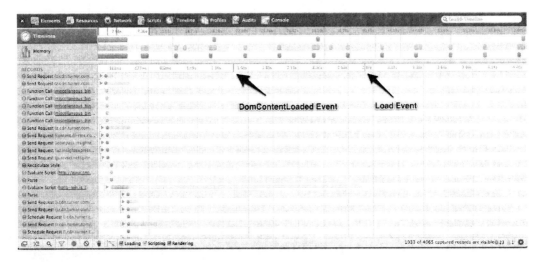

Figure 10-4. *The browser's timeline inspector*

As you can see, a lot of things happen when you hit Enter after you type in the URL. In the example, you see anything from HTTP requests and the time they take to respond, function calls within the script files, and even repaints and rendering to the DOM. Also, more importantly, you can even see what ads are doing on the page you're inspecting. What's really useful is that you can inspect when the DOM events "content loaded" and "load" fire and get a better assessment of the page's optimization before you need to dig into ad-specific optimizations. In this case, it took just shy of 1.6 seconds to fire DOMContentLoaded and about 2.8 second to fire the Load event. This is important to an ad server because the server would generally want to listen for one of these events and serve the ad after the main content is rendered to the screen. This way you can determine if the page needs to be better optimized, your ad content or both.

In addition to the "waterflow" view in your timeline, you can also inspect the memory being used to render the page contents including DOM markup, styles, scripts, and even ads. Figure 10-5 shows what the memory section would look like when you request the same page.

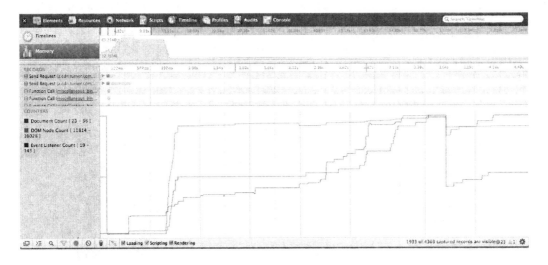

Figure 10-5. *Browser's memory usage*

With this image, you see a large spikes in the beginning of the request because the browser needs to populate all the DOM nodes and parse through the scripts and styles as quickly as possible. Also, at the beginning of the content request, you can see that close to 70MB of memory is used just to render the page to a user.

▓ **Note** These measurements are dependent on system capabilities and network connection speeds. Please do your own code optimization.

Another important tool to use in your optimization techniques is the use of the Audit tab in your browser's web inspector. The Audit feature allows developers to run a number of checks and balances against the page you're requesting. After evaluating the page contents, ads and all, the web inspector will offer tips on how to improve performance and speed up page rendering. It might recommend that you to compress your text-based files or even remove style declarations on elements that aren't being rendered. Figure 10-6 showcases an audit on my domain, `http://johnpercival.org`.

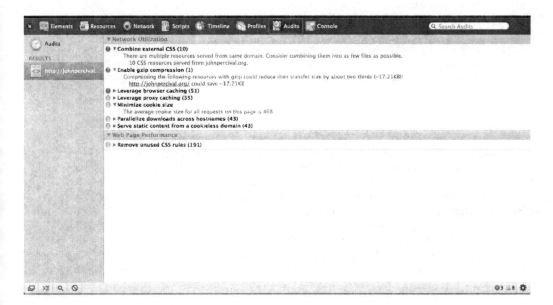

Figure 10-6. *The browser's Audits tool*

▓ **Note** I'm fully aware that my domain needs optimization, which is why it's a perfect test case.

Optimization analysis of your web content applies as much to mobile as it does to desktop and other formats using network connections. Get used to inspecting and tearing apart pages and advertisements to attempt to get the smallest digital footprint out of your content. Again, keep in mind that no one goes online to look at ads, unless you're the one building them. The same can be said about watching television for the commercials. Advertising is meant to be impactful, attention grabbing, and engaging, not something that will tax your computer or device just because some poorly written ad code is eating up system resources. Keep this in mind at all times and make the Web a better experience for everyone. Debugging and optimization are time-consuming processes that you will master only by doing them often and repeatedly. This chapter won't make you an expert, but it will give you the edge and will allow you to use a variety of great tools to help you along the way. Some of these tools will likely become your go-to favorites, and others you won't even give a second chance. I encourage you to find what works for you in your development workflow while experimenting with the others.

Mobile Tips and Tricks

Now that you have a good idea on how to debug and optimize your content, let's take a look at some of the common "gotchas" or pitfalls you typically see when dealing with HTML5 advertising, both on the desktop and on mobile devices. Let's start with HTML and CSS namespacing; if any markup in your ad is named the same as an element on the publisher's page and not wrapped in an iframe, the element's style and function could get inherited onto your ad. To avoid this, it's generally standard practice to come up with a prefix naming convention to use in all ad elements. I like to do ad serving prefixing; for example, if AdMob was serving the content, it would be `am-container`; PointRoll would be `pr-container`. Another good technique to use is to namespace from your CSS top-level element down. This could be your ad container element so all your CSS styles would be specifically set to the ads elements and none of the publisher's page. By writing something like *#adContainer .banner {...}* you can clearly target the ad container by it's ID and target nested elements like the banner class from our example.

Next I'll discuss asset caching. Caching can often be an issue on mobile applications, especially if a user is noticing dated content in your ad but you know you've updated it. Ensure that your client has exited the app/web browser, cleared their browser cache, and removed the app from any background processes. In the event of iOS, this can be done by double-clicking the device's home button, tapping, and holding down on the app until a close button appears. For Android, you'll need to go into the running applications and explicitly kill their processes.

Mobile Webkit

Webkit has a very sophisticated rendering engine, and it's the default device browser engine for iOS and Android devices. It also has plenty of useful but often hidden properties to take advantage of. If you notice that Webkit is handling your content in a strange way or perhaps even an ideal way but are not quite sure why, I recommend visiting Webkit.org to learn about the inner workings of this powerful browser. For a quick rundown, I've listed a few here that you come across most frequently in the ad world. I hope these useful properties will help you when you notice a few within your creative development, debugging, and testing. The first one is the font-rendering glitch when Webkit performs any type of CSS animation on DOM elements. This glitch is often seen when fonts look sharp and clean during the animation but on the completion they appear to get much bolder for no apparent reason and often result in an unwanted flickering effect. If you or your client notices this, try to apply the following CSS rules on the container div wrapping your text:

```
<style>
.smoothFont {
        -webkit-backface-visibility: hidden;
        -webkit-transform: translate3d(0, 0, 0);
}
</style>
```

This rule will set the GPU "on" for the duration of the ad experience, which will not result in any font glitches. Keep in mind also that as more browsers leverage the GPU, this issue could remedy itself with future browser releases. Another useful Webkit trick is to prevent Safari from adjusting text size on device orientation changes. When you rotate a device, the browser adjusts the text size. If for some reason you'd like to prevent this effect, use the following CSS rule:

```
<style>
.maintainSize {
        -webkit-text-size-adjust: none;
}
</style>
```

Note text-size-adjust is a Webkit-only CSS property that allows you to control text adjustment.

If you're a publisher, you'll often want to create a web app experience for your mobile visitors. If you're in charge of building the content that ads will run on and want to have a handy script in your arsenal for hiding the default toolbar of a mobile web page, check out the following code snippet, which can attach to the DOM load event:

```
<script>
window.addEventListener('load', function() {
        setTimeout(scrollTo (0, 1));
}, false);
</script>
```

Also, since we're talking about mobile, it's pretty safe to say you live in a touch world. While this is amazingly great for the UI, it does pose some challenges for creating traditional behaviors where users are accustomed to mouse input. One of these challenges is creating a "hover" effect, and while it's technically impossible to do, you can still have buttons in your UI respond as if they were actually being clicked. The following JavaScript example can help you mimic this effect, which can be very useful for certain design interactions:

```
<script>
var myLinks = document.getElementsByTagName('a');

for(var i = 0; i < myLinks.length; i++){
        myLinks[i].addEventListener('touchstart', function () {
                this.className = "hover";
        }, false);
        myLinks[i].addEventListener('touchend', function (){
                this.className = "";
        }, false);
}
</script>
```

As you can see, you grab all the a tags and add a class of hover on touchstart and touchend events. Now once you've added the JavaScript to your document, you can style as you normally would in CSS using the hover class.

The last mobile code snippet relates to touch events again. Often you will notice that when you are interacting with a touch-enabled object in your DOM, the entire browser window moves and not the object you're targeting.

A developer not including the preventDefault method, which tells the browser to "back off" while you're moving an element with your finger, often causes this. It's really simple to add this, so take a look at the following:

```
<script>
document.ontouchmove = function(event){
        event.preventDefault();
}
</script>
```

Keep in mind that most times publishers will include the specific HTML meta tags for locking the browser's viewport, but it's still nice to know another option should you need to address it on the ad's end.

Summary

This chapter was chock full of useful tips and tricks about storing assets offline, what goes into tracking for offline use, and general debugging and optimization. You dove into what it takes to cache assets using HTML5's AppCache and what assets you shouldn't cache because of file sizes. I discussed how this is ultimately up to publisher requirements in the in-application world, since if an application isn't supported offline, your advertisements won't be either. In addition to HTML5's application cache, you learn about what it takes to detect when your web content is online and offline using navigator.onLine as well as what it takes leveraging an SDK in the in-application world. I talked briefly about emerging APIs like the Network Connection API and how once the specification finalizes and browser adoption takes, you'll have a very nice API for offering adaptive experiences to end users. Following up on offline, I discussed how metrics could still be tallied in an offline state using offline-tracking techniques. Whether you're tracking metrics in-application using a cache file and an SDK or you're on a mobile device using DOM storage or client-side databases, rest assured you have the technology to pull this off. Lastly, I discussed the complex topic of debugging and optimization. This topic is something I'm extremely passionate about and so should you be if you aim to serve advertising content on the Web with HTML5. I covered all the tools and techniques you have at your fingertips to get the smallest file size and analyze your ad content across multiple screens.

As you wrap up your thoughts around offline, tracking, and debugging, you'll head into the enormous domain of dynamic advertising with HTML5. Things get really exciting when you incorporate dynamic elements into your advertisements, but they also get pretty complex to create and debug. However, rest assured you now have the knowledge to tackle the topics in this next chapter head on.

CHAPTER 11

■ ■ ■

Dynamic Advertising with HTML5

Dynamic advertising is nothing new in today's world. The concept of rich creative paired with relevant messaging and data is something users and marketers have grown accustomed to seeing. However, this sort of dynamic behavior was traditionally done using Flash and the ad would reference an external web service to update its creative contents, which could be updated text, new images, or even a new ad experience altogether. In this chapter, I'll focus on the same concepts that helped shape the dynamic advertising market, but I'll do it with a primary focus on HTML5 and related open web technologies.

Let's take a deeper dive into the topic of "dynamic" and figure out how you can leverage external data, publisher-passed data, public and private web services, and various APIs to manipulate creative at ad-serve time. I'll cover locally targeting users based on geolocation as well as demonstrating that advertising doesn't have to be "baked" in. I'll review how ad servers and ad-serving technology use custom macros to help speed up runtime dynamics, and I'll also showcase how ads can be timely, relevant, and efficient, creating "hot-swappable" content on the fly. Using these techniques, I'll cover the technologies in which your ads will leverage dynamic data including XML, JSON, and straight-up JavaScript. Learning these tools will ultimately open up new worlds of online advertising.

Delivery Rules

Let's kick things off with the most basic forms of dynamic advertising, which are the dynamic properties of the ad server. Typically, ad servers can place delivery rules for the users requesting the ad content. This sort of relationship goes like this: "Hey, ad server, I am a user on an iPad in landscape orientation. Deliver me a creative that isn't Flash based and is sized correctly." The ad server will then double-check that the user is in fact on an iPad by doing a browser string (user agent) lookup and then will deliver the appropriate creative type based on the request. Figure 11-1 explains the request-response relationship between the user and the ad server.

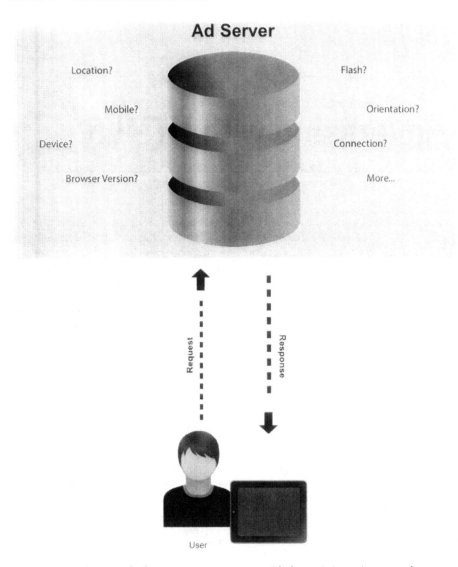

Figure 11-1. The typical ad server request-response with dynamic input/output values

Delivery rules have a lot of power in that they are the first line of entry for the ad server; ad-serving companies attempt to make this ad response super quick in order to serve an impression for every person viewing the content. They typically judge this response time in a matter of milliseconds. Ad servers don't just use browser-sniffing techniques; they can sniff out user cookies or data stored on the client side in the browser cache, as well as IP addresses, ISPs, and various other data I'll cover later. Delivery rules or settings often apply to how the ad gets served to the publisher page through the ad tag of the requesting user. Delivery rules can often have frequency, rotation, and user-has rules and specific creative types associated with them. These rules can also be paired with other variables such as time of day, location, and any other variables that the ad server can analyze. I'll cover each one of these techniques in the following sections.

Frequency is the number of times the user will see the ad. If the campaign lasts one day and the user frequents the publisher page multiple times a day, that user could "frequency capped" after the initial view and served a different creative thereafter. *Rotation* simply means how many different creatives a user can potentially see within one campaign execution. If the advertiser has multiple creative versions at the ready, the ad server can place them on a rotation so the user views fresh content with multiple ad requests. The *user-has rule* detects what the client-side browser or device is capable of rendering. This could be a static creative, Flash creative, or HTML5 creative. It is really up to what features the client-side browser can handle, including specific features of the browser. If the user can't support HTML5, can the user support Flash? If not, how about an image?

Note Each ad-serving vendor has different capabilities. Reach out to them to determine what works for you and your campaign.

Taking advantage of these ad-serving settings allows for some really crafty and dynamic use cases. For instance, you could serve a creative to an iPad user and another on a smart TV all through the same-trafficked ad tag. This allows the publisher to sell media through all of their distribution channels and makes their AdOps team rest easy because they're only required to traffic one tag. Can you imagine how hard it must be to handle multiple tags for each mobile device, tablet, computer, TV, and so on? That gets crazy quickly!

Delivery rules get more powerful as ad servers and technology vendors pump more data into them. The more data the ad server can analyze, the more custom the ad experience can be. This technique is often driven by what is known as a *dynamic creative optimization* (DCO). A DCO engine allows for serving dynamic creative on many variables and even third-party variables or inputs. Really intelligent DCO engines can factor in location, gender, age, sexual orientation, and interests, among many other input values. Using this valuable data, marketers can target their audience more effectively knowing which audience segments they want to hit (and with which creative message). Some ad servers can even detect WiFi hotspots and target advertisements accordingly based on the network service they're using. For example, Figure 11-2 was served to me while I was at a conference in San Francisco this past year. The ad server knew I was using the free conference WiFi based on my IP address and targeted ads accordingly while I visited the publisher site, Bloomberg.com. Take a look at the following sequence of images to better understand this dynamic ability.

Figure 11-2. *The initial screen on Bloomberg.com using AT&T's 3G service*

This first image was my initial request to Bloomberg.com while using AT&T's 3G network on my iPad. As you can see, I'm getting a few ads on the right side of the screen. Now if I hop onto the conference's WiFi, as you'll see in Figure 11-3, I'll see an updated experience.

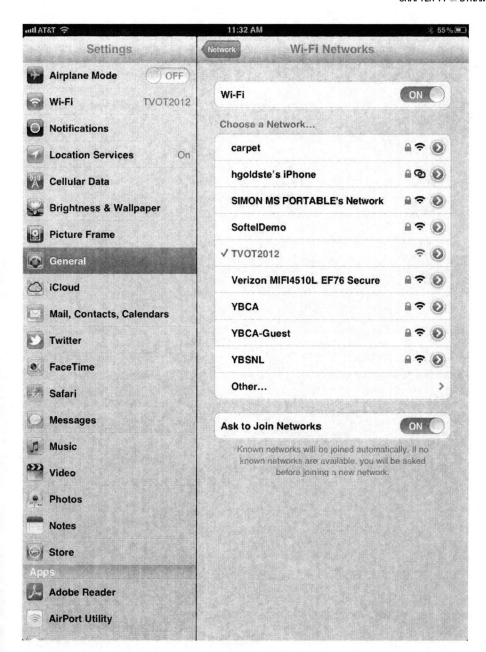

Figure 11-3. The screen to use the free conference WiFi in San Francisco

Figure 11-3 demonstrates when I went into my settings application on my iPad to switch on the free WiFi from the conference. Figure 11-4 shows the updated ad experience.

Figure 11-4. *The updated Bloomberg.com site after using the free WiFi service*

As you can see from Figure 11-4, I was targeted a specific ad based on my known location by the ad server. Because I was using the free WiFi service, the ad server knew where I was and could serve relevant ads based on that IP address. Now if I tap and hold the ad, as shown in Figure 11-5, you'll see the ad server's domain.

Figure 11-5. *The ad server responsible for showing these dynamic ads*

As shown in Figure 11-5, you can see that when I tapped and held on the ad, I was shown what the click-through destination would be for this ad unit and that `http://myturfads.com` was the ad server responsible for identifying my IP address on the free network and presenting these relevant and dynamic ads.

Publisher-Passed Data

Ad servers are pretty powerful on their own, and when used in conjunction with DCO offerings and dynamic delivery rules, they're *really* powerful. But what's interesting is that ad servers can even use publisher data to bring yet more dynamics to the ad experience. Publisher-passed data can be used in serving dynamic ads by passing information the publisher knows about their visitors into the ad server's ad tag. This information typically comes through the ad tag by way of a string value, usually comma or pipe-delimited, but it can often be encrypted on the tag pass-through from the publisher and then decrypted by the ad server. This encryption is done so no malicious behavior can be performed with the user's data unknowingly. The publisher typically gathers this data by offering a free service for a user/member to sign up for. This could be an e-mail account, free music streaming account, or even a social network. The following example could represent many values on input to the ad tag, such as age, zip, gender, and interests:

```
var adInput = "29|19428|M|Business,Technology"
```

Or Base64 encoded:

```
var adInput = "Mjl8MTkOMjh8TXxCdXNpbmVzcyxUZWNNobm9sb2d5";
```

▪ **Note** For more information on Base64 encoding, visit http://base64encode.org.

As you can see, the adInput var could be the main input into the ad server's ad tag. The publisher would then populate the data when the ad renders on its page. Publishers that take advantage of this type of data passing are Yahoo, MSN, AOL, and many, many others because it allows for more relevant advertising methods among their user bases. If you remember from the first chapter, I covered that most free services such as Yahoo and Google offer their advertisers their vast user base in exchange for media dollars. In other words, the publisher offers a free service for collecting the user's information. Hence, users are the product the publisher is selling, and advertisers are the publisher's customers. However, it's not all supposed to be negative; it's been found that using some of these rich integrations will improve your campaigns tenfold because it correlates the right messaging at the right time to the right user and users can benefit from being served ads they actually care about.

Macros and Variables

Macros are the last ad-serving feature I'll cover. Macros in software traditionally are used as temporary stand-in values that will get replaced at a later time. This may be familiar to you when you use variables where you have references to other values in your JavaScript.

A quick example of this would be var man = john, where man is the variable and john is the value. Taking this concept a step further, macros can be used for extensive server-side value replacement. For instance, say you developed a creative where all your click-out URLs were dependent on the publisher page to which the ad was served. If this were the case and you didn't have macros, the creative would need to be developed in many different ways to satisfy each placement. However, with macros, you can use these stand-in macro values, and at ad-serve time, depending on the publisher placement, the values would get switched to the correct value. The following code example demonstrates this concept more if you were to serve the same ad to both CNN.com and BBC.com:

```
Ad server assignment for CNN.com:
MACRO = "http://www.cnn.com"

Ad server assignment for BBC.com:
MACRO = "http://www.bbc.co.uk"
```

```
HTML for creative:
<a href=MACRO target="_blank"></a>
```

As you can see, it's much more scalable to develop in this fashion rather than update numerous creatives when changes need to be made down the road.

Working with XML and JSON

By now you have a fair understanding on how ads can be dynamically targeted to you as a user from an ad server point of view, but let's shift gears a bit and talk more about the technical aspects of dynamic ads as they relate to HTML5 and the open Web. This would be particularly on the creative end of things where you can manipulate the creative elements of your ad using data. But before you head down this path, you need to be clear on a few ways about how your creatives can work with external data from various services. Two of the most common communication layers when working in HTML5 are Extensible Markup Language (XML) and JavaScript Object Notation (JSON). XML and JSON are widely adopted among the industry in that they're used in many RESTful APIs for various data endpoints.

■ **Note** For good information on RESTful APIs, visit `http://blog.apigee.com/detail/restful_api_design`.

Using a common and universal language that all lower-level code languages can understand and parse allows for easy adoption, communication, and ubiquity among web developers. Anything from bringing in a brand's Twitter feed to pulling in a stock ticker, or even using a weather feed or local retail products, can be pulled into the ad creative. It's all traditionally done using XML or JSON data, and the following sections are geared toward showing the best way to work with external data providers with XML and JSON.

XML

XML is probably the most common language for web services. I'm not going to get into the nitty-gritty of XML, but in the ad world, an advertisement will make a request to some web service by way of an HTTP request, usually with some necessary URL query parameters. The response that the web service provides to that request will traditionally be in XML format. Listing 11-1 showcases a request and XML response from Yahoo's open weather service.

Listing 11-1. Yahoo's Weather API XML Example

```
HTTP Request:
http://query.yahooapis.com/v1/public/yql/jonathan/weather?zip=19428

Server Response:
<query yahoo:count="1" yahoo:created="2012-08-01T23:15:47Z" yahoo:lang="en US" xmlns:yahoo=
"http://www.yahooapis.com/v1/base.rng">
<results>
<channel>
<title>Yahoo! Weather - Conshohocken, PA</title>
<link>http://us.rd.yahoo.com/dailynews/rss/weather/Conshohocken__PA/*http://weather.yahoo.com/
forecast/USPA0326_f.html</link>
<description>Yahoo! Weather for Conshohocken, PA</description>
<language>en-us</language>
<lastBuildDate>Wed, 01 Aug 2012 6:34 pm EDT</lastBuildDate>
<ttl>60</ttl>
```

```
<yweather:location city="Conshohocken" country="US" region="PA" xmlns:yweather="http://xml.weather.
yahoo.com/ns/rss/1.0"/>
<yweather:units distance="mi" pressure="in" speed="mph" temperature="F" xmlns:yweather="http://xml.
weather.yahoo.com/ns/rss/1.0"/>
<yweather:wind chill="70" direction="0" speed="0" xmlns:yweather="http://xml.weather.yahoo.com/ns/
rss/1.0"/>
<yweather:atmosphere humidity="94" pressure="29.85" rising="2" visibility="4"
xmlns:yweather="http://xml.weather.yahoo.com/ns/rss/1.0"/>
<yweather:astronomy sunrise="5:57 am" sunset="8:12 pm" xmlns:yweather="http://xml.weather.yahoo.com/
ns/rss/1.0"/>
<image>
<title>Yahoo! Weather</title>
<width>142</width>
<height>18</height>
<link>http://weather.yahoo.com</link>
<url>http://l.yimg.com/a/i/brand/purplelogo//uh/us/news-wea.gif</url>
</image>
<item>
<title>Conditions for Conshohocken, PA at 6:34 pm EDT</title>
<geo:lat xmlns:geo="http://www.w3.org/2003/01/geo/wgs84_pos#">40.08</geo:lat>
<geo:long xmlns:geo="http://www.w3.org/2003/01/geo/wgs84_pos#">-75.3</geo:long>
<link>http://us.rd.yahoo.com/dailynews/rss/weather/Conshohocken__PA/*http://weather.yahoo.com/
forecast/USPA0326_f.html</link>
<pubDate>Wed, 01 Aug 2012 6:34 pm EDT</pubDate>
<yweather:condition code="30" date="Wed, 01 Aug 2012 6:34 pm EDT" temp="70" text="Partly Cloudy"
xmlns:yweather="http://xml.weather.yahoo.com/ns/rss/1.0"/>
<description>
<![CDATA[ <img src="http://l.yimg.com/a/i/us/we/52/30.gif"/><br /> <b>Current Conditions:</b>
<br /> Partly Cloudy, 70 F<BR /> <BR /><b>Forecast:</b><BR /> Wed - Scattered Thunderstorms. High: 82
Low: 66<br /> Thu - Partly Cloudy. High: 91 Low: 70<br /> <br /> <a href="http://us.rd.yahoo.com/
dailynews/rss/weather/Conshohocken__PA/*http://weather.yahoo.com/forecast/USPA0326_f.html">Full
Forecast at Yahoo! Weather</a><BR/><BR/> (provided by <a href="http://www.weather.com" >The Weather
Channel</a>)<br/> ]]>
</description>
<yweather:forecast code="47" date="1 Aug 2012" day="Wed" high="82" low="66" text="Scattered
Thunderstorms" xmlns:yweather="http://xml.weather.yahoo.com/ns/rss/1.0"/>
<yweather:forecast code="30" date="2 Aug 2012" day="Thu" high="91" low="70" text="Partly Cloudy"
xmlns:yweather="http://xml.weather.yahoo.com/ns/rss/1.0"/>
<guid isPermaLink="false">
USPA0326_2012_08_02_7_00_EDT
</guid>
</item>
</channel>
</results>
</query>
```

As you can see from Listing 11-1, the ad makes an HTTP request to the http://query.yahooapis.com domain with the query parameter of zip=19428 and gets a valid XML in response with detailed weather conditions for the user-defined ZIP code. This is really powerful! If you take what you've just learned from your ad server, you can have the ad server detect your location on the initial ad request, convert the location data to a ZIP code, and pass the weather service that ZIP code to provide a relevant and up-to-date ad experience that the user actually cares about all at ad serve time.

JSON

JSON is very similar to XML in that it structures data in a hierarchy, but its main difference is that it's really JavaScript objects that are parsed by the browser natively regardless of an XML manifest. Another benefit with JSON and JSON-P, is that it doesn't care what domain it's coming from. This means that XML can be crippled in its response if the domain hosting the information (in this case, Yahoo) wasn't the same as the domain making the request (in this case, the ad). There are ways around this cross-origin policy, either by using CORS, which you learned about in Chapter 6, or simply by using JSON-P. Sometimes JSON-P is not an option for a web service's response data format, but if it is, you'll never need to worry about domain security issues when working with HTML5 ads. In the case of Yahoo's weather service, making a JSON request is very similar to XML. Listing 11-2 shows the same example using JSON.

Listing 11-2. Yahoo's Weather API JSON Example

```
Request:
http://query.yahooapis.com/v1/public/yql/jonathan/weather?zip=19428&format=json

Response:
{
    "query": {
        "count": 1,
        "created": "2012-08-01T23:29:00Z",
        "lang": "en-US",
        "results": {
            "channel": {
                "title": "Yahoo! Weather - Conshohocken, PA",
                "link": "http://us.rd.yahoo.com/dailynews/rss/weather/Conshohocken__PA/*
http://weather.yahoo.com/forecast/USPA0326_f.html",
                "description": "Yahoo! Weather for Conshohocken, PA",
                "language": "en-us",
                "lastBuildDate": "Wed, 01 Aug 2012 6:53 pm EDT",
                "ttl": "60",
                "location": {
                    "city": "Conshohocken",
                    "country": "US",
                    "region": "PA"
                },
                "units": {
                    "distance": "mi",
                    "pressure": "in",
                    "speed": "mph",
                    "temperature": "F"
                },
                "wind": {
                    "chill": "72",
                    "direction": "0",
                    "speed": "0"
                },
                "atmosphere": {
                    "humidity": "94",
                    "pressure": "29.85",
```

```
                "rising": "0",
                "visibility": "5"
        },
        "astronomy": {
            "sunrise": "5:57 am",
            "sunset": "8:12 pm"
        },
        "image": {
            "title": "Yahoo! Weather",
            "width": "142",
            "height": "18",
            "link": "http://weather.yahoo.com",
            "url": "http://l.yimg.com/a/i/brand/purplelogo//uh/us/news-wea.gif"
        },
        "item": {
            "title": "Conditions for Conshohocken, PA at 6:53 pm EDT",
            "lat": "40.08",
            "long": "-75.3",
            "link": "http://us.rd.yahoo.com/dailynews/rss/weather/Conshohocken__PA/*
http://weather.yahoo.com/forecast/USPA0326_f.html",
            "pubDate": "Wed, 01 Aug 2012 6:53 pm EDT",
            "condition": {
                "code": "30",
                "date": "Wed, 01 Aug 2012 6:53 pm EDT",
                "temp": "72",
                "text": "Partly Cloudy"
            },
            "description": "\n<img src=\"http://l.yimg.com/a/i/us/we/52/30.gif\"/><br />\
n<b>Current Conditions:</b><br />\nPartly Cloudy, 72 F<BR />\n<BR /><b>Forecast:</b><BR />\nWed
 - Scattered Thunderstorms. High: 82 Low: 66<br />\nThu - Partly Cloudy. High: 91 Low: 70<br />\
n<br />\n<a href=\"http://us.rd.yahoo.com/dailynews/rss/weather/Conshohocken__PA/*http://weather.
yahoo.com/forecast/USPA0326_f.html\">Full Forecast at Yahoo! Weather</a><BR/><BR/>\n(provided by <a
href=\"http://www.weather.com\" >The Weather Channel</a>)<br/>\n",
            "forecast": [{
                "code": "47",
                "date": "1 Aug 2012",
                "day": "Wed",
                "high": "82",
                "low": "66",
                "text": "Scattered Thunderstorms"
            }, {
                "code": "30",
                "date": "2 Aug 2012",
                "day": "Thu",
                "high": "91",
                "low": "70",
                "text": "Partly Cloudy"
            }],
```

```
                "guid": {
                    "isPermaLink": "false",
                    "content": "USPA0326_2012_08_02_7_00_EDT"
                }
            }
        }
    }
}
```

As you can see in Listing 11-2, the request is pretty much the same. The only thing you change is the format in which you want the data. In this case, you add an additional query param to the request called format=json. This is, again, pretty powerful in that it will allow ads to pull in data from various domains without the need for "white listing." Think about the possibilities when you can have your ad dynamically change without "actually" changing it.

■ **Note** There are client-side XML-to-JSON formatters (see http://thomasfrank.se/xml_to_json.html), but they don't solve the cross-domain-policy issues.

Content Formatting

So, you may be asking yourself, this dynamic data is all well and good, but don't I need to handle and condition the data that gets injected into the ad? This is a great question, and the obvious answer is yes! Things like using swear filters, adding ellipses, sizing text, and inserting code for line breaks all need to be taken into consideration.

First off, swear filters can typically be done on the back-end or server-side layer. Before that data gets inputted into a service, it's generally best practice to condition for swears and negative comments against the brand. That being said, it always good to reach out to the back-end developers to ensure this technique is in place. If it's not, Listing 11-3 shows a good client-side swear filter using JavaScript.

Listing 11-3. JavaScript Swear Filter Example

```html
<html>
<head>
<script type="text/javascript">
//Grow this list for as long as you wish...
var keyWords = [D'oh,'jeez','dagnabit','boo','agh','Golly'];

function replaceChars(chr,cnt) {
  var s = '';
  for (var i=0; i<cnt; i++) {
    s += chr;
    console.log(s);
  }
  return s;
}
```

```
function checkWords() {
  var inputText = document.getElementById('textArea').value;
  var outputText = document.getElementById('conditionedText');

  for (var i=0; i < keyWords.length; i++) {
    var rg = new RegExp(keyWords[i]+' ',"ig");
    inputText = inputText.replace(rg,replaceChars('*',keyWords[i].length)+' ');
  }

  outputText.textContent = inputText;
}
</script>
</head>
<body>
<textarea id="textArea" rows="5" cols="13">
This chapter is dagnabit amazing!
</textarea>
<button onclick="checkWords()">Submit!</button>
<div id="conditionedText"></div>
</body>
</html>
```

So sweet of you to say! As you can see, you can add as many words as you'd like to the keyWords array, and you can feel free to use the words that make the most sense to you. It also may be a better idea externalizing the words in a JSON file so updates can be made easily without digging into the core script files. This could also be used using what we've learned in chapter 6 with Web Workers.

Another way to condition data is the "new to HTML5" ellipsis text property of CSS. If you're unsure about the number of words that are coming back in a web service, you can set the width and height values of the text area and set the copy inside of it to overflow: ellipsis. Take a look at Listing 11-4.

Listing 11-4. Overflow Ellipsis Example

```
<html>
<head>
</head>
<body>
<div id="textArea">
Lorem Ipsum is simply dummy text of the printing and typesetting industry. Lorem Ipsum has been the
industry's standard dummy text ever since the 1500s, when an unknown printer took a galley of type
and scrambled it to make a type specimen book. It has survived not only five centuries, but also the
leap into electronic typesetting, remaining essentially unchanged. It was popularised in the 1960s
with the release of Letraset sheets containing Lorem Ipsum passages, and more recently with desktop
publishing software like Aldus PageMaker including versions of Lorem Ipsum.
</div>
</body>
<style type="text/css">
#textArea {
  text-overflow: ellipsis;
  -o-text-overflow: ellipsis;
```

```
    -moz-text-overflow: ellipsis;
    -ms-text-overflow: ellipsis;
    -webkit-text-overflow: ellipsis;
    height: 100px;
    width: 200px;
    overflow: hidden;
    white-space: nowrap;
    padding: 5px;
}
</style>
</html>
```

Now any copy that fills the div called textArea will get an ellipsis attached to the tail end of the copy should the words overflow the div container. There is also another useful CSS tip for mobile devices called overflow: scroll. Using the following CSS on mobile devices (iOS 5+) will give you a native and elegant scrolling feature similar to the experience on the native operating system:

```
#textArea {
        overflow: scroll;
-webkit-overflow-scrolling: touch;
}
```

Next, I'll discuss the concept of text sizing as data and words grow. Again, when working with dynamic data, you have no idea what amount of data is coming to you in the response. Unless you discuss this beforehand with the back-end developers who could employ character limits, you'll need to use some text sizing code that you can leverage via JavaScript to detect the size of the div container and the number of words filling the container. Using the example located at http://jsfiddle.net/qW5h2/1 from Nikolay Kuchumov, you can reduce the size of the font to fit within the allotted space for which it's designed. This is a bit tricky to pull off and can even come back to bite you if the copy is getting reduced significantly, especially if your clients are Pharmaceutical companies (Pharma) and every word needs to be clear for legal reasons. The best bet is to communicate with your web service provider, and if the time allows, perhaps they could add a special node with a font size value. This way, the ad can check that node for its value and size appropriately without doing any logic.

There is one other trick I wanted to mention, and it's the concept of viewport size. This is increasingly important for mobile devices. In short, viewport size/scale can dynamically update the size and scale of the fonts on-screen based on the zoom level of the viewport. This is something to make note of if you're using CSS font sizing in vw. Keep in mind that this will alter the container-sizing method shown previously, but between each of these tricks, you should have a good understanding of what technique bests serves you and your campaign. For more information on viewport-sized type, visit http://css-tricks.com/viewport-sized-typography.

Note   There is also a very nice lightweight jQuery plug-in called FitText (http://fittextjs.com) for responsive font sizing.

HTML5 Data Attribute

Now that you understand how effective it can be to leverage data from within your advertisements, let's take a look at some new features that HTML5 permits you to use in the new browser market. New in HTML5 is the optional and arbitrary data attribute that can be used from within the HTML markup. Taking the example covered in the "Macros and Variables" section, you can plug these undefined macro values in your HTML without affecting your valid markup. The data attribute is a great way to add dynamic values to your markup without hacking them to the DOM through scripts. Listing 11-5 showcases how to use the custom data attribute in your ad if you were to have products dynamically added from a retail store web service like one from ShopLocal (`http://shoplocal.com`).

Listing 11-5. HTML5 Data Attribute Example

```
<!DOCTYPE HTML>
<html>
<head>
</head>
<body>
<div data-name="product" data-url="http://www.productURL.com"></div>
</body>
<script>
var element = document.getElementsByTagName('div')[0];
var name = element.dataset.name = "product"
var url = element.dataset.url = "http://www.productURL.com"
console.log('name' + name, 'url' + url)
</script>
</head>
</html>
```

■ **Note**   For more information about ShopLocal.com's retail API, visit `http://aboutshoplocal.com/products/paperboy`.

The data attribute works simply by using data-*, where * stands for whatever value you want. In this case, you use NAME and URL as they relate to product information that could be dynamically populated within your ad based on the response from the Shoplocal API. Just to reiterate, this can be any name you want! Go nuts—it's all still valid HTML!

What's really great about using the data attribute is that with all the attributes you add, you can display the information instantaneously to the user without having to worry about making any additional external requests or having to make any server-side queries. Since the data is baked into the markup, it is already present. This speeds up performance tremendously because the data is already present in the DOM. You do not need to "request more information" since the information is already there with the initial response. For more detailed information about the custom data attribute in HTML5, visit `http://html5doctor.com/html5-custom-data-attributes`.

Another really useful attribute new in HTML5 is called hidden. When using the hidden attribute, the browser should not render the element; however, the element is still visible in the markup and accessible from the DOM. When you want to show the element, you can use JavaScript to remove the hidden attribute . It's pretty straightforward; Listing 11-6 has a hidden macro value defined. After the JavaScript executes and detects that you have your value replaced by the ad server, you can render the element and its value to the screen for the user to display. This is really helpful in scenarios where you need to request the data before presenting it to a user.

Listing 11-6. HTML5 hidden Attribute Example

```
<!DOCTYPE HTML>
<html lang=en>
<head>
```

```
<script>
var output = document.getElementsByTagName('p')[0];

function onAdServerComplete (value) {
        // macro value
        var welcome = "Hello " + value;
        output.innerHTML = welcome;
        output.removeAttribute('hidden');
}

//Example Callback with value from AdServer
onAdServerComplete("John");
</script>
</head>
<body>
<p hidden>MACRO</p>
</body>
</html>
```

Content Editable

This next feature is more of an attribute than an API, but it's still an important focus on user interaction, which is a prime feature of the HTML5 specification and dynamic data. Believe it or not, *content editable* has been around since version 5.5 of Microsoft's Internet Explorer, and now it's currently supported in all five major modern browsers. When using the content editable feature, all you need to do is to set the contenteditable attribute to true on the element you want to make editable. You can also combine this feature with the ability to make pushes to a server or client-side storage and manage the changes for referencing later if the user comes back to the experience. Listing 11-7 shows the contenteditable attribute in action.

Listing 11-7. Content Editable Example

```
<!DOCTYPE html>
<html lang="en">
<head>
<meta charset=utf-8>
<body>
<header contenteditable=true>Enter Some Text Here</header>
</body>
</html>
```

Pretty, simple right? Now you can edit anything inside the header element. Really, you can add this attribute to the body element and allow the whole page to be edited. Content editable in advertising has a lot of potential. Instead of using an input field for all user entry, you can actually have the users edit the creative elements, allowing them to creatively alter their own ad experience. For example, what if you had an ad campaign that asked the user for their input, allowing them to customize, manipulate, and edit anything including the style of the ad itself? This may not be the ideal situation at all times, but for specific campaigns, it could be a unique approach. Where other advertisers are force-feeding their end users information, this could take the opposite approach and ask users for creative input. With this, you could allow a user to edit the entire ad and save the changes to the browser or a server, and the next time they view the ad in sequence, they'll see the latest saved version that they once edited. This also will allow the brand to take a good look at how their users are customizing their brand experience, which would give vital details into brand relationships. Take a look at Listing 11-8, where the user can edit the CSS styling of the ad experience and save their changes to browser storage.

Listing 11-8. Content Editable Ad Example

```
<!DOCTYPE html>
<head>
    <meta charset=utf-8>
<style type="text/css">
    * {
        -webkit-tap-highlight-color:rgba(0,0,0,0);
        outline: none;
        text-rendering: optimizeLegibility;
    }
    #cta {
        font: 175% sans-serif;
        text-align: center;
        margin-bottom: 20px;
    }
    #ad style{
        display: block;
        text-align: center;
    }
    #ad:hover{
        background-color: #999;
        width: 300px;
        height: 250px;
    }
    button {
      margin-top: 20px;
      margin-bottom: 20px;
      width: 300px;
      height: 30px;
    }
</style>
    <body align="center">
      <div id="cta">Edit Your Own CSS!</div>
        <div id="ad" contenteditable>
            <div id="style">
              <style contenteditable>
              #ad {
                  background-color: #fff;
                  width: 300px;
                  height: 250px;
                  border: 1px solid #000;
              }
              </style>
            </div>
        </div>
```

```html
<button id="clearValues">clear storage</button>
<div id="output"></output>

<script type="text/javascript">
var adStyle = document.querySelector('#style'),
    clearIt = document.querySelector('#clearValues'),
    output = document.querySelector('#output');

function adInit () {
    if (localStorage.getItem('adValue') === 'null' || localStorage.getItem('adValue') === null) {
        console.log('init')
    } else {
        adStyle.textContent = localStorage.getItem('adValue');
        console.log(localStorage.getItem('adValue'))
        output.textContent = "Values Loaded!!!";
    }

    adStyle.addEventListener('DOMCharacterDataModified', updateAdStyle, false);//Fires
everytime a character is changed
    clearIt.addEventListener('click', clear, false);

    adStyle.focus();
}

function updateAdStyle () {
    if(localStorage) {
        output.textContent = "Values Saved!!!";
        console.log(adStyle.textContent);
        //store the values
        var styleFix = "<style contenteditable>" + adStyle.textContent + "</style>";
        localStorage.setItem('adValue', styleFix);
    }
}

function clear () {
    if(localStorage.getItem('adValue') != 'null' || localStorage.getItem('adValue') != null) {
        localStorage.clear();
    }
    output.textContent = "";
    console.log('clear')
}
window.addEventListener('DOMContentLoaded', adInit, false);

</script>
</body>
</html>
```

As you can see from the previous example, you're allowing the user to edit the CSS directly on the page, or in this case the 300 × 250 ad unit. From the edits that the user makes, you store a long string value in localStorage by the name of adValue. Now, the next time the user views the ad, the values will be stored and still available to be manipulated. This really opens up the doors to truly customized ad experiences.

HTML5 Forms and Inputs

Forms were most likely the first time you realized that your web content could become *interactive*. You could not only interact with your users but also tailor your site and content based on their input. This is essentially the whole foundation of dynamic content. Allow for interaction, optimize the feedback, and represent the information specifically to the user who interacted with the ad. With that said, I can't get away with speaking about dynamic ads without mentioning the updates to the forms and inputs in HTML5. Forms and input tags have long been associated with user input on the Web. One of the most exciting new features with HTML5 forms is the ability to use client-side validation.

Here's the previous approach with HTML4:

```
<!DOCTYPE HTML PUBLIC "-//W3C//DTD HTML 4.01 Transitional//EN" "http://www.w3.org/TR/html4/loose.
dtd">
<html>
<head>
<meta http-equiv="Content-Type" content="text/html; charset=UTF-8">
</head>

<body>
<form>
        <input name="email" oninput=validate(this);>
</form>
</body>
</html>

function validate (input) {
...tons of validation code and regex magic
}
```

And here's the new approach with HTML5:

```
<!DOCTYPE HTML>
<html>
<head>
<meta http-equiv="Content-Type" content="text/html; charset=UTF-8">
</head>
<body>
<form>
    <input type=email required>
</form>
</body>
</html>
```

That's it! Did you notice it in bold? Just be sure to include the attribute required in your input element, and your browser will handle the input validation. To newcomers, this may seem logical and nothing amazing, but in reality, previous to this you would need to include some long JavaScript validation/regex function to check the string value to ensure it's well-formed for the server to handle. Now, the browser handles that all for you. Think about it! Every developer wants to ensure they have proper validation on their inputs, so if every developer is doing this, let the browser handle it natively. Why repeat yourself for every project that requires it? This, again, is what HTML5 strives to accomplish.

Along with form validation, HTML5-compliant browsers also include native data types such as date, color, e-mail, URL, and phone number form tags all with the necessary client-side validation, as you just learned in the previous example. Let's take a look at working with each of them respectively. First up, date.

date is where the browser can include a calendar picker element for a user by default in the browser's UI. Figure 11-6 showcases how the browser Chrome handles `<input type="date"></input>`.

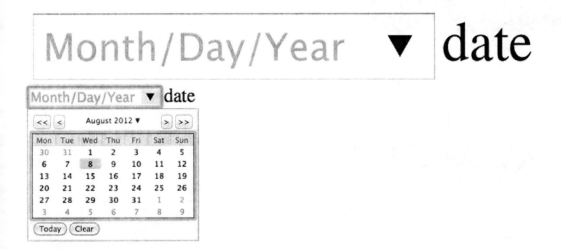

Figure 11-6. *How the Chrome browser handles the date input*

Next is the color input. Using `<input type="color"></input>`, you can tell the browser to show a color wheel for a user to select a hex value, as shown in Figure 11-7. Please note that not all browsers handle each of these inputs. Browsers will have their own visual differences for UI elements as well.

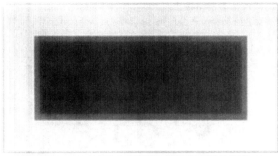

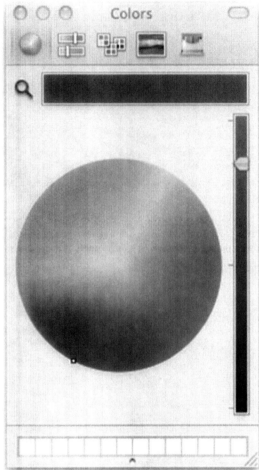

Figure 11-7. *How the Chrome browser handles the color input*

■ **Note** Any input type not recognized by a browser will gracefully degrade to a default text input.

HTML5 also supports numerical increments and sliders as inputs. Simply by adding the following inputs, you can have a user increment values and slide a simple (but CSS skinnable) UI element.

```
<input type="number"></input>
<input type="range" min="1" max="5">range</input>
```

Try the previous input tags, and you'll notice that the number type will have arrows on the right side and the range type will render a simple slider, as shown in Figure 11-8.

Figure 11-8. *How the Chrome browser handles the number and range input*

What's really interesting with these new (and old) input formats are the new attributes associated with them such as placeholder, required, and the really cool pattern. Each of these attributes has its own benefits; for example, the placeholder attribute allows the input field to display some sample text to signify what text format that user should enter. This is helpful for specific text formatting such as credit cards, phone numbers, or even Social Security numbers.

As you've learned, required is a great attribute for ensuring a user will fill out a section in the form before submitting. The browser will now check to see whether any inputs are required and flag them when the user attempts to submit the form.

The pattern attribute essentially allows you to use your own regular expressions (regex) from directly within the HTML markup. Traditionally, this was handled only via JavaScript, and if you want your user to explicitly enter something like a five-digit ZIP code, you can use a regex pattern to ensure that client-side validation is in place before the user submits their data. Listing 11-9 outlines what I am discussing.

Listing 11-9. Pattern Attribute Example

```
<!DOCTYPE html>
<html>
<body>
<form>
  Zip code: <input type="tel" pattern="^\d{5}$" title="Five digit ZIP code" />
  <input type="submit" />
</form>
</body>
</html>
```

Regular expressions are very powerful bits of code and can be conditioned to fit a wide variety of use cases. In the previous example, you are using the regex pattern of ^\d{5}$, which is ensuring that the user enters five digits for proper U.S. ZIP code entry.

Note For a useful regex tester/validator, please visit http://regexpal.com.

What's also really cool with the inputs is that you can customize your CSS based on the pseudo classes that get applied from the user interaction (or noninteraction). The following CSS example shows how you can present an error area for the form elements that weren't validated:

```
input {
    border: 1px solid #000000;
}
input:focus {
    border: 2px dashed #666666;
}
```

```
input:invalid {
     border: 5px solid #FF0000;
}
```

Looking at the previous CSS declarations, you can update the border weight and color on focus and when the value is invalid to present the user with a more significant border weight and a bright red color for "error."

Another really useful feature with these inputs is the datalist element. Have you ever started to search for something on Google and noticed that the topic you were searching for was already prepopulated in the list below the input field? Well, using an HTML5 datalist element, you can provide similar helpful hints while a user is entering information into the input tag. datalist elements can be super helpful for a user if they're trying to filter through an ad with a bunch of categories. Taking the earlier ShopLocal retail example, your user could be presented an ad with various categories and products. Wouldn't it be helpful to filter them for a user? Let's take a look at the following example to do just that:

```
<body>
<input type="text" name="categories" list="categories" />

<datalist id="categories">
     <option value="Electronics">
     <option value="Furniture">
     <option value="Office Supplies">
     <option value="Kitchen">
     <option value="Bedding">
     <option value="Bath">
</datalist>
</body>
```

As you can see from the code, you have a datalist called categories, which includes option values for all of the possible categories. Now when the user starts to type into the input field, using the list attribute called categories, you can present the users with options while they type.

Forms don't end there though, there are a lot of improvements to and even working groups are producing more content for HTML5 and HTML. That said, a full-fledged JavaScript speech API for input is in the works and is currently supported in newer versions of Google's Chrome browser. Obviously spearheaded by the folks at Google, you can start to take advantage of this in the browser by including the following in your input tag:

```
<input type="text" x-webkit-speech />
```

Using the previous x-webkit-speech attribute in your input tag will yield Figure 11-9 on your input text area.

Figure 11-9. *How the Chrome browser supports speech input*

You can also parse through the results of the input speech with the following code snippet by listening for the event being passed in and grabbing the results object off that event. Next you'll log out to the console with the result's utterance and confidence, which are two properties in the speech API that analyze the users input.

```
<script>
input.addEventListener('webkitspeechchange', function(event) {
    if (event.results) {
        for (var i = 0, result; result = event.results[i]; ++i) {
        console.log('Speech: ' + result.utterance + ' ' + result.confidence);
    }
  }
}, false);
</script>
```

Note You can learn more about Chrome's speech API by going to `http://developer.chrome.com/extensions/experimental.speechInput.html`.

If you're familiar with speech to text recognition services like Dragon diction or even Siri from Apple, this feature will be very familiar and useful to you and your users. For more information on the working spec on the JavaScript speech API, visit `http://lists.w3.org/Archives/Public/public-webapps/2011OctDec/att-1696/speechapi.html`. So, you may be thinking, "What good are these awesome attributes if some browsers won't recognize them?" Well, good question. Be sure to check out `http://caniuse.com` or leverage tools like Modernizer (if available to you); otherwise, you can always do some simple JavaScript checking like this:

```
<script>
if (!'x-webkit-speech' in document.createElement('input') ) {
    // no speech input
} else {
    // speech!
}
</script>
```

In the end, keep in mind your user base and remember that not all users will be capable of rendering all features of the modern Web.

Details and Summary Element

The details element is a great new feature in modern browsers. Have you ever wanted to show just a bit of information initially and, upon user selection, reveal more information, sort of like an accordion open/close effect? Well, the details element can help you really quickly do just that. Take a look at Listing 11-10, which incorporates the details element into the example ad. For this example, you'll assume you know where the user is and you want to show the nearest stores based on their location.

Listing 11-10. Details/Summary Example

```
<!DOCTYPE HTML>
<html lang=en>
<head>
<style type="text/css">
        summary {
                -webkit-tap-highlight-color:rgba(0,0,0,0);
                        outline: none;/*removes outline*/
        }
```

```
        li:nth-child(odd) {
                background: #CCC;
                color: green;
        }
</style>
</head>
<body>
<details>
        <summary>Closest Store Locations</summary>
        <ul>
        <li><p>500 Ford Street, East Lanford IL 12345</p></li>
        <li><p>13 West Nectar Road, Brunswick FL 12345</p></li>
        <li><p>275 Bimba Drive, Clifton PA 12345</p></li>
        </ul>
</details>
</body>
</html>
```

If you preview this in your browser, you'll see that you can open and collapse the information, which is a pretty useful UI element that can also be styled via CSS. You can even add some attributes like open, which allows the browser to open the details element by default when the document loads. You can even nest details and summary elements inside one another to create a very complex stack of UI elements. As you can see from Figure 11-10, at the time of this writing, the details element is supported only in Chrome, Safari 6, and Android 4.0. Keep an eye on this element, though, because adoption should take off very soon.

Details & Summary elements - Working Draft									Usage stats: Support	Global 35.79%

The <details> element generates a simple no-JavaScript widget to show/hide element contents, optionally by clicking on its child <summary> element.

Show all versions	IE	Firefox	Chrome	Safari	Opera	iOS Safari	Opera Mini	Android Browser	Blackberry Browser
								2.1	
						3.2		2.2	
						4.0-4.1		2.3	
						4.2-4.3		3.0	
	8.0	15.0		5.1		5.0-5.1		4.0	
Current	9.0	16.0	22.0	6.0	12.0	6.0	5.0-7.0	4.1	7.0
Near future	10.0	17.0	23.0		12.1				10.0
Farther future		18.0	24.0		12.5				

Notes	Known issues (0)	Resources (4)	Feedback	Edit on GitHub
No notes				

Figure 11-10. *The support for the details and summary element. Source:* `http://caniuse.com/#feat=details.`

You may be asking yourself, "Wait! How do we know where the user is?" That's a great question, and I'm happy to introduce you to the next section.

Geolocation

Another huge addition to the modern web stack is the Geolocation API. Geolocation data is the latitude and longitude coordinates of your user. Traditionally, you would need to leverage web services like `http://maxmind.com` and go through a process of looking up a user's IP address and tying it to an approximate location. This is not fault-proof in that it's up to the Internet service provider (ISP) to assign that IP to a user. (This would be Verizon, Comcast, and others that you're paying for Internet service.) In my current use case, using Comcast's Internet service, my IP address is assuming me to be around the Philadelphia area, and this is on WiFi, which is pretty good considering I'm just outside the city; however, I've seen in some cases where IP lookup is not even accurate about the state. It progressively gets worse when users are on cell carrier networks. So, IP location lookup is pretty unpredictable and unreliable for truly accurate uses, especially for mobile.

Luckily, with the new Geolocation API, you can grab the actual latitude and longitude of a user, which proves to be a much speedier and accurate tool than a costly (seldom reliable) lookup service. I mention the word *costly* because some of these lookup tools aren't free and because they take requests to remote servers and lookup databases to gather a user's approximate location which in turn end up being costly for timing. The Geolocation API geographically locates a user (with opt-in permission) through the browser natively. I stress "with permission" because once you attempt to detect a user, the browser's initial default action will prompt an alert to the user stating that the content's domain is asking to access their location. This prompt is a security measure employed by all browsers and devices. Figure 11-11 demonstrates how this appears in Google's Chrome browser.

Figure 11-11. *The Geolocation prompt in Google's Chrome browser*

Figure 11-12 shows it on an iDevice's mobile Safari browser.

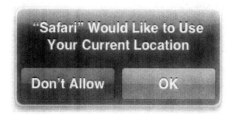

Figure 11-12. *The Geolocation prompt on mobile Safari*

If the user selects, allows, denies, or simply waits too long to reply, the developer can then handle how the user responds, by detecting for PERMISSION_DENIED, POSITION_UNAVAILABLE, or TIMEOUT based on the course of action performed. In any event taken, ensure that your ad creative is intelligent enough to adapt to the various user inputs, because not everyone will allow location-based services. Listing 11-11 shows how to work with Geolocation using JavaScript.

Listing 11-11. Geolocation API Example

```
<!DOCTYPE html>
<head>
<meta charset=utf-8>
<body>
<header>
     <h1>geolocation</h1>
     <div id="coords"></div>
</header>
<script>
function success(position) {
  var lat = position.coords.latitude;
  var long = position.coords.longitude;
```

```
    document.getElementById('coords').innerHTML = "<p><strong>lat: </strong>" + lat + "
<br><strong>long: </strong>" + long + "";
}

function error(error) {
    switch (error.code) {
    case error.PERMISSION_DENIED:
        alert("user did not share geolocation data");
        break;
    case error.POSITION_UNAVAILABLE:
        alert("could not detect current position");
        break;
    case error.TIMEOUT:
        alert("retrieving position timed out");
        break;
    default:
        alert("unknown error");
        break;
    }
}

function adInit(event) {
  console.log(event.type)
  if (navigator.geolocation) {
        navigator.geolocation.getCurrentPosition(success, error);
      } else {
        error('not supported');
      }
}

window.addEventListener('DOMContentLoaded', adInit, false);
</script>
</body>
</html>
```

As you can see from the previous code sample, you check the navigator.geolocation object, and if it's true, you know that the Geolocation API is supported in your browser or device. After that, you call navigator.geolocation.getCurrentPosition and pass in two arguments, which are a success *callback* function and an *error* callback function. Once you run this command, the user will notice the previous prompt's outline, and the user will need to take the necessary action. Assuming they select allow, it will run through the success method; otherwise, it will run through the error method, and you can handle why the error occurred by looking at the error code you receive in your callback.

Once the user allows the sharing of their location, you can grab the latitude and longitude values from the position object that comes with the success callback. With this location information, you can tie it to location-based services or geocode the latitude/longitude into a ZIP code to query against services like Yahoo's weather service or Google's mapping services. The bottom line is that geolocation provides some rich experiences within the ad environment.

Geolocation in Advertising

Location is a big part of advertising on the Web. As you are aware, advertisers want to target users by as many ways necessary to ensure a good ROI on their media investment. With this new API, developers can do just that! This location information is hugely beneficial when pairing with mapping services such as Google, Apple, or Bing or when you want to locate a user and navigate them to the nearest retail store by offering them detailed directions to get them into the store.

Timely and relevant ads go a long way; for example, if you're from Chicago and notice an ad giving you information about products and directions in London, England, that would be pretty wasteful and useless to both the advertiser and, more importantly you, the end user. Advertisers spend millions and millions of dollars a year targeting audiences by a various number of inputs. Using location as an input into the creative, advertisers are able to deliver specific and dynamic information to a user, which effectively is intended to create a much more personalized interaction with potential consumers. Brands and advertisers love this relationship because it creates repeat customers and because users end up trusting the brand.

OK, enough about the strategy. Let's take a look at an example of geolocation where you supply a specific location based on the user's location and leverage the WatchPosition API to navigate the user to the store with the offer (see Listing 11-12).

Listing 11-12. Geolocation Ad Example

```
<!DOCTYPE html>
<html>
<head>
    <meta charset=utf-8>
</head>
    <body>
        <header>
            <h1>Find The Product!</h1>
            <div id="coords"></div>
        </header>
        <script>
            var MAGIC_LOCATION = "40.068134,-75.318797"//Don't be creepy
            var location = document.getElementById('coords');
            var watch;

            function success(position) {
                var lat = position.coords.latitude;
                var long = position.coords.longitude;
                location.innerHTML = "<p><strong>lat: </strong>" + lat + " <br><strong>long:
</strong>" + long + "";

                //start watching the users location
                watch = navigator.geolocation.watchPosition(updatePosition, error);
            }

            function error(error) {
                switch (error.code) {
                case error.PERMISSION_DENIED:
                    alert("user did not share geolocation data");
                    break;
                case error.POSITION_UNAVAILABLE:
                    alert("could not detect current position");
                    break;
                case error.TIMEOUT:
                    alert("retrieving position timed out");
                    break;
                default:
```

```
                    alert("unknown error");
                    break;
            }
        }

        function updatePosition(position) {
            var lat = position.coords.latitude;
            var long = position.coords.longitude;
            var newLocation = lat + ',' + long;
            //This fires everytime the users location changes
            if (newLocation === MAGIC_LOCATION) {
                //You win!
                productFound();
                location.innerHTML = "<p><strong style='color:red'>" + newLocation + "</strong>";
            } else {
                location.innerHTML = "<p><strong style='color:blue'>" + newLocation + "</strong>";
            }
        }

        function productFound() {
            navigator.geolocation.clearWatch(watch);
            window.alert("You Win!")
            //show coupon to the user to buy the product at the store
        }

        function adInit(event) {
            console.log(event.type)
            if (navigator.geolocation) {
                navigator.geolocation.getCurrentPosition(success, error);
            } else {
                console.error('geo not supported');
                //supply different ad experience
            }
        }

        window.addEventListener('DOMContentLoaded', adInit, false);
    </script>
  </body>
</html>
```

As you can see from this example, I've extended this to make a unique game out of it. Remember the "You're Hot, Warm, or Cold" game? You know, the one where the user tried to find something blindly with the help of another? Well, this can be replicated in the digital world now! Try to take this example and update it to use a store location in your area. Maybe even set a time limit. How about if a user can find it within the allotted time, they get a special offer? The possibilities are endless with this technology.

Again, remember that geolocation is an opt-in process, and the user will have to explicitly "agree" or "allow" this feature. Make sure you handle all the responses a user could make as well as paying attention to the polling of the user's location. With this API, developers can take advantage of the watchPosition method, which will continuously check for the user's updated position if they're on the go. While great for providing accurate and real-time directions, keep in mind that the more frequent you poll and request the user's exact location, the more battery and resources you will consume because of processing the requests. It's good to keep it at a minimal threshold for mobile users or even allow the user to update their location on their own terms. As the Battery API finalizes and grows in adoption, you can use more sophisticated ways of detecting the state of the current battery percentage before going nuts on location polling. Geolocation opens up new worlds of advertising to marketers, and in the increasing mobile landscape, it's never been more important to catch your users on the go with the right message. Don't believe me? Take a look at the graphic from eMarketer.com in Figure 11-13.

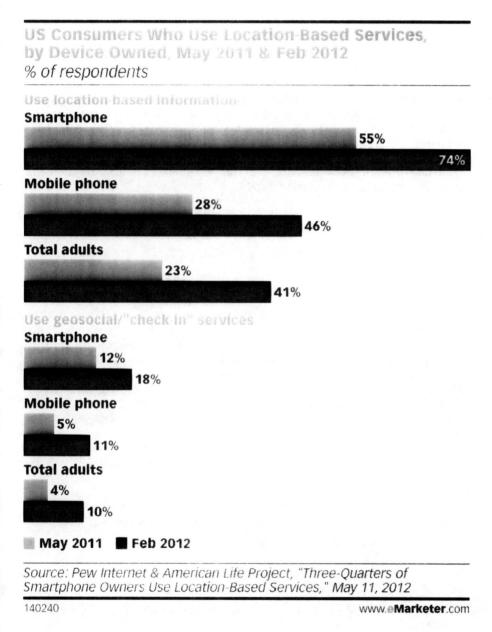

US Consumers Who Use Location-Based Services, by Device Owned, May 2011 & Feb 2012
% of respondents

Use location-based information

Smartphone
- 55%
- 74%

Mobile phone
- 28%
- 46%

Total adults
- 23%
- 41%

Use geosocial/"check in" services

Smartphone
- 12%
- 18%

Mobile phone
- 5%
- 11%

Total adults
- 4%
- 10%

■ May 2011   ■ Feb 2012

Source: Pew Internet & American Life Project, "Three-Quarters of Smartphone Owners Use Location-Based Services," May 11, 2012

140240   www.e**Marketer**.com

Figure 11-13. *The use of location-based services by U.S. consumers*

As you can see in Figure 11-13, location is pretty big, and it's getting used often! If you're not using it in your next mobile campaign, I'm sure you will shortly after by client demand. Again, the Geolocation API is a specification that often gets lumped into HTML5 even though it's separate. See for yourself at `http://isgeolocationpartofhtml5.com`. However, it does go hand in hand with many of HTML5's new features. If you'd like to learn more about the geolocation specification, visit `http://dev.w3.org/geo/api/spec-source.html`.

Web Services for Locations

I'd like to wrap this section by taking a look at some of the other web services for locations and other APIs. Keep in mind that these APIs come in both paid and free versions, so choose wisely based on your campaign goals and budget. Perhaps the most popular location API would be Google's Maps API (`http://developers.google.com/maps`); however, if you plan on using Google Maps in your production work and you expect a lot of traffic from your ad, you'll end up paying for it because Google limits the amount of requests of its free service. If you can't afford Google, another good alternative is the Open Street Maps API (`http://openstreetmap.org`), which is a great free service but often lacks the features and geographical information of Google's. A few other useful location services are IPinfoDB (`http://ipinfodb.com/ip_location_api.php`), InfoChimps (`http://infochimps.com`), and Open B Map (`http://openbmap.org/api/openbmap_api.php5`). Also, if U.S. law does not restrict you, you can take advantage of other useful data found at `http://bluevia.com/en/page/tech.APIs.UserContextAPI`.

■ **Note** Be careful with what you do with this information. As much as advertisers will beg you to track and store data about their potential customers, be aware that it may not always be in the best interest of humankind and you could face legal issues.

Social

The social market is fast growing in advertising. If you think about it, what's more dynamic and relevant than what your friends are saying? Social chatter is always happening no matter which platform it's occurring on. Using social platforms like Foursquare (`http://developer.foursquare.com/docs`), Facebook (`http://developers.facebook.com`), Twitter (`http://dev.twitter.com`), Instagram (`http://instagram.com/developer`), LinkedIn (`http://developer.linkedin.com/apis`), Google+ (`http://developers.google.com/+/api`), and SoundCloud (`http://developers.soundcloud.com`), to name a few, developers and designers can take advantage of these rich social platforms for more integrated experiences with a user's social graph. If one of your friends likes a Nike campaign, that information can be presented to you in real time. Or, if you wanted to see what the reviews were of that new movie trailer, why not bring in the hashtags from the movie's Twitter account? This is all possible with the various APIs that bring social data into your advertisement.

■ **Note** The Open Graph API (`http://ogp.me`) allows web content and ads to be tagged with metadata for social networks to create rich objects from the web content within a user's social graph.

Social APIs

Pretty much everyone and their mother is on Facebook, Twitter, or Linkedin. I mean, even the King is on it, and he's been dead for years (`http://twitter.com/ElvisPresley`)]! Social is pretty much a main vein of the Internet today; we have more access and insight into what people are saying, how they're feeling, and personal information than we've ever had in history. Even more relevant are the conversations with our friends, family, and random others we are following and who follow us. Social is pretty much a life source for many folks. Just take a look at the graphic from eMarketer.com in Figure 11-14.

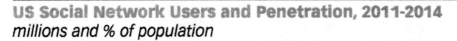

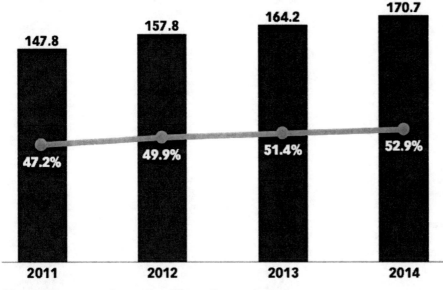

Figure 11-14. *The support for the details and summary elements*

That's proof! More than half of the United States will be tied to some sort of social network come 2014. With that data and the potential ability to add it into your advertisements, include this with geolocation . . . and I think you catch my drift; it's pretty powerful! Adding social elements into your advertisements can be a great use of dynamic content. Really, what's more "live" than the social graph that's living and breathing out there? There are numerous social platforms to take advantage of, but be sure to keep the rights and usage rules in mind when exploiting these social APIs. Companies such as Facebook, which now owns Instagram, allows developers to include their services and platform into other web applications; however, at the time of writing, Facebook (and others) does not allow you to pull users' information into third-party advertising experiences.

Synced Units

Synced ad units are when two ads on the same page seemingly communicate with each other to create a "tied together" effect to the end user. This could be an animation that starts from the leaderboard ad (728×90) unit and resolves into the box (300×250) unit. Synced units typically come sold together by the publisher, usually as a roadblock and traditionally with Flash you'd need to use external interface calls to JavaScript in order to communicate between both units across the page. Now that you aren't "black-boxed" inside the SWF container, your ads can make your own specific JavaScript calls to produce the synced effect. Take a look at Listing 11-13, where the 728×90 unit syncs up a CSS transition effect with a 300×250 companion unit.

Listing 11-13. Synced Ad Example 728 Ad

```html
<!DOCTYPE HTML>
<html lang=en>
<head>
</head>
<style type="text/css">
#ad728 {
        position: absolute;
        top: 0px;
        left: 0px;
        width: 728px;
        height: 90px;
        border: 1px solid #000;
        font-family: Arial;
        font-size: 80px;
        background-color: red;
        color: black;
        opacity: 1;
        -webkit-transition-property: color;
        -webkit-transition-duration: 1s;
    -webkit-transition-timing-function: cubic-bezier(0.5, 0.2, 0.9, 0.4);
}
#ad728:hover {
        color: white;
}
</style>
<body align=center>
        <div id="ad728">728x90</div>
</body>
<script type="text/javascript">
        var ad300 = "stop";
        var ad728 = document.getElementById('ad728');
        var ad728value = window.getComputedStyle(ad728,null).getPropertyValue("color");

        ad728.addEventListener('webkitTransitionEnd', function(event) {
                if(ad728value === "red") {
                        ad300 = "play";
                } else {
                        ad300 = "stop";
                }
        }, false );
</script>
</html>
```

In this example, you'll see that the 728×90 unit gets a transition effect on its CSS color property. Once the user hovers over the 728 unit, you'll listen for an event of webkitTransitionEnd, which fires when the transition event ends. This is useful because now you can handle these events and fire off other functions. In this case, you set a value for the 300 unit to listen for the play value on the variable called ad300. Listing 11-14 shows the 300 unit listening for this change in value from stop to play.

Listing 11-14. Synced Ad Example 300 Ad

```
<!DOCTYPE HTML>
<html lang=en>
<head>
</head>
<style type="text/css">
#ad300 {
        position: absolute;
        top: 0px;
        left: 0px;
        width: 300px;
        height: 250px;
        border: 1px solid #000;
        font-family: Arial;
        font-size: 50px;
        background-color: red;
        color: black;
        opacity: 1;
        -webkit-transition-property: color;
        -webkit-transition-duration: 1s;
    -webkit-transition-timing-function: cubic-bezier(0.5, 0.2, 0.9, 0.4);
}
</style>
<body align=center>
        <div id="ad300">300x250</div>
</body>
<script type="text/javascript">
        var checker300 = window.setInterval(check, 100);

        function check () {
                if (ad300 === "play") {
                        animate300();
                } else {
                        console.log('300 is stopped');
                }
        }

        function animate300 () {
                clearInterval(checker300);
                document.getElementById('ad300').style.color = 'white';
        }
</script>
</html>
```

As you can see, you fire an interval to check the shared ad300 value to see whether you are to stop or play your 300 unit's animation. There are a few things to keep in mind with this type of execution. First, you'll need to know how you are being served to the publisher's page. Are you in an iframe, a safe frame, an MRAID container, or a div with CSS overflow set to hidden? This all impacts how the communication via JavaScript will have to be handled. For instance, if you're served to the publisher's page in a div with overflow : hidden, all you would need to do is have both ads communicate on the same shared values within the script (like in the previous example). Again, setting a 0 to a 1 can do this, and having a "checker" interval poll for when that value changes can be helpful. Also, you can dispatch custom events from the 728 unit for the 300 unit to listen for and handle. If you are served through some container (iframe or MRAID), you'll need to communicate through that container in order for the ads to connect. This is a bit tricky considering that both ads will be wrapped at this point, and if it's run across an ad network, there's no telling what the container would be, unless you had an ad loader script file whose sole job is to detect the environment the ad is served into. If it's an iframe, you should be able to target the parent window, assuming you have access to read-write values. If it's MRAID, you'll need to see whether there are certain MRAID or publisher calls to be made in order to have the ads transfer data.

In addition, you may think that polling for a value isn't really an optimized technique. Well, it's not, and some browsers will simply castrate the reoccurring interval calls after a certain amount of time. Luckily, there is another new feature to HTML5, called the Communication API for Cross Document Messaging. It's perfect for synced ad development!

Communication API

The Communication API for Cross Document Messaging allows for transfer through the window object regardless of domain securities and if content is wrapped in an iframe on the publisher page. Basically, if you want to dispatch a message to another ad, saying "Hey, 300 unit, it's the 728 unit telling you to animate!" then you could have the publisher's page or other elements on the page (hosted from a different domain) listen for the message and react accordingly. This is done by using a method called postMessage; Listing 11-15 shows the revised synced ad example.

Listing 11-15. Communication API 728 Example

```
<!DOCTYPE HTML>
<html lang=en>
<head>
        <style type='text/css'>
#ad728 {
        position: absolute;
        top: 0px;
        left: 0px;
        width: 728px;
        height: 90px;
        border: 1px solid #000;
        font-family: Arial;
        font-size: 80px;
        background-color: red;
        color: rgb(0, 0, 0);
        opacity: 1;
        -webkit-transition-property: color;
        -webkit-transition-duration: 1s;
    -webkit-transition-timing-function: cubic-bezier(0.5, 0.2, 0.9, 0.4);
}
#ad728:hover {
        color: rgb(255, 255, 255);
}
</style>
</head>
<body align=center>
        <div id='ad728'>728x90</div>
```

```
</body>
<script type='text/javascript'>
var ad728 = document.getElementById('ad728'),
        ad728value;

function adInit () {
        console.log('adInit');
        ad728.addEventListener('webkitTransitionEnd', nudge300, false);
}

function nudge300 (event) {
        console.log(event);
        ad728value = window.getComputedStyle(ad728,null).getPropertyValue('color');

        if (ad728value === 'rgb(255, 255, 255)') {
                if(typeof window.postMessage === 'undefined'){
                        console.error('Your browser does not support the communication API');
                        //fail over to our other method
                } else {
                        //Same Domain
                        console.log('Message: ' + window.postMessage)
                        window.postMessage('play300', 'http://johnpercival.org');//Insert your
domain here

                        //Cross Domain
                        //document.getElementsByTagName('iframe')[0].contentWindow.
postMessage('play300', 'http://johnpercival.org');
                }
        } else {
                //some other color
                console.log(ad728value);
        }
};

window.addEventListener('load', adInit, false);
</script>
</html>
```

First, you set up the 728 unit much like you did prior, but the main difference is you use a postMessage call that takes two parameters. The first is the string value you want to pass, and the second is the domain for the window object (in this case, my domain, but be sure to use the domain hosting the files), which is usually the ad server.

■ **Note**   If you don't care much about the domain origin, you can pass a literal string value of *, which is the wildcard and allows all domain transfers.

Now, once the user hovers over the 728 unit, you post a message to anyone listening. In this case, it will be the 300 unit, as shown in Listing 11-16.

Listing 11-16. Communication API 300 Example

```
<!DOCTYPE HTML>
<html lang=en>
<head>
        <style type="text/css">
#ad300 {
        position: absolute;
        top: 0px;
        left: 0px;
        width: 300px;
        height: 250px;
        border: 1px solid #000;
        font-family: Arial;
        font-size: 50px;
        background-color: red;
        color: black;
        opacity: 1;
        -webkit-transition-property: color;
        -webkit-transition-duration: 1s;
    -webkit-transition-timing-function: cubic-bezier(0.5, 0.2, 0.9, 0.4);
}
</style>
</head>
<body align=center>
        <div id="ad300">300x250</div>
</body>
<script type="text/javascript">

function adInit () {
   window.addEventListener('message', messageHandler, true);
   console.log('adInit')
}

function messageHandler(event) {
   switch(event.origin) {
      case "http://johnpercival.org":
        //only listen for events from our domain
        if(event.data === 'play300') {
                animate300();
        } else {
                //not our 300's message to animate
        }
        break;
   }
}

function animate300 () {
        document.getElementById('ad300').style.color = 'white';
}
```

```
window.addEventListener('load', adInit, false);
</script>
</html>
```

In the receiver, the 300 unit, it's quite simple. You set up an event listener to listen for the message event and handle it accordingly using the `messageHandler` function. Inside that handler, you check the event's origin, making sure it came from `johnpercival.org` or the domain of your choice and finally checking whether the data attached to that event has the value of `play300`. If it does, you simply call the `animate300` method to create synced effect.

Although this is just one way to skin a cat, there are many other ways to achieve the results you want. Just keep in mind that the style could get shared between the two units. Remember, I said keep name spacing prefixed by the ad-server vendor, for example `AdServer-AdContainer`. In the event of delivering synced units to the page, I recommend prefixing the namespace with the size of the unit as well. So, `AdServer-AdContainer` becomes `AdServer-300x250-Container`. It's a bit verbose, but keeping this prefixed appropriately will ensure your styles and other events don't get shared across ads and, even more so, page content.

Note This method can be used for transferring data between the publisher's page content and the ads hosted on other domains.

Advanced Dynamics

Advanced dynamics is where it gets really exciting. When integrating multiple HTML5 features, web services, APIs, and publisher buy-in, you can create a cutting-edge campaign. There really is nothing stopping you from using location data, weather services, store lookup services, stock feeds, and even asking the user for some input to customize and craft a personalized ad experience. Sure, this takes time, effort, and money to pull off, but the execution could be amazing and really useful to the end user.

Oftentimes, you'll be stuck looking for a web service to suit your needs. When that's the case, check out the developer community on GitHub and ask around. If you have the server-side coding skills, make your own or even present the additional costs to the client for the creation of a web service. It may make the client not want the service, or they may request it and use it for many other campaigns going forward.

Dynamic Video

I covered a lot about video in Chapter 7, but I didn't mention too much about dynamic video. Before I was completely immersed in HTML5 development, I was pretty big into ActionScript and combining data from After Effects. I made some pretty cool examples where you could dynamically update and change the content superimposed over video. The content would be tied specifically to the video's movement, skew, rotation, and scale via metadata and read in by the SWF in order to create a seamless video/animation effect. Although a lot has changed in technology, the theory remains the same. Using features of HTML5 canvas and video, WebVTT, CSS3 transforms, and JavaScript, you can do very similar things. There are even useful libraries created for tying data to video content in real time. Check out PopcornJS (`http://popcornjs.org`), and you'll get a look at what I'm talking about.

Summary

I covered a lot in this chapter, including dynamically serving ads from your ad server's various inputs, using delivery rules, using publisher-passed data, using XML and JSON, using the new features in HTML5 such as the `data` attribute, using `contenteditable`, working with forms, using various useful attributes, and using the amazing new geolocation data from browsers. I even wrapped up by discussing a bit about social APIs and integration into ads, advanced dynamic executions, and the popular synced ad unit.

Feel free to take some time to visit the code samples and test on your own. There is a lot that can be done with dynamic ads, and really there is no limit as long as you have the information and data to work with. Keep in mind that not every ad should be dynamic. If you're specifically targeting users on mobile devices, keep in mind their user experience. The user could be on a significantly reduced connection where bandwidth isn't so plentiful. If that's the case, I recommend detecting for that at ad-request time and serving up alternate versions of the ad experience. *Do not tax a user's machine!* In the end, you'll really want to offer a tasteful and working ad experience as opposed to one that's hogging all the system resources and presenting a poor experience where the user would blame the brand or even the publisher. Users are smarter than ever nowadays, and they have every social outlet known to man accessible to them for making you aware that you messed up. In the end, provide a good experience for your users, understand that network conditions are a variable, and adjust on the fly. Stay dynamic and adapt to changes.

I hope you enjoyed this chapter; it was a great primer for the next discussion, bleeding-edge HTML5. Now that you know the basics of HTML5 advertising and how to include dynamics in your ads, I'll talk about layering on some really amazing features coming to you in the near future or possibly already here with the emerging web standard.

CHAPTER 12

Bleeding-Edge HTML5

This chapter is a bit different than the previous because its sole purpose is to get you excited about the new features coming soon to the browsers you use every day. Some of these features are rolled into the current HTML5 specification; others remain outside the HTML5 domain, are in specific browsers only, or are set for HTML.next (http://w3.org/wiki/HTML/next).

In this chapter, I'll cover some really amazing APIs and features such as Web Intents, WebSockets, WebGL, WebRTC, bleeding-edge CSS3, and others. I'll also focus on the emerging browsers from the Google Chrome team, Mozilla, Apple, and Opera, as well as to discuss how they, as well as Microsoft, Adobe, W3C, and WHATWG, are making specific additions to the open web standard that will impact your campaigns moving forward.

As you've learned throughout the book, HTML5 is an evolving specification, but working group members currently are determining what should stay in HTML5 and what should be pushed off until HTML.next. It may seem odd that there are two different specifications of the HTML5 specification, one managed by the W3C, which aims to make HTML5 a snapshot specification, and one managed by the WHATWG, which aims to make the HTML standard an organic, ever-growing document that builds and iterates through the years of the open Web's growth. However, it's not terribly important to get wrapped up in which specification is which; just be sure to know when the browsers have implemented these new features and when user adoption will take place.

Finally, please take this chapter with a "grain of salt." A lot of these features may not make it into the HTML5 specification and could be pushed off to the next iteration, or some could even be retired. However, be aware that working groups are committed to creating and enabling amazing things inside your browsers, and being on top of them allows you to better prepare for what your clients will eventually ask for. Whether it lands in HTML5, 6, 6.x, or something else entirely, shouldn't matter much. If you can use a feature and, more importantly, use it where your target audience is, that's the most important part to take away from this chapter. That said, let's dig into the really amazing and bleeding-edge features of the modern Web!

Emerging Browsers

In this chapter, I will showcase what's to come, in other words, the emerging and most forward-thinking stuff that's being cooked up by some really smart people and coming to your browser. As I've stressed in previous chapters, you should be working with the latest version of your favorite browser, and to be quite honest, if you've made it this far in the book using IE 6 to IE 8, God bless you, and please send me your address so I can personally come to your house and install an update for you.

For this chapter specifically, you should be working with one of the browsers shown in Figure 12-1.

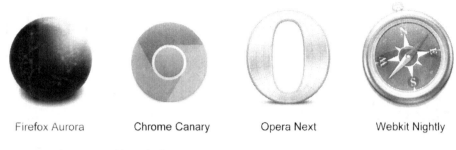

| Firefox Aurora | Chrome Canary | Opera Next | Webkit Nightly |

Figure 12-1. *All bleeding-edge browsers*

You can download these bleeding-edge browsers at one of the following locations: Firefox Aurora (`http://aurora.mozilla.org`), Chrome Canary (`http://tools.google.com/dlpage/chromesxs`), Opera Next (`http://opera.com/browser/next`), and Webkit Nightly (`http://nightly.webkit.org`). Keep in mind that these browsers are not 100 percent stable and should be used with caution in production environments because there could be bugs in the code base. It's best to use these browsers only for testing experimental features.

Note   At the time of this writing, Internet Explorer does not have a beta version of its latest browser (though IE 10 is set to be very bleeding edge).

Downloading one or all of these browsers gives you VIP access to all the beta features that these ultra-modern browsers grant access to.

New CSS Features

Now that the setup is out of the way, let's head into the important topics of this chapter, starting with emerging CSS features. The following sections are geared to many of the new enhancements of the CSS specification.

CSS Regions

First up is the new CSS feature called *regions*. Adobe has submitted a draft to the W3C for this feature, which is effectively a new specification for free-flowing text from one *region* of content to another. This allows you to have freely moving text that is device and screen independent, which allows for a great addition for copy layout in responsive web and creative designs. As you know from your knowledge of synced ad units, you could in theory have free-flowing text from one ad into another on the same page. To use CSS regions, all you'll need to do is include some empty div containers and some CSS declarations, as shown in Listing 12-1.

Listing 12-1. CSS Regions Example

```
<!DOCTYPE html>
<html>
<head>
<meta charset="UTF-8">
<style type="text/css">
```

```css
/* ad */
#ad .adContent {
  -webkit-flow-into: adRegions;
}

.adRegions > div {
  content: -webkit-from-flow('adRegions');
  -webkit-flow-from: adRegions;
  width: 30%;
  height: 250px;
  float: left;
  margin: 10px;
  padding: 30px;
  border: 1px solid #000;
  overflow: scroll;
  -webkit-overflow-scrolling: touch;
}
</style>
</head>

<body>
<div id="ad">
  <div class="adContent">
  Lorem ipsum dolor sit amet, consectetur adipiscing elit. Aliquam nec ipsum non massa vehicula
feugiat. Etiam a tempor lectus. Etiam sollicitudin commodo risus, ac hendrerit felis auctor a.
Maecenas sed sem sed libero faucibus elementum eu non sapien. Ut tellus nisl, imperdiet ut eleifend
id, lacinia et enim. Suspendisse feugiat fringilla cursus. Phasellus nisl nisi, congue ac hendrerit
eget, facilisis a nunc. Suspendisse potenti. Ut suscipit, lacus ac imperdiet lacinia, metus ipsum
placerat libero, et dictum massa arcu vitae risus. Vestibulum varius hendrerit congue.
  </div>
  <div class="adRegions">
    <div></div>
    <div></div>
  </div>
</div>
</body>
</html>
```

As you can see from Listing 12-1, you have some "lorem ipsum" content in your div called adContent and two other divs called adRegions (which could be another ad). As shown in the CSS, you instruct your adContent to flow its text content into adRegions. That's about it! Now you can have free-flowing copy independent of screen size, as shown in Figure 12-2.

299

Lorem ipsum dolor sit amet, consectetur adipiscing elit. Aliquam nec ipsum non massa vehicula feugiat. Etiam a tempor lectus. Etiam sollicitudin commodo risus, ac hendrerit felis auctor a. Maecenas sed sem sed libero faucibus elementum eu non sapien. Ut tellus nisl, imperdiet ut eleifend id, lacinia et enim. Suspendisse feugiat fringilla cursus. Phasellus nisl nisi, congue ac hendrerit eget, facilisis a nunc. Suspendisse potenti. Ut suscipit, lacus ac imperdiet lacinia, metus ipsum placerat libero, et dictum massa arcu vitae risus. Vestibulum varius hendrerit congue.

Lorem ipsum dolor sit amet, consectetur adipiscing elit. Aliquam nec ipsum non massa vehicula feugiat. Etiam a tempor lectus. Etiam sollicitudin commodo risus, ac hendrerit felis auctor a. Maecenas sed sem sed libero faucibus elementum eu non sapien. Ut tellus nisl, imperdiet ut

eleifend id, lacinia et enim. Suspendisse feugiat fringilla cursus. Phasellus nisl nisi, congue ac hendrerit eget, facilisis a nunc. Suspendisse potenti. Ut suscipit, lacus ac imperdiet lacinia, metus ipsum placerat libero, et dictum massa arcu vitae risus. Vestibulum varius hendrerit congue.

Figure 12-2. *Example from Adobe using CSS regions*

Keep in mind that this works only with percentage-set widths and not when you dictate a hard value like 300px. For this to work in the ad environment, ensure that your ad container's div has a width of 100 percent and wrap that container inside another div element with its width set to 300px (or whatever your ad inventory calls for). This could be really helpful should your client want to mimic a flipbook type of creative because elements including copy can free flow into other regions at different screen sizes.

▨ **Note**   At the time of writing, each emerging feature discussed in this chapter will more than likely need a specific vendor prefix to work correctly.

At the time of this writing, in order to utilize the CSS regions feature, you need to use Webkit Nightly, Chrome, or Chrome Canary and have the CSS regions called flags enabled in the browser settings. For Chrome, you can do this by typing chrome://flags in the address bar. Finally, restart your browser to ensure the setting took effect, and you will be able to mess around with this cool new feature. For more information on a real-world example, I suggest visiting http://css-tricks.com/content-folding, and to learn more about the specification for CSS regions, visit http://w3.org/TR/css3-regions or http://adobe.github.com/web-platform/samples/css-regions.

CSS Exclusions

Speaking about CSS regions, Adobe also submitted a new specification for a feature called CSS *exclusions*. Exclusions allow for text content to free flow around images, videos, canvases, and other elements in the DOM tree. With CSS exclusions, it's truly possible to create rich print-like magazine effects in your browser using pretty simple CSS. What's really interesting is that you can create shapes inside CSS and use them as exclusions, which can create really interesting effects with negative space. Let's take a look at an example from Adobe using CSS exclusions and adaptive text layout based on the orientation of the tablet, as shown in Figure 12-3.

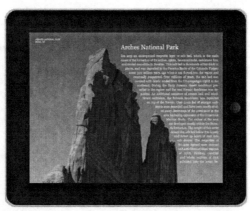

Figure 12-3. Example from Adobe using CSS exclusions (source: Adobe)

You can see by incorporating exclusions into your text layout, you can gain really amazing results that form-fit around specific content, in this case, the mountain. So, let's take a look at working with CSS exclusions in an example layout where you wrap mock publisher content around a 300x250 rectangle exclusion, which could be your ad real estate.

Listing 12-2. CSS Exclusions Example

```
<!DOCTYPE HTML>
<html>
<head>
<style type="text/css">
body, html{
    height:100%;
    width:100%;
    overflow:hidden;
}
#container{
    font-size:14px;
    text-align:justify;
    -webkit-hyphens:auto;
```

```
        /* flow the content inside this element */
        -webkit-wrap-shape-mode: content;
}
.exclusion {
        position:absolute;
        height:250px;
        width:300px;

        /* flow text around this element */
        -webkit-wrap-shape-mode: around;
}
.ad{
        top: 20px;
        left: 100px;
        border: 1px solid #000;
        -webkit-wrap-shape:  rectangle(300px, 250px 300px,250px 250px,300px 250px,250px);
}

#workspace{
        position:relative;
        width:80%;
}

</style>
</head>
<body>
<div id="workspace">
        <div id="exclusion1" class="exclusion ad"> 300x250 </div>
<div id="container">
        <p>Lo&shy;rem ip&shy;sum do&shy;lor sit amet, con&shy;sec&shy;te&shy;tur ad&shy;ipisc&shy;ing
elit. Vi&shy;va&shy;mus ac nul&shy;la ac nunc ves&shy;ti&shy;b&shy;u&shy;lum sod&shy;ales sed eget
pu&shy;rus. In&shy;te&shy;ger tris&shy;tique neque at urna eleif&shy;end por&shy;ta. Mau&shy;ris a
sa&shy;pi&shy;en augue, ve&shy;hic&shy;u&shy;la rutrum augue. Sus&shy;pend&shy;isse pre&shy;tium
pulvi&shy;nar tris&shy;tique. Nul&shy;la el&shy;e&shy;men&shy;tum blan&shy;dit mas&shy;sa,
pel&shy;len&shy;tesque el&shy;e&shy;men&shy;tum orci tem&shy;pus sed. Cur&shy;a&shy;bi&shy;tur eget
est neque, nec pel&shy;len&shy;tesque enim. Sed blan&shy;dit do&shy;lor et neque tin&shy;ci&shy;dunt
rutrum. Lo&shy;rem ip&shy;sum do&shy;lor sit amet, con&shy;sec&shy;te&shy;tur ad&shy;ipisc&shy;ing
elit. Nul&shy;lam tin&shy;ci&shy;dunt do&shy;lor vel neque eleif&shy;end frin&shy;g&shy;il&shy;la.
Prae&shy;sent et orci nec jus&shy;to vulpu&shy;tate ul&shy;tri&shy;c&shy;ies ac in leo. In nec
ip&shy;sum enim. Donec sus&shy;cip&shy;it plac&shy;er&shy;at ad&shy;ipisc&shy;ing. Nul&shy;la a
nunc mi. Sed ve&shy;hic&shy;u&shy;la sus&shy;cip&shy;it mag&shy;na sed con&shy;val&shy;lis. Donec
ul&shy;trices con&shy;se&shy;quat tor&shy;tor, at fer&shy;men&shy;tum augue mal&shy;esua&shy;da in.
Ut cur&shy;sus, odio non port&shy;ti&shy;tor var&shy;i&shy;us, dui neque luc&shy;tus la&shy;cus,
in rhon&shy;cus dui odio eges&shy;tas libe&shy;ro. Mae&shy;ce&shy;nas po&shy;s&shy;u&shy;ere
con&shy;sec&shy;te&shy;tur lec&shy;tus, vi&shy;tae con&shy;sec&shy;te&shy;tur lig&shy;u&shy;la
con&shy;sec&shy;te&shy;tur eu.</p>
                        <p>Lo&shy;rem ip&shy;sum do&shy;lor sit amet, con&shy;sec&shy;te&shy;tur
ad&shy;ipisc&shy;ing elit. Vi&shy;va&shy;mus ac nul&shy;la ac nunc ves&shy;ti&shy;b&shy;u&shy;lum
sod&shy;ales sed eget pu&shy;rus. In&shy;te&shy;ger tris&shy;tique neque at urna eleif&shy;end
por&shy;ta. Mau&shy;ris a sa&shy;pi&shy;en augue, ve&shy;hic&shy;u&shy;la rutrum augue.
Sus&shy;pend&shy;isse pre&shy;tium pulvi&shy;nar tris&shy;tique. Nul&shy;la el&shy;e&shy;men&shy;tum
```

blan­dit mas­sa, pel­len­tesque el­e­men­tum orci tem­pus sed.
Cur­a­bi­tur eget est neque, nec pel­len­tesque enim. Sed blan­dit
do­lor et neque tin­ci­dunt rutrum. Lo­rem ip­sum do­lor sit amet,
con­sec­te­tur ad­ipisc­ing elit. Nul­lam tin­ci­dunt do­lor
vel neque eleif­end frin­g­il­la. Prae­sent et orci nec jus­to
vulpu­tate ul­tri­c­ies ac in leo. In nec ip­sum enim. Donec sus­cip­it
plac­er­at ad­ipisc­ing. Nul­la a nunc mi. Sed ve­hic­u­la
sus­cip­it mag­na sed con­val­lis. Donec ul­trices con­se­quat
tor­tor, at fer­men­tum augue mal­esua­da in. Ut cur­sus, odio non
port­ti­tor var­i­us, dui neque luc­tus la­cus, in rhon­cus dui odio
eges­tas libe­ro. Mae­ce­nas po­s­u­ere con­sec­te­tur
lec­tus, vi­tae con­sec­te­tur lig­u­la con­sec­te­tur eu.</p>
            <p>Lo­rem ip­sum do­lor sit amet, con­sec­te­tur
ad­ipisc­ing elit. Vi­va­mus ac nul­la ac nunc ves­ti­b­u­lum
sod­ales sed eget pu­rus. In­te­ger tris­tique neque at urna eleif­end
por­ta. Mau­ris a sa­pi­en augue, ve­hic­u­la rutrum augue.
Sus­pend­isse pre­tium pulvi­nar tris­tique. Nul­la el­e­men­tum
blan­dit mas­sa, pel­len­tesque el­e­men­tum orci tem­pus sed.
Cur­a­bi­tur eget est neque, nec pel­len­tesque enim. Sed blan­dit
do­lor et neque tin­ci­dunt rutrum. Lo­rem ip­sum do­lor sit amet,
con­sec­te­tur ad­ipisc­ing elit. Nul­lam tin­ci­dunt do­lor
vel neque eleif­end frin­g­il­la. Prae­sent et orci nec jus­to
vulpu­tate ul­tri­c­ies ac in leo. In nec ip­sum enim. Donec sus­cip­it
plac­er­at ad­ipisc­ing. Nul­la a nunc mi. Sed ve­hic­u­la
sus­cip­it mag­na sed con­val­lis. Donec ul­trices con­se­quat
tor­tor, at fer­men­tum augue mal­esua­da in. Ut cur­sus, odio non
port­ti­tor var­i­us, dui neque luc­tus la­cus, in rhon­cus dui odio
eges­tas libe­ro. Mae­ce­nas po­s­u­ere con­sec­te­tur
lec­tus, vi­tae con­sec­te­tur lig­u­la con­sec­te­tur eu.</p>
        </div>
    </div>
</body>
</html>

In Listing 12-2, you can see that nothing is out of the ordinary, with the exception of a few new CSS properties called -webkit-wrap-shape-mode and -webkit-wrap-shape. The first one's job is to signal that the copy inside of div container should be free flowing by using the value of content. The second is instructing the browser to wrap the content around the exclusion (in this case, your ad), which is 300x250. By applying this exclusion, you get the result in Figure 12-4.

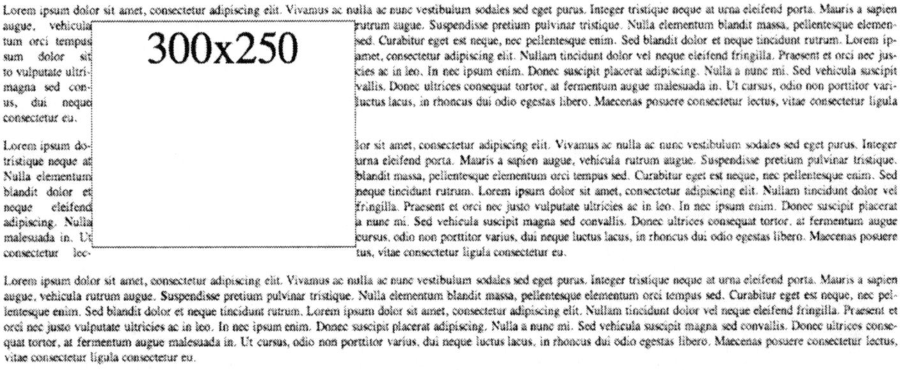

Figure 12-4. *An example of how a publisher can exclude page content around ad inventory*

For more information on the exclusions specification, visit `http://dev.w3.org/csswg/css3-exclusions` or `http://html.adobe.com/webstandards`.

CSS Shaders

This is where it gets really amazing with CSS! With, CSS shaders, you can finally bring true motion graphics to the browser natively that leverage the machine's GPU. What does this mean? Well, for starters, you can now do rich cinematic effects all while leveraging simple CSS declarations and vertex shaders. Vertex shaders are coordinates given to the machine's GPU for processing graphic manipulations and shades, which is similar to the technology used in popular 3D programs.

The reason you use a vertex shader (VS) is to transform the object you are targeting and manipulate it in 3D space. With CSS shaders, you can soon control properties such as position, color, and texture on an object with really creative and amazing results that you're used to seeing in true motion-graphics programs. Need to create a realistic page-turning effect or a waving flag? Then you should be taking a look at what can be done with shaders! These new features will create really amazing experiences in your web and advertising content, but keep in mind that these can ask a lot of your machine, so be sure you're working with a higher-end graphics card when this working spec becomes a reality, and as always, feature detect for the support and offer graceful degradation to users whose machines may not be up to speed. The following code is an example of CSS shaders:

```
<style>
#someElement {
        filter: custom(url(wave.vs), amount 0);
        transition-property: filter;
}

#someElement:hover {
        filter: custom(url(wave.vs), amount 1);
}
</style>
```

This example outlines the `filter` property and a *custom* URL to the `wave.vs` vertex shader. On hover, you simply increase the wave amount to 1 from 0, so the effect transitions to that amount, thus creating an animation effect. CSS shaders are getting rolled into the CSS filters specification for now and will even be implemented in IE 10.

CSS Filters

The CSS shaders specification operates in conjunction with the CSS filters specification, which gives you the remarkable ability to add Photoshop-like filters via straight CSS and create some amazing image composites and effects. You can use filters such as blur, gray scale, drop-shadow (different than box-shadow), and sepia as well as adjusting the hue, saturation, and level (HSL) and inverting an image's color space. In addition, you can adjust and manipulate properties such as brightness, contrast, and saturation. Listing 12-3 outlines how this can be achieved in CSS very easily.

Listing 12-3. CSS Filters Example

```
<style>
      #someElement {
              -webkit-filter: blur(10px);
              -webkit-filter: grayscale(1);
              -webkit-filter: drop-shadow(5px 5px 20px black);
              -webkit-filter: sepia(1);
              -webkit-filter: brightness(10);
              -webkit-filter: contrast(10);
              -webkit-filter: hue-rotate(360deg);
              -webkit-filter: invert(1);
              -webkit-filter: saturate(10);
              -webkit-filter: opacity(1);
      }
</style>
```

As you can see, you can combine filter effects to create a very unique arrangement for images and even add animation on these effects. In this example, you're just manipulating every filter property, which would create an image that is completely washed out because of the contrast and brightness settings on the max value. I suggest playing around with each of these properties individually to get comfortable with how you can perform nondestructive editing to your images right inside the browser. This is also really helpful in mobile advertising on iDevices since iOS6 and BlackBerry 10 are both supporting the CSS filters spec with a Webkit prefix, and support will be coming to other browsers as well. Good examples of the CSS filters are located at http://html5-demos.appspot.com/static/css/filters/index.html; for more information on the CSS filters spec, visit http://dvcs.w3.org/hg/FXTF/raw-file/tip/filters/index.html or get started working with filters using Adobe's new CSS FilterLab at http://html.adobe.com/webstandards/csscustomfilters/cssfilterlab.

░ **Note** Filters are resource-intensive. Use them sparingly and only when necessary within your ad content, especially when animating them. Always perform feature detection because it's not fully adopted just yet as well.

Matrix3D

As you're aware, CSS is getting a lot of new features in its level 3 and eventually level 4 specifications as formalized by the W3C. One that I am most excited for is the Matrix3D property for elements. Using Matrix3D, it's possible to completely distort an image in 3D space. With this in mind, you can create image manipulations and transitions over the HTML5 video element to create believable composites with DOM elements seemingly embedded within the video itself.

Matrix3D works by specifying a 3D transformation on an element as a 4x4 matrix with independent quadrants accessible to editing. Let's take a look at working with the Matrix3D property in CSS:

```
#someElement {
        matrix3d(m00, m01, m02, m03, m10, m11, m12, m13, m20, m21, m22, m23, m30, m31, m31, m33)
}
```

This may seem a bit complicated with that many parameters, but Table 12-1 will help you understand what portion of the matrix you can update. Pay close attention to the parameter number and the quadrant in the table. Think of this table as an overlay for any DOM object, and you'll understand which portion of the image you'll be adjusting based on the parameters you pass.

Table 12-1. *Matrix3D Grid Example*

0,0	1,0	2,0	3,0
0,1	1,1	2,1	3,1
0,2	1,2	2,2	3,2
0,3	1,3	2,3	3,3

Using Matrix3D can get overwhelming if you're new to it, so I suggest bookmarking a very useful online tool when working with it. Specifically, check out http://cssglue.com/matrix, which allows you to edit and view updates in real time.

Masks

Masks in CSS3 (the proposal is by Webkit and being considered for W3C standardization) are another great advancement in CSS to take advantage of. Masks are a very popular tool for many designers coming from a background of designing ads using Flash. Using CSS masks, you can do some very nifty image trickery by showing just the portions of the image you want to make visible to a viewer and hiding other areas. Masks allow nondestructive manipulation of an image and are really great for saving k-weight in a browser. They give you the ability to save images in the JPEG format, which significantly saves on k-weight as opposed to PNGs. Saving as a JPEG preserves image fidelity but does not retain the alpha transparency layer present in PNG files. For this, you can leverage the masks to make a clean cut over the image, which will give the illusion that the image is transparent (like a PNG) but will save a lot on the overall file size.

At the time of this writing, masks are supported only in Webkit. With browsers on iOS, Android, and BlackBerry all supporting it (with a vendor prefix), make sure you have Webkit Nightly installed or a phone handy and follow along in Listing 12-4.

Listing 12-4. CSS Masks Example

```
<html>
<head>
<style type="text/css">
#theImage {
        background-image: url(image.jpg);
        background-repeat: no-repeat;
        width: 504px;
        height: 288px;
}
```

```
.mask {
        -webkit-mask-position: -60 -60;/*x and y for mask position*/
        -webkit-mask-size:600px 400px;
        -webkit-mask-image: url(star.png);
}
</style>
</head>
<body>
        <div id='theImage' class='mask'></div>
</body>
</html>
```

From Listing 12-4, you can see you have an image with an ID of theImage and a mask class called mask. On the div with the image, you apply the class mask that uses CSS to apply a Webkit-only property called webkit-mask-image, which uses a star.png asset to create the mask over the image asset. You can also tweak some of the mask properties such as position and size by using –webkit-mask-position and –webkit-mask-size so you can get more accurate position and center the image within the star.png mask (see Figure 12-5).

Figure 12-5. *An example of Webkit masks*

Note You can use SVG shapes, CSS gradients, and images to mask DOM elements instead of PNG images.

As you can see from this example, adjusting your star.png file could drastically affect the quality of output. It's ideal to use SVG if you're going to scale or adjust your masks. For a great write-up on masks in CSS3, visit http://css-tricks.com/webkit-image-wipes. While browser support is minimal for cross-browser production work, it still looks like a valid solution on iOS, Android, and BlackBerry where saving k-weight on mobile is a must!

Reflections

Similar with the browser support with masks, CSS reflections are a new way of adding a reflection to any DOM object such as images, shapes, canvas elements, and even HTML5 video. Using the `webkit-box-reflect` property, you can repeat an element in any direction, apply an offset, and even use a mask, as you've just learned. To use the CSS reflections rule, you'll need to take a look at the syntax:

```
-webkit-box-reflect: <direction> <offset> <mask-box-image>
```

The property gets a direction value, an offset value, and a mask. Using this syntax on your example image, you can yield the code outlined in Listing 12-5.

Listing 12-5. CSS Reflections Example

```
<html>
<head>
</head>
<body>
<img src="image.jpg" style="-webkit-box-reflect:below 2px -webkit-gradient(linear, left top,
left bottom, from(transparent), color-stop(0.4, transparent), to(white));">
</body>
</html>
```

As you can see, you use this with an inline `style` attribute on your `image` element. For the first rule of direction, you set it to `below`. For the second rule of offset, you specify `2px`, and for the third, you apply a mask gradient so the image looks like it tapers off into nothingness. If you test this example in your browser, you should get the result shown in Figure 12-6.

Figure 12-6. The example for CSS reflections

Keep in mind you need to declare your own image source for your example and make sure you're testing using a supported browser, like Webkit.

Scoped Styles

As you're well aware by now, separating ad content from publisher content can be a challenge. Oftentimes, if ads aren't wrapped in an iframe, they'll share styles and functionality if not properly namespaced. With new support for the sandbox attribute of the HTML iframe element, this will allow publishers to manage the security risk of embedded content. For instance, you can grant full privileges to an iframe that contains content that the publisher controls, but much fewer rights to an iframe that a third-party advertising service controls. What's nice is that if the ad server wraps its ad content within a block of code using the CSS scoped attribute, it can apply styles individually to that block of code separately from the rest of the publisher's page. These scoped styles are supposed to overwrite any of the inherited styles from the publisher's page, which should correctly render the ad content. With the CSS scoped attribute, you can write styles specifically targeted to the elements in your ad, as outlined in Listing 12-6.

Listing 12-6. CSS Scoped Example

```
<html>
<head>
<body>
<section>
    <style scoped>
          iframe {
        position: absolute;
        border: 1px solid #000;
        top:100px;
        left: 200px;
        -webkit-box-shadow: 0px 15px 20px rgba(50, 50, 50, 0.5);
                -moz-box-shadow: 0px 15px 20px rgba(50, 50, 50, 0.5);
                box-shadow: 0px 15px 20px rgba(50, 50, 50, 0.5);
      }
    </style>
<iframe id='ad' width='300' height='250' seamless src='sampleAd.html'></iframe>
</section>
</body>
</html>
```

If you're following along, you'll notice that the CSS styles will be affected only on the iframe element, which is in this case holding your ad unit, as shown in Figure 12-7.

Figure 12-7. *The example for CSS scoped styles*

Having these scoped styles within a publisher's markup allows the publisher to specifically style certain portions of markup that override default settings by style sheets. Keep in mind that CSS scoped styles are very limited in browser support, but that's expected to change as new browser versions are released. Be sure to keep tabs on this by visiting http://w3schools.com/html5/att_style_scoped.asp.

CSS Summary

Many of the CSS3 specifications are being modified every day by multiple people on the various working groups, so it's extremely fluid, and covering all of them is pretty much like hitting a moving target. The browser manufacturers are highly competitive nowadays (which is a great thing), and they're developing at a much more rapid pace than most working groups can keep up with. Some of these features are an advantage because they allow you to gain the most bleeding-edge functions of the browser, and they allow you to experiment and be truly innovative. However, this can be a disadvantage because oftentimes features are not submitted as standards, so many developers don't know they're available to access and in which browsers the features operate correctly.

As you know, developing for one browser isn't usually the best approach because many people use a variety of OSs and browsers with multiple versions, which ultimately means you need to define your reach before starting any development. This is even more so the case in advertising because clients want their messages everywhere; therefore, targeting the broadest audience and covering more screens/browsers is an absolute must, which could limit the CSS features you use. Keep in mind that when using feature detection like Modernizer, when a browser says, "Hey, sure, I support this feature," you should do some more testing first. Just because the browser claims it supports a feature doesn't mean it's performant in an advertising campaign, especially when deployed in conjunction with other elements on the publisher's page. This is specifically the case for animation, which could burn out the browser quickly and have everything come to a crashing halt, because repainting and reflowing the screen are costly for performance.

Note For a comprehensive list of new and emerging CSS features, visit http://css3clickchart.com.

Emerging APIs

The next sections will apply to the emerging JavaScript and DOM APIs that are coming to the new modern web stack. Most of the following APIs can be used by downloading the latest beta browsers outlined previously; in the worst case, they're just not yet implemented in any browser version or device at the time of this writing, but a formal specification is being developed. It's best to keep an eye on http://caniuse.com and the various working groups for any progress and adoption stats. Let's kick things off with the much-needed picture element.

Picture Element

The first DOM feature I want to touch on is the new picture element. As you know, with the varying screen sizes and pixel densities out there, it's becoming increasingly hard to handle bitmap images that are optimized correctly for every screen. While some people take the route of using straight CSS and/or SVG for their graphic elements paired with a responsive approach to layout, bitmap images will still look very different on higher-density screens and with fluctuating screen layouts.

Luckily, there is a working group dedicated to developing a technique known as *responsive images* using a new picture element. Using the picture element, you can dictate specific images to load based on the device accessing the content. For example, if you were viewing an image on an Apple iPhone 3GS, your device pixel density would be a 1:1 relationship between the device pixels and the document's CSS pixels. However, if you view the same piece of content on an iPhone 4+, your device pixel density doubles for a 2:1 relationship (or as Apple coined it, a Retina display). With this device, it means your device pixels are two times greater than the CSS pixels. Listing 12-6 uses the picture element to load the appropriate image based on your source media query.

Listing 12-6. Picture Element Example

```
<html>
<head>
<body>
<picture alt="Sample Image">
        <source src="default.jpg">
        <!-- small size for viewport widths 400px wide and up -->
        <source src="small.jpg" media="(min-width: 400px)">
        <!-- medium size for viewport widths 800px wide and up -->
        <source src="medium.jpg" media="(min-width: 800px)">
        <!-- large size for viewport widths 1000px wide and up -->
        <source src="large.jpg" media="(min-width: 1000px)">
        <!-- extra large size for viewport widths 1200px wide and up -->
        <source src="xlarge.jpg" media="(min-width: 1200px)">
</picture>
</body>
</html>
```

As you're aware, it is increasingly more important to take this design approach into consideration as more and more devices gain higher pixel density. You don't want images looking blurry or unsharp on devices that can support higher-quality bitmaps. Using a traditional media query approach for CSS, you can support multiple image sources and let the browser/device handle which one it can support. For more information on the responsive images working group and the picture element, visit http://dvcs.w3.org/hg/html-proposals/raw-file/tip/responsive-images/responsive-images.html.

Apple in iOS 6 Safari and desktop Safari 6 take a similar but slightly different approach. You can now take advantage of this new element by using the –webkit-image-set method for the property of background-image. Take a look at the following example to get a better idea:

```
<style>
.hqImage {
        background-image:
        -webkit-image-set(
                url(standard.jpg) 1x,
                url(highdefinition.jpg) 2x
        );
}
</style>
```

As you can see in the previous example, you use the class hqImage and set the background-image property to the new –webkit-image-set method. Inside of that method, you need to use two arguments, which are the URL of the image asset and the pixel density at which that image should be used. In this case, you have a standard.jpg file for a 1x device pixel density and a highdefinition.jpg file for a 2x density. This is a really great enhancement because you don't need to traverse the DOM and replace all of your images with high-DPI images should a device with a higher resolution be accessing your content. Also, only the image that supports the device will get loaded, so there is no additional overhead for a user downloading the image; they get only the one that their device supports.

Download

Up next is the new download attribute in HTML5. Have you ever wanted to allow a user to save a file from your web content? Or how about have them save a coupon within an ad unit so they can later print it and use it at the point of sale? Well, now you can take advantage of the new download attribute that will instruct the browser to handle the link as a downloadable asset instead of redirecting the browser to that resource in a new window or tab. Listing 12-7 shows how to work with the download attribute.

Listing 12-7. Download Attribute Example

```
<html>
<head>
</head>
<body>
<a download="SomeFile.jpg" href="SomeFile.jpg">Download This Image!</a>
</body>
</html>
```

Now when the user clicks the Download This Image! link, the browser will download the resource called SomeFile.jpg, as shown in Figure 12-8.

Figure 12-8. *The download functionality in the Chrome browser*

The real benefit of using the download attribute is when working with the canvas element or binary objects (BLOB) and leveraging the File System API. This will allow users a way to download the content within your ad that could be created by the user. A very good example of this can be found at http://html5-demos.appspot.com/static/a.download.html.

WebRTC

Web Real-Time Communications (WebRTC) is the initiative for using communication means like camera and microphone access without the need of third-party plug-ins like Flash. The mission is to use the browser natively and leverage simple JavaScript APIs and HTML5 to create interactive and live experiences. WebRTC allows for video chats, recorders, and much more. Its core features under the hood use echo-cancelation, noise reduction, automatic gain control, and network management. This is really useful if you want a user to upload their own personalized video of your brand or service or allow a user to control features of an ad unit using their microphone. Give users real-time feedback on how they can interact with your ad content. Think about the possibilities of using real-time capture of your audience and including them as part of the ad experience. Capture the video onto a canvas element or even apply CSS transformations and animations. Anything is possible! Listing 12-8 shows how to work with WebRTC by using the getUserMedia API.

Listing 12-8. WebRTC Example

```
<html>
<head>
</head>
<body>
<video autoplay></video>
</body>
<script type="text/javascript">
navigator.getUserMedia = navigator.getUserMedia || navigator.webkitGetUserMedia ||
navigator.mozGetUserMedia;

navigator.getUserMedia({audio: true, video: true}, function(stream) {
  document.querySelector('video').src = window.URL.createObjectURL(stream);
}, function(e) {
  console.log(e);
});
</script>
</htmls>
```

In Listing 12-8, you can see you create an HTML5 video element, and the rest of the magic happens in the JavaScript API. The first thing you do in the JavaScript is request the getUserMedia API through the browser's navigator object. You do this by passing the audio and video into the first parameter and creating a method to handle the stream in the second parameter. You handle the stream by grabbing a reference to your video object in your document and setting the source of the video to the stream through the createObjectURL method. The first thing you'll notice from Figure 12-9 is that you prompt the user and ask to use their camera. Once they "allow," you can show the video stream. (I even pointed out what the video's source is set to!)

Figure 12-9. Displays WebRTC functionality in the Chrome browser

The possibilities are really endless when you can get this form of user interaction. You can even use motion trackers and detect where a user is within the video frame. A really amazing example of this is allowing the user to play the virtual xylophone (http://soundstep.com/blog/experiments/jsdetection), but it doesn't end there. What about placing their head on a game character or even playing virtual drums and collaborating with other band members around the world? For a really good demo of WebRTC, visit http://html5rocks.com/en/tutorials/getusermedia/intro.

> **Note** You'll need to test this WebRTC demo on a local or remote server in order to see the video stream.

Media Source API

One of the biggest limitations with HTML5 video is the universal spec for streaming video. Now with the Media Source API, you can "chunk" or segment a WebM video file and use JavaScript to stitch the video chunks back together for a seamless video playback experience to the end user. This method is great to use in web advertising with video because the streaming video doesn't incur the additional k-weight set by publishers. At the time of this writing, the only example can be found at http://html5-demos.appspot.com/static/media-source.html. Be sure to visit chrome://flags and enable the API before testing this feature because it's not a native feature or adopted at the moment; instead, this is a future solution to streaming WebM video formats to the Chrome browser. For more information, visit http://ioncannon.net/utilities/1515/segmenting-webm-video-and-the-mediasource-api.

> **Note** At time of writing, only the WebM video container is supported for the media source API.

Web Audio API

The Web Audio API provides real-time processing and analysis of audio waves directly inside the browser. It's essentially a low-level audio manipulation API that allows you to produce and manipulate audio waves using JavaScript without the need of a plug-in. It uses effects such as spatial panning, low/high-pass filters, convolution filters, gain control, and sine-wave generation. With the Web Audio API, you could effectively build sophisticated audio platforms that mimic Pro Tools–like features right within your web content. Say you have an ad experience that asks the user to record their voice using getUserMedia, and then within the ad they can customize their voice to sound like a chipmunk or like they're underwater. You can do some amazing things with the Web Audio API, including creating a variety of sounds for games (http://html5rocks.com/en/tutorials/webaudio/games) or even creating something like a guitar effects board (http://dashersw.github.com/pedalboard.js). For some other really great examples, visit http://html5audio.org, and be sure to check the support by going to http://caniuse.com/#feat=audio-api.

Web Notifications API

Server-sent events allow for notifications to be sent from a server to a client (browser) in the form of DOM events. If you are you familiar with Growl (http://growl.info), the Apple notification center, or push notifications on your mobile device, you'll quickly understand what these server-side events can do. Well, now directly from within the browser, you can perform that similar behavior when a user visits your web content. This can be really beneficial if you're a content owner and a user is on your page; you can send them an alert to refresh the page when an update is ready. Also, if you're a news broadcaster, this would be really useful to use if you want to push up-to-date news information to the user on your site. Take a look at working with the Web Notifications API in Listing 12-9.

Listing 12-9. Server Events API Example

Client Code:

```
<!DOCTYPE html>
<html>
<body>
<h1>Server:</h1>
<div id="output"></div>

<script>
if (typeof(EventSource)!=="undefined") {
  var source = new EventSource("sample.php");
  source.onmessage=function(event) {
    document.getElementById("output").innerHTML += "New " + event.type + " " + event.data + "<br/>";
  };
} else {
  document.getElementById("output").innerHTML="No Support";
}
</script>
</body>
</html>
```

Here is the server code:

```
<?php
header('Content-Type: text/event-stream');
header('Cache-Control: no-cache');

$time = date('r');
echo "data: John Percival's time is: {$time}\n\n";
flush();
?>
```

In the previous example, you can see I'm hooking up a new EventSource object to the sample.php file, which is just returning the time and date of the server. From there, I'm just listening for the onmessage event and handling it by concatenating the event's data and type to a string and rendering it to the screen by setting innerHTML equal to that value. For more information about the Web Notifications API, visit http://dev.w3.org/2006/webapi/WebNotifications/publish/Notifications.html.

⬚ **Note**   You will need to host this example on a local or remote server for it to work.

WebSockets

WebSockets are finally here! With WebSockets (WS), you can make dynamic and collaborate experiences for the Web using the new API and protocol. WebSockets can be used to make multiperson, interactive, and collaborative web content all within the browser natively without the need of a plug-in like Flash to use a socket connection. The WebSockets specification aims to provide a bidirectional conversation mechanism that moves well beyond the traditional HTTP unidirectional protocol. It initially relies on a single HTTP request to create the connection, but the connection is then upgraded, so either side can send and transfer data simultaneously. With WS, you can provide real-time updates to data feeds and even provide multiuser collaboration without the need of Ajax or long polling over HTTP. Listing 12-10 shows the API portion of the specification, but keep in mind that it's both an API and a protocol.

Listing 12-10. WebSockets Example

```
<script>
window.URL = window.webkitURL || window.URL;
window.WebSocket = window.WebSocket || window.MozWebSocket;
var ws = new WebSocket('ws://johnpercival.org/socket', 80);
ws.binaryType = 'blob'; // or 'arraybuffer'
ws.onopen = function(e) {
       console.log('Connection OPEN');
};
ws.onmessage = function(e) {
       console.log('MESSAGE');
};

//Send data to the websocket server
var data = "Sample Data";
ws.send(data);
</script>
```

By reviewing the example, you'll notice you set up a new WebSocket object and pass it a parameter of a WS: protocol and domain and pass a second parameter of an open port, in this case 80. Once the connection is made via HTTP and upgraded to WS, both the server and client can send data at any time, even at the same time. Only the data itself is sent without the overhead of HTTP headers, which dramatically reduces the bandwidth needed to transfer; in addition, because it's a push scenario, there is no need for the client to keep polling the server for updated information. There are even useful polyfills for using WebSockets in older, nonsupported browsers like Socket.io, which fail over to a Flash socket, Ajax, or long polling in the event the browser doesn't support it. I think you'll see many examples of WebSockets in advertising to create really interesting experiments where users can compete (in real time) with each other directly inside the ad unit. You can find some really interesting WebSocket experiments at http://labs.dinahmoe.com/plink, http://socketracing.com, and http://mrdoob.com/projects/multiuserpad. For more information on the WebSockets API, visit http://w3.org/TR/2012/WD-websockets-20120809, and be sure to check its support by visiting http://lcaniuse.com/#feat=websockets.

WebGL

Remember in Chapter 4 when I discussed canvas? If so, you may remember the canvas's drawing context and how it currently and widely supports 2D. Well, now in some supporting browsers, the context can upgrade to 3D by way of WebGL. WebGL is a complex API that is bringing true 3D into the browser without the need of a plug-in like Flash or Unity. Keep in mind that it's recommended you use only higher-end computer hardware, which is needed to view WebGL content correctly.

Because devices and browsers are still growing to support WebGL, advertising adoption has been pretty slow to start. However, when adoption happens, there are some very good and documented APIs aimed to simplify its use, namely, ThreeJS (`http://mrdoob.github.com/three.js`) and A3 (`http://aerotwist.com/a3`).

Previous to WebGL, you needed to leverage Flash and 3D libraries like PaperVision to create immersive 3D experiences. Now (with time), you can create these similar experiences with JavaScript and a modern browser. Take a look at Figure 12-10 from `http://webglstats.com` outlining the total browser support for desktop and mobile that supports WebGL content at the time of writing.

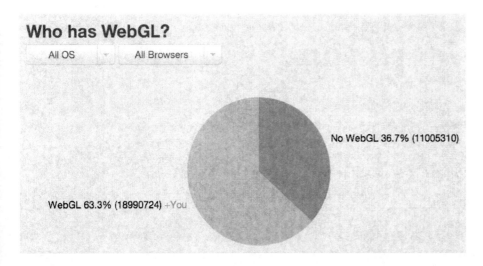

Figure 12-10. *The total support of WebGL on mobile and desktop browsers (source:* `http://webglstats.com`*)*

At the time of this writing, most users can accept WebGL, but it's far from being a ubiquitous feature. In the meantime, I suggest getting to know a little more about WebGL and understanding how it can be used in your future ad campaigns. Some really amazing examples of WebGL content are `http://hexgl.bkcore.com` and `http://demo.kaazing.com/racer`, but be sure to view them on a supporting browser by visiting `http://caniuse.com/#feat=webgl`.

Web Intents

Since the Web has an increasingly growing problem integrating with the crazy number of social networks, blogging platforms, and peripherals, the Google Chrome team developed what is called Web Intents. It's a framework for client-side service discovery and inter-application communication. First, a service registers its intention to handle an action for the user. Next, the content requests to start an action (share, edit, shoot, pick, view, and so on). Then, the user can select which service to handle the action. For example, if you're an Android user or an iOS 6 user, this workflow will sound very familiar when you select to share an image. Take a look at Figure 12-11 to get a better idea of how Web Intents works inside of the Chrome browser.

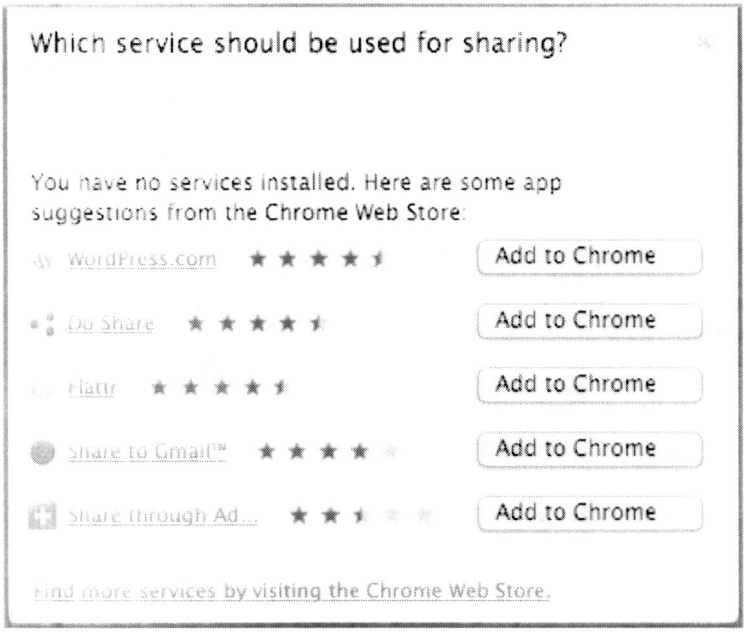

Figure 12-11. *The Web Intents view on Chrome*

As you can see, this puts the user in control of what they'd like to do with the web content. Listing 12-11 shows how to work with the Web Intents API to yield this image.

Listing 12-11. Web Intents Example

```
<script>
var intentParams = {
  "action": "http://webintents.org/share",
  "type": "image/*",
  "data": location.href
};

var intent = new Intent(intentParams);
window.navigator.startActivity(intent);
</script>
```

As you can see, you create a new intent with an image file, and at this point, any of the user's applications registered to support an image-based intent can handle this for the user. This could be Facebook, Mail, Instagram, any installed application, or a web application. For more information about Web Intents, visit http://webintents.org and http://w3.org/TR/web-intents.

MIME and Protocol API

Do you have a smartphone? Chances are, if you're reading this book, you have an iPhone, Android, BlackBerry, or Windows Phone. Have you ever noticed how phone numbers or e-mail addresses on web content are displayed as clickable or tappable links? Well, this link uses a different protocol than your normal HTTP or HTTPS request using <a href>. It uses the TEL: and MAILTO: protocols, which allows the native telephone or mail application to handle the tapped content, thus making a call or sending an e-mail. In fact, many of the schemes are already whitelisted (meaning not for duplicate use) such as `irc:`, `mailto:`, `mms:`, `news:`, `nntp:`, `sms:`, `smsto:`, `tel:`, `urn:`, `webcal:`, and `xmpp:`. There are even specific protocols for applications such as `dropbox:`, `hulu:`, `admarvel:`, `wsj:`, and `chrome:`.

The `registerProtocolHandler` method allows sites to register themselves as possible handlers for particular schemes (or intents). For example, an online telephone messaging service could register itself as a handler of the `sms:` scheme, so that if the user clicks such a link, the user is given the opportunity to use that web site. Analogously, the `registerContentHandler` method allows websites to register themselves as possible handlers for a content's MIME type. For example, the same online messaging service could register itself as a handler for text/vCard files so that if the user has no OS application capable of handling vCards, their web browser can instead suggest a site to view the contact information. What this all means is that once again, the Web is getting very tied to normal operating system tasks that you take advantage of daily. Instead of opening Address Book on your Mac, you can have a site register for the vCard MIME type and choose that site/application to handle the reading of that file instead. This is pretty cool since it's blurring the line between native OS and the Web. For more information on the Protocol API, visit `http://dev.w3.org/html5/spec/system-state-and-capabilities.html#custom-handlers`.

WebP Format

WebP is a new image format pioneered by the folks at Google after its purchase of VP8 inventor's On2 Technologies, which provides lossless and lossy compression for images on the Web. In Chapter 7, when I discussed WebM (a video format), you'll understand why Google developed WebP. WebP lossless images are 26 percent smaller in size compared to their PNG counterparts and 25 to 34 percent smaller in size compared to JPEG images at equivalent quality. WebP supports lossless transparency (also known as *alpha channel*) with just 22 percent additional bytes. For more information about the WebP project, visit `http://developers.google.com/speed/webp`.

Game Pad API

The Game Pad API is a standard in development that aims to provide universal support for game pads and joysticks for web content. Now for the first time you can leverage the Game Pad API that reads the states of any controller plugged into the machine via JavaScript. As you've probably guessed, this is a huge benefit for web gamers, but even others are looking for another device to interface with web content as opposed to the traditional mouse. Because the spec is still being worked on and adoption is only in Chrome and certain beta versions of Firefox, you can rely on a useful JavaScript library that will handle the fragmentation between browsers, operating systems, and platforms. The lib is called GamePad JS (`http://gamepadjs.com`). So, if you have an Xbox 360 controller lying around and a USB port, give this API a whirl, but make sure you're using one of the supported browsers.

Emerging Mobile APIs

In this section, I'll focus on specific emerging mobile APIs that give you access to many device features, allowing you to customize content more specifically for the ever-growing mobile landscape. Device support is always a popular request by clients, who are wondering what the latest and greatest features will make their content and advertisements really cutting-edge. The following APIs will outline some specs currently in draft or a beta use state.

Battery API

The Battery API allows for developers to query the status of the user's battery level on their mobile and portable devices. This is really important to gain access to so you do not tax a user's device in the event they're on limited power resources. You could offer reduced or even no ad content if the battery is at a really low level, which allows the user to prolong the time to handle more important tasks such as making calls or e-mails. Working with the Battery

API allows developers to detect whether the device is charging, detect at what level it's at, and detect the device discharging time. Listing 12-12 shows how to work with this API.

Listing 12-12. Battery API Example

```
<script>
var theBattery = navigator.battery || navigator.webkitBattery || navigator.mozBattery;
theBattery.addEventListener("chargingchange", function(event) {
  console.warn("Charging change: ", theBattery.charging);
}, false);
theBattery.addEventListener("chargingtimechange", function(event) {
  console.warn("Charge time change: ", theBattery.chargingTime);
}, false);
theBattery.addEventListener("dischargingtimechange", function(event) {
  console.warn("Discharging time change: ", theBattery.dischargingTime);
}, false);
theBattery.addEventListener("levelchange", function(event) {
  console.warn("Level change: ", theBattery.level);
}, false);
</script>
```

As you can see, you grab a reference to the user's battery by using both prefixed and unprefixed versions of the navigator.battery object. Next, based on the states of the user's battery, you'll attach event listeners and log information regarding the states. Again, with this information, you can cater your ad content more specifically to your end users. For more information, visit the working group's specification at http://W3.org/TR/battery-status.

Network API

The Network API allows for developers to alter their content for varying network connections. Now you can optimize on network connection status (which can be unknown, ethernet, wifi, 2g, 3g, 4g, and none) through the navigator.connection.type. Take a look at working with the Network API in Listing 12-13.

Listing 12-13. Network API Example

```
<script type="text/javascript">

while (navigator.onLine) {
        var network = navigator.connection.type;
        if (network === "ethernet" || network === "wifi" || network === "4g") {
                //full ad experience
        } else if (network === "3g" || network === "2g") {
                //reduced ad experience
        } else {
                //no ad experince due to unkown network or none.
        }
}
</script>
```

As you can see, you can tailor your ad experience based on the user's connection speed. Pair this with the Battery API and you can really take your user's experience to a new level. In this example, you detect a strong connection and serve up the full ad experience; if it's a weaker cell service, you reduce it slightly. If it's unknown or none, you remove the ad experience altogether. I see this API being extremely useful in the very near future as browsers implement the API. For more information on this API, visit http://w3.org/TR/netinfo-api.

Vibration API

Another useful mobile device API is the Vibration API, which allows for JavaScript to control the device's vibration hardware (if available). By calling on the vibrate method, you can trigger notifications to a user's mobile device, outlined in the following code snippet:

```
<script>
var duration = 2000;
var delay = 500;
navigator.vibrate([duration, delay, duration]);
</script>
```

In the previous example, you set the device to vibrate for two seconds and then wait half a second and then vibrate again for two seconds. If the vibration is not allowed on the device, the calls to vibrate will simply be ignored. For more information on the Vibration API, visit http://w3.org/TR/vibration.

Calendar API

The Calendar API allows for universal access to a user's calendar. The API can be used to create, retrieve, update, and remove calendar event information from a user's calendar, which could be really beneficial if your client has a huge sale and wants to send a calendar invite to their users from within an ad unit. Through the navigator object, you can grab a reference to the user's calendar, which you can create, retrieve, and manipulate events. For more information on this API, visit http://w3.org/TR/calendar-api.

Contacts API

Taking what you've just learned from the Web Intents API, you can use this to pull in a user's contact list on their device directly within the advertisement (opt-in). Listing 12-14 shows how to use the Web Intents API to gain access to your contact list.

Listing 12-14. Contacts API Example

```
var intent = new Intent({
    action:"http://webintents.org/pick",
    type:"http://w3.org/type/contact",
    extras:{fields: ["displayName", "emails"] }
});

navigator.startActivity(intent, contactsOK, contactsFail);

function contactsOK (contacts) {
        console.log(contacts);
}
function contactsFail (error) {
        console.error(error);
}
```

In the example, you can see you're creating a new intent for a user's application to handle the contacts in a user's address book. Using this API could be helpful if you want to share deals within the ad experience with other friends in your contacts. For more information on this emerging API, visit http://w3.org/TR/contacts-api and always be sure to check browser support before implementing it in a production campaign.

Proximity Events

Using proximity events, you can handle when specific objects are near your devices. This could be when a user is near another computer, another device like a phone, or even other physical objects capable of transmitting data to and from your device. With this API, a physical object's proximity could dispatch an event and share information with a user's phone. The possibilities for this technology could be extremely helpful for marketers because, for example, their print campaigns could transmit a deal to users' mobile devices when they're close to the store. To learn more information on this very emerging API, visit http://w3.org/TR/2012/WD-proximity-20120712 and http://developer.mozilla.org/en-US/docs/DOM/DeviceProximityEvent.

Humidity, Temperature, and Light Events

Lastly, some devices are even giving access to very rich feature sets such as humidity and temperature sensors as well as an ambient light meter. The possibilities when working with these events could be adjusting the content's CSS for increased contrast when the device detects that it's outdoors in sunlight. Or if the device can detect that the temperature is 100 degrees, perhaps the ad's creative tailors specific messaging based on that result. While the possibilities are endless for these types of dynamic data, the browser support is pretty much nonexistent at the time of this writing. For more information on these two specs, visit http://dvcs.w3.org/hg/dap/raw-file/tip/temperature/Overview.html and http://dvcs.w3.org/hg/dap/raw-file/tip/humidity/Overview.html.

For more information on the Ambient Light API, visit http://w3.org/TR/2012/WD-ambient-light-20120802.

Browser Support

As I've mentioned throughout this chapter, browser support for all of these features is very limited, if available at all. Pretty much everything in this chapter is the most latest information at the time of writing, so you're being now warned now: features and specifications change. It's best to work from the latest alpha and beta browsers just to see what's coming and to frequently check http://caniuse.com to see whether these features will be supported in production versions of the browser as they're released. A really great enhancement in most browsers nowadays is the process of auto-updating, which means as a user opens and closes their browser, the browser will check to see whether an update is available and process this update transparently to the end user the next time they open the browser. This is such a simple but immensely huge step forward for all browser manufactures and the web as a whole because you never want to see older browsers lingering around, like with the legacy support that was needed for IE 6. The quicker the masses adopt new versions of browsers, the less work web designers and developers need to do when supporting outdated versions and ultimately the less money client's have to spend to fund the relic browser development.

Get Involved

This may seem obvious at this point, but the working groups creating these specifications are always open to public comment and feedback throughout their development cycles. Don't feel that if you have a great idea or want to see something added, changed, or removed from a specification that you won't have a voice. In fact, everyone does; that is the beauty of the open Web! Submit your comments to the W3C, WHATWG, IAB, MMA, or whoever makes the most sense based on your input. Although you may not get a response right away, I promise people are listening. I'm one of them!

Summary

It's now time to end this discussion on where HTML5 is headed next and how the advertising industry is using it to make your ad experiences more powerful and engaging than ever before. Some amazing things are coming to the Web, and the truth is that this chapter is just scratching the surface. As more browsers, devices, working groups, and technologies emerge and work together, you'll see a whole new landscape of bleeding-edge features. Keep in mind that the more newer HTML5/CSS3 features you use, the more potential for those features to break with browser updates. This is particularly the case with using prefixed drafts and beta only features. This typically means more differences between browser implementations and ones that are more likely to change between their actual releases.

Lastly, it's pretty difficult to manage each and every API because there are just so many of them being developed (`http://dret.typepad.com/dretblog/html5-api-overview.html`). If you want to keep up with the most bleeding-edge features, I strongly suggest reading the browser manufacturers' blogs, developer advocate articles, and the W3C's and WHATWG's evolving specs. As you start to head into your final chapter, you'll be taking a holistic look at the entire web advertising landscape and how HTML5 is impacting it all on every screen going forward.

CHAPTER 13

HTML5 Advertising Going Forward

As you know, advertising on the Web has been through many changes, from static images to animated GIFs to rich media with Flash to present day HTML5. It's fair to say this was fueled by the dawn of affordable, web-centric mobile devices and tablets—but what's to come? What other platforms will take advantage of the new open web standard? This chapter will demonstrate the possibilities. HTML5 will eventually be everywhere a browser is: televisions, appliances, game consoles, vehicles, set-top boxes, outdoor displays, billboards, screens in elevators and even in the back of taxicabs—basically, every screen both indoors and out! Have you ever seen that movie *Minority Report*? Yeah, like that! Anywhere there's a browser and network access you'll see HTML5 and most certainly advertising.

HTML5 adoption is already omnipresent in our industry; soon every device and appliance will work on the same technology as our desktop computers and mobile devices. This will be a huge paradigm shift in traditional media buying because everything will become a "digital buy". The walls between traditional and digital you currently see in agencies will crumble, and you'll be able to gain the reach of broadcast with the measurement of digital. This will be a huge disruption in the advertising industry; many new companies will emerge, and there will be many casualties. Through user adoption, HTML5 will quickly bring ubiquity and continuity across all screens, allowing marketers to develop a unified marketing message and measure ad campaigns much more effectively across channels. With this knowledge, ad servers and data providers will soon be able to have a viewer/user *fingerprinted* (or tied) to a few TVs, a game console, a tablet, a phone, and a desktop computer. With this sort of information, it's certain that privacy concerns will arise because users' data will need to become much more protected. With all that said, let's look at HTML5 advertising today and more importantly, going forward.

HTML5 Advertising Circa 2012

In 2012, HTML5 had a pretty big year. It has been through many changes, including a separation of specifications from working groups (http://w3.org/QA/2012/07/html5_and_htmlnext.html), additional features added to the specification, removed features, and new browsers supporting various levels of compliance. However, you and I both know that this is just the beginning because HTML5 has been a long time in the making.

Specifically, the developments of 2012 have brought much confusion to the advertising industry regarding how to efficiently bring scale with this new way of ad development. Between businesses small and large, we as an industry have a lot of improvements to make; in fact, don't think for a minute that just because a company is a Fortune 500 that it knows what it's doing in this realm. HTML5 is a huge, game-changing shift, and everyone both big and small needs to adapt! Advertisers and marketers either are clueless on how to target users on the growing mobile landscape or are just unsure that HTML5 (which is now more than a buzzword) is going to drastically impact their businesses now and in the years to come. To better illustrate this, I've been compiling a list of questions I've heard in the past year regarding HTML5 and advertising. Here are a few (and note that most of these questions came from director and chief-level executives of huge web properties):

- "What is HTML5?"
- "How much does HTML5 cost?"

- "Can Flash run on my iPad?"

- "Can you help me install HTML5?"

- "The client needs this to be in HTML5." —Me: "None of the features in the ad requires it to be HTML5." —Client: "It just needs to be HTML5." —Me: "Oh, OK, that makes sense now."

- And my all-time favorite, "I can't see my HTML5 ad!" —Me: "What browser are you using?" —Client: "Internet Explorer 8." —Me: "Thank you."

While some of these are comical, as you can see, we are still at the infancy of this technology, especially in the digital advertising business. This presents great opportunity, but we as an industry still have much to learn, build, adopt, and fix with HTML5 and, much more so, in the way advertising is bought, sold, developed, and measured using the new open web standard.

Note   You can find a few very good articles on this topic at `http://bit.ly/Nuc1tv` and `http://rww.to/SOxQr3`.

HTML5 Platforms

HTML5 platforms are becoming more and more abundant, and it's much more than the traditional Web that people are used to interacting with every day. With the latest operating systems and devices doing away with the plug-in model, more browser vendors and platform developers are relying solely on the open Web to power their application and advertising experiences. Two examples of this are Microsoft's new platform, Windows 8 and Microsoft's new tablet, the Surface. The new user interface within the Windows 8 OS, provides an HTML, CSS, and JavaScript front end, which means so does its advertising model. Platforms like Windows 8 will become the norm as more and more people understand that there are limitless possibilities with HTML5 (once adoption occurs). This can even be said for web editor tools because they're being built inside the browser now. In other words, you don't need to install a special application on your computer to write and design for the Web. Take the Adobe project Brackets, for example (`http://github.com/adobe/brackets`). This showcases a great web-editing tool that is built right inside your browser.

Note   Plug-ins are supported in Windows 8; however, they need special privileges to run. For more information, visit `http://msdn.microsoft.com/en-us/library/ie/hh968248(v=vs.85).aspx`.

Platforms like Windows 8 resemble a similar environment to in-application mobile apps, where you get your applications from an online shop or storefront and view ads through an instance of the browser or web view within the downloaded app. With that said, it's safe to assume that these advertising models will need to rely on web standards for creating interactive and emerging experiences within those environments.

Speaking of phone applications, some are even being built on HTML5 using frameworks like PhoneGap (`http://phonegap.com`) to compile down to native code for the app stores to accept. This again demonstrates the true power (as well as the flexibility) of HTML5 because it can be used in almost any digital environment.

Publishers are even taking advantage of the new open standard, by offering progressive enhancement approaches to their web design, by using the power of HTML5 to provide richer experiences to users whose browsers support them, and by maintaining basic support for legacy browsers. In fact, I am sure you'll see many publishers in the coming year implement HTML5-only solutions to both web content and advertising. This chapter focuses on new implementations of HTML5 and where you'll see browsers and advertising moving toward very soon.

Think of this as the new frontier of digital advertising powered by HTML5, and you are the pioneer!

Connected TVs

Up first are connected, or *smart*, TVs; they've been really blowing up on the scene this past year. These are television sets that are connected to the Internet and can support applications and web browsers. Lately, if you're in the market for a new television, you'll find your options will more than likely have some form of wired or wireless network access, and you can expect to see many more televisons using this approach going forward. With much anticipation from providers like Google and Apple to get into this space and disrupt the conventional television model of viewing, the more traditional manufacturers such as Samsung, LG, and Sony have already begun implementing browsers and their own apps into their television sets, but what's most interesting is that the browsers on these screens are scoring a pretty high rank on the HTML5 Test (http://html5test.com). In fact, just take a look at Figure 13-1 showcasing some of the top HTML5 television browsers at the time of this writing.

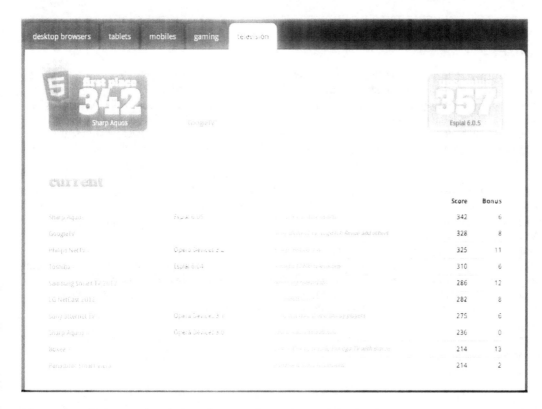

Figure 13-1. *Showcases the television browsers that support HTML5 features (source: http://html5test.com/results/television.html)*

After reviewing Figure 13-1, you can see that these televisions are getting pretty high numbers for HTML5 compliance. There's also a lot of budding competition in this market, which is really untapped and pretty new to the masses. It's reminiscent of the early days of mobile, and I believe we're not even at the beginning of what to expect with television sets in the years to come, and that includes how web advertising is built, bought, sold, and deployed to this screen in conjunction with the traditional advertising approaches. Connected TVs will eventually become the norm among consumers, and with approximately 38 percent of users already working with these sort of TVs (http://multichannel.com/article/482912-TV_Sets_Are_Connected_To_Internet_In_38_Of_Homes.php), it's only a matter of time before content providers start selling ad inventory to marketers for premium prices. What's really interesting is that most of these platforms are taking web standards and HTML5 into account out of the gate!

In fact, Samsung's smart TV apps are heavily HTML5- and CSS-driven for platform-agnostic web apps that can gain specific device access through various APIs (`http://fiveminutes.eu/a-birds-eye-view-on-samsung-smart-tv-apps-development`). This is exciting news for developers because it provides another opportunity to get their content in front of users, and companies such as Opera and Google are taking notice and offering tools to get you prepared for this imminent shift. Check out Opera's TV emulator (`http://opera.com/business/tv/emulator`), which can assist in your development process for CE-HTML and HTML5 content for the big screen and Google's guidelines for television designing (`https://developers.google.com/tv/web/docs/design_for_tv`).

■ **Note** You can find more information about HTML5 adoption for television at `http://w3.org/2011/07/w3c-webtv-nem.pdf`.

Set-Top Boxes

What about the "nonsmart" televisions that can't access the Web on their own? Great question. Those users won't be left behind—trust me, those eyes are too valuable to advertisers and content owners!

In addition to buying television sets with browsers that support HTML5, consumers are also looking to many set-top boxes (STBs) such as Logitech's Revue with Google TV to complement their existing television experiences. These forms of TV/web capabilities are known in the industry as *over-the-top* (OTT), and many hardware manufacturers are offering TV experiences through a network-connected set-top box with various applications that a user can install to personalize the viewing experience. Some of the more popular devices at the time of this writing are Apple TV (`http://apple.com/appletv`), which comes with a variety of Apple-related applications including YouTube, Netflix, Hulu, and Vimeo; and Roku (`http://roku.com`), which offers similar experiences but a much wider variety of content. There is even the Boxee (`http://boxee.tv`) and Slingbox (`http://slingbox.com`) that offer similar experiences, all with their own contracts to provide users with featured content through partnerships with content providers such as MLB.com, HBO, Amazon, Netflix, and WSJ Live.

What's really interesting about these STBs is that most of them allow for traditional ad serving of in-stream video ads, as you learned in Chapter 7, using VAST. This means you can serve dynamic and addressable advertising content to these devices through the IAB's standard video delivery specification. Equally interesting is that if the STBs allow for a browser, there is no reason you can't use and leverage web standards to create even more engaging or interactive experiences using a JavaScript-based VPAID API within the HTML5 video environment.

■ **Note** You can find more information on the JavaScript VPAID API at `http://iab.net/vpaid`.

Cable Platforms

Cable is another major piece of the television experience, and this is where it gets really interesting and just a bit tricky. Cable has long been a protector of its content, forcing users to buy a package of channels when the user may not necessarily watch all of them. This model has worked for years, and cable companies have been really comfortable "managing" everyone's content through a single distribution model. However, times are rapidly changing, and users are going to other platforms and screens for their content and getting it when they want it instead of operating on the linear broadcast model of delivery. As cable becomes disrupted by this change, the huge corporations are fighting to maintain exclusive rights to their content while also trying to accept the impending reality of the Web and its impact on their traditional business models.

I think in the future users will be able to create their own channel package through a cable provider and pay only for the content they view. If viewers want a channel, they pay or get it for free through the advertising model. This approach is similar to the free, ad-driven applications you find in app stores. Think about it—currently you're paying big cable companies top-dollar to view a bunch of content, most of it you'll never watch and you're being advertised toward! I predict this will eventually shift in the years to come, especially as content gets pushed across all of the different screens a user has.

For me and where I am located, I use Verizon for my cable and Internet services, and even though I'm a paying customer, Verizon still requests my permission to sell targeted advertising to me. Refer to Figure 13-2, which is an e-mail from Verizon that I received shortly after signing up for the service.

Dear JOHN,

Your privacy is an important priority at Verizon. We want to let you know that Verizon will soon participate in a program that will improve the ability of advertisers to reach our Verizon Online customers based on your physical address. The goal is to provide online ads that may be more relevant to you.

This program uses your address to determine whether you reside in a local area an advertiser is trying to reach. However, Verizon won't share your address with advertisers as part of this process. Advertisers won't know it's you specifically or where you actually live. If you do not want us to allow advertisers to send you ads based on your geographic area you can let us know by selecting here.

What does this mean for you?

Certain ads you'll see while browsing the Internet may be directed to you and other Verizon Online customers in your area, so these ads may be of more interest to you. For example, a pizza chain may want to deliver their ad to give a special offer to people living in a particular area. Using this program, national brands and local businesses can tailor their offers, coupons, and incentives to your local area.

Protection of Your Personal Information

Verizon protects your personal information as described in our privacy policy. You can learn about Verizon's ad practices or let us know that you do not want to participate by selecting here. If you don't want to participate, you will need your User ID and Password to access the opt-out page. Please note that declining to participate won't impact the number of ads you see, just their potential relevance to you.

For answers to your frequently asked questions, select here.

Thank you for choosing Verizon. We look forward to serving you.

Sincerely,
Verizon

This message was sent from a notification only email address that cannot accept incoming email messages. Please do not reply to this email. ©2012 Verizon.

Figure 13-2. *A Verizon e-mail asking for permission to serve targeted third-party ads*

As you can see, this polite e-mail from the folks at Verizon stress that they're sharing my information to provide relevant online ads, but if you recall from the beginning of the book, Verizon is really selling that information to advertisers for top-dollar in return for targeted advertising campaigns on their network. While I think this model needs to change (especially because customers like myself pay an ungodly amount of money to cable companies), there is room for both models in the market. Cable should sell premium and live content to users such as sporting events and the Olympics, but there also should be free ad-supported models. Ultimately, users should be able to control their content on demand while paying for what they actually consume. I predict the web having a huge impact on this change.

With all that said, cable is rapidly moving toward a browser-based world. Let's face it, it's the most ubiquitous platform in the household today, and big names in the U.S. arena like Comcast/Xfinity are taking advantage of this by launching a platform called X1 (http://xfinity.comcast.net/x1). X1 is a revolutionary new platform for controlling your cable set-top boxes connected through the Web. It features a variety of applications including Search, DVR, On Demand Movies, Sports, Weather, and Social, including wireless controllers via your phone or tablet device. With plans to integrate with applications like Microsoft's Skype (http://bit.ly/OPxPNf), X1 could be an ideal candidate to leverage web technologies such as WebRTC and other HTML5 APIs to develop a unified cross-screen experience while preserving privacy for users; this would offer the ability to interact and target users like never before.

And if you're a Skype user, be sure to check out your preferences—Skype is about advertising as well. Remember that if you're using services for free, you'll likely see targeted third-party ads, as Figure 13-3 outlines.

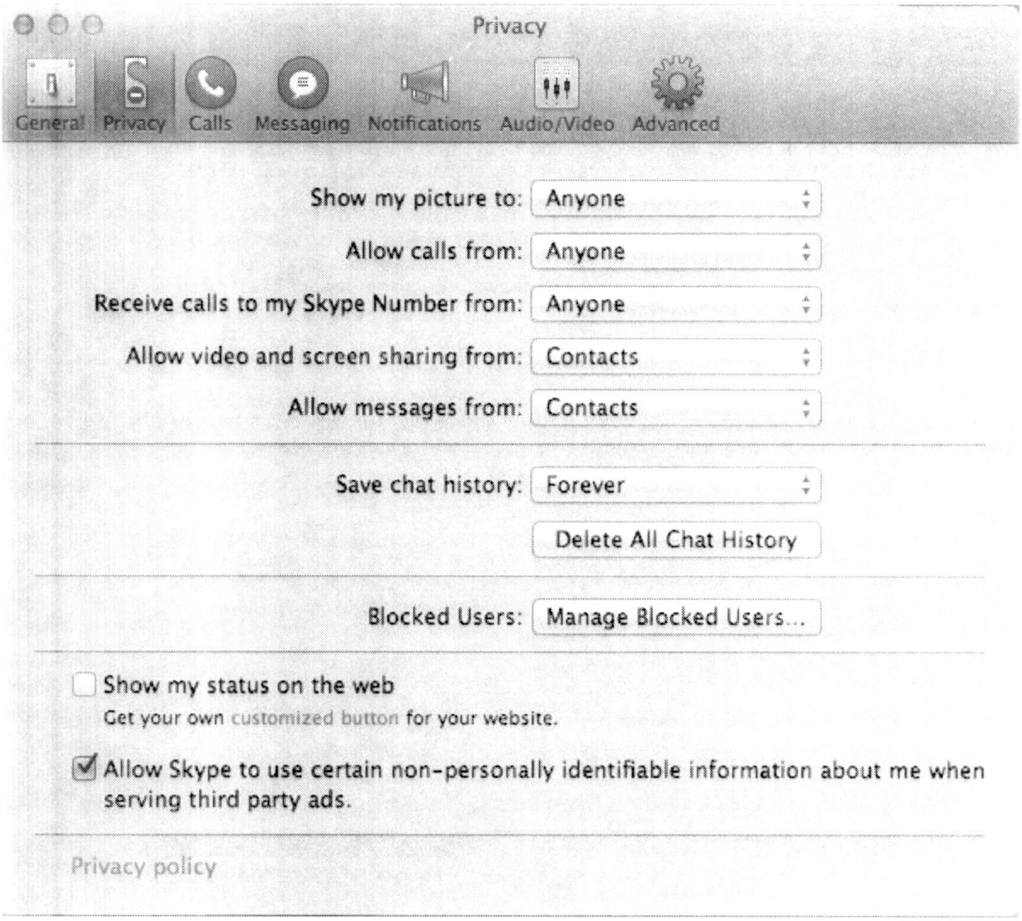

Figure 13-3. Skype's default settings for serving third-party ads

So, with this information about Comcast and Skype, you can see advertisers can learn quite a bit about you and target their ad campaigns much more effectively. What's also exciting is that big web players like Google are getting into the cable and Internet provider market. Google started rolling out a huge initiative in Kansas City, Missouri, offering gigabit-speed Internet access and offering fiber-optic network access with cable packages. Google is in a great spot to offer a cohesive experience across channels if it can ramp up this offering across the nation—we'll see in the months and years to come. For Google users, this could mean cross-screen experiences via your single Google+ or Gmail login, and being that Google is heavily fueled by advertising (remember, it's a free service), expect to see a lot of marketers and advertisers leveraging Google if this offering becomes a reality.

While all this is occurring in the United States, it's not the only area bringing cable and Internet together as one uber-platform. In fact, the Hybrid Broadcast Broadband TV (HbbTV; `http://hbbtv.org`) is a huge European initiative bringing television, video on demand, interactive advertising, gaming, and social elements (among others) together in a standardized way. HbbTV leverages open web standards with traditional broadcasting techniques that serve as an alternative to proprietary technologies that don't scale. Services using HbbTV can operate over different broadcasting technologies, such as satellite, cable, or terrestrial networks.

Currently, you more than likely have a cable subscription, an OTT STB like Apple TV or Roku, and maybe even Google TV along with a Blu-ray Player that connects to Netflix or Hulu. Wouldn't it be nice to have one device that does it all, including the broadcast of user-generated content? Well, that's what HbbTV aims to accomplish! I personally love it! I believe this is where the industry needs to go and, more importantly, where it's headed. With web technologies such as HTML5, WebRTC, and video delivery specifications like MPEG-DASH, you'll be sure to see revolutionary improvements in this arena.

Note For a great article on this topic, visit `http://bit.ly/PEZfZ6`.

Broadcast mediums entering the Internet age raises many questions. For instance, how will these platforms track users? Will privacy remain the same as online, or because the experience is more personal and "in the living room," will it become much stricter? If if becomes stricter (which I believe it will), it will take a full agency shift, where traditional creative and media agencies need to adopt the usual "asks" of digital and remove the barriers that were once present. These "asks" would be any form of measurement that digital offers over traditional broadcast such as impressions, interaction time and activites. This also begs the larger question of how the media will be bought and sold in the new market. CPM models may work for some but may not work for all; especially when one campaign will span across the interactive and linear broadcast channel. One thing is for certain: user experience will win overall, and the ad servers that can measure across screens will come out on top.

With all of these amazing technologies coming to cable platforms, Enhanced TV Binary Interchange Format (EBIF), a model for deploying interactive experiences over broadcast, shouldn't go unnoticed. Leveraging EBIF, the future holds some amazing things for the cable industry. Developed and maintained by Cable Labs (`http://cablelabs.com`), EBIF is currently deployed in more than 40 million U.S. households by companies like Comcast/Xfinity and TimeWarner. EBIF enables everything from interfacing with the Web to phone services such as caller ID to even household alarm systems. The home is now hyper-connected! It's pretty amazing that we live in a world where your television can notify you when someone is at your door , and you can change the channel to view who's at the front door. Utilizing EBIF to control cable STBs from second screens and never having to interact with the TV guide again offers really interesting cross-screen opportunities for users, developers, and marketers. Use your tablet or phone to do the searching and cue up your favorite shows. Make your own video playlist for a rainy day, or even find out more information on your second screen while watching a film on your TV.

Note Cable Labs is an open consortium for the cable industry, much like the W3C is for the Web.

Game Consoles

After learning about OTT devices and STBs, you may have wondered about the other devices attached to your television. A game console such as Microsoft's Xbox, Sony's PlayStation, or the Nintendo Wii is no stranger to this growing market either; these consoles are not just for the "gamers" anymore. With more of these consoles taking an approach to entertainment as a whole, they're offering more than just a game experience since you can install applications much like you would using other OTT STBs, watch movies, surf the Web, and be social with your communities. With the anticipated release of IE 10 on Xbox and with Xbox's new advertising initiative called NUads (`http://bit.ly/PtZUJu`) leveraging the Kinect, you should see amazing experiences within ads on these new platforms. Microsoft is in a very good position to offer amazing living room entertainment experiences through web standards from the likes of WebRTC while using device hardware such as Xbox and the Kinect. We're not too far off from interacting with web-based content through body movements, gestures, and voice commands.

The Xbox, PlayStation, and the Wii consoles are all very sophisticated hardware and devices for gamers and people who enjoy entertainment. Sony's PlayStation 3 with firmware update 4.10 gives the device a "sort of" compliant HTML5 browser. I state "sort of" for the sole fact that it scores pretty low (80) in the overall grand scheme of HTML5 browsers, according to the ACID3 test (`http://acid3.acidtests.org`), which is a measurement tool for testing a browser's accordance to web standards. However, a score of 80 is still a really nice achievement in the game console market, and it ranks as one of the highest HTML5-compliant browsers in the gaming category on HTML5test.com at the time of writing, as shown in Figure 13-4.

Figure 13-4. HTML5test.com's ranking for gaming console browsers

As you can see, the Nintendo devices are among the leaders in this category after the Xbox, with roughly 100-point scores across the board. As you look ahead to the newer consoles soon to be released, you'll see huge advancements in HTML5 with Nintendo's WiiU (`http://nintendo.com/wiiu`) and Sony's PlayStation Vita (`http://playstation.com/psvita`), which offers a web browser, application, and another solution to the second screen experience—much like Microsoft's Smart Glass (`http://xbox.com/smartglass`).

Digital Signage and Billboards

So, I've been speaking a lot about the indoor living room experience, but let's not forget outdoor. Every day we see screens fighting for our attention, whether it be driving down the road, in the back of a taxicab, or strolling through Times Square in New York City. Billboards and outdoor displays are becoming no stranger to the digital landscape, and in an industry fueled by advertisements, more and more displays are powered by the digital screens. With more displays becoming digital along with web access, it is becoming cheaper and much more effective to run campaigns to these media properties.

Think about it—you no longer need to have a person install anything to the site of the billboard, so that cuts down on operational costs, and because the screen is connected, you can run multiple ad campaigns throughout the day and even display relevant information such as the recent lottery numbers, closest stores to a nearby exit ramp, or even the most wanted criminals in the area. Using these media properties from companies such as Clear Channel (`http://clearchanneloutdoor.com`), Adams (`http://adamsoutdoor.com`), CBS (`http://cbsoutdoor.com`), Lamar (`http://lamar.com`), Captivate (`http://captivate.com`), and RGB (`http://rgbnetworks.com`), you can tailor location-based and timely advertising to these large screens. Pair this with the idea that users can interact with the display via a smartphone, and you have previously unavailable creative options. Imagine driving down the road and noticing that the billboard is detecting how fast you're moving through the beacons implanted in the road. From there, the outdoor display can show messaging to slow down, to be safe, or that a cop is on the way! Again, these are just thoughts, but we're not too far off from this becoming a reality and having the ability to tap into this sort of data from within advertising units. In fact, some emerging companies are taking a web approach to powering their outdoor displays now. Iadea (`http://iadea.com`) develops hardware for digital displays that run on web standards using SVG, SMIL, and HTML5. With this company and others in the market, you'll be seeing really engaging creatives around Times Square and other locations very soon.

■ **Note** For an interesting article on the topic of outdoor advertising and web standards, visit `http://bit.ly/Qc13WR`.

Vehicles

So, you now know that outdoor screens are becoming more enhanced through digital technologies and the Web. What would you say if I told you that your car or truck will eventually have a browser? You know, right where your fancy navigation system is. Actually, some vehicles are already coming with applications such as Pandora Internet Radio and Google Maps, and they can already make calls, read SMS messages and update your Facebook status for you while you drive. Soon, you'll see vehicles with browsers, and rest assured that the browsers will have some form of HTML5 compliance. For an advertising model, maybe it doesn't make the most sense to have flashy on-screen ads while a person is driving, but through the use of technology and various device APIs, you will be able to detect when a user is sitting idle and perhaps have the ability to advertise. A company called Webinos and the W3C have started documentation on it (`http://bit.ly/Pu4DLn`) and a standardization process. For more information, visit `bit.ly/O5zVNw`.

Cross-Screen Initiatives

As you learned in previous chapters, advertisers and media agencies want metrics to measure how well a campaign performed. While publishers and advertisers join in launching cross-screen campaigns across channels in a timely matter through ad scheduling, in the growing landscape of connected screens, it's proving more and more challenging to roll up all of these analytics into a single unified campaign analysis for strategists and producers to digest. Companies like Zeebox (http://zeebox.com) offer truly interactive second-screen experiences, and as more people maneuver their digital lives across devices, the need for a cross-platform measurement tool is an absolute must. Whether it is by use through a shared network or an amalgamated login screen, the need to measure across screen and device is real, and solutions are emerging. I'll review some of the technologies that are powering this shift in the next few sections.

ACR

One technology that's doing cross-screen effectively is Automatic Content Recognition (ACR). ACR reads audio information from one source and displays relevant information on the receiving end. Companies like Shazam (http://shazam.com) and Soundhound (http://soundhound.com) do this in the mobile market where users can listen to a song and figure out what song is playing. The technology samples the audio from the source and can detect what file it is through its metadata, whether it be a music track, television show, or commercial. This technology can be paired to the second screen for showing relevant messaging to a user, who could be passively watching television while surfing the Web on their tablet device. ACR is a technology that is currently being rolled into the original equipment manufacturers (OEMs) of set top boxes and phones so that a third-party install won't be needed for a user—if this were to happen, it would surely disrupt the business models of the companies mentioned. Users face a similar barrier with QR codes when they need to install an app to read the QR code before participating. A few of these companies working with ACR include Audiblemagic (http://audiblemagic.com), Gracenote (http://gracenote.com), TvPlus (http://tvplus.com), and Ensequence (http://ensequence.com).

Device Fingerprinting

Another cross-screen initiative to allow advertisers to track users across device is the concept of device fingerprinting. *Device fingerprinting* is a technology that detects information about a user's device or machine, and the information can be saved for later analysis. Think about this in regard to online tracking—if you're viewing an ad on your iPad, that device identifier can be saved, and the next time you view another ad, the ad server would know who you are based on the previous ads you've seen. From that information, more data can be collected about your location, behavior, and interests, offering a really nice audience segment for marketers to target campaigns toward.

In the early days of mobile development, applications and ad creatives by way of an SDK could access what is known as a *unique device identifier* (UDID), which is a device-specific string of characters identifying a particular device in the world. It's like a device's Social Security number. This is important to know because with this intelligence, web content can pair this information with the stored data in a database to clearly match a user and offer more targeted messaging. This is a huge advantage in tracking users across screens and devices, but some mobile device manufacturers such as Apple put an end to doing this because they didn't want to breach users' privacy. While the technique through HTML5 is to use localStorage or some other client-side storage technique along with a remote database, there is an initiative called OpenUDID (http://github.com/ylechelle/OpenUDID) that allows for an open way to track users via an open device identifier that isn't tied to a user's personal information. The OpenUDID is currently backed by 17+ mobile ad companies such as Appsfire and Greystripe (http://github.com/ylechelle/OpenUDID).

Note As of iOS 6, Apple has launched an "Advertiser ID" aimed to replace the UDID approach. You can find more information at http://businessinsider.com/everything-we-know-about-ifa-and-tracking-in-apples-ios-6-2012-10.

Now many other companies like AdTruth (`http://adtruth.com`) use a technology that generates unique hashes based on users' online behavior and available device information, among other values, using sophisticated statistical analysis for targeting audiences with a small margin for error. With companies like this emerging and with companies like Apple (which is a leading device manufacturer and operator of the mobile ad network iAds), a market is emerging that many will look to take advantage of. We'll see if it remains siloed in the walled garden of Apple, though . . . my guess is it will.

Near-Field Communications

Near-Field Communications (NFC) is a technology used to detect proximity and specific sensors via a piece of hardware like your mobile phone. Using NFC, people can share information between devices such as two phones, a phone and a television, or even a tablet and a car, which can open up a whole new world for users interfacing with screens and displays. The screen powered by HTML5 in the browser environment can detect and receive information about users passing by with an equipped phone or device. This sort of transfer can bring a whole new world of interaction to advertising.

The primary business model for this has been through the financial vertical; for instance, Google uses it for Wallet and MasterCard uses it for Paypass, where the device can swipe over a "tag" for a secure wireless data transfer. But in regards to advertising, the tag could hold specific information relating to the ad on-screen or based on contextual or location data to display to the user.

So, with all of this information, you might be wondering what this has to do with HTML5 or HTML.next? The truth is, it all relates, because the Web has many APIs (and will have more in the future) that can tap into this information as more devices adopt NFC. In addition, with the release of new mobile devices supporting proximity events, you should see interesting uses very shortly. It's also been said by Doug Turner of Mozilla that he wants to bring device proximity support to mobile Firefox. To get an early look at working with proximity within the DOM, visit `http://dvcs.w3.org/hg/dap/raw-file/tip/sensor-api/Overview.html`.

Facial Recognition Software

Facial recognition is a technology that has been a long time coming. It's a technology that allows video cameras and webcams, along with software and hardware, to detect face structure, distance, gender, and even attention time of a user. Companies like Immersive Labs in the digital signage space and Face.com, recently acquired by Facebook, are already using this technology, and with more and more computers and devices already coming equipped with cameras, you should see a huge growth in the market for years to come.

So again, what does this have to do with HTML5?

Well, if you remember back to Chapters 7 and 12, HTML5 has a new video tag, and along with the WebRTC specification, using facial recognition can open up amazing new worlds for creative user interaction. Pair this with the information you've just learned about from device manufacturers like Microsoft with the Kinect, and I think you see where I'm going with this. In fact, some really smart developers have already begun working with facial detection within HTML5 and WebRTC. Take a look at the example by Neave at `http://github.com/neave/face-detection`.

Another interesting feature of this is to pair with social data using Facebook, Twitter, LinkedIn, and others. Using these social APIs and facial recognition technology, you can pretty accurately learn a whole lot about a user by just the information they post online. An interesting product is Facedeals, which pushes offers to people via their Facebook account when they walk into a store that has the Facedeals camera installed at the entryway. To read more on this, visit `http://bit.ly/RSUhKb`.

Do Not Track (DNT)

As I talk about all of this amazing technology, I'd like to bring it home by discussing user privacy and security and the industry-wide emerging theme of Do Not Track (DNT). In short, DNT is a bit of information attached to all HTTP request headers, and without going into extreme detail about HTTP headers, just know that every time you visit Google, Amazon, Facebook, and so on, your browser provides an HTTP request to retrieve information located at the server of those domains. The new DNT information attached to the browser request currently has three values: 1 means "Don't allow websites to track me," 0 means "Allow websites to track me, and Null is the default setting should the user not take any action to set their browser preference to a 1 or 0. Now, because this information is attached to every single request from a user's browser, the server on the receiving end has to handle this information accordingly, and this is where it gets even more interesting. Right now the industry is trying to adopt DNT into newer browser versions while also trying to figure out what the receiving servers should do with that DNT data (`http://read.bi/TXBz4N`).

At the time of this writing, Internet Explorer 10 on the Windows 8 operating system is set to have DNT set to 1 by default, which means without the user taking any action, all websites, ads, and data providers will see the request header of "don't track me." As you may have guessed, this is a huge concern in the advertising industry since IE 10 is set to be a large chunk of the browser market in the coming months and years. To shed a little more light on this from an advertising standpoint, the CEO of the IAB, Randall Rothenberg, issued a statement to all IAB colleagues when this information was made available.

> *"Dear IAB Colleague, Today, Microsoft announced that the newest version of Internet Explorer, packaged with the Windows 8 Release Preview, will have a so-called "Do Not Track" flag set to "on" by default. This represents a step backwards in consumer choice, and we fear it will harm many of the businesses, particularly publishers, that fuel so much of the rich content on the Internet."*

—Randall Rothenberg, IAB

In that abridged quote, you can see this is being taken very seriously because many ad networks, publishers, and data providers fear that they will not be able to grab metrics from users on the IE 10 browser by default.

However, keep in mind that this is not a standard yet. The W3C is currently working on it, and most of the major browsers to date include some sort of DNT toggle so each request has a DNT value included. Some of the DNT settings from the major browsers are demonstrated in Apple's Safari in Figure 13-5.

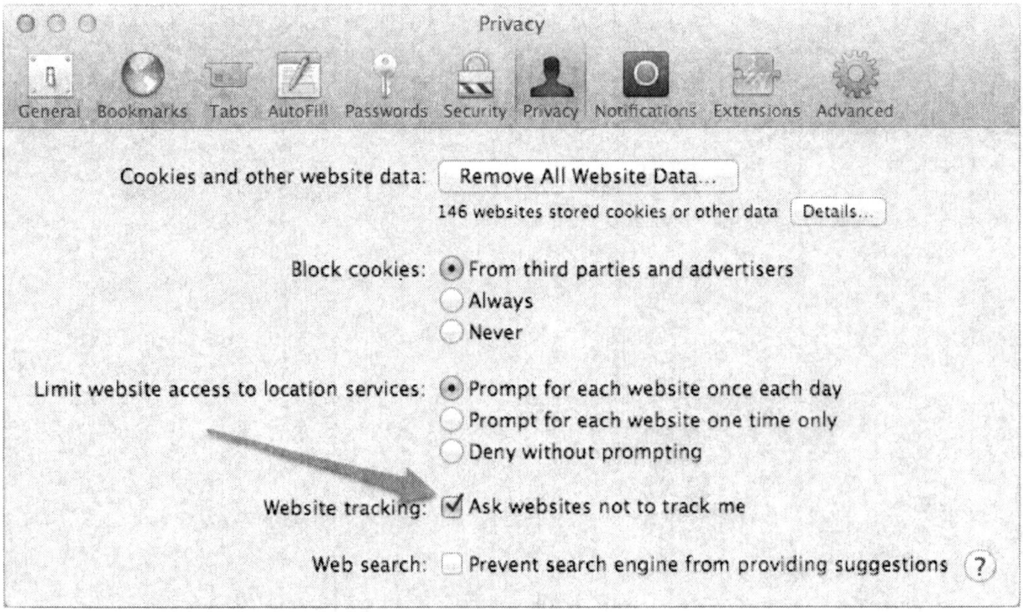

Figure 13-5. The DNT setting in Apple's Safari browser

Figure 13-6 shows the setting in Firefox.

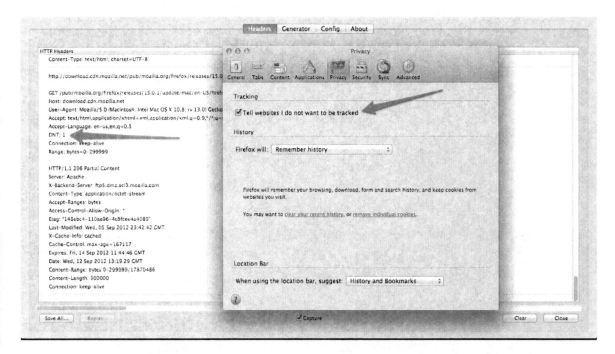

Figure 13-6. *The DNT setting in Mozilla's Firefox browser with DNT set to 1 using the Firefox plug-in, HTTP LiveHeaders*

I believe it's not as black and white for a DNT value. Users, when they open their browsers for the first time, should be presented with a few questions on how they'd like to have ads, sites, and networks track them. From this initial screen, they will need to set the options before they're allowed to move on and use the browser to its full experience. And rather than doing this for every browser you use, there should be a centralized location for accessing and updating the data so it's known across all of your browsers and devices.

As of September 2012, Apache developer Roy Fielding has released a patch that will bypass the Do Not Track setting in the upcoming Internet Explorer 10, which has it set to 1 by default. The basis of doing this is that Fielding believes it is against everything open standards stand for, which is the foundation of Apache, a huge provider and contributor of server-side architecture and the Web. For more information on this important industry topic, feel free to visit http://donottrack.us and http://ftc.gov/opa/2012/05/donottrack.shtm.

■ **Note** You can find more information on the Apache server patch at http://bit.ly/QBcwng.

Summary

Obviously, this chapter was intended to make you ask questions and to think about what's possible rather than focus on the current limitations within the space. With Internet advertising revenue setting 2012 records of $8.4 billion in a single quarter (http://bit.ly/NupSQs), there will be no shortage of competition in this industry. This means, like it or not, advertising is here to stay!

As I close out this book, I want you to be aware that there is a whole world out there eagerly waiting tasteful online advertising, and it's one that hasn't even been dreamed up of yet. While I know most people frown upon advertising as an evil, keep in mind that it offers a great revenue model for content providers offering premium free content to a wide variety of audiences and so we're at a very good transitioning point to make the digital advertising industry effective again and redefine a lot of what has failed us and our users in the past. So, please be receptive to the change and offer guidance in how you'd like to see this industry take shape in the coming years as it makes its move into using web standards.

Lastly, know that the Web is becoming more open, and we're all on the cusp of many great things ahead in web development, web applications, and digital advertising. Now that the Web is on phones, desktops, laptops tablets, and televisions, the market has exploded with more growth and opportunity than ever before. Today it's on your television, but tomorrow it will be on billboards, cars, elevators, appliances, and more places we haven't even thought of yet, which will mean much more competition and more needs from advertisers to measure the effectiveness of their marketing goals. We've learned a lot from our digital past with HTML4 and Flash, but one thing is for certain: web standards won't go away, so learning the new features of HTML, CSS, and JavaScript is one of the best thing you can do for yourself and your career.

I personally want to thank you for reading *HTML5 Advertising*. This is a fairly new topic, and the book was an attempt to set a baseline for strategy and development throughout the transition in the industry. As we all push forward, the information will undoubtedly need to adapt but I hope you found this informative and fun to read. Please feel free to reach out to me with any questions or comments when you begin your next digital campaign. As we continue to narrow in on a complete HTML5 specification and complete browser support, you'll be in a great place to take this entire industry head-on. It's going to be an exciting few years to come, and I really hope you're looking forward to the developments as much as I am.

Keep experimenting!

Index

CPSIA information can be obtained at www.ICGtesting.com
Printed in the USA
LVOW110440211212

312722LV00012B/928/P